The Minds of Gods

Scientific Studies of Religion: Inquiry and Explanation

Series editors:
Luther H. Martin, Donald Wiebe, Radek Kundt and Dimitris Xygalatas

Scientific Studies of Religion: Inquiry and Explanation publishes cutting-edge research in the new and growing field of scientific studies in religion. Its aim is to publish empirical, experimental, historical, and ethnographic research on religious thought, behaviour, and institutional structures. The series works with a broad notion of scientific that includes innovative work on understanding religion(s), both past and present. With an emphasis on the cognitive science of religion, the series includes complementary approaches to the study of religion, such as psychology and computer modelling of religious data. Titles seek to provide explanatory accounts for the religious behaviors under review, both past and present.

The Attraction of Religion
Edited by D. Jason Slone and James A. Van Slyke

The Cognitive Science of Religion
Edited by D. Jason Slone and William W. McCorkle Jr.

Connecting the Isiac Cults
Tomáš Glomb

The Construction of the Supernatural in Euro-American Cultures
Benson Saler

Contemporary Evolutionary Theories of Culture and the Study of Religion
Radek Kundt

Death Anxiety and Religious Belief
Jonathan Jong and Jamin Halberstadt

Gnosticism and the History of Religions
David G. Robertson

The Impact of Ritual on Child Cognition
Veronika Rybanska

Language, Cognition, and Biblical Exegesis
Edited by Ronit Nikolsky, Istvan Czachesz, Frederick S. Tappenden and Tamas Biro

The Learned Practice of Religion in the Modern University
Donald Wiebe

The Mind of Mithraists
Luther H. Martin

Naturalism and Protectionism in the Study of Religion
Juraj Franek

New Patterns for Comparative Religion
William E. Paden

Philosophical Foundations of the Cognitive Science of Religion
Robert N. McCauley with
E. Thomas Lawson

Religion, Disease, and Immunology
Thomas B. Ellis

Religion Explained?
Edited by Luther H. Martin and Donald Wiebe

Religion in Science Fiction
Steven Hrotic

Religious Evolution and the Axial Age
Stephen K. Sanderson

The Roman Mithras Cult
Olympia Panagiotidou with Roger Beck

Solving the Evolutionary Puzzle of Human Cooperation
Glenn Barenthin

The Study of Greek and Roman Religions
Nickolas P. Roubekas

Understanding Religion Through Artificial Intelligence
Justin E. Lane

The Minds of Gods

New Horizons in the Naturalistic Study of Religion

Edited by
Benjamin Grant Purzycki and Theiss Bendixen

BLOOMSBURY ACADEMIC
LONDON • NEW YORK • OXFORD • NEW DELHI • SYDNEY

BLOOMSBURY ACADEMIC
Bloomsbury Publishing Plc
50 Bedford Square, London, WC1B 3DP, UK
1385 Broadway, New York, NY 10018, USA
29 Earlsfort Terrace, Dublin 2, Ireland

BLOOMSBURY, BLOOMSBURY ACADEMIC and the Diana logo are
trademarks of Bloomsbury Publishing Plc

First published in Great Britain 2023
This paperback edition published 2024

Copyright © Benjamin Grant Purzycki, Theiss Bendixen and contributors, 2023

Benjamin Grant Purzycki and Theiss Bendixen have asserted their rights under the
Copyright, Designs and Patents Act, 1988, to be identified as Editor of this work.

For legal purposes the Acknowledgments on p. xvii constitute an extension
of this copyright page.

All rights reserved. No part of this publication may be reproduced or transmitted in
any form or by any means, electronic or mechanical, including photocopying,
recording, or any information storage or retrieval system, without prior
permission in writing from the publishers.

Bloomsbury Publishing Plc does not have any control over, or responsibility for, any
third-party websites referred to or in this book. All internet addresses given in this
book were correct at the time of going to press. The author and publisher regret any
inconvenience caused if addresses have changed or sites have ceased to exist, but can
accept no responsibility for any such changes.

A catalogue record for this book is available from the British Library.

Library of Congress Control Number: 2022942225

ISBN: HB: 978-1-3502-6570-7
PB: 978-1-3502-6574-5
ePDF: 978-1-3502-6571-4
eBook: 978-1-3502-6572-1

Series: Scientific Studies of Religion: Inquiry and Explanation

Typeset by Newgen KnowledgeWorks Pvt. Ltd., Chennai, India

To find out more about our authors and books visit www.bloomsbury.com
and sign up for our newsletters.

For Ezra and Edward

Contents

List of Figures	xi
List of Tables	xii
List of Contributors	xiii
Acknowledgments	xvii

Introduction Studying the Minds of Gods: State of the Art   1
Benjamin Grant Purzycki and Theiss Bendixen

1. Toward a Cognitive Science of the Gods: A Brief Introduction   5
   Benjamin Grant Purzycki and Uffe Schjoedt
2. Growing the Minds of Gods   17
   Emily Reed Burdett
3. The Divine Projector: How Human Motivations and Biases Give Shape to Gods' Minds   29
   Joshua Conrad Jackson and Kurt Gray
4. The Personality of the Divine   41
   Kathryn A. Johnson
5. Night Visions: The Cognitive Neuroscience of Dreaming about Supernatural Agents   51
   John Balch and Patrick McNamara
6. Animatism Reconsidered: A Cognitive Perspective   63
   Jesper Frøkjær Sørensen and Benjamin Grant Purzycki
7. The Minds behind the Ritual: How "Ordering Gods" Reinforced Human Cooperation   77
   Matt J. Rossano
8. The Mind of God and the Problem of Evil: A Cognitive and Evolutionary Perspective   89
   John Teehan
9. From Watching Human Acts to Penetrating Their Souls   101
   Anders Klostergaard Petersen
10. Cultural Models of Minds and the Minds of Gods   111
    Rita Anne McNamara

11	Moralistic Gods and Social Complexity: A Brief History of the Problem *Benjamin Grant Purzycki and Ryan McKay*	121
12	Game Theoretical Aspects of the Minds of Gods *Aaron D. Lightner and Benjamin Grant Purzycki*	133
13	Accounting for Cross-Cultural Variation in the Minds of Gods *Theiss Bendixen and Benjamin Grant Purzycki*	149
14	Environmentalism and the Minds of Gods *Adam Baimel*	159
15	Approaching the Minds of the Gods through AI *Wesley J. Wildman and Justin E. Lane*	169
16	Never Mind the Gods: Explaining Unbelief and Nonreligion *Anne Lundahl Mauritsen and Valerie van Mulukom*	183

Notes	195
References	203
Index	257

Figures

1.1 Müller–Lyer illusion (a), in a carpentered world (b), and intervened upon (c) 6
3.1 Aggregates of the images that young participants and old participants associated with how they viewed God 35
4.1 Mean ratings for God's personality as dominant/authoritarian, benevolent, limitless, ineffable, and playful by religious type 47
4.2 God's personality expressed in cultural artifacts. (a) God in Michelangelo's "Creation." (b) Jesus as "Sacred Heart." (c) Jesus as the infant of Prague. (d) Krishna the butter thief. (e) Krishna with Radha the *gopi* milkmaid. (f) Bhairava, god of destruction 49
9.1 Penetrability of gods' knowledge at varying analytical levels 107
11.1 (a) Causal model of original society size, having a moralistic god, observer effects, and actual data from quantitative databases. (b) Proportions of absent/unreported and moralistic high gods across levels of jurisdictional hierarchy among 186 societies in the Standard Cross-Cultural Sample (SCCS). (c) Probability plot from logistic regression predicting probability of having a moralistic high god. Vertical line marks the maximum possible value in SCCS data and horizontal line marks the 50 percent chance. (d) Moral interest scale of "local deities" from twelve societies around the world 126

Tables

11.1	Raw Frequencies of Levels of Jurisdictional Hierarchy by High God Type across All Societies in the SCCS ($n = 186$)	127
12.1	Payoffs in a Game of Pure Conflict	134
12.2	Payoffs in a Game of Pure Coordination	135
12.3	Pascal's Wager Payoff Matrix	135
12.4	An Example of a Payoff Matrix for Guthrie's Best Bet Hypothesis	138
12.5	Prisoner's Dilemma (PD) Payoff Matrix for Player 1	139
12.6	Payoff Matrix for the Stag Hunt Game	141
12.7	Payoff Matrix for the Coordination Problem Faced by Upstream and Downstream Subaks in Bali	143
12.8	Payoff Matrix for Player 1 in a Martu Burning Dilemma	144
12.9	Hawk–Dove Payoff Matrix for Player 1	145

Contributors

Adam Baimel is currently an early career research fellow at Oxford Brookes University, UK. He studies the cultural evolution of religion and is currently working on a series of projects identifying when (and in what ways) socioecological challenges create changes in religious systems with a particular focus on how (and with what consequences) religious systems are adapting their concerns to the rising threats associated with the climate crisis.

John Balch is a doctoral candidate at Boston University and a Lindamood Research Fellow at the Center for Mind and Culture. His research utilizes tools drawn from computational social science and the cognitive sciences to analyze the evolution of religious ideologies over time, particularly as individuals respond to the challenges posed by climate change.

Theiss Bendixen is a psychologist and PhD fellow at Aarhus University. His PhD project involves developing and testing accounts of how and why religious beliefs, appeals, and rituals vary across cultures using cognitive and cultural evolutionary theory and statistical modeling of large cross-cultural datasets. He has written two popular science books and is also involved in research on meta-science, science communication, and the evolution of intelligence in the animal kingdom.

Emily Reed Burdett is Assistant Professor at the University of Nottingham and retains a research associate post at the University of Oxford. She is currently investigating the development of belief across thirty different sites globally (developingbelief.com) as well as the developmental origins of creativity. Her research interests include science and religion, child development, the developmental origins of creativity and learning, morality, and social cognition. Her work has been published most recently in *Journal of Experimental Child Psychology*, *Philosophical Transactions of the Royal Society*, and *Child Development*.

Kurt Gray is Professor of Psychology and Neuroscience at the University of North Carolina at Chapel Hill. He studies people's deepest beliefs and how to best increase moral understanding.

Joshua Conrad Jackson is a postdoctoral research fellow in the Kellogg School of Management at Northwestern University. He studies the coevolution of culture and social cognition, with a focus on religious belief, emotion, and moral cognition. He has also developed and taught methods for studying cultural evolution, such as in vivo spatial tracking, agent-based modeling, quantitative ethnographic analysis, and natural language processing.

Kathryn A. Johnson is Associate Research Professor in Psychology at Arizona State University. Her research focuses on the social perception of nonhuman agents with expertise in representations of God and their influence on values, social attitudes, and prosocial behavior.

Justin E. Lane is the cofounder and CEO at CulturePulse, an AI company focused on the development of advanced forms of AI for social prediction. Justin has pioneered new approaches using AI to study human cultures at large scales. He has helped develop grants with an awarded value of over US$85 million. His work has been covered globally in outlets such as the *New York Times*, *BBC News*, *Vice News*, *The Atlantic*, *New Scientist*, and *The Telegraph* and he has been a featured speaker at research, technology, and policy conferences in North America, Asia, and Europe. He's also the author of the book *Understanding Religion through Artificial Intelligence* (2021).

Aaron D. Lightner is a postdoctoral researcher in the Department of the Study of Religion at Aarhus University. His research has focused on religion, cooperation, and knowledge specialization from cross-cultural and evolutionary perspectives. He is working on a series of articles about how and why religious systems often reflect the social and ecological challenges that people encounter around the world.

Anne Lundahl Mauritsen is a PhD student in the Department of the Study of Religion at Aarhus University. Her primary research areas are nonreligion and cultural religion in Scandinavia. She works in the fields of sociology of religion and the cognitive science of religion, employing qualitative and quantitative methods and interdisciplinary approaches in her work.

Ryan McKay is professor of psychology at Royal Holloway, University of London. He is the primary investigator of the Morality and Beliefs Lab (MaB-Lab) and is also a member of the COVID-19 Psychological Research Consortium (C19PRC). He is interested in the causes and consequences of dysfunctional beliefs.

Patrick McNamara, PhD is Full Professor of Psychology at Northcentral University; Associate Professor of Neurology, Boston University School of Medicine; President Emeritus, Center for Mind and Culture, Boston, MA; and Founding Editor at *Religion, Brain and Behavior.*

Rita Anne McNamara is a senior lecturer in cross-cultural psychology in the Victoria University of Wellington School of Psychology, where she is director of the Mind in Context Lab. She is also a fellow of the Victoria University of Wellington Centre for Cross-Cultural Research.

Valerie van Mulukom is Assistant Professor at the Brain, Belief, and Behaviour Lab at Coventry University, UK. She does research on imagination, memory, and belief and their overlaps from the perspectives of cognitive science and experimental and social psychology. Main recent points of focus have been religious and nonreligious rituals and worldviews, and their psychological functions and effects. As part of this research she has conducted fieldwork on rituals in churches and nonreligious assemblies throughout the UK, and a large cross-cultural survey on nonreligious beliefs and worldviews with one thousand participants from ten countries around the world. She is an editor of the *Journal for the Cognitive Science of Religion*.

Anders Klostergaard Petersen is Associate Professor for the Study of Religion at Aarhus University. He has written extensively on early Christ-religion, Second Temple Judaism, matters relating to philosophy of science in the humanities and social sciences, and biocultural evolution in the general history of religions. Among his most recent books are *The Emergence and Evolution of Religion: By Means of Natural Selection* (2018, with Jonathan H. Turner, Alexandra Maryanski, and Armin W. Geertz) and *Theoretical and Empirical Investigations of Divination and Magic: Manipulating the Divine* (2021, edited with Jesper Frøkjær Sørensen).

Benjamin Grant Purzycki is Associate Professor at Aarhus University's Department of the Study of Religion. Trained as an anthropologist, he engages in the cognitive, evolutionary, and ethnographic sciences of sociality and cultural variation. He works mostly on topics of religion, morality, and their coevolution. He has conducted fieldwork in the Tyva Republic and managed large cross-cultural projects. Purzycki's recent book is *Religion Evolving: Cultural, Cognitive, and Ecological Dynamics* (2022, coauthored with Richard Sosis).

Matt J. Rossano is an evolutionary psychologist at Southeastern Louisiana University who specializes in the evolution of ritual and religion. He has authored, coauthored, or edited over fifty scholarly papers, books, book chapters, commentaries, and reviews. His work has appeared in both highly respected academic journals as well as more popular outlets. His books include: *Supernatural Selection: How Religion Evolved* (2010); *Mortal Rituals: What the Story of the Andes' Survivors Tells Us about Human Evolution* (2013); *Ritual in Human Evolution and Religion* (2020); and *Handbook of Cognitive Archaeology: Psychology in Pre-History* (2020, coeditor).

Uffe Schjoedt is Associate Professor at the School of Culture and Society, Aarhus University. His research focuses on the relationship between social cognition, neuroscience, collective rituals, and religious experience.

Jesper Frøkjær Sørensen is Associate Professor in the Department of the Study of Religion at Aarhus University. He has published books including *A Cognitive Theory of Magic* (2007) and *Theoretical and Empirical Investigations of Divination and Magic: Manipulating the Divine* (2021) and numerous articles and book chapters on magic, ritual, research history, and theoretical issues pertaining to the application of cognitive theories and methods in the study of religion.

John Teehan is Professor of Religion at Hofstra University, where he also teaches in the Department of Philosophy, and the Cognitive Science Program. His research focuses on an evolved cognitive scientific study of morality and religion, and its philosophical implications. He is the author of *In the Name of God: The Evolutionary Origins of Religious Ethics and Violence* (2010), as well as numerous articles on these topics.

Wesley J. Wildman is Professor in Boston University's School of Theology and in the Faculty of Computing and Data Sciences, and Executive Director of the Center for Mind and Culture. Author of two dozen books and numerous articles, he is a philosopher and ethicist specializing in understanding complex human social systems, including those involving religion, and he uses high-tech computational and data science methods to study the seemingly intractable problems that arise within those systems. For more details, visit www.wesleywildman.com and www.mindandculture.org.

Acknowledgments

It has been a genuine delight to work with the contributors of this volume. Just as with their other work, they have taught us a great deal in their contributions to this book. We appreciate their steadfast enthusiasm and effort and hope they are pleased with this collection.

We also thank Luther Martin, Lily McMahon, Don Wiebe, our reviewers, and the fine folks at Bloomsbury for their support, guidance, and patience.

We also extend our appreciation to Lotte Varnich and the faculty at the Department of the Study of Religion at Aarhus University for providing a warm and welcoming place to work. Many thanks also go to our students in the Minds of Gods classes who inspired us to organize this book.

The Aarhus University Research Foundation generously supported us throughout the preparation of this volume and its related works. Purzycki also acknowledges support from the Max Planck Institute for Evolutionary Anthropology and the Culture of Schooling grant funded by the Issachar Fund (#TIF0206).

Introduction: Studying the Minds of Gods: State of the Art

Benjamin Grant Purzycki and Theiss Bendixen

Our species' ability to infer the mental activities of other entities is probably not unique. However, the apparently compulsive human propensity to infer the existence of powerful, spiritual minds ranks among the more curious novelties of our lineage. As a consequence of this ability, we are also the only known species that appeals to divine minds and engages in various behaviors believed to alter their dispositions, curry their favor, soothe their anxieties, and use them against our enemies. All societies postulate the existence of spirits and engage in corollary behaviors devoted to them. Presumably, all human societies of the past maintained similar traditions. Despite the fact that what gods know, desire, and care about have comprised a lasting human obsession in all societies throughout history, only until recently have thinkers and scientists begun to approach understanding this obsession seriously and rigorously from a naturalistic perspective. The present volume is a wide-ranging sample of works showing just how seriously the topic can be taken from this vantage point and why it matters in our modern world.

Here, we take up many compelling questions: *Why are humans so interested in divine minds? How do beliefs in gods emerge, evolve, and affect human lives and relationships? Why do gods have the dispositions they do? What do gods know and what do they care about? What happens to us and our relationships when gods are involved? How are beliefs in gods produced? How do they develop throughout the life course? Are there cross-cultural similarities in how individuals appeal to their gods? What do the gods of nonliterate or traditional societies care about? What accounts for religious diversity across cultures? Do local beliefs about minds affect religious worldviews? Do leaders appeal to gods merely as rhetorical flourish? Are norms more likely to be followed when couched in such appeals? Does following such norms hold societies together? And what happens when gods are supplanted by governments?*

This volume is a general-but-targeted survey of the topic, one we designed to be educational and inspiring for experts and curious bystanders alike. Each chapter offers brief intellectual histories of their respective topics, summarizes current cutting-edge approaches to various questions, and, through argument and implication, points to areas in need of attention. We encouraged the contributors to write inviting and accessible pieces that did not shy away from requiring some technical engagement to get more out of them.

Drawing from neuroscience, evolutionary, cultural, and applied anthropology, social psychology, religious studies, history, philosophy, the computer, cognitive, neurological, and political sciences, the contributors to this volume probe the mysteries of the minds of gods from a multitude of naturalistic perspectives. They highlight the manifold ways in which we can address the aforementioned questions. Also as evinced herein, our contribution to this ongoing conversation is one that transcends the so-called "two cultures" problem (Snow 2012); without sacrificing their colorful accents, dialectical idiosyncrasies, and eccentric fascinations, social scientists and humanists can learn to speak a common language.

We organized the chapters into three general sections. The first section (Chapters 1–7) focuses on the mechanics and processes that underlie the perception of gods and the formation of religious beliefs. It includes discussions of what it is about *our* minds that make the minds of gods possible and why specific aspects of gods' minds are predictable. The second section (Chapters 8–13) focuses more on the social side of beliefs and religious expression. Homing in on problems of cooperation and social scale, it brings theological problems, religious history, and cross-cultural psychology together with evolutionary theory, behavioral ecology, and ethnography. The third section (Chapters 14–16) situates the study of gods' minds in contemporary issues including artificial intelligence, climate change, and secularism.

While the chapters refer to each other explicitly, there are many connections we leave for thoughtful readers to make. Indeed, we think this is a rare edited volume in that it can be interactively read cover to cover. In Chapter 1, Purzycki and Schjoedt discuss important models of human cognition and point to how they relate to each other, their limitations, and their relevance to the social scientific study of religion. They lay some of the groundwork that informs some of the subsequent chapters that might assume or adopt particular models of human cognition. For example, just as Chapter 1 details cognitive theory's growing appreciation for flexibility and culture, Chapter 2 provides an overview of the developmental processes that contribute to conceptions of and beliefs in what gods know. There, Burdett highlights the growth of the field, and details an abundance of studies aimed to unravel the way the child's mind generates and culturally inculcates aspects of their religious traditions. These chapters address agency detection and theory of mind in a variety of ways.

These two systems, however, are not the only mental systems potentially undergirding beliefs in gods. By assessing our tendency to anthropomorphize, our egocentrism, and motivations, in Chapter 3, Jackson and Gray examine how individuals attend to the minds of gods by projecting aspects of their own minds onto the gods'. Similarly, Chapter 4 homes in on gods' personalities and dispositions. There, Johnson surveys a range of traditions and posits that gods' temperaments are dynamically linked to individuals' social lives in important ways. While these two chapters highlight how individual psychological profiles can seep into representations of gods, Chapter 5 probes questions about the generation of gods' minds by examining the content and functions of dreams. In it, Balch and McNamara show both how cross-culturally, dreams can be both the source of religious inspiration and beliefs, as well as place social cognition as central in the production of dreams. In Chapter 6, Sørensen and Purzycki shift the scope from the minds of gods to spiritual forces more generally, such as *mana* and *wakan*. Drawing upon the ethnographic record and anthropological thought, they frame the link between *mentalized* and *non-mentalized* spiritual agency as fundamentally exploiting more fundamental causal cognition and one that naturally demands human intervention.

One important way in which people believe they enact change in the world is through rituals devoted to gods. Building a bridge between the first and second sections of the book, Chapter 7 closely examines the evolutionarily deep relationships between gods, ritual, and human cooperation. Drawing from the archeological record, Rossano pinpoints beliefs in gods as central to maintaining the ritual order that, in turn, has served societies since before the dawn of modern humans. In Chapter 8, Teehan moves us into the realm of theology to address the age-old problem of theodicy. Rather than approach the Problem of Evil theologically, however, Teehan reframes the question to address the deeper assumption that gods have some moral role in the first place by applying contemporary insights from the cognitive and evolutionary sciences of religion. Chapter 9 is an historical examination of beliefs in omniscience. Critically assessing various popular ideas about pivotal changes in the history of religions, Petersen posits that a central shift in religious thought was not only that gods' knowledge covered more political territory, but that it also reached deeper into human thoughts. These shifts, he contends, correspond to human group living. While Teehan and Petersen draw upon theology, history, and biblical studies, Chapter 10 widens the scope and considers various culturally expressed models of mind. Contrasting standard approaches that focus on Western conceptions of mental activity, McNamara discusses models of mind from India, Oceania, and Amazonia, arguing that religious beliefs are reflections of these more general models.

Building on some of the themes in previous chapters, Chapter 11 questions the view that only a narrow subset of religious traditions posit that gods care about morality. Drawing on the ethnographic records and anthropological intellectual history, Purzycki and McKay introduce us to the question of the ubiquity of gods' and spirits' moralistic punishment and cast doubt on the founding assumptions of this area. In addition to morality and ritual, Chapter 12 focuses on the narrow range of behaviors that gods care about. Examining various cross-cultural religious behaviors such as Balinese ritual, Australian field burning, and Siberian ritual, Lightner and Purzycki show how game theoretical models can be useful for coming to terms with a cross-culturally diverse range of behaviors associated with the gods. Chapter 13 takes and runs with this baton and evaluates various cultural evolutionary approaches to religious diversity. There, Bendixen and Purzycki contend that the behaviors that gods care about are reflections of pressing threats to cooperation and coordination, so-called "god problems." They derive a set of hypotheses from this account, and wager that much of the appeals to gods' minds we find in the ethnographic world can be accounted for by these threats to sociality.

The final section brings three pieces together that point to future horizons not only in the scientific study of religion but also in the state of the world we all share. Chapter 14 focuses on one pressing threat that affects us all, namely, the collapse of the natural environment. In it, Baimel examines the role beliefs in gods have played on the modification of the natural world and what its current and future roles might be in softening the blows of climate change. In Chapter 15, Wildman and Lane discuss the promise, power, and application of simulating theoretical models to understand the social dynamics of religious thought and practice and profile emerging software that simulates human interactions with gods through an artificial intelligence intermediary. They provide a rich history of simulating religious systems and point to ways in keeping our models sophisticated, our thinking clear, and our technology useful. We close the volume with Chapter 16, where Mauritsen and van Mulukom point to some ways toward an *absence* of religiosity. Along the way, they survey current approaches to when the minds of gods lose traction and are no longer the targets of individuals' and communities' devotions.

As all the chapters of this book attest, the minds of gods are a window into the human mind—its social and epistemic needs, its cognitive quirks, cultural malleability, and evolutionary contingencies. More importantly, however, the minds of gods also tell us quite a bit about relationships within and beyond human communities. We hope you find these essays as inspiring as we do.

1

Toward a Cognitive Science of the Gods: A Brief Introduction

Benjamin Grant Purzycki and Uffe Schjoedt

Introduction

How can we account for humans' ubiquitous and exceptional propensity to believe in gods? Many in the cognitive sciences of religion posit that there is dedicated machinery or a suite of task-specific mechanisms that make the representation of gods' minds both possible and probable. Yet, there are growing movements in the field that challenge these views. Here, we detail the models of cognition that guide these disparate views and discuss current limitations and blind spots. We first provide an overview of various models of human cognition from cognitive modularity to predictive processing (PP). We then discuss how these models have shaped—and continue to shape—the cognitive sciences of religion and point to some avenues for future thought and research.

Models of Cognitive Architecture and Processing

Modularity and Symbolic Input Systems

One view that has had a lasting influence in the cognitive sciences of religion is that the human mind is *modular* in structure. While what exactly this means varies considerably across sources (e.g., Anderson 2007; Barrett and Kurzban 2006; Callebaut and Rasskin-Gutman 2005; Chomsky 1980, 2000: 117–19; Fodor 1983, 2000, 2005; Karmiloff-Smith 1992; Pinker 2005a, 2005b; Segal 1996; Sperber 1996, 2002), one of the most influential views of cognitive modularity is presented by Jerry Fodor (1983) in his now-classic text *The Modularity of Mind*.

Introducing a notably conservative view, Fodor emphasizes four features of modular systems: *encapsulation*, *inaccessibility*, *domain specificity*, and *innateness* (Fodor 1998: 127–8). *Encapsulation* refers to information that is locked-in and released upon exposure to the right inputs. To be processed, these inputs are converted into some form of symbolic "mentalese" and transformed into intelligible outputs (Fodor 1975). This information is *inaccessible* both to reflective human manipulation as well as other cognitive systems. They may interact and interfere with each other, but only by interfacing at other phases of processing. Modular input systems are *domain-specific* inasmuch as they attend to a relatively narrow range of information and are *innate* to the extent that they are a typical and untutored feature of human development (see Margolis and Laurence 2013; cf. Samuels 2004).

Fodor (1983) uses the Müller–Lyer illusion to illustrate (Figure 1.1a). When we view the two lines, line AB appears shorter than CD. This visual input is automatically interpreted in this manner; we have an innate predisposition to interpret this specific kind of input in this fashion. Even if we measure and reflectively know that these lines are the same length, we cannot perceive them any other way without intervention (see below). In other words, the encapsulated information that informs our awareness that CD is longer than AB is inaccessible to conscious thought.

While this example intuitively illustrates the features of modularity, it is intuitive only to the extent that we are fooled. Yet, many traditional populations in Africa are not (Segall, Campbell, and Herskovits 1963, 1966), and this may be linked to features of their environment. Specifically, in "carpentered worlds," similar lines indicate spatial depth or proximity (Stewart 1974). This regularity therefore alters our perceptual inferences about simple 2D images; we *anticipate* line AB is shorter in Figure 1.1a because we regularly witness line CD of Figure 1.1b as farther away. Once we appreciate Figure 1.1b, we can actually see some depth in Figure 1.1; AB looks *closer*. This suggests that input regularities in one's environment can subtly influence how perceptual systems diachronically change over an individual's life course. As such, while perceiving

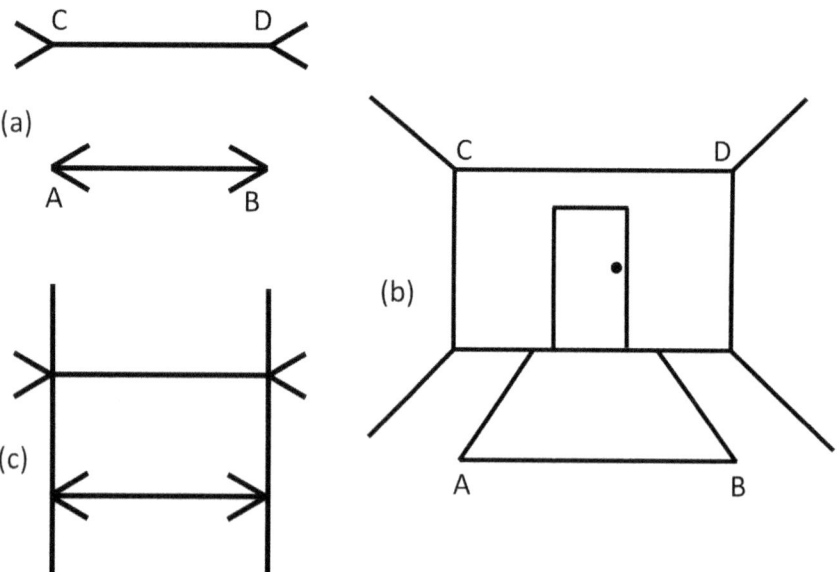

Figure 1.1 Müller–Lyer illusion (a), in a carpentered world (b), and intervened upon (c). Created by Benjamin Grant Purzycki.

this illusion (or not) is domain-specific, innate (i.e., untutored, not socially learned or individually learned through trial and error), and inaccessible, it is not necessarily as rigidly encapsulated as Fodorian modules (see McCauley and Henrich 2006). Instead, there are ontogenetic processes that attend to environmental regularities and thus incorporate information from the environment into their functioning.

In the subsequent decades—particularly in the then-emerging field of the cognitive science of religion (see below)—Fodor's notion of modularity became more popularized and underwent some considerable conceptual drift. While Fodor explicitly restricted modular cognition to only a few systems such as emotions and perception, others repurposed the idea to address a wide range of systems (see Barkow, Cosmides, and Tooby 1992; Hirschfeld and Gelman 1994; Premack and Premack 2003: 17–37 for cross-domain surveys), something Fodor (1987) characterized as "modularity gone mad" (27; cf. Pietraszewski and Wertz 2021; Samuels, Stich, and Tremulet 1999). Some even characterized concepts and their development as modular. For example, Sperber (1996) suggests that we have "an initial template module for living-kind concepts that gets initialized many times, producing each time a new micro-module corresponding to one living-kind concept (the DOG module, the CAT module, the GOLDFISH module, etc.)" (131). In other words, we have a built-in system that, when exposed to incoming stimuli, creates new, more specific iterative members of the same general category. In other words, rather than socially learned, conceptual development largely springs from directed inner processes that attend to relatively uninformative inputs (see the "poverty of the stimulus" argument; Berwick et al. 2011; Laurence and Margolis 2001). While this process might be innate, a process that "produces new micro-modules" or new concepts as described here is still a domain-general process, the production of living-kind subconcepts is likely to be the same process as the generation of nonliving-kind subconcepts. Furthermore, if we assume it is the same process, the fact that we can readily produce new concepts suggests far more accessibility than Fodor's modules. As we discuss below, this divergence is precisely where other approaches to cognition already had much to say.

Modular accounts tend to assume that cognition consists of a set of predisposed procedures either in the shape of inductive and deductive inferences made explicit by propositional representations or in the shape of rule-based systems. Two further points are worth noting here. First, the proposed cognitive procedures are assumed to function relatively independently of the physical properties of the brain; their workings are *analogous* to features of the brain, but they are not themselves constrained by any physical substrate. Second, the proposed systems operate much like computer code using abstract representational units in sentence-like structures, regardless of what information is being processed or how the specific system is organized. Indeed, modules are often thought of "as a set of information processing machines" (Chomsky 1980: 60; Cosmides and Tooby 1997). Modules are assumed to convert analogical signals from sensory input systems into symbolic forms, which are then subject to logical or rule-based procedures. These procedures are made explicit in propositional representations where the symbols are placed in grammatical structures. According to Eysenck and Keane (2000), the propositional representations are characterized by being discrete (made of arbitrary unit, e.g., letters), explicit (symbols are represented explicitly in propositions), subject to strong combination rules (the function of particular symbols depends on the grammatical position in the proposition), and amodal (they consist of arbitrary symbols independent of the brain's visual, auditory, olfactory modalities, etc.): "Thus, they constitute a universal, amodal, mentalese [i.e.,] propositions are a fundamental language or code that is used to represent all mental information" (246–7). In this view, activities in the sensory modalities prior to the transduction into symbols are simply excluded from the cognitive process. The sensory motor systems are reduced to mere input/output channels for an amodal information processor.

The modularity of mind was an immensely successful idea in the first decades of the cognitive science of religion (White 2021). Yet, the abstractness of these proposed modules is increasingly challenged by new theories in which cognition is constrained by the physical brain, including neural processes, networks, and anatomy.

Connectionism and Simulation Theory

Instead of having discrete and arbitrary symbols as the fundamental unit of representation, proponents of connectionism and simulation theory use neurons (e.g., Barsalou 1999; Damasio 1994; cf. Balch and McNamara, present volume). Unlike most modularity accounts, connectionist models of the mind tend to emphasize flexibility, domain-generality, and the generation of rules and procedures as emerging from the dynamic interaction of inputs.

In connectionism, neural networks are modeled on the physical properties of neuron (e.g., axons, dendrites, action potential, etc.), using concepts like input/output units, activation values, "weighted connections," and rules for learning (Bechtel and Abrahamsen 2002: 20) including Hebbian learning (1949), in which units in the neural networks "wire together, if they fire together." Rather than focusing on devoted machinery to evaluate a given situation and provide the appropriate output, then, connectionist models take in multiple inputs and weigh their relevance to produce an output. According to Bechtel and Abrahamsen (2002), connectionist systems learn "not by adding or modifying propositions, but rather by changing the connection weights between the simple units" (38). So, rather than a module computing a particular input and transforming it into perceptual information with a relatively stable system, connectionist networks flexibly incorporate new incoming information for further use.[1]

While connectionism uses the properties of the neuron to model cognition, models still tend to be abstracted from the anatomical brain. To address this limitation, simulation theories situate the activities proposed by connectionist models in the physical brain and body. Simulation theory proposes that cognition takes place directly in the brain's sensory motor modalities by simulating concepts and propositions in perceptual systems. Vision, for example, discriminates topographically between particular colors, shapes, and contrasts, and stores each component of the optic field separately in specific neuronal populations. Barsalou calls these components perceptual symbols, and proposes that these represent the base unit of the representational system, serving as parts of the simulation of objects, concepts, and categories. Perceptual symbols are organized hierarchically linking colors, shapes, and contrasts into more complex structures (Barsalou 1999: 586). A symbol consists of any given neural activity during a particular perception (582–3) so that specific colors and contrasts each make up one symbol (e.g., *red* or *vertical contrast*), while objects and concepts consist of several components (e.g., *a red triangle*). Thus, rather than being mere input channels for an amodal information processing unit, *the physical systems in the brain are assumed to simulate concepts based on prior experience and associative learning.* Simulation theories therefore explore the neural connections being simulated, instead of looking for specific syntactic and grammatical rules. Furthermore, emotional content is integrated in simulations of concepts as reenactments of homeostatic states relevant to a given situation. Damasio (1994) proposes that such somatic markers are crucial for the way the organism responds to its surroundings. In this way, the homeostatic systems of the body hold a kind of automatic intentionality that functions to optimize the organism's interaction with the environment. Thus, the executive system that remains a puzzle for neo-Cartesian models of the mind may be described in terms of simulation theory, as the homeostatic intentionality of the body.

Simulation theory effectively explains how humans simulate the world in order to understand and navigate it, and it has also been used in the cognitive science of religion to understand the embodied nature of religious cognition and behavior (e.g., Barbey et al. 2005; Schjødt 2007). However, it views inferences about the world as automatic multimodal pattern completions that are fundamentally passive. This makes it difficult to account for the brain's ability to actively evaluate and test its own models of the world against incoming sensory input. The predictive processing (PP) framework, which appears to be becoming the standard model of cognition in neuroscience, does exactly that.

Predictive Processing

Many cognitive neuroscientists no longer view the brain's perceptual system as a passive receiver of sensory input. Instead, they view the human brain as a scientist that perceives the world by generating predictive models based on prior experience and then actively tests these models against incoming evidence. The brain attends to the most reliable information for testing its prior expectations, and mismatches elicit prediction error signals that force the system to update its predictive models. This general framework is often called PP. Elements of PP can be found quite early (Helmholtz 1867; cf. Westheimer 2008; Kant [1787] 1929: 92; cf. Swanson 2016), but recently it has been reconceptualized and formalized by theoretical neuroscientists (Friston and Kiebel 2009).

According to PP, the brain is a Bayesian inference generator (Clark 2016; Hohwy 2013; Wiese and Metzinger 2017). What this means is that the mind interacts with incoming information and produces perceptions (or *posterior* perceptions) that are partly informed by prior information we have (hypotheses, predictions, or *priors*). Rather than processing symbolic input using modules or necessarily activating networks of units, PP posits that the brain constantly generates and tests *prior* predictions about the world and informs *posterior* outcomes through the interaction of *priors* and data. The primary reason why this processing is named after English mathematician Thomas Bayes (1764) is that this updating process approximates his famous theorem. We express this theorem in a few common ways:

$$P(A|B) = \frac{P(A)P(B|A)}{P(B)} \tag{1.1}$$

$$P(\text{predator}|\text{rustling bushes}) = \frac{P(\text{predator})P(\text{rustling bushes}|\text{predator})}{P(\text{predator})} \tag{1.2}$$

$$\text{posterior} = \frac{\text{prior*likelihood}}{\text{marginal likelihood}} \tag{1.3}$$

$$P(\text{hypothesis}|\text{data}) = \frac{P(\text{hypothesis})P(\text{data}|\text{hypothesis})}{P(\text{data})} \tag{1.4}$$

$$P(h|d) \propto P(h)P(d|h) \tag{1.5}$$

The first equation reads that the probability of A given B equals the probability of A times the probability of B given A divided by the probability of B. The second equation is the same but with an example. To illustrate, say you see some bushes rustling, B, and you want to know the probability that there is a predator afoot, A, given the rustling, thus P(A|B). If you know that the probability of there being a predator is quite low in general, say, P(A) = 10%, but a very strong likelihood that when predators are present, they rustle bushes (e.g., P(B|A) = 90%), and since bushes rarely rustle in general, say, P(B) = 10%, then you should consider leaving the premises because P(A|B) = 90 percent (0.1*0.9/0.1).[2] What's important here is that the prevalence of a predator in this example can be thought of as *prior* information about the state of the world and the bush rustling can be thought of as incoming data.

The third equation employs Bayesian terminology: the *posterior*—what we should think or perceive *now* is the result of our *prior* information times the *likelihood* of an observation given our prior knowledge divided by the likelihood of the *observation* in the first place. In the first predator example, then, our *prior* is the regularity of predators in your vicinity. The *likelihood* refers to the *likelihood of rustling bushes, given that there is a predator*. The *marginal likelihood* is simply the regularity of rustling bushes. As indicated in the fourth equation, we can further reframe this equation in a predictive coding framework. Specifically, we can treat our *posterior* as the perceived probability of a hypothesis given some data. Our minds calculate this with a prior probability value to our inferences about the world, its product with the likelihood of seeing such data, given that our hypothesis is true, marginalized over the likelihood of seeing the actual data. In other words, the *posterior* represents our updated knowledge; to the extent that it has changed from our *prior* hypothesis, we have learned something. The more informative and precise our *priors*, the less we have to lean on our perceptions. The reverse is also true, the less informative and precise incoming stimuli are, the more we rely on our *priors* to guide our thinking.

We can dispense with the *marginal likelihood*, $P(B)$, on the grounds that it is typically a number that ensures that $0 \leq P(A|B) \leq 1$ (and it often means the average probability of getting an observation—something beyond the scope of this illustration). We express this simplification in equation (1.5), which reads that the *posterior* is proportional to the *prior* times the likelihood. This simplification helps us illustrate how competing *priors* or hypotheses interact with the *likelihood* of data given the *prior* to produce different *posteriors* that we can evaluate. Here, the probability of a predator given bush rustling (0.09) is proportional to the *likelihood* of bush rustling given the presence of a predator (0.9) weighted by your prior (0.1). If, however, you're somewhere where predators are ninja-like and hardly ever rustle bushes, say, 0.1, then your *posterior* is 0.01, which makes sense since the *probability of a predator given bush rustling* is less likely if they rarely rustle bushes. So, the context changed. Now, imagine that you have a hypersensitive friend who warns you about rampant predators, say, 0.5. Here, the *posterior* is 0.45. Without any other criteria to go on, since 0.45 > 0.09, it makes sense to act upon your friend's advice. If our *priors* are different across predictions, we have to be able to weigh these competing posteriors, that is, learn, based on other criteria. This comes in the form of a process of error reduction.

As our *prior hypotheses* about the world are manifold, we are always producing batches of predictions (e.g., that wall is solid or that person is bound by space). Our nervous systems handle incoming data and, in a process that approximates Bayes' theorem, interact with our priors to produce a *posterior* (cf. Thornton 2017). Our brains detect divergences between *priors* and *posteriors*. These divergences—prediction errors—ultimately feed back to our *priors*; insignificant divergences maintain the inference the *prior* provides, whereas dramatic divergences will update the *prior* so that it is closer to incoming data (see Kwisthout, Bekkering, and Van Rooij 2017 for discussion of the importance of precision in prediction).

In the PP account of mental development, there might be abstract *hyperpriors* upon which new information is scaffolded. These *hyperpriors* might be learned or innate, and can guide the elaboration of networks of multilayered packages of hypotheses. Furthermore, PP accounts suggest that the brain is rapidly anticipating the world not with a single *prior* but with bundles of hierarchically structured *priors* and deeper *hyperpriors*. This makes some sense; we don't serially have to evaluate each stream of incoming information at a time. But as we navigate the world, we also don't necessarily need to deploy *hyperpriors* if we are learning. Similarly, we can rely on early-stage *priors* and their correspondence to data (i.e., the prediction error) to do the interpretive work for us, despite *knowing* what reality is. Hohwy (2013) suggests that the kind of cognitive impenetrability posited by Fodor in his illustration of the Müller–Lyer illusion is when prediction error is treated as minimized at a fairly early phase of processing. In effect, "we can be stuck with false beliefs because they can explain away prediction error more efficiently down the [processual] hierarchy—they provide better control over the actual sensory input than do the competing true beliefs" (128). In such cases, we're driven to intervene and act upon the world in order to satisfy those competing true beliefs; we *know* the illusion is an illusion, and we can alter the environment in ways that correspond to our true belief (e.g., Figure 1.1c; see Sørensen and Purzycki, present volume, for a discussion of how ritual corresponds to this process).

The PP framework offers an attractive model of the mind, which can be used to explain very specific cognitive processes, for example, within visual (Rao and Ballard 1999) and reward processing (Schultz 1998), but for some (e.g., Friston, Kilner, and Harrison 2006), PP is much more than that. PP may express life's way of creating structure in chaos by minimizing the free energy of the biological system to a limited number of states. Most PP proponents, however, take more moderate positions. Some see PP as a general framework for understanding perception, while others see PP as a unifying framework for all cognitive processes (Sims 2017). Regardless of position, the PP framework forces scholars of religion to reconsider how religious experience works in predictive minds: "Why do people report vivid supernatural encounters like apparitions, trance, possession, and mystical union if subjective experience is dominated by inferences that cause the least prediction error?" (Schjoedt and Andersen 2017).

Detecting Spirits and Reading the Minds of Gods

These models provide abstract tools to think through various problems, but at the end of the day, how useful are they in the study of religion? As discussed below, most cognitive scholars of religion approach god beliefs from a modular logic positing that human minds are equipped with several submodules that enable relationships with spirits and gods. Two of the most widely used constructs are the capacities for *agency detection* and *theory of mind*. In the following, we introduce these constructs and evaluate the current state of cognitive research into the minds of gods.

Detecting Spiritual Agents

Heider and Simmel (1944) examined the tendency for individuals to detect agents in their environment even when none are present. The now-famous Heider–Simmel illusion illustrates the ease with which humans attribute agency to nonliving things like geometrical shapes. Agents are the most important objects (e.g., predators, prey, partners, etc.) that humans encounter in their environment, and since the perceptual system is set up for survival rather than accuracy, it is hardly surprising if humans are especially attentive toward agency in the world. Agency detection also plays a vital role in human social cognition. Once agency is detected, one can begin to make inferences about its mental states (beliefs, intentions, desires, etc.). From a modular perspective, agency detection is the product of task-specific cognition in one of the submodules involved in social cognition.

In the cognitive science of religion, the idea of a hardwired cognitive bias toward agency detection has become one of the most widely used ideas to explain why humans believe in supernatural[3] or spiritual beings. In particular, Guthrie's (1980, 1993) influential work argues that at its core, religion is anthropomorphism; we ascribe humans' symbolic forms of thought and communication to nonhuman entities. Guthrie argues that the systems that give rise to such a generalized application of mentalizing were selected as a "better-safe-than-sorry" perceptual strategy; as it is better to have a false-positive of a predator than not have the ability at all, not having this ability meant survival (see Lightner and Purzycki, present volume). Drawing directly on Guthrie's theory and on Baron-Cohen's modular approach to social cognition (see below), Barrett (2004) popularized the idea that an important cognitive device responsible for religious thought is the "hyperactive agency detection device" (HADD), a mechanism that provides the foundations for perceiving the minds of gods. Detecting mental activity behind mysterious natural phenomena can contribute to the generation of god concepts. False-positives can sometimes be interpreted as evidence of supernatural agency, either to support already-held beliefs or to produce attribution of new kinds of supernatural entities (Barrett 2004: 39–42; Barrett and Lanman 2008).

While the HADD theory is perhaps the most widely used cognitive explanation for why humans believe in gods, it remains underspecified in terms of actual cognition. What are the neurocognitive processes involved in HADD? How many basic agency detections lead to religious beliefs? Experimental evidence offers limited support to Barrett's theory. No distinct network for agency detection has been located, and no direct association between agency detection and religious beliefs has been found (for a review of evidence, see van Leeuwen and van Elk 2019). In fact, participants who are exposed to ambiguous or threatening stimuli show no clear bias toward agency detection (Maij, van Schie, van Elk, 2019; van Elk et al., 2016). Instead, what is consistently found is that expectations seem to determine what is perceived in the environment (e.g., Denison, Piazza, and Silver, 2011). Andersen et al. (2019), for example, found that participants who strongly expected agents in a virtual forest were much more likely to falsely detect agents. Most detections were typical forest animals (e.g., squirrels, deer, foxes, and birds), which illustrates how the context induces prior expectations, which in turn drive experience. Andersen (2019) notes that "religious systems communicate estimates of the distribution of supernatural agents in certain environments or, rephrased in Bayesian terms, *religious systems often provide their users with estimates of the prior probability of the occurrence of supernatural agents*" (77; emphasis in original).

The PP framework is better equipped for handling such expectation-driven effects on agency detection including experiences of supernatural agents. The PP framework has already been used to analyze ingredients in religious contexts that appear to enhance the probability of triggering religious experiences (Schjødt 2018; Schjoedt et al. 2013a; 2013b; van Elk and Aleman 2017). Sensory deprivation, for example, reduces access to reliable input for testing one's prior expectations. Prior expectations that include supernatural agents are therefore left unchecked in dark or noisy contexts, which may explain why such encounters often happen in the dark (Andersen et al. 2014, 2019). Another ingredient may be source credibility, where accepting a piece of information is often conditional on who expresses it (Hoogeveen et al. 2022). Trust in religious experts appears to reduce individual efforts to monitor for evidence against religious realities and therefore increases the probability of experiencing rituals according to prior beliefs and expectations, for example, of god's presence (see Rossano, present volume). For example, Schjoedt et al. (2011) used functional magnetic resonance imaging to show that Pentecostal Christians downregulate brain areas involved in error monitoring in response to a charismatic authority. Remarkably, the amount of neural downregulation predicted the extent to which participants reported religious experiences when listening to prayers. Van Leeuwen and van Elk (2019) argue that the HADD theory should in fact be inverted in line with the PP framework; agency detection does not create beliefs, but religious people seek out contexts with these ingredients to gain empirical support for those prior beliefs and expectations that they consider crucial for their world views. Detecting agents, however, is but one component of the greater process of mentalizing.

Processing Minds

Descartes posed what is now called the "problem of other minds," when he pondered how we could ever possibly know that others have internal states (Cottingham, Stoothoff, and Murdoch 1998: 85). He emphasized that when we view others, we view more than mere objects and events. Rather, we commonly explain observable human behavior by appealing to hidden mental states such as goals, beliefs, and perceptions. When humans infer mental states of others, we say that they have theories of mind. Research into this ability in nonhuman animals (e.g., Call and Tomasello 2008; Krupenye and Call 2019; Penn and Povinelli 2007; Premack and Woodruff 1978) evolved into a wide-ranging literature on human "mind perception" and "mind reading" (see Jackson and Gray, present volume; Teehan, present volume; Epley and Waytz 2010; cf. Heyes and Frith 2014; Veissière et al. 2020).

Baron-Cohen (1995) delineates a variety of modular subprocesses that comprise the mind reading system. These subprocesses include inferring mental states from behaviors (*theory of mind*), detecting intentions in mobile entities (*intentionality detection*), inferring that one is thinking the same thing (*shared attention*), and *eye detection*. According to this model, once triggered, these modular systems tap into relevant mental state concepts that help us ascribe internal states to the behaviors of others including gods and spirits. Indeed, it has been virtually axiomatic to hold that mentalizing is a prerequisite to religiosity. If anything, gods *are* perceived minds (Atran 2002: 59–71; Boyer 2001: 137–67; Cohen 2007: 190–204; Pyysiäinen 2009: 3–42; Tremlin 2006: 73–106).

The fact that all humans develop mentalizing abilities as they grow does not mean that the cluster of abilities termed "theory of mind" is similar across populations. Indeed, as with the case of the Müller–Lyer illusion, our mind reading systems also attend and acclimate to regularities in our environments. For example, Perner, Ruffman, and Leekam (1994) found that children with more siblings are better at attributing false beliefs to characters in stories. Research suggests that some components of the mind reading system develop variably across populations (Shahaeian et al. 2011). In other words, while one social environment might emphasize mastery of false-belief detection during childhood and another might emphasize eye detection, children of both populations appear to converge when they reach adulthood (see Burdett, present volume). Like the variation found in susceptibility to the Müller–Lyer illusion, then, mentalizing exhibits diachronic, cross-cultural patterns of variation.

But culture also provides explicit and variable models of what minds do; general units in one cultural model of the mind might include phenomena such as "thinking," "feeling," "perceptions," and so forth, while others might include phenomena like experiencing "*hygge*" or "*schadenfreude*" (D'Andrade 1987). In her seminal paper, Lillard (1998) proposes that the cluster of abilities we know as theory of mind is in fact specific to Western psychological science and a European American science-oriented culture (see McNamara, present volume). For example, thoughts in the Western theory of mind are understood as private if not expressed in overt behavior. Following the Cartesian tradition, the mind is exclusively what generates thought. Other populations, however, adopt a theory of mind in which thoughts may also come from other sources, for example, from witches and ancestors. In some cultures, the mind is perceived as porous—thoughts are not considered private and inaccessible—and may be accessed directly through the skull by religious experts, spirits, ancestors, and so on. Luhrmann et al. (2021) has recently explored this variation in her cross-cultural work on religious experience. Indeed, a porous model of the mind seems crucial for individuals who interact with supernatural beings through prayer or other religious practices. While this may come naturally to people brought up with non-Western theories of mind, Luhrmann (2012) convincingly argues that Western believers need to *delearn* part of the Western theory of mind in order to connect with their gods and spirits.

Research into theory of mind serves as a prominent example of modular thinking that has become popular in the cognitive science of religion (see Maij et al. 2017 for review). Inspired by Baron-Cohen, Leslie, and Frith (1985), who proposed that the inability to understand intentions of others in autism results from an impaired theory of mind system (for a noteworthy critique of this view, see Gernsbacher and Yergeau 2019), scholars of religion have theorized that people on the autism spectrum may be constrained in their personal relationships with gods, and found preliminary but mixed correlational support (Caldwell-Harris et al. 2011; Gervais and Norenzayan 2012; Gervais, Norenzayan, and Trzesniewski 2012; Reddish, Tok, and Kundt 2016; Schaap-Jonker et al. 2013; see Mauritsen and van Mulukom, present volume). This naïve use of theory of mind as an evolved module has been heavily criticized by those who observe that children on the autism spectrum routinely imagine supernatural beings. For example, Visuri (2018) found that seventeen high-functioning adults on the autism spectrum actually had more experiences of supernatural beings compared to neurotypical individuals. She argues that such beings are attractive to autistic people because they are perceived as relatively simple agents, whose intentions, unlike those of real humans, are often unambiguous and categorical. Moreover, a large multinational replication study (Maij et al. 2017) with 67,000 participants found no correlation between mentalizing and religiosity but corroborated another important finding, namely, that being exposed to religious activity is by far the most important predictor of god beliefs. While mentalizing systems might ultimately make representing and reasoning about the minds of gods possible, depending on the task, mentalizing may not be as important for god beliefs at the proximate level, and proposed direct links between religiosity and mentalizing effectively illustrate how modular thinking can lead to oversimplified models of god beliefs.

Future Horizons

Appealing to modularity to account for the underlying evolved mechanics that make gods possible might be reasonable, but it can neither be the entire story nor take us very far in accounting for many aspects of religious thought, including diversity in beliefs and the various contexts in which they become relevant. Without clearly testing the idea, postulating a particular modular faculty underlying a behavior always runs the risk of being upended by an explanation with some culturally represented corollary (and vice versa). As is the case with PP, deep questions about the role of hyperpriors and their source (i.e., learned or innate) remain open in the case of perceiving gods and their minds (Maij and van Elk 2019). Connectionism, however, can be very useful empirically, particularly when exploiting its insights in application to specifically cultural data. Work increasingly focuses on the specific content and structure of mental models of gods' concerns (e.g., Bendixen, Apicella, et al. forthcoming; McNamara et al. 2021; Purzycki 2011, 2013; Singh, Kaptchuk, and Henrich 2021; White and Norenzayan 2022). As cultural schemas, these models tell us about what is being socially learned in a community and how they correspond to salient features of one's environment.

Yet, while detailing the content and structure of beliefs is important, explaining them, their variation, and utility requires linking cognitive theory to other bodies of theory. Simulation theory and PP focus more on the anticipation and processing of stimuli. They do not, however, tell us much about how religious cognition predictably becomes relevant in particular socioecological conditions (see Baimel, present volume; Bendixen and Purzycki, present volume). If, for example, agency detection is differentially "triggered" across religious contexts, any modular approach would still have to acknowledge some interface between socialization and this faculty. Unless there were some physical resemblance, there is no a priori reason, a particular tree or mountain, for example, would trigger mentalizing without some cultural scaffolding. What makes mentalizing possible may be some modular faculty that is ultimately part of our genetic endowment. However, ontogenetic processes of enculturation develop the conceptual repertoire required to associate such entities with mental agency. This conceptual repertoire can be appropriately modeled as a conceptual network of interconnected notions. Yet the active, synchronic processing of engagement with and perception of spirits may be best handled by a PP framework insofar as it draws from the ontogenetically incorporated *priors* and perhaps deeper *hyperpriors* responsible for perceiving minds more generally.

Acknowledgments

We acknowledge support from the Culture of Schooling grant that was funded by the Issachar Fund (#TIF0206) and Purzycki thanks the Aarhus University Research Foundation for generous support. Thanks also go to Theiss Bendixen for his feedback on a previous draft of this chapter.

2

Growing the Minds of Gods

Emily Reed Burdett

Introduction

One of the puzzles of the scientific study of religion is the widespread prevalence and ubiquity of God/s across all societies. Why is God, or particular gods, so pervasive in so many societies? One answer to this question has been to look at the common cognitive biases in humans that scaffold our thinking about supernatural agents. However, if we really want to understand these cognitive biases one of the best approaches is to understand how these biases develop. In other words, studying children and the processes of their cognitive development illuminates some fascinating insights into these cognitive biases and how humans conceptualize similar supernatural agents, especially across diverse societies. By studying the development of cognitive processes in children, we can understand which biases develop early; which attributes of God are commonly given among young children; which attributes are given based on social, experiential, and/or cultural learning; and the interplay between how cultural and cognitive processes form and develop to influence their concept of God/s.

This chapter begins by surveying the history of the study and theories regarding the development of the mind of God. Next the chapter evaluates the theories that suggest that particular cognitive biases influence the early conception of gods and describes more recent work that examines the crucial interplay of sociocultural input and cognitive biases. I highlight that research examining the complexities of cognitive scaffolding and cultural learning involved in the formulation of supernatural agents is in the germinal stages of its research with plenty of potential for future work.

A Brief History: Children's Concepts of Supernatural Agents

Early Approaches

Some of the first theories that speculated about children's early conception of God and supernatural agents were from the research and writings of Sigmund Freud, the famous psychoanalyst, and Jean Piaget, one of the earliest developmental psychologists.

Sigmund Freud argued that God is an exalted father figure (Freud 1927). At first an infant seeks the mother to meet all of its needs but she is later replaced by the father as the primary protector figure. Freud believed that the father symbolized the ultimate protector from the outside world. When an adult feels helpless and seeks protection, they may be attracted to God, the strongest father-like figure.

Another important figure that theorized about early conceptualization of God was Jean Piaget. Like Freud, Piaget emphasized that children begin to conceptualize God by thinking about their parents. Piaget diverged from Freud, however, by suggesting that it is due to conceptual limitations that children base their understanding about God through their concept of "parent," rather than the Freudian idea that a concept of God stems from a psychological need for a father. Piaget developed his theory based on extensively recorded observational data. He noticed that young children first attribute omniscience and divine attributes to parents and God (Piaget 1929). As young children age and realize that humans are fallible, a child's concept of God remains anthropomorphic.

Modern Approach: Cognitive Science of Religion

Piagetian theory on how children develop concepts of God largely dominated in psychology until the 1990s. During the subsequent development of the Cognitive Science of Religion (CSR), there was rapid movement toward the use of methods from many disciplines (e.g., anthropology, neuroscience, psychology, etc.), and toward empirical work to study specific phenomena related to religious cognition. One of the earliest areas to be studied in this field was the development of supernatural agent concepts (Barrett, Richert, and Driesenga 2001).

The early founders of CSR suggested that a belief in God (among other religious concepts) is a natural consequence supported by cognitive processes used in everyday activities to understand and interact with the world (Barrett and Nyhof 2001; Bloom 2007; Boyer and Ramble 2001; Guthrie 1993; McCauley 2000). Three cognitive biases in particular are the building blocks for understanding other minds and agents, and are theorized to encourage conceptualization of supernatural agents: a tendency to detect agency, teleological thinking, and *theory of mind* (ToM).

The first cognitive bias hypothesized to be a building block for the conceptualization of supernatural agents is a tendency to detect agency (Guthrie 1993). This bias not only identifies human and nonhuman agents in the environment but also sometimes causes humans to *over*-attribute agency. For example, in some experiments adults have attributed agency to shapes moving around a screen with seemingly goal-directed behavior (see Heider and Simmel 1944 for a classic experiment) or to unseen agents, such as ghosts or God, when faced with unexplained events (e.g., an object that falls off the shelf) (Bering and Parker, 2006). Uncertain events may predispose humans to attribute supernatural agency when natural agency is not sufficient. This bias is controversial as some researchers (McKay and Efferson 2010) have claimed that although this bias would have been useful to Paleolithic ancestors (e.g., for detecting dangerous agents in the environment), humans in the modern day no longer need this level of hypervigilance for detecting agents. Regardless, although this bias is not sufficient to explain solely how humans come to conceptualize agents, it contributes to an understanding of the origins of supernatural ideas.

The second hypothesized cognitive bias is a default to attribute a purpose or design to the origin of objects and other beings. This *teleological bias* is supported by a strong research program that demonstrates this bias is a universal (i.e., across several cultures) and naturally emerging cognitive bias in both adults as well as children. In these experiments, young children ascribe a function to objects and beings. For example, four- and five-year-old children when asked "what's this for?" say that "rocks are for sitting," lions are meant "to go in the zoo," and "clouds are for raining" (Kelemen 1999b). Seven- and eight-year-old children also opt for teleological explanations when asked to select a response for a science task: they choose responses that ascribe a function to objects and beings, such as claiming that "mountains are for climbing" and "babies are for loving" (Kelemen 1999c). Adults also fall prey to this bias when asked similar questions under timed pressure (Kelemen and Rosset 2009), and also adults who have Alzheimer's disease (Lombrozo, Kelemen, and Zaitchik 2007) or who lack formal education (Casler and Kelemen 2008). Responses are also similar in adults in China (Rottman et al. 2017) and Finland (Järnefelt, Canfield, and Kelemen 2015). In addition to asserting that artifacts, natural objects, and nonhuman animals were created for a purpose, children also prefer explanations that humans are intentionally created by an agent, and were created by God (Evans 2001; Kelemen 2004; Rottman et al. 2017). This intentional account of how humans and other beings originate makes more "creationist" accounts attractive to young children. In other words, both religious and nonreligious children as old as ten years favor origin explanations that say that humans were made by God. From eleven years, responses from children raised in nonreligious homes start to diverge from children raised in religious homes by responding with evolutionary explanations (Evans 2001).

The third cognitive bias hypothesized to underlie supernatural concepts is the human capacity for a ToM: the ability to take the perspective of other minds. More specifically, ToM is the capacity to attribute mental and emotional states to agents. This capacity develops across the preschool years and is a universal phenomenon in normally developing children (Liu et al. 2008; Wellman, Cross, and Watson 2001) although the onset may be slightly different across cultures (Callaghan et al. 2005; Lillard 1998; Shahaeian et al. 2011). ToM is flexible and enables a person to think about agents that are unseen (and unseeable!). The same methods to test children's understanding of other human minds have also been used to test whether they understand nonhuman animal and supernatural minds. These studies, and the methodology for testing ToM, will be discussed more fully below, but in brief, it appears that children follow a similar developmental trajectory as they do for understanding human thinking (Barrett and Nyhof 2001; Burdett, Wigger, and Barrett 2019; Giménez-Dasí, Guerrero, and Harris 2005; Kiessling and Perner 2014; Knight et al. 2004; Lane, Wellman, and Evans 2010; Nyhof and Johnson 2017; Wigger, Paxson, and Ryan 2013).

These three cognitive biases—agency detection, teleological thinking, and ToM—serve to provide the foundations for understanding both natural and supernatural agency. Researchers engaged with exploring the early development of supernatural agency concepts agree that these cognitive processes are the basic cognitive building blocks that support early conceptualization of God, deities, and other supernatural agents. However, disagreement primarily lies in how children use these biases during normal developmental cognitive processes to reason and develop a more robust concept of God. Much of this disagreement surrounds the third bias, ToM, especially how children use their developing ToM to think and form a concept of supernatural agents. I will next discuss four different theories for how children may use ToM to come to conceptualize supernatural agent concepts followed by a review of some of the studies behind each of these theories.

Four Hypotheses for How Children Come to Conceptualize God

The first hypothesis is called the *Preparedness Hypothesis*. Some proponents of the naturalness of religion suggest that certain cognitive processes and biases enable children to be particularly *prepared* to conceptualize supernatural agents (Barrett and Nyhof 2001; Wigger, Paxson, and Ryan 2013). In particular, this theory posits that children find the notion that God is omniscient fairly intuitive. In other words, children can default to knowing that whatever the piece of knowledge, a supernatural mind would know. Typical experiments use a false-belief task where children are asked to reason whether a certain supernatural or ordinary mind would have knowledge of the contents of a box when they have not looked inside. Studies supporting this approach show that young children respond that both a human and God know the contents of a box, whereas older children only respond that God would know (Barrett and Nyhof 2001; Knight et al. 2004; Wigger, Paxson, and Ryan 2013).

A second hypothesis is called the *Anthropomorphism Hypothesis*. This hypothesis suggests that children first learn to conceptualize God as human-like, based on their own experiences of observing themselves and others (Heiphetz et al. 2015; Lane, Wellman, and Evans 2010). This approach was promoted by Freud and Piaget, but is also supported by recent studies (Heiphetz et al. 2015; Lane, Wellman, and Evans 2010, 2012). These scholars suggest that children first form concepts of the ordinary human minds around them. Children develop and construct increasingly rich and complex understandings of how other human minds think based on the accumulation of experience, observation, and interaction with peers, caregivers, strangers, siblings, and so on (Carpendale and Lewis 2004; Lane 2021). Then, children use their understanding of humans as an anchor to differentiate other types of minds. Studies supporting this approach also use false-belief tasks but suggest that younger children's responses are inconsistent or more likely to show that God does not have certain knowledge, similar to a fallible human (Heiphetz et al. 2015; Kiessling and Perner 2014; Lane, Wellman, and Evans 2010, 2012; Lane, Wellman, and Evans 2014).

A third hypothesis is *Agent-Specific*, or *Anthropocentric*. Other recent data suggests that it is possible that an infant's earliest understanding of agency is more abstract rather than human-first or anthropocentric. In other words, children will reliably develop and apply a sense of agency to other things, but each agent or class of agents is subsequently treated differently. This approach is supported by psychologists who trust the methods used to test infant cognition. Other psychologists may be more skeptical because one can only infer what infants are thinking based on measuring infant behavior. As an example, developmental psychologists test infants by designing experiments that use looking-time procedures that measure the amount of time infants watch a display, event, or agent. Longer looking time usually correlates with more interest or surprise. When infants are bored or not surprised, they look away. This work shows that twelve-month-old infants will track the gaze of blobs and attribute goals and intentions to moving shapes (e.g., Csibra and Gergely 1998; Luo and Baillargeon 2010), indicating an abstract understanding of agency. This agent-specific theory is similar to the preparedness hypothesis, in that children can attribute agency to nonhuman entities, but differs by suggesting we are neither born nor destined to develop these concepts. It is also different from the anthropomorphism heuristic in that children do not first use human attributes as an anchor to think about supernatural agents. The agent-specific heuristic does not have as large a consensus because there are only a limited number of studies. It seems implicitly, based on timed experiments and infant studies, that humans can conceptualize a nonhuman agent.

A fourth hypothesis is the *Constructivist Approach* or *Sociocultural Hypothesis*. The most recent theory for understanding early conceptualizations of supernatural minds focuses on the interplay of both cognitive and sociocultural processes for constructing a concept of God. In other words, researchers propose the development of supernatural ideas is supported by ordinary cognitive processes in addition to the acquisition of specific religious and folk ideas from the child's social and cultural world (Burdett, Wigger, and Barrett 2019; Lane 2021; Legare and Souza 2012; Richert et al. 2017; Shtulman et al. 2019). Most developmental researchers are likely to agree that some portion of cultural input has a role in cognitive development, but proponents of this approach suggest a much larger role of cultural input and its role in the development of understanding other minds.

In the next section, these theories are integrated through a description and summary of both seminal and also new experimental work on children's developing concepts of God.

Precedent Research

A Brief History of the Conceptualization and Construction of God Concepts

Piagetian ideas that children use anthropomorphism to conceptualize God dominated developmental psychological thinking until the 1990s when several different labs found conflicting results. In a seminal paper, Barrett and colleagues (2001) asked children whether they thought various nonhuman (e.g., bear, God) and human agents (e.g., Mom) would know the contents of a cracker box. Minutes before children were asked this question, they were shown that instead of crackers, rocks were inside the cracker box. This so-called "false-belief task" tests whether children understand that other agents would have a false belief that crackers are inside the box. Children pass this test (and are presumed to have developed a more complex ToM) when they respond that other agents would have a false belief that crackers are inside the box. Children do not pass the test (and are presumed to still be developing an understanding of ToM) if they respond that an agent would know there are rocks inside the box. Children in Barrett, Richert, and Driesenga's (2001) study responded similar to a well-documented pattern of responses: the youngest children (around age three years) were captivated by their own privileged knowledge that there were rocks inside the box and responded that all agents knew that there were rocks inside the box. Older children (>4.5 years), on the other hand, differentiated knowledge abilities and attributed false beliefs to the nonhuman and human agents. Children's responses for God were an exception. Children of all ages responded that God knew there were rocks inside the box. These results, that all children attributed "omniscience" to God, prompted Barrett, Richert, and Driesenga (2001) to make the provocative conclusion that children find understanding divine knowledge conceptually easier than understanding more limited human knowledge abilities, and that children might be *prepared* to think of supernatural ideas. This first study argued heavily for the preparedness hypothesis.

This study inspired many follow-up studies, a few replicating this pattern of results but many also challenging these findings. Several follow-up studies supported Barrett, Richert, and Driesenga's (2001) findings with Christian children in America (Richert and Barrett 2005; Wigger, Paxson, and Ryan 2013) and Muslim children in Indonesia and Mormon children in the United States (Nyhof and Johnson 2017). The first study to challenge Barrett and Nyhof's (2001) findings was a study that gave three- to five-year-old Greek children both a false-belief task as well as an *ignorance* task, a task where children remained ignorant of the contents of the box (Makris and Pnevmatikos 2007). They were curious whether children would reason about humans and God differently when children did not know the contents of the box. They suspected that when presented with a false-belief task, children find it difficult to suppress their own knowledge and the pattern observed by Barrett and colleagues (2001) was reflective of children overattributing knowledge based on an inability to suppress their own knowledge rather than a cognitive default to attribute omniscience. Similar to Barrett and Nyhof (2001), three-year-old children attributed knowledge to all agents and they only differentiated more limited knowledge to humans between four and five years. Differentially, three-year-old children in the ignorance task attributed ignorance to all agents, whereas four- to five-year-old children attributed knowledge to God and ignorance to the human agents. They concluded that children cannot represent a supernatural mind until they have developed a fully representational understanding of a human mind, typically sometime after five years of age. Children used anthropomorphism as a heuristic to conceptualize God. The anthropomorphic hypothesis has been replicated with American children (Lane, Wellman, and Evans 2010), Spanish children (Giménez-Dasí, Guerrero, and Harris 2005), and Austrian children (Kiessling and Perner 2014).

The above experiments claim to be examining children's understanding of God's "omniscience." But do young children really understand "omniscience" and its implications, especially considering adults can barely think consistently about it (Purzycki 2013b; Purzycki et al. 2012)? One study asked three- to five-year-olds to answer question about a fictional supernatural agent (Mr. Smart) that "knows everything about everything" (Lane, Wellman, and Evans 2014). Children were asked whether they would attribute different types of knowledge (e.g., knowledge about facts) and also the depth of knowledge (e.g., knowing all information about a particular topic such as the mechanics of a car) to God, Mr. Smart, and Mr. Powerful. If children reason consistently about omniscience, or that a being should know everything, children should attribute all knowledge to Mr. Smart. Only the oldest children (age five) attributed all knowledge characteristics to Mr. Smart. The youngest children only attributed some knowledge to Mr. Smart (factual knowledge) and found it difficult to attribute depth of knowledge in favor of attributing other experts (e.g., mechanics) with more expertise (e.g., knowing all information about the mechanics of a car). Two of the cognitive competencies that aid children in being able to think about omniscience are (1) being able to imagine improbable phenomena as well as (2) being able to understand the concept of infinity (Lane et al. 2014). These results suggest that as young children develop an understanding of others they learn to differentiate between more limited and divine minds. A fuller understanding of omniscience develops across the life span and crucially with cultural input.

For the first two decades of the twenty-first century, the preparedness and anthropomorphism hypotheses dominated experiments examining children's conceptualization of God's mind. These experiments largely focused on children's understanding of whether God is all-knowing (e.g., Barrett and Nyhof 2001; Lane, Wellman, and Evans 2010), or whether God has particular divine cognitive characteristics such as keen perception (e.g., Burdett, Barrett, and Greenway 2020; Richert and Barrett 2005) or is able to hear and answer prayers (e.g., Lane and Shafto 2017; Woolley and Phelps 2001). As detailed above, these studies suggest that older children (usually after four years of age) differentiate among supernatural and human minds. Further work has examined whether children attribute other types of properties. Below I describe this other work and also describe how researchers are moving more toward testing more constructivist-conceptual development theories of children's development of God concepts.

Examining God's Other Attributes

In the last decade, researchers have shifted away from using theory-of-mind tasks to examine whether children understand if another agent has privileged knowledge. Some of this shift is to try to use new tasks to explore children's attributions of other psychological properties (i.e., besides knowledge) as well as biological and physical properties to gods.

In one study, five-year-old children were shown cards with depictions of different psychological (e.g., thinks, talks, dreams), physiological (e.g., sits, stretches, jumps), and biological properties (e.g., eats, grows, sneezes) and asked whether these could be attributed to supernatural and fictional agents (Shtulman 2008). Unlike adults who attributed more psychological properties to both types of agents, five-year-olds attributed all types of properties to both types of agents. In a different cultural sample, younger Indian children (eight to eleven years) also attributed more anthropomorphic properties to supernatural agents than older ones (twelve to fifteen years) (Shtulman et al. 2019). Other interesting patterns emerge with cultural background and religion. Both Christian (Richert et al. 2017) and Hindu children (Shtulman et al. 2019) are more likely to attribute human properties to God than Muslim children. Researchers conclude that the differences in responses may be reflective of the different theological teachings of each religion. For example, Allah is not depicted in human form, whereas Jesus and the Hindu gods, Ganesha and Krishna, all have (by and large) human forms. Further work has also shown that some children may be more likely to anthropomorphize based on how much the child ascribes "animacy" to agents, and therefore infer more properties based on the perceived "aliveness" of the agents (Saide and Richert 2021). Thus, there are interesting patterns that emerge depending on age (i.e., younger children are more likely to attribute more human-like properties than adults), religious background (i.e., Muslim children anthropomorphize less than children of other traditions), and individual variation in concepts (i.e., children who see God as "alive" attribute anthropomorphic properties). This pattern suggests other variables are influential in concepts of God beyond just cognitive biases.

Moral Action

In addition to types of knowledge and power that is attributed to God, other work has examined the type of moral knowledge that God knows and cares about. In studies with adults in the United States and the Tyva Republic, a culture where not all gods care about the moral behavior of humans, adults were more likely to affirmatively respond about statements that said gods cared about moral behavior (e.g., giving to the homeless) rather than other knowledge attributions (e.g., knowing that someone's cat is hungry), and at least among American Christians, they are quicker to respond to questions about God's knowledge of moral information than nonmoral information (Purzycki 2013b; Purzycki et al. 2012). Building on this work, Heiphetz et al. (2018) asked five- to eight-year-old American children whether God and humans would find either good (e.g., helping another person) or bad behavior (e.g., hitting another person) acceptable. Children responded that both God and humans would find the good behavior acceptable and the bad behavior unacceptable. However, in another study, six- to seven-year-olds were more likely to respond that God would know whether they and others had bad behavior (Wolle, McLaughlin, and Heiphetz 2021), whereas four- to five-year-olds did not make this distinction. In a second study, four- to five-year-olds responded that God would know their own transgressions but not know the transgressions of other people (Wolle, McLaughlin, and Heiphetz 2021). In short, this says that young children can distinguish good and bad behavior but only older children understand that God would know both the transgressions of all people.

The Sociocultural Construction of a Concept of God's Mind

In addition to exploring children's attributions of various other properties, extant research is exploring the sociocultural impact on the development of religious concepts (Burdett, Wigger, and Barrett 2019; Kapitány et al. 2020; Richert et al. 2017; Richert et al. 2016; Saide and Richert 2020). Cultural acquisition processes are necessary because of the unobservable nature of supernatural agents. The early beginnings of the work in the CSR were dominated by theories that suggested that children are "intuitive theists" (Barrett and Nyhof 2001; Kelemen 2004), and that cognitive biases support the conceptualization of religious concepts. However, more researchers are recognizing that religious concepts are *in part* supported by particular cognitive biases (e.g., via anthropomorphism, agent-based, or preparedness) and capacities (e.g., ToM, executive function), and also constructed by cultural input (Lane 2021; Saide and Richert 2020). Indeed, cognitive content biases are important for how people mentally represent gods, but cultural learning biases are key to explaining why children and adults commit to and believe in God and other supernatural agents (Gervais et al. 2011). Particular social and cultural learning mechanisms, such as learning through testimony (Harris and Koenig 2006), imitating behaviors or rituals (Kapitány and Nielsen 2015; Legare and Watson-Jones 2015), and observing others (Nielsen and Blank 2011), serve to provide the context and cultural information that the basic cognitive framework needs for religious ideas and potentially belief (Harris and Corriveau 2014; Richert et al. 2017; Saide and Richert 2020).

The idea that sociocultural input influences cognition is not new. In most areas of conceptual development, cultural input scaffolds the development of key cognitive abilities. For example, an understanding of death, life, and existence requires some experience to understand that life ends and that some species go extinct (Burdett, Barrett, and Greenway 2020; Poling and Evans 2004). However, historically researchers examining religious cognition tend to examine the universality of many religious concepts to help explain the ubiquity and transmission of religion and do so by examining cognitive processes. In a current trend, researchers are going beyond exploration of the cognitive processes that bias us to think about supernatural agent concepts by trying to understand how cultural input, testimony, participation in rituals, and so on change and form our conceptions of God and influence many people to commit to religious traditions.

Observation and testimony are two examples of early sociocultural learning about both the natural and supernatural world. For believing that an entity is real, testimony plays an influential role. The endorsement from an influential role model, such as their mother, teacher, favored peer, and so on, is a powerful advertisement for a particular belief. By age five, children are able to distinguish the reality status of unobservable entities (Kalish 1996; Lane and Shafto 2017; Woolley and Cox 2007). And four- to eight-year-old children are not gullible (Woolley and Ghossainy 2013); they can distinguish between unobservable entities that are endorsed by others (e.g., God, Tooth Fairy), not usually endorsed (e.g., witches), impossible entities (e.g., barking cats), and scientific entities (e.g., germs) (Harris and Koenig 2006). Children responded confidently about the existence of scientific entities compared to the endorsed beings, and this confidence seems to be influenced by the quality of testimony (Harris and Koenig 2006).

In one of the earliest studies that explored the interplay between children's ToM and sociocultural input, Lane and McCorkle (2012) found that younger children raised in Christian homes were more accurate in their attributions of knowledge to God compared to secular counterparts who were not consistent in their responses. Indeed, growing evidence supports the idea that cultural input influences the early conceptualization of God concepts. In one of the first comparisons of three- to seven-year-old children's understanding of God in two different religious traditions in the

United States (Mormonism and Christianity) and two different religious traditions in Indonesia (Catholicism and Islam), Nyhof and Johnson (2017) found that the youngest children distinguished between God, ghosts, and angels in all cultures and religious traditions and attributed special mental properties to God and not to other agents. However, as children aged, they continued to make more sophisticated distinctions among the agents. In another study, Burdett, Wigger, and Barrett (2019) asked three- to five-year-old children in four different cultures to respond whether they would attribute knowledge or ignorance to God and other supernatural agents. Results showed different cultural patterns. For example, Catholic children from the Dominican Republic attributed God with knowledge from an early age but older Modern-Orthodox-Jewish-Israeli and Christian British children consistently attributed God with knowledge. Christian Kenyan children responded at chance levels for God at all ages. For all other supernatural agents, responses were variable from all cultural groups, with inconsistent responses even in the older age groups. Burdett, Wigger, and Barrett (2019) argued strongly for more work to examine the role of cultural influences on both cognitive and conceptual development. Specifically, further holistic data collection is needed for each child participant's religious participation intensity, parent's views on God, family dynamics, parent and children's tendency to anthropomorphize, and who teaches children about God.

In a suite of studies, Richert and colleagues (2017) have shown that four- to seven-year-old Muslim children are more likely to attribute omniscience to God (Allah) than Protestant, Catholic, and Non-Affiliated children. And, children's ability to differentiate between God's mind and a human mind (regardless of their religious tradition) was predicted by the degree of anthropomorphism in their parent's concept of God (as measured by an eight-item questionnaire from Shtulman (2008). Parents and community consensus play a large role in early conceptualizations of God concepts. Indeed, children are attuned to subtle linguistic markers from parents' speech (e.g., "I believe in…" vs. "I know about…") (Canfield and Ganea 2014).

Future Directions

A growing consensus among developmental researchers is that understanding the processes of cultural learning is crucial for understanding the variations and similarities in the formation of God concepts. New work can go in several different directions.

One avenue is to explore the influence that peers, parents, and other role models have on learning (e.g., Harris and Corriveau 2011). For example, preschool children are more likely to learn from influential role models such as those who are competent (e.g., Burdett et al. 2016), accurate (e.g., Koenig and Harris 2005), familiar (e.g., Lucas et al. 2017), or composed of a majority (e.g., Haun, Rekers, and Tomasello 2012). Much of this work has examined human-based models. However, there is a small body of work that has shown that children accept information from an informant who produced a magical event over an informant who produced an ordinary one (Kim and Harris 2013), and that children prefer to learn from someone who can read minds compared to someone who cannot (Kim and Harris 2014). These studies are notable because these show how attractive and powerful role models are in learning and accepting information. These types of studies can help illuminate how people acquire knowledge about religion and other cultural information in addition to the degree of influence they have. For example, further work could explore the type of information (e.g., facts, knowledge of future events) children will choose to learn from extraordinary minds over ordinary ones. In addition, work could explore the attributes of different influential religious leaders in different traditions and how they influence belief and behavior.

Another area is how children understand and acquire cultural and religious actions through imitation and ritual (Watson-Jones and Legare 2016). This work highlights how important ritual is to group cohesion (Watson-Jones and Legare 2016) and sustaining norms (Rossano 2012) and group membership (Wen et al. 2020). In other words the more one engages in the same actions as a group of people the more one affiliates with these group members and carries out these actions in the future. However, we do not know the extent to which children will continue to carry out a ritual or practice. One theory is that humans reliably measure the importance of a certain belief or cultural norm to a community by attending to the actions of particular individuals. These credibility-enhancing displays (CREDs) are actions that demonstrate a person's degree of commitment to a type of belief or value (Henrich 2009). CREDs can signal particular normative, cultural, and religious beliefs of the community and can help stabilize these actions across the community as others transmit the same displays. Recent empirical work with adults has shown that exposure to CREDs predicts religiosity, belief in God's non/existence, and theism vs. non-theism (Lanman and Buhrmester 2016). We might predict that children who notice and witness rituals, especially more frequently and by notable others, will be more likely to participate and potentially believe in the values the ritual represents. Other work could explore how sensitive young children are to CREDs, whether certain particular learning biases influence religious transmission, such as the frequency or intensity of the display of ritual or if CREDs are made by particular individuals (e.g., who are prestigious, familiar).

A new area worth exploring would be the different cultural facets that influence conceptual development of supernatural agents such as the degree to which children learn these concepts from social interactions (Richert et al. 2017). Traditionally, work has looked at differences between nations rather than variation within them (although see Richert et al. 2017). A new review paper by Heiphetz and Oishi (2021) outlines several different ways that researchers measure culture. Many researchers think of culture as a particular nation (e.g., the UK or China). Other researchers have described culture along different terms, such as more feminine or masculine (Hofstede 1980), tight or loose (Gelfand et al. 2011), collectivistic or individualistic (Triandis 1995), or heterogeneous or homogeneous (Muthukrishna et al. 2020). Heiphetz and Oishi (2021) further propose that studying development may be best in light of the shared values and norms that surround developmental milestones. For example, understanding shared language, social norms, and how these are transmitted (e.g., peer-to-peer, across generations, parent-to-child, expert-to-child) can inform how culture and especially how cultural ideas form. This type of approach may shed light on how children are introduced and continue to formulate their concepts of supernatural agents across their development.

Finally, what is really needed are studies that consider development across time and across populations that can compare religious traditions beyond WEIRD (Western Industrialized Educated Rich Democratic) and Christian nations. Studies need to conduct work longitudinally to understand the cognitive maturational process alongside cultural influence. Longitudinal work has many challenges, including that it is expensive and time-consuming, especially keeping participants over long periods of time.

We are only at the beginning of understanding the development of God concepts. As suggested in the examples above, more work is needed in understanding the acquisition, development, and cultural transmission of religious ideas and supernatural minds, including God. Some answers may be forthcoming. A new network of developmental psychologists, the Developing Belief Network, has formed in order to test the cultural, social, developmental, and longitudinal processes of the development of religious cognition and behavior using a multi-method approach (www.developingbelief.com). It is my hope that in a few years we will know much more about the formation of supernatural agent concepts as researchers tackle many of the above gaps in understanding the development of religious cognition.

3

The Divine Projector: How Human Motivations and Biases Give Shape to Gods' Minds

Joshua Conrad Jackson and Kurt Gray

"Behold, God is exalted, and we do not know Him"

—Job 36:26

Introduction

Many believers, like the biblical character Job, believe that gods transcend human knowledge, and that human minds cannot grasp the true nature of the divine. But this has not stopped us from guessing what gods may look like, how they may behave, where they may live, and what they might think of our choices and behaviors on earth. From the Epic of Gilgamesh and the ceiling of the Sistine Chapel to the *Book of the Dead* and the great Pacific Island totems, humans have conceptualized gods on countless occasions, in countless mediums.

Human views of gods have also been tremendously diverse. Some gods are perceived as malicious and cunning, such as the Hindu God Badi Mata who attacks children during puberty. Others are benevolent and kind, such as the Navajo (*Diné*) fertility god Estsanadehi who sends gentle rain to help crops grow during the summer, or the Inuit god Ignerssuak who helps to guide mariners home when they are lost at sea. Some gods possess physical desires and flaws, such as the blind Norse god Hoder or the drunk Chinese war god Zhang Fei. Others transcend worldly sensation, such as Greco-Roman god Chaos, whom the Roman poet Ovid styled as an unformed mass of elements. Some gods are emotional and expressive—such as the Celtic god Aengus who fell deeply in love or the Polynesian god Ruamoko who flew into rages that caused earthquakes. Others are unbound by feeling, such as the unknowable Ugandan creator god Bunyoro.

We still do not have a full grasp on why gods' minds—defined here as their character traits and thoughts—vary as much as they do. Nearly a century ago, Floyd Allport (1937) outlined a framework for studying human psychological variation when he combed through a dictionary and documented English-language personality traits (Allport 1937). However, we are only beginning to develop methods of capturing divine minds with survey and ethnographic data (Bendixen and Purzycki, present volume; Purzycki and Jamieson-Lane 2017; Watts et al. 2021), and there are still wide disciplinary differences in how scientists of religion estimate this variation. Psychologists have developed methods of dimension detection and reduction in survey data and applied these methods to the study of religion and spirituality (Gorsuch 1968; Johnson et al. 2015, 2019; Johnson, present volume). However, these studies have predominantly focused on Western Christian samples. Anthropologists have been much more devoted to studying religious diversity through fieldwork and ethnography, but this research seldom uses quantitative methods that can identify the broader dimensions of gods' characteristics and test the socioecological correlates of these dimensions. These disciplinary divides have been barriers to a broadly accepted approach to studying gods' minds, and by extension, unifying theories of gods' minds in the social sciences.

If there were a comprehensive theory of gods' minds, however, it would surely place the role of human psychology front and center. The human mind not only allows us to envision and communicate information about divine minds, but it also allows us to modify this information based on our cognitive biases and motivations. A surge of research on cognition and culture is beginning to shed light on exactly how we shape and reshape our views of gods, and why religious beliefs vary so much across cultures. The goal of this chapter is to gather much of this evidence in one document that cohesively describes (a) how humans can perceive gods' minds, (b) how these perceptions are influenced by cognitive biases, and (c) how ecological and cultural context interacts with human motivation to change how people view gods. Taken as a whole, this research paints views of humans as "divine projectors" of gods' minds.

While the term "projection" has a long history with different connotations in psychology, we use the word to describe the process in which humans' personal biases and motivations (e.g., a motivation for attachment, a bias toward egocentrism) and awareness of collective pressures and ecological features (e.g., the pressure to cooperate, the salience of natural hazards) explicitly or implicitly influence how they perceive gods' minds. Not all divine projections are self-serving, but they often arise from people's motivations to preserve cognitive control, well-being, and to address their concerns about society. In this chapter, we begin by describing the human capacities to conceptualize and communicate about gods. We next describe how cognitive and motivational factors can influence these conceptualization and communication processes, and we close by describing future directions that can broaden and refine how we think about the complicated relationship between human and supernatural psychology.

Cognitive and Cultural Mechanisms Underlying Conceptualizing Gods' Minds

As it was, every time that the parasol slightly moved, the dog growled fiercely and barked. He must, I think, have reasoned to himself in a rapid and unconscious manner, that movement without any apparent cause indicated the presence of some strange living agent, and that no stranger had a right to be on his territory.

> The belief in spiritual agencies would easily pass into the belief in the existence of one or more gods.
>
> —Charles Darwin ([1871] 2008: 118)

Humans have most likely believed in supernatural agents since the dawn of our species. According to archeological evidence, humans have been ritualistically burying their dead, creating religious iconography, and making sacrifices to gods and spirits for tens of thousands of years (see Rossano, present volume). The historical and cross-cultural prevalence of human religious belief has led many scholars to suggest that ancient evolutionary mutations predisposed humans to religious belief. In the *Descent of Man* ([1871] 2008), for example, Darwin compares human religious belief to his dog's distrust of a parasol moving in the wind.

In the early twenty-first century, these intuitions blossomed into a cognitive science of religion (CSR), in which scholars investigated how evolutionary adaptations in human prehistory may have predisposed people to supernatural beliefs (Atran and Norenzayan 2004; Barrett 2004; Boyer 2001). CSR continues to provide interesting hypotheses about the early development of belief in gods. However, these claims are now complicated by a growing realization that religious beliefs are the product of at least two interactive evolutionary systems: biological evolution and cultural evolution (Acerbi and Mesoudi 2015; Boyd and Richerson 1985; Jablonka and Lamb 2007). To understand the mechanisms that allow people to conceptualize gods' minds, we must therefore recognize both the basic psychological capacities that allow humans to perceive minds and the cultural processes that allow us to transmit religious beliefs across time and place. We begin by briefly reviewing these two sets of processes.

Mind Perception, and the Capacity to Conceptualize Divine Minds

All people appear to have access to their own minds but not to the workings of other minds. We cannot even be certain that other agents have minds at all, a dilemma that philosophers call the problem of other minds, or "Descartes Problem" (Overgaard 2006). The problem of other minds does not stop people from detecting minds in surrounding agents, and inferring the preferences, values, and beliefs of these minds (Epley and Waytz 2010; Waytz et al. 2010; Wegner and Gray 2017). Children as young as three months of age will show preferential treatment toward other people, animate objects, and biological motion (Bertenthal, Proffitt, and Cutting 1984; Crichton and Lange-Küttner 1999; Legerstee 1991). By age five, children will show evidence of understanding that agents have separate minds that can hold information beyond the child's awareness or can fail to grasp something that the child knows, an ability that is measured through the false-beliefs task (Dennett 1971; Wimmer and Perner 1983).

These mind perception abilities are important building blocks for perceiving supernatural minds. Belief in supernatural agents such as gods requires attributing agency to a mind, acknowledging that this mind has unique capacities and contents, and inferring that the contents of a supernatural mind are guiding the behaviors of that supernatural agent. The complexity of these processes may be an important reason why religious beliefs appear to play an outsized role in human life compared to the life of other animals There are famous examples of animals attributing agency to inanimate objects, other than Darwin's dog. For example, Jane Goodall described chimpanzees who would break sticks to scare away a passing storm (Goodall 2000) and other studies have observed vervet monkeys making eagle calls after seeing falling leaves (Cheney and Seyfarth 1988). However, there is still debate about the nature of agency detection in nonhuman animals or the extent that these animals infer psychological qualities in the agents they detect, let alone supernatural qualities.

Cultural Transmission, and the Evolution of Religious Diversity

Basic mind perception capacities can help us understand why religious beliefs are universal, but they do not explain the tremendous scope of religious diversity. Cultural evolutionary models are therefore critical for understanding how shared religious beliefs can emerge in populations, how these beliefs are transmitted and modified over time, and how events in the environment can shape the cultural transmission of supernatural agents.

Cultural evolutionary models arguably date back to Darwin's *Descent*, but they were popularized in the 1970s and 1980s in population genetics as a framework for understanding how behavioral differences could arise in groups without genetic variation (Boyd and Richerson 1985; Cavalli-Sforza and Feldman 1981). According to these models, cultural information can be transmitted and modified as in Darwinian evolution, meaning that cultural transmission is defined by variation, inheritance (social learning), and competition (between groups, and between sources of cultural information). In the years since these early contributions, cultural evolutionists have pointed out similarities between cultural and biological evolution (e.g., both cultural and biological variation can frequently be traced along evolutionary phylogenies) (Gray and Watts 2017), and crucial differences between these evolutionary systems (e.g., cultural evolution is subject to higher rates of nonrandom modification than genetic evolution) (Jablonka and Lamb 2007) that make cultural evolution worth studying as a unique process.

One reason why cultural evolution models are useful for explaining religious differences is because of the attention they give to environmental differences. Just like the environment shapes the traits that genetically evolve in species, it will also shape the traits that culturally evolve in gods (Bendixen and Purzycki 2020). Some of these traits are more mundane: human groups living along the banks of rivers may be more likely to believe in river spirits or bathing taboos. But other environmental influences on cultural evolution can be more nuanced. For example, theories of "big gods" suggest that people developed beliefs in gods who monitor human behavior and punish defection because these religious beliefs helped humans live in large agricultural societies without large-scale free riding (Johnson 2016; Norenzayan et al. 2016; Norenzayan and Shariff 2008; Purzycki and McKay, present volume).

Cultural evolutionary models are also useful because they help explain why some religious belief systems have evolved to be so similar. One reason for this similarity can be ancestral interdependence: Islam, Christianity, and Judaism share very similar views of God as monotheistic, all-knowing, and moralizing, but this is because these religious belief systems share a common Abrahamic ancestor (Gray and Watts 2017; Watts et al. 2015; White et al. 2021). Another reason for similarity can be because of forces of cultural "attraction" that lead people to remember and transmit some religious beliefs at the expense of others (Sperber 1996). For instance, theories of "minimal counterintuitive" transmission suggest that people will remember information about supernatural agents who violate key principles of lay physics (e.g., walking on water) or lay biology (e.g., living without food) more than supernatural agents who violate none of these principles (e.g., an ordinary human) or agents that violate all these principles (e.g., a spirit with an unintelligible name who can neither be seen nor heard) (Boyer 2007). Theories of minimal intuitive transmission are controversial (Purzycki and Willard 2016), but we use these theories as an example here because they illustrate a typical CSR approach to studying why some aspects of religious belief have proliferated at the expense of other aspects.

Forces of cultural evolution are constantly interacting with individual-level preferences and beliefs. For example, humans may have a common bias toward viewing their gods as sharing their environment and appearance (see below), but ecological and cultural variation in ecology, clothing, and adornment will interact with these biases to produce diverse religious beliefs (McNamara and Purzycki 2020; Purzycki and McNamara 2016). Similarly, people may believe in gods that are well-suited to address collective threats. However, each community will face a different set of collective threats to survival and resource availability, which will result in widespread variation in how people conceptualize gods' concerns and capacities (Bendixen and Purzycki, present volume; Lightner and Purzycki, present volume). In these cases, and other cases described below, properties of gods' minds emerge from the interaction of common psychological mechanisms and differentiated regional ecologies and cultural norms.

How Human Cognitive Biases Influence Gods' Minds

> If cows and horses had hands and could draw, cows would draw gods that look like cows and horses would draw gods that look like horses.
> —Xenophanes

Humans are a unique species in part because we share much of the same cognitive hardware. Whereas many nonhuman animals have speciated to adapt to their environments, human cultural adaptations have allowed us to settle the globe with a relatively universal genome (Collins, Morgan, and Patrinos 2003; Henrich 2016). The universality of our hardware means that many of our religious beliefs may be affected by the same cognitive tendencies, even in diverse religious groups from different world regions.

Anthropomorphism

As Xenophanes pointed out long ago, one of these biases may be to perceive gods as humanlike. In religions around the world, people appear to anthropomorphize the bodies, minds, and familial histories of their gods. The cross-cultural scope of anthropomorphism is still debated, and some religious groups do not appear to personify their gods as much as others (Medin and García 2017b, 2017a; Ojalehto et al. 2015; Ojalehto mays, Seligman, and Medin 2020). However, hundreds of religious groups across world regions show at least some tendency to anthropomorphize gods (Murdock 1967), and new theories of anthropomorphism suggest general mechanisms that could encourage such anthropomorphism (Epley, Waytz, and Cacioppo 2007). The first of these mechanisms, elicited agent knowledge, proposes that human beliefs are constrained by what people already know. Since people know more about humans than any other kind of agent, they are most likely to ascribe humanlike traits and capabilities to a nonhuman mind. Studies on "theological correctness," for example, find that people implicitly assume that God shares human limitations (e.g., answering prayers one at a time) even though they explicitly claim that God is limitless (J. L. Barrett 1999). Even when humans ascribe nonhuman traits to their gods, they tend to borrow traits from animals in their local environments: Whale cults can be historically traced to religions in Japan and Alaska (Lantis 1938), whereas cattle cults arose in Southern Asia and Northern Africa (Brass 2003; Di Lernia 2006), near where humans may have first domesticated cattle.

A second mechanism of anthropomorphism is effectance, the drive to understand one's environment. Effectance may be one reason why active high gods who intervene in human life are most common in regions of the world with unstable weather patterns (Botero et al. 2014; Skoggard et al. 2020), or why many agricultural societies believe in gods that regulate weather and crop yield. And a final mechanism for anthropomorphism is sociality, or the bias toward perceiving gods with whom we can have humanlike relationships. Some studies suggest that people develop attachment relationships with gods the same way that we develop attachment relationships with parental figures and romantic partners (Granqvist and Kirkpatrick 2013; Kirkpatrick 1998; Kirkpatrick and Shaver 1992; Rowatt and Kirkpatrick 2002). Since it is easier to conceptualize attachment with a humanlike figure than an unknown agent, people are biased to perceiving gods as humanlike.

Egocentrism

Elicited agent knowledge, effectance, and sociality may not only lead people to infer anthropomorphic traits in their gods but may also lead people to conceptualize gods' attitudes, preferences, and even physical appearances egocentrically (i.e., similar to their own). For example, Christians assume that God shares their views on social issues such as affirmative action and abortion (Epley et al. 2009). People even assume that God shares some aspects of their physical appearance. One study asked Christians to choose images that resembled their view of God, and then statistically aggregated these images into composites. Analyses revealed that younger participants produced composite images of God that appeared younger than older participants' composites (see Figure 3.1), African American participants produced composite images of God that had darker skin tones than white participants, and participants who identified as physically attractive produced more physically attractive images of God than participants who identified as physically unattractive (Jackson, Hester, and Gray 2018).

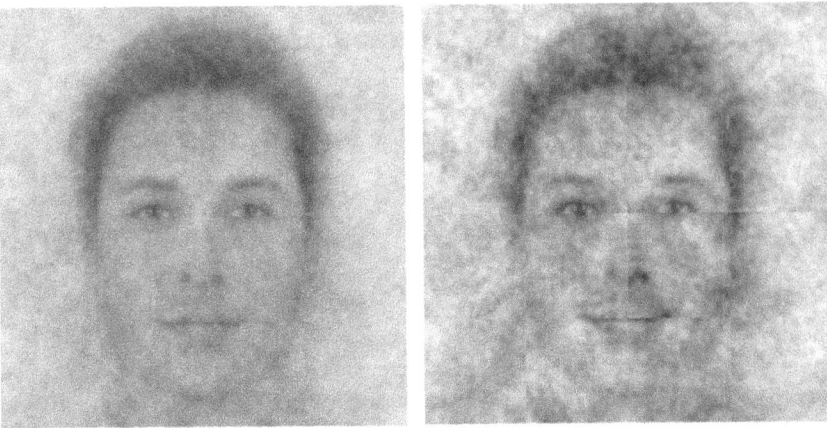

Figure 3.1 Aggregates of the images that young participants (left panel) and old participants (right panel) associated with how they viewed God. Reproduced from Jackson, Hester, and Gray (2018).

Egocentric religious beliefs can have wide-ranging implications beyond religion. In the United States, for example, white men have disproportionate power in society, and this position of power leads many people to assume that God is a white man (Roberts et al. 2020). However, perceiving God as a white man perpetuates assumptions that white men are better suited to lead. One study tested this assumption with a creative design in which kids were taught that a foreign planet with two ethnicities was created by a God with "Hibble" ethnicity or with "Glerk" ethnicity. Results showed that children consistently believed that aliens with the same ethnicity as the creator god should be responsible for ruling the planet (Roberts et al. 2020).

This research has intriguing implications for the historical development of religious beliefs, and it may explain cross-cultural differences in how people perceive gods' minds. However, a major limitation of this research is that it has sampled nearly exclusively from Christians in the United States and Europe. Given evidence that anthropomorphism is not common in some religious traditions (Medin and García 2017b, 2017a; Ojalehto et al. 2015; Ojalehto mays, Seligman, and Medin 2020), we encourage future research to explore the kinds of biases that may influence the diffusion of gods in these other traditions.

How Human Motivations Influence Gods' Minds

Whatever your heart clings to and confides in, that is really your God.
—Martin Luther

Humans are constantly using their religious beliefs to manage their motivations. This process may take the form of behaviors such as prayer or ritual in which people directly ask supernatural agents to act on the world. But in other cases, people will reconstruct their views of gods based on a motivation to overcome problems facing their groups. This process was perhaps best documented in fieldwork with the Tyvan people of Siberia. Across several studies, Purzycki asked Tyvan believers about the salient problems in their community, and then asked them to free list what gods care about (Purzycki 2013b). These studies showed that people commonly ascribed their salient communal concerns to their gods.

The Motivation to Punish Norm Violators

The motivation to outsource salient community concerns to gods may have broader implications for the cultural evolution of religious beliefs. The last several thousand years have been marked by a rise in punitive and moralizing high gods (cf. Purzycki and McKay, present volume), and many theories have now speculated about the origins of these gods (Johnson 2016; Norenzayan and Shariff 2008; Watts, Greenhill et al. 2015). Belief in punitive gods is also puzzling from a psychological standpoint, as it is unclear why people should believe in gods that punish them. Until now, the most popular theory of this trend has relied on "distal" mechanisms of cultural evolution, meaning that it has focused on the population-level functions of punitive gods for large-scale cooperation. However, distal explanations do not explain why individuals will embrace and share punitive religious beliefs. Some of our recent studies build on Purzycki's fieldwork to suggest that the motivation to regulate community norms and punish norm violators may be a proximal explanation of why people adopt beliefs in punitive and moralizing gods in the first place.

Our theory of punitive religious beliefs draws from tightness–looseness theory, which is a theory of why some societies have more restrictive cultural norms than others (Gelfand, Harrington, and Jackson 2017). A prominent finding in tightness–looseness theory is that societies typically become more restrictive after large-scale collective threats such as warfare or famine (Gelfand et al. 2011). Another crucial finding in this literature is that, as societies become culturally tighter, individuals living in these societies become less tolerant of people who violate community norms and more personally motivated to punish these individuals (Mu et al. 2015). The cost of third-party punishment makes it unappealing for individual people to themselves act as secular norm enforcers (Jordan et al. 2016; McAuliffe, Jordan, and Warneken 2015). For this reason, people living in tight societies may find norm-enforcing punitive gods and spirits appealing, since supernatural norm enforcers have the advantage of punishing norm violators at a minimal perceived cost to their believers (so long as believers think of themselves as rule-followers).

Following this theorizing, we made two basic predictions: punitive religious beliefs may be most common in culturally tight societies, and these beliefs may also be most common in regions of the world with high levels of socioecological threat. In many ways, these dynamics resemble the individual-level projections that we summarized earlier in this chapter. Just as people projected their disapproval about abortion to beliefs in gods who punished abortion (Epley et al. 2009), so too might they project their disapproval of selfish norm violators to beliefs in gods who punish people who refuse to follow cooperative norms.

A range of studies have now provided support for each of these predictions. For example, an analysis of conflict over two hundred years of human history found that, during periods of intense intergroup conflict (measured through number of deaths due to warfare), literary corpora are most likely to contain citations to Bible chapters depicting God as punitive but were no more likely to cite Bible passages depicting God as loving (Caluori et al. 2020). Historical changes in cultural tightness within the United States over that same period closely mirrored shifts in how punitively people viewed God. A series of follow-up studies showed that historical levels of ecological threats, including natural hazards, resource scarcity, and pathogen prevalence, could explain regional differences in punitive religious beliefs across US states—effects that were mediated by state-level cultural tightness (Jackson, Caluori, et al. 2021). Even manipulating people's perceptions of—the value of—cultural tightness leads people to rate punitive traits of God as more important relative to loving traits (Jackson, Caluori et al. 2020).

Many of these findings have replicated in analyses of small-scale societies. Studies analyzing the distribution of moralizing gods in the ethnographic record have found that gods are most likely to have moralizing and punitive attributes in societies facing high levels of pathogen prevalence and natural hazards (Botero et al. 2014; Jackson, Gelfand, and Ember 2020; Skoggard et al. 2020), an association that appears to be at least partially mediated by variation in cultural tightness across societies (Jackson, Gelfand, and Ember 2020). These findings reflect how aspects of people's cultural groups can influence what they think is best for society.

The Motivation to Maintain Cognitive Control

People may be motivated to uphold societal norms and values, but they are also motivated to preserve their own well-being, and these personally focused motivations may also shape views of gods. One line of reasoning, dating back to Freud (1927) and Nietzsche (2005), is that the motivation for cognitive closure and control may explain why some people view God as all-powerful. Theories of compensatory control have experimentally tested this intuition by manipulating people's sense of personal control and testing for their views of gods (Kay et al. 2009, 2010). According to these studies, people who perceive a lack of control tend to view gods as more powerful, perhaps as a way of outsourcing control to a higher power. Replication efforts have failed to reproduce some of these findings, however, meaning that the true relationship between personal control and religious beliefs is an important area for future research (Hoogeveen et al. 2018).

The Motivation to Maintain Psychological Safety

Many people also appear to believe in gods that directly watch over them and ensure their safety, happiness, and prosperity (Johnson, Cohen, and Okun 2016). For example, many Christians appear to implicitly assume that God will protect their well-being when they take risks (Kupor, Laurin, and Levav 2015). These beliefs may stem from the motivation for psychological safety (Edmondson and Lei 2014). However, it can sometimes have negative consequences for ethical behavior. One such consequence involves "passive immorality," in which people perpetuate immorality by failing to correct unethical circumstances because they think that God has arranged for circumstances that benefit the individual. A series of thirteen studies found that, when Christians believe that God intervenes in everyday life, they are more likely to commit acts of passive immorality (e.g., failing to return a lost wallet to its owner) because they believe that unethical circumstances are God's will (Jackson and Gray 2019).

These findings are striking because they show how the same gods can be reimagined depending on the needs and circumstances of believers. Christians can either view God as forgiving, loving, and benevolent, or as wrathful and vengeful depending on whether they are motivated to view God as an attachment figure or a dispenser of righteous justice. Collective motivations may have interacted with environmental factors to produce many current-day religious differences, but they also continue to produce variation and division within the same religious traditions.

Future Directions in the Psychological Study of Gods' Minds

The science of religious beliefs has a long history. Some of the first social scientists were fascinated with religious beliefs, ranging from James (1958), Durkheim ([1915] 2001), and Tylor ([1871] 2016), to Darwin ([1871] 2008) and Weber (1993). But an interdisciplinary study of religious beliefs has only truly accelerated in the last twenty years as cognitive scientists and anthropologists have begun collaborating. In the spirit of encouraging this interdisciplinary science, we offer two critical directions in the future study of gods' minds.

Building a More Inclusive Study of Gods' Minds

A vast majority of studies on gods' minds have studied people's perceptions of the Christian God, and most of the remaining studies have sampled other Abrahamic faiths (see McNamara, present volume). On the other hand, folk religions and polytheistic world religions are vastly underrepresented in the science of religion (Apicella 2018; Boyer 2020; Hartberg, Cox, and Villamayor-Tomas 2016; McNamara and Purzycki 2020; Singh, Kaptchuk, and Henrich 2021). A consequence of this disproportionate focus on Abrahamic believers is that many key findings in our field may only apply to a particular set of people. For example, people who worship polytheistic faiths may be less likely to project anthropomorphism onto their gods because these gods are more likely to be associated with specific animals or features of nature. Moreover, gods from smaller-scale societies may be more likely to be linked with specific collective action problems (e.g., managing flooding) rather than broad behavioral prescriptions that can apply to a range of diverse groups (e.g., to be charitable, to be honest) (Hartberg, Cox, and Villamayor-Tomas 2016).

A natural way to build a more representative science of religion is to increase the availability of data from non-Western religious groups. Databases such as Pulotu

(Watts, Sheehan, et al. 2015), D-PLACE (Kirby et al. 2016), and the Database of Religious History (Slingerland and Sullivan 2017) now offer access to hundreds of world cultures but are relatively unheard of in the psychology of religion and spirituality. The "Human Relations Area Files" offers thousands of pages of carefully annotated ethnographic material that researchers can use to develop datasets that sample small-scale societies and extinct religions (Ember 1997). We are in the process of building a large ethnographic database of gods' characteristics across nonindustrial societies, which will hopefully facilitate research on diverse religious traditions. We also encourage research that examines whether the same religious traditions may vary across different cultural groups (White et al. 2021).

Forecasting the Future of Gods' Minds

Most studies of religious belief have used explanatory models, in which researchers explain differences between religious groups or differences over some period of the past. But we may soon be in a position where we can speculate about the future of gods' minds. Will people view gods as more personal or more distant figures in the future? Will people view gods as more punitive or more benevolent? How widely will these trends vary across cultural groups?

Methodological limitations have previously kept these questions out of reach, but new advances in time series modeling mean that predictive studies of religious beliefs are within reach. For example, autoregressive integrated moving average (ARIMA) models can decompose a time series into gradual trends, intertemporal dependences (autoregressive components), and errors in these dependencies (moving averages). With these components, ARIMA models can forecast future changes in a time series (Grossmann and Varnum 2015). For example, these models have been used to project a rise in religious "nones" in America, and a shift toward viewing God as more of a benevolent figure and less of an authoritarian figure (Jackson et al. 2021). Popular ARIMA models in cultural change research are still quite simple, seldom modeling nonlinear dynamics or incorporating exogenous variables. However, these models have great potential for studies that predict future changes in gods' minds based on the changing needs and preferences of religious individuals.

Conclusion

People's views of gods influence their moral values, beliefs about the world, and goals for the future, but the reverse is also true. Here we have reviewed a growing science of how believers' cognitive biases and motivations color their religious beliefs in general and their perceptions of gods' minds more specifically. We have argued for a multilevel approach to this science where basic cognitive and evolutionary theories of human mind perception are integrated with cultural evolutionary models. We have also reviewed several studies that exemplify this approach and encouraged future studies that build on these studies' findings with samples of non-Abrahamic religions and dynamical methods. This is an exciting time to pursue this work. Social science is growing more interdisciplinary, psychological studies are becoming more replicable, and methods of studying religion are becoming more sophisticated. With these advances, we are prepared to fully understand the capacities and limits of the divine projector, and to use this knowledge to predict the gods' minds of the future.

4

The Personality of the Divine

Kathryn A. Johnson

Introduction

Personality can be defined as the set of motivational, intellectual, emotional, and behavioral characteristics that distinguish each person. For example, we might say that a trusting, thoughtful, and friendly person has an agreeable personality. However, "person" is a term that transcends the biological category *human* (Johnson et al. 2015), and the notion of personhood can be extended to include angels, demons, ancestors, and the Divine.

If the Divine can be thought of as a person with thoughts, feelings, and behaviors, one might ask, "What is the personality of the Divine?" What is God like? Is God concerned with administering judgment or with granting favor? Is God incomprehensible—or playful? Can God even be known? In this chapter, I discuss four characteristics attributed to the Divine that are commonly described in the psychological literature—dominance, benevolence, limitlessness, and ineffability (e.g., Benson and Spilka 1973; Johnson, Okun, and Cohen 2015; Johnson 2019; Krejci 1998; Kunkel et al. 1999; Noffke and McFadden 2001; Spilka, Armatas, and Nussbaum 1964). I then present new data assessing beliefs about the Divine as a playful trickster god. I conclude with a brief overview of research regarding the antecedents and outcomes of beliefs about the personality of the Divine.

In discussing the minds of gods, I will refer to representations of "the Divine" across several religious traditions. Regardless of the doctrinal positions in each of these traditions, research shows that many theists also have idiosyncratic ways of representing the Divine that may not be theologically accurate (e.g., Davis, Moriarty, and Mauch 2013; Froese and Bader 2010; Silverman, Johnson, and Cohen 2016; Babb 1975). However, most Jews, Christians, Muslims, and Hindus would agree that the Divine is the ultimate governor of the world who is concerned with human morality and the enforcement of moral codes. This view of the Divine has been referred to as a "high god" by social scientists (Murdock and White 1969). For Jews, this most high god is YHWH (Yahweh), or G-d who revealed Himself to the Hebrews as described in the first thirty-nine books of the Bible. Christians revere three persons of the Divine Trinity as one sovereign deity: God the Father, Jesus Christ the Son, and the Holy

Spirit. Borrowing from the Greeks' description of the gods, Keller (2008) has likened the persons of the Trinity to being in a dance of mutually self-giving love that, in turn, pours out love to others. Islamists (Muslims) worship Allah (translated as "God"; Stark 2009) who is One but is described by ninety-nine epithets, including the Merciful and the King of the Day of Judgment (Qur'an 1:4). Although Hindus have often been described as polytheists, most Hindus believe there is one supreme deity, and the many gods and goddesses are different forms of the one high god (Babb 1975; Ward 1998). For example, Ramanuja of the Sri Vaishnava sect taught that Brahman is Ultimate Reality comprised of a triad of supreme deities (the *Trimurti*): Brahma the Creator, Vishnu the Preserver, and Shiva the Destroyer.

The Divine's Personality as Dominant

A common belief among Jews, Christians, Muslims, and Hindus is that the Divine is *dominant*—commanding and capable of punishing human transgressors (Teehan, present volume). For example, most monotheists are familiar with the Ten Commandments (e.g., honor the Sabbath, do not steal, honor your father and mother). However, the divine imperatives that might incur God's wrath are often thought to be more extensive. Jewish scholars have identified over six hundred commands given by G-d that cover a range of ethical, legal, and ritual behaviors in addition to specialized laws governing food consumption (Regenstein, Chaudry, and Regenstein 2003).

Yet, the Divine's commands are not necessarily seen as burdensome (1 John 5:3). The Bible/Tanakh instructs that "The fear of the LORD is the beginning of knowledge" (Proverbs 1:7). Here, the writer stresses reverence for God coupled with the need for obedience (Goodfriend 2013) but is also inferring that obedience is beneficial. When asked which is the greatest commandment, Jesus (a Jew) replied, "Love the Lord your God with all your heart, with all your soul, with all your mind, and with all your strength" (Mark 12:30).

Muslims also revere the Divine's commands and are governed by Sharia law that combines laws from the Qur'an, the Hadith (sayings of Muhammad), and rulings of Islamic scholars (Janin and Kahlmeyer 2007). Hindus, too, articulate humans' many ethical and social obligations in the compendium *Manu* (Doniger 1992). Each of these and other religious law codes is deemed to represent the expectations of a commanding God, and these commands are given with the promise of a better life now and in the hereafter.

High gods not only issue moral imperatives; they (and lesser deities) are also capable of observing and punishing transgressions (including those done in secret). Social scientists have documented that disease, death, and misfortune are often supposed to be punishment levied by an angry deity (Shweder et al. 1997; Wilt et al. 2016). In the Bible, God is described as flooding the world, destroying Sodom and Gomorrah, and sending earthquakes and plagues. And the Apostle Paul warns, "The wrath of God is being revealed from heaven against all the godlessness and wickedness of men who suppress the truth by their wickedness" (Romans 1:18). The majority of Muslims, too, believe in eternal punishment (Lugo et al. 2012).[1]

Social scientists have theorized that beliefs about the Divine as moralizing, all-knowing, and *punitive* have benefited humans by facilitating interpersonal cooperation (Johnson 2005; Norenzayan et al. 2016; Swanson 1960). From an evolutionary perspective, selfishness should be adaptive because it affords more resources; however, selfishness would be constrained if one's actions could be discovered and punished by powerful others—particularly if that "other" is an all-knowing, punitive, high god. Ethnographic data seem to support the theory that belief in a punishing and wrathful deity facilitated cooperation between strangers and, consequently, enabled the development of large-scale societies (see also Lang et al. 2019; Purzycki et al. 2016; Purzycki and McKay, present volume; Andersen, present volume).

The Divine as a Benevolent Caregiver

The Divine is not always represented as dominant, commanding, and punitive. Certainly not exclusively so by most theists. On the contrary, most contemporary theists believe the Divine is loving and supportive (Fincham, May, and Kamble 2019; May and Fincham 2018; Silverman, Johnson, and Cohen 2016). Although there are both individual and religious group differences regarding belief in divine benevolence (Johnson, Okun, and Cohen 2015; Noffke and McFadden 2001), theists often rely on the Divine for help in times of trouble or when seeking forgiveness for moral transgressions (Escher 2013). Others may seek relationship or existential union with the Divine just as they seek to be close with cherished human persons (James 1958).

There are multiple Hindu gods associated with health practices, including the goddess Shitala Mata who carries a pitcher of healing water. In the Bible, God is referred to as the God who heals (Jehovah-Rapha) (e.g., Psalm 103:3). Christians believe that Jesus Christ healed people of blindness, deafness, and disease. Many theists believe that the sacred writings themselves carry healing power (e.g., *Al-Israa* 17:82; Proverbs 4:22).

Whether seeking wealth, wisdom, safety, blessings, or boons, theists also look to the Divine for provision. The Bible refers to God as Jehovah-Jireh (God will provide; Genesis 22:14) and as a Father who gives abundantly (Matthew 7:11). The Qur'an also identifies God as "the Provider" (51:58), and Hindus frequently turn toward the elephant god Ganesha for success, wealth, and the removal of obstacles.

When blessings are not forthcoming, believers may look to a benevolent deity for strength and endurance; trust that the Divine has a more excellent (yet perhaps unseen) plan; or view one's troubles as a lesson to be learned. Turning toward a benevolent deity for healing, comfort, and forgiveness is indicative of what psychologists refer to as positive religious coping (Pargament et al. 1998).[2] One important method of religious coping is intercessory prayer directed toward the Divine as a form of interpersonal communication (Baesler 2003; Bänziger, van Uden, and Janssen 2008). There is evidence that such prayers can improve pain tolerance (Dezutter, Wachholtz, and Corveleyn 2011), increase optimism (Schafer 2013), and strengthen interpersonal relationships (Skipper, Moore, and Loren 2018).

In addition to seeking healing or blessings, theists may look to a benevolent deity for forgiveness and mercy. In both ancient and modern times (Govindrajan 2015), theists have offered sacrifices of animals, produce, time, or money to appease the Divine. However, the Divine may also be thought of as forgiving regardless of sacrifice. Muslims revere Allah, the Compassionate and Merciful. Protestants, a sect of Christianity, consider divine forgiveness (i.e., divine grace) a defining characteristic of God's personality. Emmons et al. (2017) describe grace as a gift of forgiveness and reconciliation given by the Divine, without limits, to an otherwise undeserving person, without expectation of repayment. Divine grace represents God's unmerited favor toward humans, offering forgiveness through the sacrificial death of Jesus Christ so that humans may have a close relationship with God.

To at least some theists, the Divine person has been a Father, Lover, Charioteer, Guide, Teacher, Shepherd, King, Warrior, Savior, Friend, and more. In each of these social roles, the Divine's personality is thought to be revealed in new and different ways, and beliefs about these social roles and personality traits can be complex (Sharp, Rentfrow, and Gibson 2017). As mentioned, beliefs about the Divine as dominant and benevolent are not mutually exclusive (Johnson, Okun, and Cohen 2015). The Divine can be thought of as both the Lion and the Lamb; the Merciful and the Avenger; malevolent and benevolent. God can be "loving without compromising his ethical rigor, … but weeps when he must punish" (Seltzer 1980: 290). Like many other human persons in authority (e.g., parents, police, teachers), a person-like deity may be seen as quite capable of all-at-once providing rules for life and administering adverse consequences to transgressors all for the ultimate benefit and well-being of humans.

The Limitless, Ineffable, Unknown God

Beliefs about the Divine as dominant and benevolent are grounded in thinking of God, gods, and goddesses as intentional, person-like beings (Gervais 2013; Heiphetz et al. 2018; Kapogiannis et al. 2009; Schjøedt et al. 2009; Willard and McNamara 2019). Yet God is more than a person, and beliefs about God can vary in level of abstraction (Shaman, Saide, and Richert 2018).

In addition to human-like attributes, nearly all theists would describe the Divine in terms of "omni-ness" (Trimèche, Vinsonneau, and Mullet 2006). That is, the Divine can be thought of as limitless (e.g., eternal, infinite), omniscient (knowing all things), omnipresent (in all places at one time), and omnipotent (having unlimited power). The Christian philanthropist Sir John Templeton (1981) argued that as humans learned more and more about the universe and the human condition, God would seem to be more and more limitless. Indeed, some theists contend that the Divine should not be thought of as a "person" at all (Johnson et al. 2022). Instead, God is too great to imagine in concrete terms. For example, although Allah is spoken of in personal terms (e.g., having a Divine will, Qur'an 64:9; hurling thunderbolts, 11:9), Muslims are forbidden to create any likeness of Allah for Allah is unimaginable and "There is nothing comparable to Him" (Qur'an 112:4)—although, of course, this prohibition may not prevent personified representations of Allah from springing up in the mind of the believer.

For others, it may be that words utterly fail in expressing the awesomeness of God; God is best described as *ineffable*. The Jewish theologian Abraham Heschel (1976: 22) explains that when humans experience God, "We are struck with an awareness of the immense preciousness of being; a preciousness which is not an object of analysis but a cause of wonder; it is inexplicable, nameless, and cannot be specified or put in one of our categories." Echoing descriptions of God as ineffable, Christian theologian Keith Ward (1998: 154) writes about the greatness of God as being "the asymptotic goal, which will never be finally attained; the unlimited source of endless being."

Still, for others, God may simply be *unknown*. For example, an individual may profess belief in God but, regardless of what may be theologically correct, this same individual may have never given much thought to the person-like attributes of the Divine. Others may view G-d as inattentive (Rosmarin, Krumrei, and Andersson 2009), disengaged (Degelman and Lynn 1995), and/or relationally distant (Exline, Grubbs, and Homolka 2015). Thus, for some theists, the Divine may not seem to have a "personality" at all, at least explicitly.

The Divine as a Playful Trickster

In some religious traditions, the cosmos and everything in it—the sun, earth, bear, eagle, trees, and even rocks—may be regarded as sacred or as persons who are deserving of respect, relationship, and reverence (Bird-David 1999; Johnson, Cohen et al. 2015; Morrison 2000). Moreover, other-than-human persons such as dream visitors, spirit guides, and thunderstorms are believed to be capable of providing wisdom and good fortune (Hallowell 1975).

Beyond the attribution of personhood to natural things, there is evidence for belief in a creator deity in animist societies. This Supreme Being is often thought of as distant and unconcerned (Radin 1992). However, in certain Native American Indian traditions, the *Wakan Tanka* (the unity of the "god persons") is thought to be personable and involved in human affairs (e.g., fond of music; Sword and Walker 1992; Sørensen and Purzycki, present volume). Moreover, much has been written about the playful personality of trickster gods in American Indian and other indigenous traditions (Hynes and Doty 1997). For example, Coyote, a trickster god in the American Southwest, can take an animal or human shape. His irreverent antics include gluttony, sleeping with family members, and stealing the moon (Erdoes and Ortiz 1999).

Trickster gods are often thought of as having been involved in the creation of the world, humans, and culture and yet remain on the earth, engaging in clever but often child-like pranks, challenging social norms (particularly sexual taboos), changing appearance at will, making people laugh, and frequently providing a contrast between the sacred and the lewd (by engaging in forbidden antics). Trickster gods have both divine and human traits or are sometimes thought of as divine messengers for superior gods.

Many Hindu gods and goddesses are well-known as playful tricksters (O'Flaherty 1975). As a child, the Hindu god Krishna loved butter and would regularly steal the freshly churned butter from the houses of the milkmaids (Hawley 1979). Thus, Krishna is often pictured as a child with his hand in the butter pot. As a young adult, Krishna mischievously steals the milkmaids' (*gopīs*) clothing as they bathe in the river. In the Rasa Lila, a favorite story from the *Bhagavata Purana*, an older and more powerful Krishna playing his flute captures the hearts of the *gopīs*. In a state of rapture, the women leave their husbands to be with Krishna, who flirts, teases, dances, and amorously touches them. Eventually, Krishna sends them back to their homes and their husbands—for that is the highest duty and calling (*dharma*) of the *gopīs*, a duty that does not contradict the love of their god Krishna.

There is no equivalent representation of the Divine as a playful trickster in monotheism. However, there are references to God's laughter (Psalm 2:4); and some see God's playfulness in nature (God's creation) or find humorous incongruity in some of the scriptures (Mir 1991; Trueblood 1964). Nevertheless, the notion of a playful deity is at least downplayed, and perhaps this is why there is a paucity of research regarding this aspect of the Divine's personality.

Assessing Beliefs about the Divine's Personality

People have a multitude of beliefs about the minds of gods, and psychologists have been interested in assessing individual differences in these beliefs for decades (Sharp et al. 2019). Most recently, Johnson et al. (2019) developed the twenty-five-item LAMBI measure of God representations to assess five dimensions of the Divine's personality: Limitless (characterized as *vast, immense, boundless, infinite,* and *limitless*); Authoritarian (*commanding, strict, stern, punishing,* and *wrathful*); Mystical (i.e., abstract; *nature, energy, cosmic, consciousness,* and *the universe*); Benevolent (*compassionate, merciful, forgiving, gracious,* and *tolerant*); and Ineffable (*inconceivable, unimaginable, incomprehensible, unknowable,* and *unknown*). However, despite advances in assessing these five dimensions of the Divine's personality, belief in the Divine as playful has been insufficiently investigated.

To begin to address this gap in the literature, I conducted an exploratory study using the extant LAMBI scale (Johnson et al. 2019) and adding the descriptors *playful, funny, amusing, mischievous,* and *trickster* as indicators of belief in the Divine as playful, which I will refer to as the K-Factor (recognizing the Hindu god Krishna as a prototypical divine trickster). Participants were 406 theists living in the United States, Canada, and India recruited via email or snowball sampling. The religiously diverse sample consisted of 101 nonreligious theists, 203 Christians, 46 Muslims, and 56 Hindus.

A principal components analysis of the scores for the thirty items revealed the expected six-factor solution, and the mean ratings for the five relevant dimensions, by religious type, are shown in Figure 4.1. As can be seen, Christians and Muslims tended to believe that God is benevolent and limitless—but not so much playful and amusing. In contrast, Hindus attributed all five personality traits to the Divine, including belief

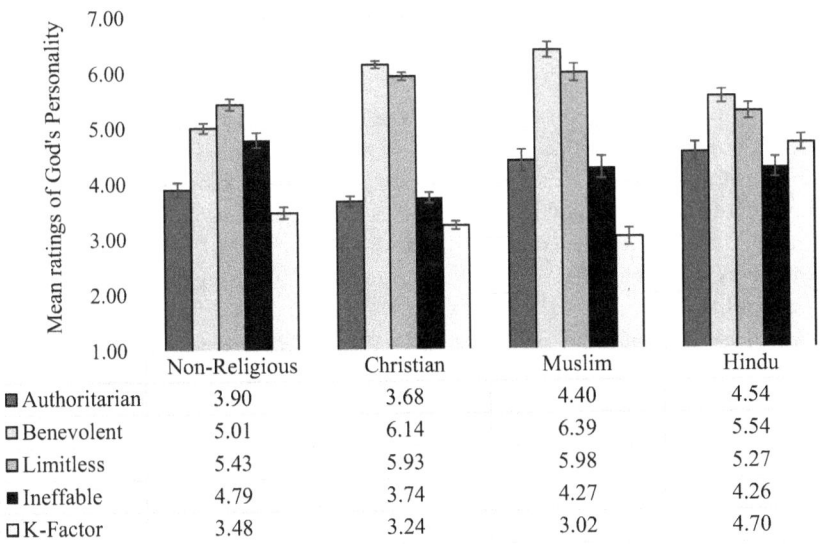

Figure 4.1 Mean ratings for God's personality as dominant/authoritarian, benevolent, limitless, ineffable, and playful by religious type. Created by Kathryn Johnson.

Note: Error bars indicate standard errors; means for the mystical dimension are not shown.

in the Divine as a playful trickster. Notably, Christians tended to have the lowest scores for Authoritarian God. Thus, the results of this exploratory survey suggest that the "K-Factor"—the playful, trickster dimension—may be an important but neglected aspect in thinking about God's personality across cultures.

Antecedents of Beliefs about the Divine's Personality

How do theists come to have particular beliefs about the personality of the Divine? In her seminal work on God representations, Rizzuto (1979) used object relations theory to argue that the representation of God is an illusory and special kind of transitional object that is shaped and reshaped over a lifetime of experiences with primary sources. These primary sources may include caregivers, religious instruction, and even self-representations. In childhood, beliefs about God are formed during exchanges between the child and her primary caregivers. For example, monotheists who developed a secure attachment style are likely to ascribe benevolence to God (Granqvist, Mikulincer, and Shaver 2010). Throughout their lives, theists continue to be influenced by social interactions with their families (Cooper et al. 2018), teachers (Nyhof and Johnson 2017), peers, and religious leaders.

As Rizzuto (1979) theorized, the traits people ascribe to God are also closely related to the way people think about themselves (Mikloušić and Lane 2019; Roberts 1989). For instance, Christians' certainty about the nature and attributes of God are associated with a clear, consistent, and cohesive view of oneself (Kitchens and Phillips 2018). Research confirms that believers often imagine that the face of God resembles their own or those they value (Jackson, Hester, and Gray 2018). Hodges, Sharp, Gibson, and Tipsord (2012) found that believers used the same adjectives to describe themselves and God. Positive self-evaluations are related to belief in a benevolent God, and negative self-evaluations are associated with belief in a punishing God (Smither and Walker 2015; see also Jackson and Gray, present volume). Additionally, people have rated Jesus Christ as caring and concerned with a degree of detachment (Piedmont, Williams, and Ciarrochi 1997) and much like themselves (Oishi et al. 2011; Strawn and Alexander 2008) using the Big 5 inventory of personality traits.

Another critical but understudied source of beliefs about the Divine's personality is the physical environment. Research suggests that culturally relevant images of God can influence beliefs about God (Barrett and Van Orman 1996; Shtulman et al. 2019). In India, for example, images of gods and goddesses can be seen in temples, markets, homes, and street corners. The Hindu gods and goddesses are believed to embody their images made of clay and stone, and, therefore, images are created to reveal certain personalities (Waghorne, Cutler, with Vasudha Narayanan 1985). Consider how the diverse images in Figure 4.2 might influence theists' beliefs about the Divine's personality. The presentation of images of an angry deity (Figure 4.2a, far left) have been shown to increase aggression, whereas images of a benevolent God (Figure 4.2b and 4.2c, left of center) inspired benevolence (Johnson et al. 2013). Similar images of the Divine as benevolent or malevolent can be found in the Hindu tradition (Figures 4.2d, e, and f).

As mentioned above, beliefs about the Divine's personality can and do shift with the vicissitudes of life (VanTongeren et al. 2018). For example, people may have awe-inspiring experiences that initiate or enhance belief in the positive attributes of the Divine (Cohen, Gruber, and Keltner 2010; James 1958). In contrast, people may ascribe relatively more authoritarian traits to God following a natural disaster (Aten et al. 2019), international conflict (Caluori et al. 2020), or adverse life events (Grubbs and Exline 2014).

Social and Psychological Outcomes

Beliefs about the Divine's personality as dominant or benevolent can, in turn, influence mental health (Schaap-Jonker et al. 2017). A meta-analysis revealed that views of God as benevolent and supportive were positively associated with subjective well-being (Stulp et al. 2019). Theists who think of God as supportive are more likely to engage in positive religious coping strategies (Pargament et al. 1998; Phillips III et al. 2004), have higher self-esteem (Francis, Gibson, and Robbins 2001), are more likely to self-forgive (Fincham and May 2019), and, consequently, often experience less death anxiety (Krause 2015). It should be noted, however, that theists also experience religious struggles that may include religious doubts, guilt about moral transgressions, or negative emotions toward God (Bockrath et al. 2021; Exline et al. 2014; Rosmarin, Krumrei, and Andersson 2009).

Personality of the Divine 49

Figure 4.2 God's personality expressed in cultural artifacts. (a) God in Michelangelo's "Creation." (b) Jesus as "Sacred Heart." (c) Jesus as the infant of Prague (credit: Mr. Tobin/iStock). (d) Krishna the butter thief (credit: D. Shelare/iStock). (e) Krishna with Radha the *gopi* milkmaid (credit: T. Bhadresh/iStock). (f) Bhairava, god of destruction (credit: R. Tortelli/iStock).

The varied beliefs about the Divine's personality are also associated with a range of social attitudes and behavioral outcomes (Froese and Bader 2010). For example, the belief in hell and a dominant, punitive deity is associated with moral objectivism (Sarkissian and Phelan 2019), the value of social dominance (Johnson, Okun, and Cohen 2015), aggression (Bushman et al. 2007), militarism (Thomson and Froese 2018), and support for capital punishment (Unnever, Cullen, and Bartkowski 2006). However, the divine commands—which typically require self-regulation—can also foster prosocial outcomes including lower crime rates (Shariff and Rhemtulla 2012), honesty (Shariff and Norenzayan 2011), ingroup solidarity (Norenzayan et al. 2016), and prosociality toward strangers observed around the world (Purzycki et al. 2016).

Yet, in a study of "high gods" in twenty countries, Barrett et al. (2019) found that most theists emphasized the moral goodness of the Divine as a benevolent role model rather than the fear of a dominant, punitive deity. Similarly, other studies have shown that belief in God's benevolence (but *not* God's punishment) is associated with prosocial behaviors such as forgiveness (Johnson et al. 2013), helping behaviors (Johnson et al. 2013; Johnson, Cohen, and Okun 2016), and religious group inclusivity (Johnson, Memon et al. 2015).

Belief in a benevolent God is not without a downside. People who attribute their good fortune to God's benevolence often engage in selfish behavior (e.g., keeping a lost and found wallet, parking across multiple spaces) (Jackson and Gray 2019), and less religious people who rely on God's forgiveness may not value physical fitness (Krause and Ironson 2017). Other research suggests that theists who view God as person-like (e.g., dominant and benevolent) are less likely to engage in sustainability practices (Johnson et al. 2017), often explaining that "God will take care of this world" or that one will leave this world and go to a better place after death (Johnson, Minton, and McClernon 2021). In contrast, individuals who think of God as limitless or ineffable are often more supportive of sustainability policies (Johnson et al. 2017, 2019). Moreover, these more abstract views of the Divine are associated with more positive attitudes toward science (Ecklund, Park, and Sorrell 2011; Johnson et al. 2019; Longest and Smith 2011).

There is much more to learn and understand about how theists represent the personality of the Divine. For example, what are the possible beneficial or adverse consequences of obedience to an *authoritarian* deity when divine imperatives go against one's immediate self-interest (e.g., requiring costly ritual commitments, prohibitions against food or sex)? What do people mean when they say that a *benevolent* God provides "strength"? Do representations of God as *limitless* or *ineffable* correspond with beliefs that God has a mind? Why do monotheists generally think of God as somber, whereas Hindus and indigenous people often believe in a more *playful* deity? To what extent do cultural artifacts—music, architecture, art, social media—both reflect and influence beliefs about the minds of gods?

Conclusion

In addition to the Divine as discussed in this chapter, people have feared, worshiped, been awed, or been amused by many other divine personalities throughout the ages, including contemporary local deities, the deities of East Asia, and the ancient Egyptian, Greek, Roman, and Celtic gods and goddesses.[3] Indeed, theists have long sought to understand the minds of the gods as dominant, benevolent, limitless, ineffable, or playful so that they might have some assurance of a healthy, abundant life both now and in the hereafter. Thus, devotees and social scientists alike will want to continue to investigate the different aspects, sources, and social outcomes of beliefs about the personality of the Divine.

5

Night Visions: The Cognitive Neuroscience of Dreaming about Supernatural Agents

John Balch and Patrick McNamara

Introduction

The claim that the brain is a prediction or simulation machine is now ubiquitous throughout the cognitive and neural sciences (Clark 2015; Hohwy 2013; Purzycki and Schjoedt, present volume). But where does all this "simulating" appear or occur? The neurocognitive simulations that guide our everyday strivings and perceptions are laid out for us to examine in our dreams. Yet oddly enough the cognitive science and neuroscience communities have until recently been slow to take up the challenge to unravel the secrets of the mind/brain by examining dreams. This has changed in the last few decades, as predictive coding/processing models of brain function have become more prominent, and as the pace of the interdisciplinary field of dream research has increased.

Inspired by predictive processing, some of this new dream research has focused on the cognitive mechanisms that enable individuals to cognize interactions with human-like spiritual agencies in dreams. It should not be surprising that dreams constitute a unique data source for understanding the neurocognitive mechanisms undergirding supernatural agent (SA) cognitions. Both religious studies scholars and psychologists (Abraham and White 1912; Bulkeley 2001, 2008, 2016; Freud 1913; Jung 1964; McNamara and Bulkeley 2015) have suggested that religious ideas and myths are rooted in dream imagery and narratives. Moreover, generations of ethnographers and anthropologists have produced ethnographies, dream compilations, and documentary accounts of dream-based sources of religious ideas and myths in small- and large-scale societies around the world (D'Andrade 1961; for references see McNamara 2017; Mageo and Sheriff 2020). We take it therefore as largely established that there are interesting links between dreams and religious SAs. The question is: *are these links in some way causal, mediatory, or simply non-trivial?* Why might dreaming serve as a uniquely important arena for cognizing the thoughts and feelings of gods?

We approach this issue by providing an overview of the scientific study of dreaming, which we believe contains important insights for understanding religious cognition. Advances show that dreams are very deeply and intimately involved in simulating social life and updating how individuals perceive their relationships with significant others. We argue that it is a natural next step to include SAs among these significant others, and that our relationships with SAs are emotionally worked on in the rapid eye movement (REM) dream state. These dynamics are further influenced by the interaction between dreaming minds and culture; dreams are often the source of cultural myths and imagery, but dreaming is also structured by cultural models and narratives. Consequently, we contend that dreaming is a crucial medium through which individuals simulate their social interactions with the minds of gods, and that the time is ripe for new research that integrates scientific models of dreaming with perspectives from cultural anthropology and religious studies.

Dreaming Minds: A Brief History of the Psychology of Dreaming

What Are Dreams?

Dreaming is a universal and crucial aspect of human experience. Even dreams that are not consciously recalled are nonetheless encoded into long-term memory systems and affect daily functioning. People experience an average of three to four REM cycles per night. If we assume one dream per cycle, then people experience twenty one to twenty eight dreams per week. While the majority of these dreams are not remembered, three to five are recalled on average per week, and 37 percent of young adults report that they recall a dream "every night" or "very frequently" (Belicki 2017; Goodenough 1991; Strauch and Meier 1996). Many dreams are also highly significant to the waking life of the dreamer, and in representative samples of the general population between 40 and 75 percent recall between one to five intense and "impactful" dreams per month (Knudson, Adame, and Finocan 2006; Krippner, Bogzaran, and Carvalho 2002; Kuiken and Sikora 1993; Kuiken and Smith 1991; Stepansky et al. 1998). In traditional societies it is not uncommon for people to recount several dreams per night for others in detail (Laughlin 2011). In modern societies most people share at least one dream every couple of weeks with others, usually intimate others (Stefanakis 1995; Vann and Alperstein 2000). As discussed below, once a dream is shared it can become a social fact and a potential cultural artifact.

Until relatively recently, the majority position in the behavioral and cognitive sciences has been that dreams are bizarre and epiphenomenal states that have little resemblance to or impact on waking life (see Domhoff 2017 for a discussion). This position has been overturned by a new consensus that dreams very reliably and consistently produce remarkably detailed simulations of everyday social interactions that are known to influence waking cognitions (Blagrove 2007; D'Agostino and Scarone 2011; Domhoff 2003, 2017; Kuiken et al. 2006; McNamara 2004; Palagini and Rosenlicht 2011). Content analysis of long-term dream diaries has been shown to be a reliable method of tracking the ongoing concerns and ideas that occupy dreamer's waking lives, and these concerns often vary systematically with social factors such as age, gender, and ethnicity (Domhoff 2017). As we discuss below, however, this does not mean that dreams are simply a one-to-one mirror of waking cognition. The key insight is that even in dreams that seem bizarre or otherworldly, the exaggerated or incongruent versions of people and places that populate dreams usually reflect the cognitive and emotional frameworks that structure waking thoughts.

Do Dreams Have a Function?

Even with this new consensus among researchers that dreams are a form of embodied simulation, there is still ongoing debate over whether have functional role in human life, with three broad hypotheses dominating the discussion. The first set of theories postulates that dreaming is simply the result of the forebrain attempting to make sense of neural activation patterns that occur during REM (e.g., Hobson 1999). In other words, dream experiences are simply neurocognitive interpretations of random neural stimuli and impulses, with no inherent coherence or stability. The second group of theories proposes that dreams draw upon cognitive schemas, the frameworks that guide thought, and episodic memories of waking events to produce experiences in a similar manner to those found in mind-wandering and daydreaming (see especially Domhoff and Fox 2015). On this account, dreaming is a coherent-but-random walk through these networks, reliably simulating everyday experience. Theorists in this camp contend that dreaming has no primary function, although they concede that dreaming can be utilized for cultural or therapeutic purposes. The third group of theories defends a functional role for dreaming, whether as a threat simulator, a means of emotional processing or memory consolidation, or an "off-line" arena through which the brain can process past events and prepare for novel situations (Tuominen et al. 2019; Valli et al. 2005).

Hobson and Friston (2012) propose that the brain utilizes sleep as a time to take the predictive model of the world that guides waking perception "off-line," and to prune and reorganize it in order to update this model to improve future predictions. Dreams emerge from the brain's attempts to make sense of the inputs triggered by REMs and the side effects of this pruning process. Therefore, while dreams are a consequence of the brain's need to work through multiple simulations of waking content in order to build novel perceptual predictions, they in part reflect this work in updating predictive models. Dream content as experienced by the individual in this narrative is depicted as largely epiphenomenal and bizarre, with only an incidental resemblance to waking cognition.

Domhoff's continuity theory of dreaming directly challenges Hobson and Friston's contention that dream content is comprised of random impressions that are a side effect of internal neural processing. In his view, dreams are far too consistent with waking cognition to be random or epiphenomenal:

> Dreaming simulates waking life in a reasonably coherent fashion, dream content consists of simulations of both personal concerns and adventure fantasies, and dream content reflects panhuman as well as gender, cross-national, and individual differences. In addition, there is consistency and continuity in people's dream life to the extent that there is consistency over time in their conceptions and personal concerns. (Domhoff 2017: 116)

Domhoff has extended this approach by locating the neural correlate of dreaming in the default mode network, with augmentation by the sensorimotor and secondary visual cortices (Domhoff and Fox 2015). The default mode network includes nodes in the ventral medial prefrontal cortex, the dorsal medial prefrontal cortex, the posterior cingulate cortex and adjacent precuneus, and the lateral parietal cortex (Raichle 2015). It has been shown to become active during resting states, as well as during mind-wandering, daydreaming, and spontaneous thinking (Fox et al. 2015). The link between the default mode network and the sensorimotor cortex during dreaming supports Domhoff's contention that dreams are "embodied simulations," involving a reuse of sensorimotor areas to accompany mental imagery (Noë 2004).

Thus, while dreaming and mind-wandering are presented as similar processes, dreams are more dramatic and active forms of simulation, referred to as *immersive spatiotemporal hallucinations*, by philosopher Jennifer Windt (2010, 2015; Windt and Noreika 2011). Dreaming occurs when "an augmented portion of the brain's default network is highly activated at the same time that external stimuli are occluded," yielding a strong sense of self within a hallucinatory context of mind-wandering that draws upon memory and cognitive schemas (Domhoff and Schneider 2018: 2). Dreaming is thus a type of "cognitive workout, in which self-location must be generated with respect to continuously shifting and unfamiliar environments" (Windt 2015: 611). In Windt's view, dreaming bolsters two computational needs of the human brain: (1) the maintenance of self in relation to other agents in a constantly changing world and (2) the ability to engage in simulation and planning by partially dissociating from the regular world in order to engage our imagination. On Windt's account, "(d)reams … are the most vivid reflection of our mental capacity to simulate imaginary worlds, as well as imaginary selves in them" (Windt 2015: 616).

Despite being a firm proponent of the coherence of dreams as embodied simulations, Domhoff clearly claims that dreaming itself is a by-product of human evolution, with no primary adaptive function. While he accepts that dreaming can play an important role in social and therapeutic contexts, Domhoff argues that these are cultural uses of dreams as experiential phenomena, and denies that dreaming has a biological function. Domhoff justifies his position by contending that children under the ages of nine to eleven have very few dreams, despite their brains undergoing rapid cognitive and neural development, a hypothesis that remains controversial among dream researchers. In addition, neurological patients who lose the ability to dream still maintain healthy levels of cognitive and personal function. Any adaptive theory of dreaming must contend with the existence of significant populations of humans who function well despite not dreaming.

Nevertheless, there are a wide range of proposed evolutionary functions for dreams, including memory consolidation (Schredl 2017; Wamsley and Stickgold 2011), emotional processing (Scarpelli et al. 2019), threat modeling and simulation (Valli et al. 2005), and creative problem-solving (Barrett 2017). Here we focus on the Social Simulation Theory (SST) laid out in Tuominen et al. (2019) and the relationship between dreaming and emotional consolidation of attachment relationships. If, as we believe, SAs are important relational figures for many individuals, then these theories help us understand why dreaming likely plays a key role in shaping and updating these relationships.

Dream content is highly social, with 95 percent or more involving one or more individuals other than the dreamer (McNamara 2019). Tuominen et al. (2019) refer to this as the Sociality Bias, which hypothesizes dreaming to be "specialized in the simulation and rehearsal of social perception and interaction" (Tuominen et al. 2019: 104). A recent study found that this bias still holds even when subjects were placed in seclusion, strongly supporting the hypothesis that dreams are primarily an arena for simulating social interaction, not processing waking content generally (Tuominen et al. 2022).

Simulation of social life in dreams differs in important ways from waking reality. Social network analyses of the co-occurrence of characters in dreams undertaken by Schweickert and his collaborators have repeatedly demonstrated that dream social networks more accurately reflect an individual's cognitive map of their significant social relations than their real-life network (Han et al. 2016; Han and Schweickert 2016; Schweickert 2007; Schweickert et al. 2020). They found that people who are emotionally closer to the dreamer will tend to appear in the same dreams, even if those people do not know each other in real life. In the well-studied dream series reported by a woman given the pseudonym "Barb Sanders" (publicly available at the *DreamBank* website, https://www.dreambank.net) her current and past romantic interests often co-occur in dreams, even though they never knew each other in real life. Domhoff (2017), who has conducted several content analyses of the Barb series, argues that this result lines up well with Barb's waking preoccupation with past relationships and disappointments. The co-occurrence of disparate elements (in this case social relations) thus corresponds to the cognitive and emotional schemas of the dreamer that they also employ in making sense of their everyday waking life. The social life of our dream selves is consequently closely related to reality but also involves unusual juxtapositions and relational elements.

There is also a substantial body of research linking dreams to emotional processing and attachment orientations. REM sleep, for example, facilitates consolidation of emotional experiences and dreamed elements into long-term memory (Almeida-Filho, Queiroz, and Ribeiro 2018; Hu, Stylos-Allan, and Walker 2006; Levin and Nielsen 2009; Walker and van der Helm 2009; Wamsley and Stickgold 2010). Dream story elements are memorable not merely because they contain ideas with counterintuitive characteristics but because REM biology promotes emotional memory consolidation. Recent advances in the science of sleep and dreams have demonstrated that REM dreaming not only facilitates but may also be required for emotional memory consolidation and for emotional attachment to others (for reviews see Almeida-Filho, Queiroz, and Ribeiro 2018; Tempesta et al. 2018; Walker and Stickgold 2006). Sleep periods rich in REM sleep as opposed to periods during daytime are associated with significantly greater amounts of emotional memory consolidation and recall (van der Helm and Walker 2011; Wagner, Gais, and Born 2001). REM sleep is associated with intense activation in the amygdala (Maquet and Franck 1997) and is rich in acetylcholine activity (which is known to be crucial for memory encoding processes) and may act to decontextualize emotionally intense memories (due to cessation of arousing noradrenergic neurochemical activity; Levin and Nielsen 2007), thus making them easier to consolidate into long-term memory stores. REM dreams appear to facilitate this "decontextualization of memory episodes" effect (Hartmann 2000; Nielsen and Powell 1992).

We and others (Keller 2011; McNamara 2004; McNamara et al. 2001, 2010, 2014; Mikulincer et al. 2009, 2011; Selterman, Apetroaia, and Waters 2012; Selterman et al. 2014; Selterman and Drigotas 2009) have also shown that REM dreaming facilitates attachment orientations and emotional commitment to others. For example, Selterman et al. (2014) showed that if the dreamer in a romantic relationship dreamed of positive social interactions with the partner, then both partners within the relationship rated the relationship as close the next day. Conversely, if the dreamer had no dream of the partner or dreamed a negative interaction, distancing between the partners occurred the next day in the relationship. Thus, dreaming possesses the neurocognitive architecture to promote emotional commitment to selected others, such as those felt with significant SAs. Kirkpatrick (2005), Granqvist (2010; Granqvist, Mikulincer, and Shaver 2010) and others have shown that internal working models of attachment orientations (secure, anxious, preoccupied, and avoidant; Bowlby 1983) operate with respect to an individual's relationship with SAs or God. In short, dreams appear to play a crucial role in constructing and adjusting internal working models of attachment orientations to significant others, including perhaps significant SAs.

In summation, dreaming provides relatively coherent simulations of an individual's emotional and cognitive states, especially in relation to their social context. In dreams, the mind experiments with a variety of counterfactual social situations as well as emotionally significant encounters with other agents, exercising its abilities in establishing the self against the background of a dynamic simulated reality and running through different models of social relations to others. Dreaming is similar to daydreaming and mind-wandering but it is distinct for both its immersive quality and its lack of voluntariness. As discussed below, this sense of "happening" to the individual from the outside is a key aspect of how dreams give rise to SA perceptions, as a felt lack of agency is significantly correlated with the appearance in dreams of powerful and otherworldly SAs in dreams. Overall, we contend that the role of dreams as social simulators indicates that they are likely to be intimately involved in the way individuals experience, represent, and update their relationships with significant SAs, which in turn influences waking processes of religious cognition and practice.

Simulating the Supernatural: Dreams and Religious Cognition

Linking Dreaming to SAs

We contend that REM dreams are naturally conducive to production of SAs because they (1) regularly generate emotionally vivid stories of dreamer interactions with both significant others and with unusual supernatural characters, (2) modulate social attachment processes during the daytime with characters dreamed about the night before, and (3) act to consolidate emotional memories into long-term memory systems.

But can we say anything more about the *cognitive mechanisms* associated with production of dreamed SAs? Our investigations (McNamara 2016; McNamara et al. 2018) of this question focused on dreams where SAs appear to the dreamer. The end result of these investigations suggests that dreams spontaneously produce SAs because dreaming is naturally associated with a transfer of cognitive agency from the dreamer to a different unfamiliar but salient character who then (frequently though not invariably) assumes supernormal forms of agency in the dream. Because REM is associated with both periodic bodily movements and fluctuating activation levels in midline and ventromedial and supplementary motor cortex (sites associated with the sense of agency; Macrae et al. 2004; Northoff et al. 2006), the sense of agency itself fluctuates during REM dreaming. McNamara et al. (2018) noted that loss or reduction in the sense of agency within the dreamer (e.g., "I was stuck in quicksand and could not move!") corresponds with a sense of increased agency for one of the dream characters the dreamer is interacting with—typically a dream character hitherto unknown to the dreamer. If this reduced agency in the dreamer is extreme or prolonged some other dream character will frequently assume supernormal forms of agency and become monstrous (e.g., "Then I noticed that the stranger was actually a monster coming toward me but I could not move due to the quicksand"). This is most clearly the case in bad dreams or nightmares. We found that when SAs appear in a dream or nightmare they are reliably associated with diminished agency in the dreamer. Diminished agency within the dreamer occurs in over 90 percent of dreams (whether nightmares or unpleasant dreams) *that have overt SAs* and virtually never occurs without SAs. In about half of nightmare reports the SA appears suddenly with no clear emergence pattern, aside from reduction of agency in the dream self. In some two-thirds of unpleasant dreams, however, the SA emerges from a human character. In most nightmares, the SA intended to harm the dreamer and in one-third of nightmares the dreamer was the victim of physical aggression by the SA. SA intentions in unpleasant dreams were more varied and actually benign in 13 percent of cases (McNamara et al. 2018). These patterns in the ways in which SAs appear and act in dreams are consistent with character transformation in dreams in general (Rittenhouse et al. 1994) and suggest that there may be a principled way to study their cognitive dynamics and origins in dreams.

Dreaming with Others: Cultural Frameworks for Dreaming

Anthropological research often seeks to contextualize individual dream narratives within social contexts of interpretation. This approach highlights that although the act of dreaming itself is internal and individual, the impact dreams have on an individual is structured by cultural patterns of dream sharing and interpretation. Cultural variation in dream interpretation is fundamentally structured by underlying beliefs in dream ontology, as observed long ago by Irving Hallowell (1966; 1975). In a review of ethnographic studies of dreaming, Lohmann and Dahl (2013) identify six distinct social folk theories of dreams:

1. Nonsense theory: Dreams are products of the imagination that are not inherently significant
2. Discernment theory: Dreaming is a heightened perception of reality
3. Message theory: Dreams are symbolically encoded communiques
4. Generative theory: Dreaming affects and contributes to ways in which reality unfolds
5. Soul travel theory: Dreams are what one's soul experiences as it wanders
6. Visitation theory: Dreaming images are presented by another being (69)

These folk theories provide the building blocks for constructing more complex cultural assemblages of interpretation. For example, both Poirier (2003) and Glaskin (2005, 2011, 2015) found that Aboriginal models of dreaming include both visitations with ancestors and spirits as well as soul travel to the primordial Dreamtime. Similarly, Groark (2020) presents the Tzotzil Mayan view of dreaming as a type of soul wandering that leaves the dreamer in "a state of heightened vulnerability to the often-hostile intentions of others, both social and supernatural" (175). Different folk theories of dreaming may also enhance diminished senses of agency, which thereby increases the likelihood of dreaming about SAs or extraordinary figures.

When cultural models of dreams consider them the waypoint for encounters with supernatural presences, dreams often empower the dreamer while stimulating cultural innovation for the group. For example, Plains Native Americans trace the origins of many of their ritual forms to visionary individuals, and they also ascribe personal power based on the ability of individuals to experience and interpret important dreams (Irwin 1994). In Australia, Glaskin (2005) shows that ritual and artistic innovations among the Bardi are framed within the context of oneiric revelation. Within the dream, supernatural beings communicate and "reveal" new designs and dances, which (when accepted) are considered by the group "to have always existed 'from the beginning,' and are not considered to be 'new'" (2005: 299). Consequently, Bardi tradition is exceptionally open to creativity and novelty as it is mediated through revelatory dreaming, which may stimulate a greater openness and adaptiveness for individuals (Glaskin 2015). Importantly, however, as in many indigenous contexts, revelatory dreams are only accepted within Bardi tradition after a lengthy process of exegesis, negotiation, and interpretation that involves a diverse set of actors within the social group. While not all religious traditions place the same importance on dreaming, there are similarly dynamic processes of authentication, disagreement, and innovation at play when communities determine which dreams should be considered as legitimate religious experiences or communications from important SAs.

Certain dreams may also take on an iconic role in large religious traditions, such as the dream of the Old Testament Patriarch Jacob in Genesis (Lipton 1999). After he shared it with others it became an enduring narrative within all three Abrahamic traditions. Jacob left his homeland and his father Isaac in order to find a wife. On the journey he stopped at "a certain place," which he later named "Bethel," then slept and had a dream (Genesis 28:13-18). God appears in the dream and speaks to Jacob directly. The image of the ladder with angels appears to be symbolic as the ladder is a portal to the supernatural realm. The dream had the effect of not only sanctifying the place now called Bethel but specifying its religious significance for centuries as "the gate of heaven." The dream of Jacob's ladder illustrates how a dream element or trope can become a cultural mytheme and how recordings of experiences of supernatural agency while dreaming can grant importance to specific places.

Of course, most dream encounters with SAs will not become central narratives of religious traditions. The success in dream "visitations" or revelatory narratives depends on their coherence with the social context in which they are reported. Conflicts over dream interpretation are common in religious traditions, and they can reveal distinct fissures over the nature of which kind of religious experiences are considered authentic. Amira Mittermaier's (2007, 2010, 2012) ethnographic research on dreaming among Muslims in Cairo highlights the precarious position of Sufi devotional believers who experience direct communication from Muhammad and other religious figures in their dreams. These dreams are viewed as threatening from Islamic reformers, who view these interpretations as un-Islamic. Consequently, while they are highly salient sources of identity and personal formation for the devotional believers, they also may serve as a point of tension within a larger social context that seeks to unilaterally control access to the important information that the minds of gods possess.

Crucial to the social function of dreams is their tendency to be interpreted as "anomalous" events, which lie outside conventional everyday models of reality. Experience of the anomalous tends to naturally lead to the ascription of the event to supernatural or unnatural agencies, as recently highlighted by Luhrmann's cross-cultural study of spiritual experiences (2020). In Luhrmann's view, spiritual experiences engage with the "paracosm," or a "private-but-shared imagined world" (Luhrmann 2020: 26) in which individuals feel as though they are inhabiting the same imaginary reality. Paracosms occur when the imaginary world becomes sufficiently familiar to a group of individuals that it begins to become seamless with the social reality. Luhrmann gives the example from her fieldwork with evangelical Christians in a Bible study group who would "read a passage about the Israelites fighting with the Midianites and talked about it as if it were something that had happened to them that afternoon at work with a colleague" (Luhrmann 2020: 32). What makes a paracosm distinctly "religious" is the codification of rules of engagement with the alternate reality. Religions authenticate experiences, provide means of communicating with supernatural beings, and distinguish between types of entities.

These shared imaginal spaces may vary substantially within cultures on the basis of differing religious affiliation or expertise. In a recent study conducted in China, a comparative analysis of the dreams of monks and nonreligious participants found a marked divergence in appearances of SAs. Monks reported more frequent appearances of divine beings and teachers, while the nonreligious participants reported more frequent conversations with relatives and animals (Zhang et al. 2018). Cultural frameworks thus structure both dream content as well as social interpretations of SA visitations in dreams. Dreams are a distinct area for interacting with the minds of spiritual agencies, even though their overall function will depend on the cultural setting of the dreamer.

Drawing the preceding threads together, we can conceptualize religious dreaming as social simulation within a culturally postulated paracosm; it affords the possibility for interaction with characters and entities from mythic narratives or stories that the individual will perceive as *real* especially when the dream is authenticated by the group. The natural function of dreaming as imaginative play in a socially rich hallucinatory environment thus naturally gives rise to experiences of culturally schematic supernatural encounters, which feeds back to bolster the individual's tie with group doctrine and strengthen group belief in the existence of the divine. If an individual's experiences are significantly out of alignment with the group's beliefs, then anomalous experiences can lead to the formation of new religious communities. This process has been mapped by Ann Taves (2016), who attributes the growth and success of new religious movements onto the acceptance of believers of the unusual experiences described by their charismatic leaders (Taves 2016).

Conceptualizing the relationship between dreams as social simulations and religious cognition requires a definition of religion that foregrounds relationships with SAs. A classic formulation by anthropologist Robin Horton is "religion can be looked upon as an extension of the field of people's social relationships beyond the confines of purely human society" (Horton 1997: 12). Another way of framing has been put forth by William Paden, who defines religion as "communicative, information-exchange signaling between social beings" that includes interactions with "invisible, supposed superhuman beings such as ancestors, souls, saints, spirits, buddhas, demons, and gods" (Paden 2017: 705, 2018). Understanding the development of religious systems over time thus requires considering this larger behavioral niche of interaction between religious traditions and the SAs for which they have established practices of communication. In many cultures, dreaming is a vital component of this communicative sphere, as dreams provide the most consistent and universal medium for nonspecialists to receive images and interactions with the supernatural. In part due to the prestige of these supernatural beings based on their perceived more-than-human powers, religious dreaming can be a means for individuals to gain authority or prestige within their social group as a mediator with the divine power. In all of the above ways, dreams provide a distinct avenue through which the "real" world of social relationships and the imaginal realm of cognized social reality intersect.

Directions for Future Research

What is the importance of the finding that SAs appear frequently in dreams and are in fact significantly associated with daytime cognitions? Such a finding would pave the way for future systematic studies of the precise ways dreams contribute to mythic narratives and cognitions about religious SAs. One important implication is the possibility that many of the mythic stories that underlie cultural belief systems, including religious stories about SAs, might originate within dreams. The finding would advance theories of acquisition of god concepts by identifying a brain/mind system (REM dreaming) that naturalistically facilitates that acquisition. This means that one promising avenue for future work is to bring the tools and findings of sleep and dream science to bear upon questions in the scientific study of religion. This research would also help to explain numerous phenomena associated with the scientific study of religion such as why dreams figure so often in accounts of religious ideologies or why dreams figure so prominently in theological traditions and sacred scriptures of most religions.

Another potential area for study is that of children's dreams. Studying SAs in children's dreams could provide a window into real-time acquisition of SA cognitions in all kinds of environments. Do children still acquire SA concepts from dreaming even if they receive no overt instruction about SAs? Sándor, Szakadát, and Bódizs (2014) recently reviewed the literature on children's dreams and methodological issues in collecting and analyzing children's dreams. Key findings from their review (and these are consistent with our own experience; Colace 2010) are that (1) children as young as three can reliably distinguish dream from reality and reliably report their dreams; (2) parent-collected dreams are preferred over lab- or school-collected dreams as children feel safer with parents and divulge more information with parents. Parents in addition can provide reliable background information on the sources of their child's dream content; (3) Colace (2010) and Sándor, Szakadát, and Bódizs (2014) created a checklist of eight features of the child's report that will increase confidence that that report is an actual dream rather than a confabulation. Thus the tools are now available to look at the acquisition of SA concepts in dreams versus waking states over time in children, which could also be compared with the development of social cognition and Theory of Mind skills, both of which are known to be essential for religious cognition.

In conclusion, researchers would greatly benefit by engaging with and drawing upon the wealth of insights emerging from the scientific study of dreams. Dreams, as we have seen, play a vital role in both personal experiences of interacting with the minds of gods, as well as providing the raw material for generating and substantiating cultural myths involving encounters beyond the human.

6

Animatism Reconsidered: A Cognitive Perspective

Jesper Frøkjær Sørensen and Benjamin Grant Purzycki

Introduction

Many contemporary approaches posit that religion originated, is maintained by, and/or covaries with our ability to mentally represent other minds (Andersen 2019; Schjoedt and Purzycki present volume). Many hold that the ability to detect minds where there are none—particularly minds that can understand human communication—is the hallmark of human religiosity (Barrett 2004; Boyer 2001; Guthrie 1980, 1993). Yet, to the extent that "agency" implies a "mind," a considerable amount of the beliefs and practices we might call "religious" are *not* obviously agentic at all. Instead, many traditions include abstract forces that are central aspects of religious cosmologies and commitment. In this chapter, we examine the cognitive underpinning of these beliefs and how non-agentive representations relate to more full-fledged agentive ideas.

Based on a short introduction to the British anthropologist Robert R. Marett's concepts of preanimism and animatism, we first discuss two ethnographic cases of animatistic forces. We then proceed to suggest a cognitive model of how humans represent "forces" as inherent in objects belonging to distinct ontological domains of the human environment before examining the close relationship between such force representation and representations of minds of both humans and spiritual agents. Drawing from this, we suggest that *mana* representations, that is, the attribution of special forces within distinct entities, agents, objects, or actions, emerge as an effect of fluctuations in frequency distributions of perception, and that these can be manufactured, harnessed, and stabilized by means of cultural technologies, such as gods and rituals. In short, while it can appear independently, animistic force is easily attached to representation of gods, spirits, and ancestors. This orientation amends the tendency of other theories to overemphasize full-fledged representations of "agency" as an evolutionary underpinning of religion, and favors a more perception-directed approach that emphasizes the role of human–environment motor interactions.

Animatism, Agency, and the Foundations of Religion

In an inquiry about religious origins that was typical of the times, Marett (1900, 1914) suggested that the essential—if not original—constituent of religious expression was not *animism* but *animatism*. Marett thereby critically assessed the prevalent understanding of the origin of religion in Britain before the turn of the twentieth century, Tylor's theory of animism, and found it wanting (Tybjerg 2018). Too many cases in the ethnographic record did not fit a model emphasizing spiritual agency, and nothing indicated that these could be explained by implicit assumptions of personal agency. Hence, unlike animism—expressed in Tylor's minimum definition of religion as "the belief in spiritual beings" (Tylor [1871] 2016a: x)—Marett hypothesized a preanimistic stage in human cultural evolution and suggested the term *animatism* to account for the belief in spiritual *powers* or *forces* not (yet) expressed in a personal idiom. To use one of Marett's distinctions, in practice, an *animist* might make a sacrifice toward a spirit that is "out there" (e.g., spirits of the forest or river who appreciate your offering), whereas *animatistic* practices are directed toward natural objects and phenomena (e.g., paying respects to a river, or utilizing sacred stones) believed to wield *power* of some sort without any implicit or explicit personal idiom (Marett 1914: xx). Animatism thus posits that these objects are imbued with or controlled by a supernatural or spiritual substance or force that makes them powerful, without ascribing these a mind. Humans do not merely seek to engage such objects in order to control their effect. Rather, this power is also often transferrable; people, objects, and even actions can have different amounts of the animatistic force and can deposit it elsewhere. This prospect points to social institutions that subsequently (re)distribute the force inherent in powerful objects (see below).

For a few reasons, Marett is still relevant for us today. First, he expressed cogent reasons for avoiding overly "agency-centric" and intellectualist accounts of religion in favor of a broader approach that focuses on the emotions stirred by experience of the nonordinary, unusual, and uncanny. Second, by emphasizing the role of perception and motor behavior, Marett outlined a model where humans react to fluctuations in their environment by representing these as initiated by impersonal "forces" rather than agents. Some of these will stabilize into cultural representations, but such representations will span a spectrum from impersonal immaterial forces to the personified and spiritual representations characteristic of animism.

While animatistic beliefs such as magic stones or powerful storms might appear to be relatively mundane, others are—or are portrayed to be—central to broader belief systems (e.g., *wakan* of the American Great Plains or the Polynesian concept of *mana*; see below). In these cases, animatistic forces and properties are often glossed as "sacred" or "holy" and people often claim they pervade the natural world and even vary in their manifestations and/or concentrations. In accordance with sentiments expressed by Durkheim ([1915] 2001), objects with concentrations of such qualities distinguish them from their more mundane or secular counterparts, thus affording them a religious or spiritual significance (see Sørensen 2020, 2021). As such, Marett was part of a general trend reacting against the narrowness of Tylor's orthodox explanation of the origin of religion, and looked to a more multifaceted account that would allow for other causes and origins.

On the basis of its cross-cultural ubiquity, grounding in natural phenomena, and the idea that while all spiritual agents are forces of change, not all spiritual forces of change are agents, Marett argued that *animatism* predates animism (see, too, Durkheim [1915] 2001: 142–7).[1] This argument would at least problematize the tendency to overemphasize the role of agency detection and anthropomorphic god representations in more recent cognitive and evolutionary approaches to religion. Indeed, this approach is not without its more recent champions. For instance, Vine Deloria Jr. (1979) echoes Mauss and Hubert (2001) and Durkheim ([1915] 2001) by suggesting that rather than the agentic spirits of animism, the unifying belief among indigenous peoples is the nonpersonal force of animatism:

> It is with the most common feature of primitive awareness of the world—the feeling or belief that the universe is energized by a pervading power. Scholars have traditionally called the presence of this power mana, following Polynesian beliefs, but we find it among tribal peoples, particularly American Indian tribes, as wakan [Sioux; see below], orenda[2] [Iroquois], or manitou[3] [Ojibwe]. Regardless of the technical term, there is general agreement that a substantial number of primitive peoples recognize the existence of a power in the universe that affects and influences them. (Deloria Jr. 1979: 152–3)

Note, however, that Deloria (1992) recognizes that it is effortless to *talk* about these forces as though they are humanlike and agentic:

> The overwhelming majority of American Indian tribal religions refused to represent deity [sic] anthropomorphically. To be sure, many tribes used the term grandfather when praying to God, but there was no effort to use that concept as the basis for a theological doctrine by which a series of complex relationships and related doctrines could be developed. While there was an acknowledgment that the Great Spirit has some resemblance to the role of a grandfather in the tribal society, there was no great demand to have a "personal relationship" with the Great Spirit in the same manner as popular Christianity has emphasized personal relationships with God. (79)

So, while these vast sacred forces might be a unifying idea among many traditions around the world (if not the "overwhelming majority of American Indian" traditions), there are nevertheless some anthropomorphic, even personal relationships posited or implied about them. Deloria also notes that whatever anthropomorphic aspects were casually ascribed to a sacred force, they played no role in the broader canonical beliefs and postulates. If anything, personification was a bastardization of canonical views. Do people actually do this? As we examine with two ethnographic examples, they do. But herein lies a problem: *why would individuals refer to an abstract entity anthropomorphically when their traditions don't explicitly endorse such views?* Where does this distortion come from and why does it appear to be common, intuitive, and effortless? We argue that even though force representations are often evoked without agentive properties, they are often linked to representations of spiritual or supernatural agency and, hence, to mentalizing.

Mana, Wakan Tanka, and Agency

The mixture of and interplay between spiritual, agentic, animatistic, and purely non-agentic representations of forces is a ubiquitous feature of religion; hence, rather than postulating the foundational nature of representations of minds for religions, a more nuanced approach models the various cognitive pathways that lead to representations of special forces active in the world and how specific cultural representations might oscillate between these as a function of local context. To illustrate this interplay, we examine two important ethnographic cases: the Melanesian concept of *mana* and Siouan notions of the Great Spirit, *wakan tanka*.

Mana and Social Life

To a large extent, early discussions of animatistic forces in religion took their point of departure with the Melanesian concept of *mana*. While it had entered discussions ongoing for a century, *mana* is typically hailed as entering the popular imagination through Codrington's (1891) ethnographic treatise *The Melanesians*. According to him, Melanesians believed

> that there is a supernatural power about belonging to the region of the unseen; and, as far as practice goes, in the use of means of getting this power turned to their own benefit ... There is a belief in a force altogether distinct from physical power, which acts in all kinds of ways for good and evil, and which it is of the greatest advantage to possess or control. This is Mana ... It is a power or influence, not physical, and in a way supernatural; but it shews itself in physical force, or in any kind of power or excellence which a man possesses. This Mana is not fixed in anything, and can be conveyed in almost anything; but spirits, whether disembodied souls or supernatural beings, have it and can impart it; and it essentially belongs to personal beings to originate it, though it may act through the medium of water, or a stone, or a bone. All Melanesian religion consists, in fact, in getting this Mana for one's self, or getting it used for one's benefit—all religion, that is, as far as religious practices go, prayers and sacrifices. (1891: 118)

As described by Codrington, *mana* is an impersonal force, but it "is always connected with some person who directs it; all spirits have it" (119). *Mana* is transferrable between persons and objects, so that specific objects—when touched by certain agents—can possess *mana*. Successful people owe their success and status to *mana*. This "force" became an entity, which conferred a particular power. Here, then, is one way in which an otherwise "impersonal force" is directly linked to the minds of humans and spirits.

According to Mauss and Hubert (Mauss 2001), "*mana* is power, *par excellence*, the genuine effectiveness of things which corroborates their practical actions without annihilating them" (137). This conception of *mana* emphasizes the potentiality of an entity's ability to alter the status of something else. Thus, *mana* is not only relational but also *differential*, in the sense that it implies something else's relative *inability* or *lack* of effectiveness. To Mauss and Hubert, *mana* represents a hidden layer of reality that intellectually unifies otherwise disparate worldly entities into a more sensible and coherent cultural logic. Coupling this with the idea that such notions are common in traditional societies, Mauss and Hubert treat *mana* as a fundamental property of human thought, in general, and religion specifically; *mana* concepts are essential aspects of how human beings categorize the world.

Generations of researchers treated *mana* as a cross-cultural catch-all and frequently listed it among ostensibly similar notions (see above). However, others have since questioned such liberal uses of *mana*. Keesing (1984), for example, suggests that it "was an invention of Europeans, drawing on their own folk metaphors of power and the theories of nineteenth-century physics" (148). In fact, Keesing points out that *mana* has many secular uses and often refers to things working successfully, becoming engaged, or simply a matter of good fortune (see Firth 1940; Meylan 2017; Tomlinson and Kāwika Tengan 2016 for more comprehensive treatment of how researchers have misused *mana* over the years). However, even though this criticism might be pertinent to emic descriptions of Melanesian and Polynesian worldviews, it does not directly affect the use of *mana* as a *universal* concept referring to representations of animatistic force cross-culturally. Further, while *mana* might not be as central to native theological perspectives as generations of scholars may have suggested, having or being *mana*—this "potential" or "good fortune"—was nevertheless important to Polynesians and Melanesians who explained its distribution with appeals to spirits.

Wakan tanka, Agency, and the Siouan Pantheon

We now turn our attention to another concept that has often been described as comparable to *mana*, namely the myriad Siouan (American Great Plains) traditions' use of the notion of *wakan*. Often glossed as "power" or "sacred" (Powers 1975: 45-7), *wakan* might very well be "the core of Lakota [one of the three major linguistic branches of the Sioux] belief ... [it is] the animating force of the universe, the common denominator of its oneness" (Neihardt 1984). Like *mana*, the use of *wakan* often appeals to something that is powerful, strange, and/or mysterious; it can mean "sacred, holy, consecrated, incomprehensible, special, possessing or capable of giving *ton* [which is] a spiritual quality received or transmittable to beings for making what is specially [*sic*] good or evil" (Buechel and Manhart 2002: 333). According to one elder, "*Wakan* was anything that was hard to understand. A rock was sometimes *wakan*. Anything might be *wakan*. When anyone did something that no one understood, this was *wakan*" (Walker 1991: 70). Another notes that "A *wakan* man [*wichasha wakan*] is one who is wise. It is one who knows the spirits ... has power with the spirits ... communicates with the spirits ... can do strange things. A *wakan* man knows things that the people do not know" (69). Like *mana*, *wakan* can be concentrated in special objects and people with ties to the spirits.

If *wakan* is the unifying force underlying the mystery of the universe, the notion of *wakan tanka* represents a very small step closer to comprehensibility and a stronger animist undertone. *Wakan tanka* (lit. "sacred vastness" or "big holiness") is synonymous with "the Great Spirit" or "Great Incomprehensibility" (Eastman [1911] 1980: 3). While some abstractly refer to *wakan tanka* "the all-pervasive force" that "was conceived of in various graded levels of manifestation", it is also just as readily personified (Hassrick 1964: 206–7). Eastman ([1911] 1980) notes that "the spirit pervades all creation and … every creature possesses a soul in some degree" (14); and that "the spirit which the 'Great Mystery' breathed into man returns to Him who gave it, and that after it is freed from the body, it is everywhere and pervades all nature" (156).

One scholar (DeMallie 1987) posits that *wakan tanka* "was the sum of all that was considered mysterious, powerful, or sacred … Wakan Tanka never had birth and so could never die. The Wakan Tanka created the universe … Rather than a single being, Wakan Tanka embodied the totality of existence" (28). Indeed, this "sacred vastness" often represented the abstract totality of everything *wakan* but also included a multitude of relatively concrete entities (*wakanpi*) with agentic properties, including addressing prayers and enhancing the lives of people (Mails 1979: 16; Standing Bear [1928] 1975: 113). And, the Great Mystery regularly communicates to the Sioux either directly through visions or indirectly through the animals and the elements (e.g., "the storm wind is … a messenger of the 'Great Mystery'"; Eastman [1911] 1980: 34).

Aspects of the Great Mystery are almost entirely framed anthropomorphically. In fact, *wakan tanka* functions as an organizing principle that unifies otherwise disparate spiritual entities in the Siouan pantheon. In a compendium of passages dated to 1896, recorded views of Lakota elders are replete with agentic conceptions of *wakan tanka*. According to some of these accounts, *wakan tanka* "was everywhere all the time and observed everything that each one of mankind did and even knew what anyone thought, that he might be pleased or displeased because of something that one did" (George Sword, 1896 cited in DeMallie and Jahner 1991: 75). Others note that the Great Spirit "is like sixteen different persons … they are all only the same as one" (George Sword, Bad Wound, No Flesh, and Thomas Tyon, 1905 cited in DeMallie and Jahner 1991: 93).

These passages contain agentic elements of "observing," "knowing," and "punishing."[4] Yet, they also suggest a concept with degrees of complexity beyond immediate comprehension; the Great Spirit is multidimensional ("like sixteen different persons"), omnipresent, and omniscient. These "different persons" are concentrations of the distributed *wakan* force. Indeed, other passages specify more precise features of *wakan tanka*, inconsistently reporting its material manifestation(s):

> Some of them do not have a body of matter. These are all spirits that do good to mankind … There is one *wakan tanka* who is evil … The *Wakan Tanka* are the superior and the inferior and there are four of each kind … The *Wakan Tanka* that have material bodies are the Sun, the Earth, the Rock, the Moon. Those which have no material bodies are *Taku Skan Skan* (the Sky), *Tate* (the atmosphere or the

wind), *Wakinyan* (the Winged), and *Wohpe* (the Meteor). (George Sword, 1896 cited in DeMallie and Jahner 1991: 99)

While some deistically suggest that the Great Spirit "was above all spirits. He did nothing. He was the chief of all things. Indians did not know much about him. They invoked only the spirits that were under him," others are explicit about *wakan tanka*'s role in creation:

> The animals and plants are taught by Wakan Tanka what to do. They are not alike ... The Great Spirit likes it that way. He only sketches out the path of life roughly for all the creatures on earth, shows them where to go, where to arrive at, but leaves them to find their own way to get there. He wants them to act independently according to their nature, to the urges in each of them. (Lame Deer and Erdoes 1972: 156–7)

Clearly, *wakan* and *wakan tanka* play a central, even unifying role in the Siouan religious worldview. Elders who are likely the most knowledgeable of their traditions nevertheless freely communicate these notions in a personified fashion, despite being inconsistent with the idea that the *wakan* and Great Spirit are spiritual forces.

Animatism and Social Life

The preceding discussion demonstrates the confused state of *mana*-like concepts. Both *mana* and *wakan* are described as abstract, impersonal forces; they also have direct associations with spiritual *and* human agents. In fact, as these spiritual forces are the powers of the gods themselves, they are arguably represented as inseparable (Radin 1914). The American Indian Iroquois concept of *orenda*, for example, was classically defined as "the fictive force, principle, or magic power ... inherent in every body and being of nature and in every personified attribute, property, or activity, belonging to each of these and conceived to be the active cause or force, or dynamic energy, involved in every operation or phenomenon of nature, in any manner affecting or controlling the welfare of man" (Hewitt 1912: 147). The gods wielded this "dynamic energy"; indeed, "the possession of orenda or magic power is the distinctive characteristic of all the gods" (Hewitt 1912: 147). Yet, because this possession exerted influence on people, individuals had to propitiate these gods in order to increase their welfare who did so with the power of *orenda*. Here, then, we have two more clear cross-culturally expressed links between spiritual forces and spiritual minds; not only do the gods wield such forces, but these forces have a direct bearing on "the welfare of man."

One reason for this apparent duality might be found in their origin. Indeed, *animatistic* notions are believed to be intertwined with social life (i.e., other *human* minds). Mauss and Hubert (Mauss 2001) characterized animatistic forces as "unconscious categories of understanding" and as it "is present in an individual's consciousness purely as a result of the existence of society," it is undoubtedly "a category of collective thinking" (146). Durkheim ([1915] 2001) suggested that "the psychological roots" of animatistic beliefs are the human tendency to explain our "collective feeling of respect" toward something or someone identified as sacred (196). We appeal to culturally postulated forces and beings to account for the feelings of social force shared by individuals in any given group. Like Durkheim, Mauss and Hubert argued that the unconscious entertainment of animatism not only helps people organize their world into sacred and profane (as well as demarcate better hunters, shamans, leaders, and so forth), but it also marshals their value systems; as magic and religion stem from satisfying the intellectual and social needs of one's community, animatistic forces like *mana* and *wakan* can be appealed to in order to reaffirm one's social milieu and to direct attention toward special or unique phenomena and people in the world (see Bendixen and Purzycki, present volume, for discussion of cultural models of appeals to gods' concerns).

Both *mana* and *wakan tanka* are inextricably linked to—if not represented as—mental entities. Deloria suggests this link might have communicative utility and that we might anthropomorphize forces in order to convey them. In other words, communicating these notions through the idiom of agency might reduce the kinds of variation that would otherwise arise. Yet, in both cases, these powers are also directly linked to human individuals and their needs. In other words, these powers are not impersonal but socially relevant. Why, then, are they socially relevant? In order to address this problem, we need a better understanding of the cognitive mechanisms underlying both representations of force and the manifest human tendency to ascribe agency to the world. We discuss a host of mechanisms that both generate and maintain the social relevance of force concepts.

Animatism and Cognition

Force representations are an essential aspect of categorical perception and as such, an integral part of the motor-representation enabling us to engage the world. This unification makes some sense in a predictive processing account of human cognition (see Purzycki and Schjoedt, present volume). In short, predictive processing argues that that central function of our neurocognitive system is to predict "whatever next" (Clark 2013, 2016; Hohwy 2013). By means of mental models, so-called priors, we generate expectations of perceptual input and thereby gauge causal structure in the world. For instance, we have a model of "cat" that gives us certain expectations. As long as the input is matched by the model, information need not ascend further up the processing hierarchy. In a way, we see the cat that we expect to see. However, should models fail to predict stimuli, new information presents itself as an error signal that prompts an updating of our model, or that, alternatively, entices us to act and thereby change the world. If the cat has only three legs (new information), we might update our cat-model to include three-legged cats; should the cat go missing (new information), we might move our bodies until our expectation of seeing the cat is once again fulfilled. In both cases, prediction error is minimized, either by modifying our model so that it better fits the world, or by acting in the world, to have better fit our expectations.

We do not just represent abstract features of categories such as "stones," "cats," or "people." Instead, our predictive models involve expectations about force dynamic characteristics informed by stable expectations. Often resulting from innate structures, these domain-specific hyperpriors are targeted and informed inferences upon which other inferences are built. Stones are supposed to be heavy (e.g., they are predicted to sink if immersed in water), but as inanimate objects they are expected to be immobile unless moved by an *external* force. By contrast, we characterize both cats and persons as self-propelled and are thus able to exert force upon the environment (e.g., moving otherwise immobile stones). Interestingly, the movements of "cats" and "persons" are themselves represented as driven by *internal* forces; besides the obvious exertion of force expressed through muscular-skeletal contraction, agents' behaviors are intuitively represented as caused by internal and invisible mental states such as desires, wishes, dispositions, and "will" (Baron-Cohen 1995). In short, we expect the living to be driven by their own models of the world. These psychological forces are translated into behavior, that is, into concrete physical force that can in turn exert itself onto other entities. Some of these entities are other humans.

Of central importance in this context is therefore the relation between force representations and domains of application. Predicting the inherent force in a stone—its weight, density, solidity, and so on—does not obviously entail predictions involving agency. Even when a stone falls after rolling off of a cliff or sinks when immersed in water, we do not obviously posit a "will" to it. But *something* is happening in both cases; a state of the world is changing. The world is full of such impersonal forces understood as inherent force dynamic potentialities and our cognitive system would indeed be overwhelmed by false positives should these systematically be endowed with agency (cf. Guthrie 1980, 1993). Therefore, we have no a priori reason to assume that representations of "magical" stones necessarily involve concomitant representations of agency. As already claimed by Marett, Hubert, and Mauss, magical stones are stones that are somehow unusual, surprising, or uncanny; they contain a special inherent force-potential that defines their unusualness. It might be up to humans to extract or utilize the inherent quality, but the quality is *potential* (and, thus, "impersonal"). A more parsimonious hypothesis would thus posit that humans readily ascribe special but non-agentive forces to special exemplars of categories in the world, and that animist representations require additional contextual cueing and cultural elaboration in order to be evoked. Those cues and elaborations are grounded in the minds of other people who in religious contexts are "motivated" by the minds of spirits.

Research into causal representations might give us an indication of what types of contextual cues are relevant and why our models of force often take an agentive direction. If we commence at the most basic level, studies of representations related to simple causal relations of the billiard-ball type expose a consistent pattern: when asked to explain a simple causal scenario, subjects relate these as "the red ball making the white ball move"; they rarely, if ever, account for the same event as "the white ball made the red ball stop" even though this description is equally correct in terms of mechanics (Bender and Beller 2011; White 2006). Human causal representations are asymmetric; we tend to emphasize the dynamic side of an event, most likely as this supplies more urgent and potentially relevant information. This makes good sense, if we understand human cognition in broad terms as engaged in trying to predict the world by means of generative models (Clark 2016). As it elicits prediction error relative to the prevalent model, movement involves changes in the perceptual field that, in turn, necessitate that the generative model used to predict incoming stimuli is updated. In short, in contrast to mobility, movement is information rich.

This causal asymmetry is enhanced as the "effectors" of dynamic changes in the environment are typically agents (in contrast to inanimate objects, these are self-propelled); more complex representations are therefore likely to take on an increasingly agentic form. Further, the prototypical agent in this regard is likely to be oneself. Force dynamic representations are based in proprioceptive models of one's own body moving within a physical environment replete with resistance (White 2006). Lifting a stone from the ground demands the exertion of force, whereas its movement toward the ground when released appears to rely on a force inherent in the stone. This is in line with both models of developmental psychology as well as in cognitive linguistics. Developmental psychologists argue that children initially understand force as an inherent property of things, and more recent research indicates that, even though these representations are later modified as a result of education, at the core also adults understand forces as part of things (Vosniadou 2002). And, as we represent relations in the world as the dynamic unfolding of mutual relations of internal force, force representations are abundant in language (Talmy 2000). *Dynamic changes in the world are therefore prototypically represented as agentive, as they entail an exertion of force met by inertial resistance from the environment.* We therefore argue that rudimentary representations of agency are grounded in a bodily experience of interacting with entities—persons or inanimate things—governed by inherent forces.

If basic representations of force are related to the actions of bodies—including one's own—we might ask how forces in the world relate to moral intuitions. Gods, spirits, and ancestors are generally thought of as agents that relate to human behavior on moral grounds. But what about the animatistic forces? As alluded to above, while a force in and of itself might be amoral or "impersonal," associated representations of how people and the gods use them are very much moral. Propelling or obstructing human goals, whether individual or collective, will necessarily imply at least a rudimentary moral dimension, particularly if those goals are to affect others in beneficial or costly ways. As such, to the extent that they further one party's agenda at the expanse of another, forces both ordinary and special will readily enter the moral domain regulating interaction between people. The gods use such forces not only to mediate morally relevant social dilemmas (see Petersen; Purzycki and McKay; Lightner and Purzycki, present volume) but also to maintain social status of individuals (see above). However, forces in themselves are often represented as less morally neutral and as having an essential moral dimension. When *wakan tanka* is described as the spirit that pervades all creation, this force has a "direction." Working "together" with it will be considered harmonious and proper in contrast to working against it, which is rendered unnatural and bad.

If we take these observations into account, we can present a few tentative ideas accounting for the ubiquity of *mana* representations in the world as well as their tendency to be associated with agency. First, as we saw above, things are always endowed with inherent forces, and special objects, persons, actions, or events are therefore likely to be ascribed equally special forces that set them aside from those normally experienced. Second, forces ascribed due to an infrequency in ongoing experience—setting aside *this* particular stone as different from other stones, or this person as especially lucky—can be utilized to further the goal of human agents. Thus, *mana* representations are not based in disinterested observations of "supernatural" forces but in interested, motivated, and emotionally fueled conceptions of how particular forces might be helpful, or inhibitory, in reaching particular goals. Like appealing to the minds of gods (Bendixen and Purzycki, present volume), appealing to or roping in special forces is a way to affect *others'* behavior. They are therefore inherently moral—or at least morally relevant—forces. Magical stones are only magical if they further some goal (e.g., increase the catch of fish or prevent one from being shot during battles), and persons contain a special force if they are strong or lucky, that is, if they have power to bring their will about and therefore represent powerful allies or strong opponents to other agents. *Mana* is ascribed based on potential or observed impact on the environment of human agents and can therefore be both acquired and lost (see Section "*Mana* and Social Life").

Third, as ancestors, spirits, and gods are presented as especially powerful agents able to impact the success of humans, these are, naturally, considered to contain this force in greater proportions. This does *not* entail those representations of force originate with these agents, but, rather, that they will attract *animatistic* representations already present (see Section "*Wakan tanka*, Agency, and the Siouan Pantheon"). Fourth, instigating changes in our environments is prototypically the role of agents. It follows that if entities containing *mana* are considered to be the *main* instigator of changes—if they are understood as more than merely instrumental in reaching a goal—they are more likely to be represented as agents. If, further, concepts of the "special force" are generalized into broad concepts such as the local versions of *mana*, *orenda*, or *wakan*, these are more likely to be endowed with agentive qualities as this will account for the distribution of force related to human goals (and hence with a moral[5] quality) among many instances, thus forming a recurrent pattern normally ascribed agency. Fifth, structural features of perception and communication might themselves push toward agentive representations. As Deloria suggested above, personification is efficient communication, and inanimates will function as subject and thereby agents in the sentence structure of many languages.[6]

These five points lead us to a fundamental aspect of animatism that might help explain its cultural success: *animatistic representations allow the creation, accumulation, and distribution of force*. This point is crucial, as humans thereby circumvent a fundamental limitation of animistic agency: that the force inherent in an agent is limited to its own action. Ancestor, spirits, and gods may act upon the world, but this would restrict religion to different modes of influencing or directing "the acts of gods" flying in the face of the many aspects of religion concerned with generating, accumulating, and distributing force. Even the gods depend on the ability of their power to accumulate as a non-agentive force in material objects that can be distributed among believers.

Future Directions

If *mana*-like representations solely arose as a product of experienced "oddity" in the social and natural environment, it would possibly not play such an important role. Humans need methods to generate animatistic representations. In line with Mauss and Hubert, we argue that ritual is the prime, but not sole, cultural technology engaged in generating representations of special force. Numerous studies have pointed to the special characteristics of ritual action (Rappaport 1979; Staal 1979) and how this impacts cognitive processing (Boyer and Liénard 2006; Legare and Souza 2012; Nielbo and Sørensen 2011; Sørensen 2007b). These studies unanimously argue that ritual conflicts with the canonical models guiding cognitive processing of both performed and observed actions. In human rituals, actions are causally opaque; the actions performed are not causally represented as related to their purported result. Further, rituals are intentionally underdetermined and goal-demoted; the intentions of the performers have very little impact on the content and sequential unfolding of the action. Rituals are stipulated action sequences guided by conventional rules and whose alleged effects are based on either associative relations between action and goal, such as similarity and contagion, or available conventional interpretations.

Sørensen (2007a) argued that these features make participants ascribe "magical agency," that is, the force responsible for the efficacy of the ritual, into different parts, persons, actions, or objects, depending on the ritual in case. Take, for example, the transubstantiation of the Catholic Eucharist where, by virtue of institutional power, a priest ostensibly alters the *essence* of bread and wine to the body and blood of Jesus (100–5). Its physical form is maintained while its essential character is supposed to be thought of as literally transformed allowing it to function as the agentive force in subsequent rituals—legitimate in communion and illegitimate when placed under the doorstep of a house to prevent theft (Thomas [1971] 1991).

Focusing on the role of force dynamic representations allows us to expand this view considerably and account for how ritual behavior in itself is likely to lead to ascription of special inherent force in one or several ritual elements. Besides eliciting a search for an agentive force to account for ritual efficacy, the central features of ritual are, in themselves, likely to evoke representations of special force. The reason for this is simple, even if the underlying cognitive processing might follow more complicated patterns: *all actions involve the expenditure of energy*. In canonical, instrumental actions, the expenditure of energy is regulated by a feedback loop relating this investment with the effects of the actions. Having reached the goal, the agent will stop spending energy. By contrast, no such feedback controls the expenditure of energy in ritual. Rather, the range of energy that should be invested is generally specified by tradition. The crucial thing is, however, that the effect of the ritual is non-perceivable. No perceivable change takes place in the phenomenal world as an effect of the energy invested. To account for the missing energy, we predict that it accumulates in one or several of the elements, objects, and persons, taking part in the ritual. We see this when thousands of pilgrims circumambulate the Kaaba in Mecca, when the sanctified host is lifted and spoken over in a Christian church, and when shamans sanctify sacred places. In these cases, we see the generation of *mana* in particular objects: representations of inherent force that can later be redistributed to the community from whose action it arose. This effect can be produced by individuals' ritualistic interaction with objects, but it is likely to multiply its effect when the rituals are performed by a group whose combined expenditure of energy in the ritual action can be accumulated within a ritual object.

Acknowledgments

The authors thank Theiss Bendixen for his feedback on a previous draft of this chapter. Purzycki acknowledges generous support from the Aarhus University Research Foundation (AUFF).

7

The Minds behind the Ritual: How "Ordering Gods" Reinforced Human Cooperation

Matt J. Rossano

Introduction

Looming silently over the desolate Harran plain of southern Turkey are the 12,000-year-old ruins of Göbekli Tepe (Dietrich 2011; Dietrich and Schmidt 2010). They include over two hundred stone pillars, some over twenty feet tall and nearly ten tons in weight, arranged in a series of circles encompassing a space of about a thousand feet in diameter. There is no evidence of long-term habitation at Göbekli Tepe. Instead, it appears to have been a pilgrimage site where collective rituals were enacted (Dietrich et al. 2019). Clues regarding the nature of these rituals may be found in the site's abundant iconography.

Göbekli Tepe's stone pillars are adorned with engravings of threatening and dangerous animals such as snakes, leopards, scorpions, and wild boar, often shown in aggressive stances or attacking motion (Dietrich et al. 2019). The pillars themselves have humanlike qualities being composed of a long vertical slab, topped by another horizontal one, forming a T-shaped body with a faceless head. Many have representations of arms, hands, belts, or loincloths on them, giving them the appearance of giant, abstract humanoids. Researchers speculate that they might be gods or watchful ancestors. Abstract symbols are also present on the pillars as well as on various bowls, shaft straighteners, and tablets found at the site. The regularity of these symbols suggests that they are a text relating some, as of yet, unknown story. Buildings decorated with animal images have also been found here. Interestingly, different buildings appear to be specifically associated with particular animals. For example, at one building (called A), snake images predominate, while at building B it is foxes. One hypothesis is that the animal images marked buildings set aside for different groups that gathered at the site.

The copious imagery devoted to themes of power, danger, and fear would have created a strong emotional setting for initiation rituals or other rites of passage (Dietrich et al. 2019). Further evidence of emotive ritual can be found in the large amount of broken and burned game-animal bones present at the site. Celebratory feasting, possibly at the conclusion of traumatic rituals, clearly occurred at Göbekli Tepe. These rituals likely also reinforced the narrative present in the iconography, celebrating the common mythological framework that united the different groups that congregated there. The fact that similar pillars and imagery have been found at other sites surrounding Göbekli Tepe suggests that this cultural framework extended region-wide (Dietrich et al. 2019).

The proprietors of Göbekli Tepe faced a problem. How to get diverse, independent-minded hunter-gatherer groups to coalesce into a unified tribe? To address this, they used ritual—ritual that transmitted a canonical message about the divine order of the universe and each group's place within that order. By all indicators, that ritual was emotionally compelling by virtue of its "specialness"; that is, the fact that it occurred at a special place (an especially constructed pilgrimage site) involving special actions (initiating, celebrating, feasting, storytelling, etc.) using special objects (pillars and other ritual accoutrements) and imagery (engravings on the pillars).

My argument in this chapter is that Göbekli Tepe is not unique. Our ancestors prior to Göbekli Tepe faced the same problem only on a smaller scale. They had to convince group members that they were duty-bound participants in a divinely ordained cosmic order, and they use ritual to do it. But why ritual? Because they perceived that that is what the gods responsible for this order demanded. Our ancestors were not deists. The minds of their gods were keenly aware of human thought and behavior. Indeed, it was the recognition of the gods' presence and the order emanating from this presence that compelled a ritualistically enacted human sign of commitment to what the gods had wrought. The proper enactment of this sign of commitment catalyzed the evolutionary transition from primate ritualized behavior to human ritual.

The basic elements of the argument are as follows:

1. The evolution of ritual involves a change from an indexical message (ritualized behavior) to a canonical one (rituals).
2. This canonical message described the divine (shamanistic) order of the cosmos and what the gods required of humans in return for this order.
3. Individuals ritually committed to this order and in doing so rendered important psychological resources to their groups (loyalty, sacrificial service, concern for fellow group members, etc.).

I conclude by addressing the question: can rituals be taken seriously if they lose this canonical message? The answer to this question requires that we appreciate that part of what makes humans distinct from other species is our hyper-cooperativeness (Tomasello et al. 2012). Ritual was the mechanism we used to construct our unprecedented level of in-group cooperation and cohesion (Rossano 2019). Buttressing these rituals was a belief that the mind(s) of god(s) was (were) responsible for cosmic order. If rituals lose their credibility without these gods behind them, then what becomes of the uniquely human prosocial sentiments that rituals foster?

Ritual and Ritualized Behavior

Hobson et al. (2018: 261) define ritual as "(a) predefined [gestural] sequences characterized by rigidity, formality, and repetition that are (b) embedded in a larger system of symbolism and meaning, [and] (c) contain elements that lack direct instrumental purpose." Part (a) of the definition describes what makes *ritualized behavior* different from ordinary behavior—it is (among other things) rigid, formalized, and repetitious. These characteristics are designed to attract and hold one's attention while conveying an important social message.

For example, an American president laying a wreath on the Tomb of the Unknown Solider will approach the wreath at a slow marching pace escorted by a military honor guard. Then he will stand erect before the wreath with his hand over his heart as the National Anthem is played. After which he will very deliberately approach the wreath, place it upon its stand, step back, and once again place his hand over his heart, eyes locked on the wreath, while taps is played. These rigid, formal, and repetitious behaviors convey a solemn message of respect and gratitude for fallen soldiers. Ritualized behavior is not unique to humans, however. Baboons use a rigid, deliberate approach gait as a prelude to alliance formation (Smuts and Watanabe 1990), and dogs will often repeat the play-bow gesture numerous times while roughhousing with other dogs and humans to reinforce their intention to play, not fight.

It is part (b) of the definition that distinguishes rituals from ritualized behavior. Human ritualized behaviors are often embedded within a larger system of symbols and traditions that give them a broader, more enduring meaning than animal ritualized behaviors. Geese have ritualized mating dances, but they do not have weddings, replete with all the cultural symbols, traditions, and meanings that weddings entail. This difference was elaborated by anthropologist Roy Rappaport in his discussion of the indexical versus canonical messages that rituals transmit.

Indexical versus Canonical Messages

Anthropologist Roy Rappaport (1999: 52–3) argued that rituals convey two distinct messages to witnesses and participants. The first was an *indexical* message about present states of mind or intentions. For example, by their participation in the wedding ceremony the marrying couple is expressing something about their present state of mind—they are "in love" and willing to commit to one another. Likewise, by their attendance at the ceremony, witnesses convey approval and support of the marrying couple (which is probably why those who have serious objections to the marriage often opt not to attend—they're in the "wrong" state of mind). Animal "rituals" also convey this message. The play-bowing dog is in a playful state of mind. A chimpanzee doing a begging gesture is in a submissive state of mind and no longer "wants" to fight. The two geese doing a mating dance "intend" to find mates. Thus, the "indexical message" is shared widely across the animal kingdom.

Ritual's *canonical* message is a cultural expression of an existent universal order from which important ideals and values emerge. This message is typically conveyed using special, often symbolic, objects, venues, and actions. For example, a religious wedding ceremony takes place on sacred ground (church, synagogue, etc.) using symbolic objects (rings, a white wedding gown, etc.) and involves special actions (readings from scripture, vows, lighting candles, etc.). This "specialness" transmits and reinforces a message about the divinely ordained nature of marriage and the values (fidelity, purity, family, etc.) associated with it. Thus, in the wedding ceremony both an indexical message (the couple's mutual love) and a canonical message (the community's enduring values associated with marriage) are being expressed. It is the presence of the canonical message that distinguishes rituals from ritualized behavior. Indeed, it was the inclusion of this canonical message that led to the evolution of ritual out of already-present primate ritualized behaviors.

Archeology of Ritual

While we can never be certain about the beliefs of our long-dead ancestors, archeological evidence of ritual (presumably associated with belief) is present. Often these remains appear to be motivated by a desire to acknowledge and honor the supernatural forces responsible for creating the order our ancestors perceived around them. For example, Göbekli Tepe contains all the elements that are typically found in rituals. As already mentioned it was a special place—rituals often occur in locations deemed to be extraordinary (holy places, graveyards, elaborate banquet halls, etc.). Additionally, Göbekli Tepe contained special objects, images, and activities. While evidence of special objects, images, and activities can be found in the archeological record attesting to the evolutionary emergence of rituals, this chapter will focus primarily on special places (a discussion of objects, images, and actions can be found in Rossano 2021: 57, 61–4).

Over the course of hominin evolution, there is increasing evidence that our ancestors began to recognize certain geographic locations as having extraordinary significance. By itself, this recognition may not be entirely unique to hominins. Though certainly debatable, chimpanzees might associate a primitive sense of "specialness" with certain natural features and may even perform ritualized behaviors at those sites (Kühl et al. 2016). But in time, hominins began to understand special places as indicators of a supernaturally designed cosmic order. These were natural inflection points in the landscape teeming with spiritual power. In all likelihood, it was at these places that the first gestural acknowledgment of cosmic order (a canonical message) was incorporated into the ritualized behaviors performed there.

Liminal Places

Overactive agency detection appears to be common throughout the animal world (Rossano and Vandewalle 2016) and is especially acute in humans (Guthrie 1993; Purzycki and Schjoedt, this volume). Unsurprisingly then, evidence indicates that animism is the oldest form of supernatural belief (Peoples, Duda, and Marlowe 2016). Thus, it is highly likely that our hominin ancestors understood the natural world as being thoroughly pervaded by consciousness(es). Nearly as old as animism is shamanism, which entails the additional belief that the natural world is not just conscious but *consciously ordered*. The shamanistic world is three-tiered, with the earthly realm set between supernatural realms both above (the heavens) and below (the underworld; Hayden 2003: 77–9).

An important step in the evolutionary transition from primate ritualized behaviors to human rituals was the recognition that the natural world's consciousness was especially present or sensitive in certain places. These places have been termed "places of power," or "shrines of the land" (Scarre 2011: 10). Frequently, these were "liminal" places, ones that mark boundaries, thresholds, or transitions in the landscape. These included mountains, hills, bogs, swamps, shorelines, and caves. These liminal places provided access to the spiritual realms of the heavens and the underworld. Furthermore, they were connected to human transitions of birth, death, and maturation (Haaland and Haaland 2011). This connection led to bogs, rivers, lakes, and caves frequently being used as burial sites. Caves, portholes to the underworld, appear to be the oldest burial sites.

Caves

Some have argued that the first hominin grave site is the 400,000-year-old "pit of bones" (Sima de los Huesos) found deep in the Atapuerca Mountains in north-central Spain (Pettitt 2011). Here, the remains of over thirty hominins have been found, most likely of the species *Homo heidelbergensis* (Arsuaga et al. 1997). Although it is unclear how the bones ended up in the pit, one possible scenario is that bodies were deliberately placed near the pit over an extended period of time and natural process swept them into it, preserving them (Andrews and Fernández-Jalvo 1997; Fernandez Jalvo, and Andrews 2003). The dead were deposited here possibly because hominins associated the transition from life to death with the liminality of the cave. It was a place where earth and underworld met.

Caves served as burial grounds for both Neanderthals and *Homo sapiens*. Multiple bodies have been found at numerous Neanderthal cave sites dating from 130,000 to 50,000 years ago such as Krapina in northern Croatia (twenty to thirty bodies), La Ferrassie in France (seven bodies), and Shanidar in Iraq (seven to nine bodies; Pettitt 2011). Similarly, for *Homo sapiens*, beginning about 100,000 years ago, multiple bodies have been found at such places as Skhul and Qafzeh caves in the Levant, and Cussac Cave in France (Aujoulat et al. 2002; Riel-Salvatore and Clark 2001).

Two nonburial cave sites also appear to have been ritual venues. The first is Bruniquel Cave, a Neanderthal site in France dated to about 175,000 ybp (years before present; Jaubert et al. 2016). About two hundred meters deep in the cave, after a very tight crawl through a narrow passage, there is a small (approximately 14 m^2) enclosed floor space that appears to be a ritual site (Hayden 2003: 100–2, 2012). Hundreds of stalagmites and stalactites have been broken off and formed into two circles on the cave floor. Evidence of a fire is present in the larger of the two circles along with bear or large herbivore bones. There is little evidence that the space was used for habitation, reinforcing the notion that it was a ritual or ceremonial space.

The second is Rhino Cave, a *Homo sapiens*' site dated to around 70,000 ybp (Coulson, Staurset, and Walker 2011). Rhino Cave is located in the visually prominent Tsodilo Hills of Botswana (Southern Africa), the only major outcropping for over a hundred kilometers in any direction. Archeologists have argued that the Hills may have served as an assembly site for hominin communities in the region (Coulson, Staurset, and N. Walker 2011). Inside Rhino Cave is a natural serpentine outcropping—a "snake" rock—which has been intentionally modified to enhance its snake-like qualities. By flickering torchlight (how it would have been observed in the past), the snake rock conveys the illusion of movement (Coulson, Segadika, and Walker 2016). While it is impossible to know how this scene was interpreted by ancient people, similar contexts from more recent sites have been interpreted shamanistically—as signifying entry points to the spirit world (Lewis-Williams 2002).

It may be that Rhino Cave represents the first site where the consciousness-altering rituals associated with shamanism were practiced. Further reinforcing the ritual interpretation of the site are the unusually large number of burnt, broken, and abandoned tools found on the cave floor. Many of these tools were produced from carefully selected, colorful, nonlocal ("exotic") raw materials (Coulson, Staurset, and N. Walker 2011: 30). The raw materials were brought to the cave from distances ranging from fifty to several hundred kilometers. Once inside the cave, the raw materials were "delicately worked" (48) into tools (points) and then intentionally destroyed or abandoned in the cave. From a practical standpoint, this behavior is odd and costly. Time, energy, and valuable material resources were exhausted for no clear utilitarian gain. But, as Coulson, Staurset, and Walker (2011) point out, these are precisely the hallmarks of human ritual.

Upper Paleolithic Cave Rituals

With the onset of the Upper Paleolithic about 35,000 years ago, evidence of ritual activity in caves becomes increasingly abundant. There are hundreds of painted caves across Europe that suggest ritual activity. Shamanistic themes are present at some of them. For example, deep in Chauvet Cave (France), an image of a half-human/half-bison has been painted in black on a natural limestone panel (Whitely 2009: 70). The legs and torso are human, while the head is that of a bison with horns extending upward. The image could represent the transformation a shaman undergoes while in a trance state, where he or she is inhabited by a powerful animal spirit. The paintings in Chauvet Cave are some of the oldest in Europe, dating 30,000 ybp or more.

A similar, even more compelling, therianthropic (part human, part animal) image is present at Les Trois Frerer Cave (also in France) in a deep recess aptly named "the sanctuary." Ten feet high on the cave wall, engraved in black paint is the famed "Sorcerer" image. Cave art researcher Count Henri Begouen described the image as "an amazing masked human figure with a long beard, the eyes of an owl, the antlers of a stag, the ears of a wolf, the claws of a lion, and the tale of a horse" (as quoted in White 2003: 51). In the isolated sanctuary chamber, the Sorcerer stares down at hundreds of other animal images adorning the cave walls. Some, including Begouen, have interpreted the image as a shaman being ritually transformed into the spirit of a powerful animal (Dickson 1990: 116).

Possibly the most celebrated potential shamanistic image is the famous bird-man from the shaft at Lascaux Cave. Here, a human male with a bird-head has been painted on the cave wall. The man is falling backward while apparently hunting or fighting with a bison. In close proximity is an image of a bird perched on a staff. Some have argued that this is a shaman battling with an animal spirit (see discussion, for example, in Lewis-Williams 2002: 264–5). The physical setting for this image, as well as those of Chauvet and Les Trois Frerer, is a dark remote cave recess, highly conducive, both visually and acoustically, to bringing about the altered states of consciousness integral to shamanistic rituals.

Finally, El Juyo Cave in northern Spain contains one of the most enigmatic of ancient ritual venues (Freeman and Gonzalez Echegaray 1981). Near the cave's entrance, an elaborate altar was constructed that is at once both visually arresting and concealing. Arresting, because the 120-square-foot-space, with its focally placed half-human/half-feline face, has clearly been constructed to captivate an audience. Concealing, because what are apparently offerings of animal bones, spear points, and bone needles have been buried out of sight, beneath two huge stone slabs. Simultaneously, the ritual space grabs the attention of those entering the cave, while hiding from them the complete nature of the space. Rituals are typically rule-governed activities where custom dictates how the ritual is conducted. The El Juyo sanctuary appears to have structurally incorporated rules about what aspects of the ritual were public knowledge versus what may have been exclusive to certain elites or ritual specialists.

The rock slabs composing the altar are so large and heavy that a dozen or so individuals would have been needed to put them into position. A foot-tall half-human/half-feline face keeps watchful gaze over the space "presiding from its dominant position over the whole complex" (Freeman and Gonzalez Echegaray 1981: 15). The right half of the face appears to be a bearded human male, while the left side is feline—maybe a leopard or lion, both of which would have been present in the local area at the time. Archeologists studying the site claim that the face depicts a supernatural agent who was likely the target of the offerings and rituals performed in the cave.

Mountains

More recently, evidence of ritual activity associated with mountains and hilltops (portholes to the heavenly realm) has also been found. For example, on the western side of the island of Crete stands Korakias peak, part of the Kourourpas mountain group. Around four thousand years ago, Minoans used the mountain as a sanctuary (Peatfeield 1992). Thousands of fragments of terracotta animal and human figurines along with jars, bowls, cups, and other pottery have been found at the site, many of which were deliberately broken. Broken pieces were then placed in the clefts of the two natural terraces on the mountain. Some human figurines have upraised arms, as if in worship. Detached arm and leg representations have also been found, suggesting that some of those traveling to the site may have been seeking healing for damaged limbs, possibly from shamans who frequently serve as healers for their social groups (McClenon 2001). Upturned cups found at the site suggest offerings of libations.

Over seventy deliberately broken human figurines have also been uncovered at the five-thousand-year-old "woman man stone" site at Meotoshi, Japan (Kaner 2011: 459–60). The site is located on an elevated terrace set beneath the shadow of three spectacular peaks of the Kofu Kamagadake mountain range. Much of the ritual activity at "woman man stone" site appears to have been focused on a massive 2.5-meter-long by 1.7-meter-high (over 8 ft. × 5½ ft.) boulder positioned in the center of the terrace.

Humans often sought to simulate mountains through mound-building and monument construction. For example, at the three-thousand-year-old San'nai Maruyama site in Japan, decorated pottery was found on both large artificially constructed mounds and an elevated twenty-meter-high platform (Hayden 2003: 163–4). Presumably, these structures were used for ceremonies and offerings of some sort. Monumental structures on an even more impressive scale were not uncommon in more recent times including the sixty-meter ceremonial structures built for feasting by the Māori in New Zealand and the well-known Egyptian Pyramids and Aztec and Mayan temples of Mesoamerica (Hayden 2003: 363–5).

Finally, watery sites such as riverbanks, lakes, and bogs were also singled out for ritual offerings and activities. One of the most impressive is the (roughly) eight-thousand-year-old site of Lepenski Vir in Serbia. It is located on a high bank along the Danube River about two hundred kilometers above the Danube's mouth at the Black Sea (Hayden 2003: 159–60). About fifty structures are present at the site, many of which contain large stone-slab hearths. At numerous hearths, one end is decorated with engraved boulders bearing strange abstract humanoid faces. Human jawbones and stone engravings of jawbones surround the hearths. The size of hearths (larger than comparable ones in similar settings) along with the eccentric deliberately placed items around them indicate ritual activity.

At other sites such as Llyn Cerrig Bach and the River Witham in England and the confluence of the Havel and Spree Rivers in northern Germany, human and animal remains, broken weapons (sometimes in the hundreds), and other deliberately deposited artifacts have been found indicative of ritual activity (Bruck 2011; Joy 2011). In some cases, elevated human-made structures were used in making the deposits.

This is but a brief review of the many liminal geographic locations that were targeted as ritual sites in the ancestral past (more extensive reviews can be found in Haaland and Haaland 2011; Pettitt 2011; Rossano 2021: 52–64; Scarre 2011). It is quite likely that our ancestors chose liminal sites because they represented transition points in a shamanistically ordered cosmos. Mountains and hilltops beckoned to the heavens above, where gods and ancestors resided. Caves, bogs, and shorelines were passageways to the underworld of the dead. The living had their place in this ordered cosmos—between Heaven and Hades. Recognizing one's place in the cosmos amid its myriad spiritual inhabitants went hand in hand with the duties assigned to that place.

Ritually Committing to an Ordered Cosmos

Our ancestors didn't just recognize the shamanistic order of the universe, they behaviorally committed to it. Their gods were not detached, impersonal forces. They were conscious entities with desires and concerns that demanded satisfaction. Our ancestors believed that an ordered universe had important behavioral implications. Order wasn't free. In return for order, the gods required certain human actions such as the observance of taboo, the offering of sacrifices, the honoring of ancestors, and a strict adherence to tradition. Ritual was the means they employed for compelling those actions. But again, the question can be posed, why ritual? Elsewhere (Rossano 2020), I argue that the answer is that ritual is a resource management tool. That is, it cultivates, directs, sustains, and replenishes the psychological resources necessary to maintain in-group cohesion. Additionally, as will be discussed in more detail later, putting a divine mind behind the ritual appears to serve as a powerful motivating factor compelling both ritual participation and group commitment.

Humans possess a wealth of communal, prosocial sentiments. But to be useful, these sentiments must be harnessed and directed. Loyalty, for example, means loyalty *to something or someone*, such as one's tribe and/or its values. Similarly, empathy or goodwill only translates into action when they are directed to specific others or groups. Identifying the objects of emotional commitment is one of the important functions of ritual. Consider, for example, a simple oath-taking ritual. The person taking the oath is required to pledge loyalty to the group or organization he or she is joining. This loyalty can be understood as a state of mind that the oath-taker promises to maintain in order to help build greater solidarity within the group and efficacy in its functioning (Rossano 2020). Indeed, ritual activity can be so powerful that it produces a sense of group identity and commitment capable of supporting acts of extreme self-sacrifice when one believes his or her group is under dire threat (Ginges, Hansen, and Norenzayan 2009; Whitehouse and Lanman 2014).

The psychological states mobilized by ritual activity are, in many ways, analogous to material resources such as food or fuel (Rossano 2020). As with material resources, emotional commitment to group values can be "built up," "depleted," and "replenished." It takes effort to be a good group member. Selfish interests must be regularly set aside so that one can adhere to group norms of cooperation. A substantial body of research has shown that ritual activity increases levels of prosocial psychological states such as goodwill, empathy, trust, liking, perceived unity, and similarity (Hobson et al. 2018; Morgan, Fischer, and Bulbulia 2017). Increased ritual participation is associated with greater generosity and in-group normative behavior (Branas-Garza, Espın, and Neuman 2014; Fischer et al. 2013; Power 2017; Soler 2012).

Ritual doesn't just generate prosocial sentiments; it replenishes them as well. For example, ritual behavior, such as meditation or prayer, has been shown to restore dwindling reserves of self-control (Friese, Messner, and Schaffner 2012; Friese et al. 2014). Ritual activities, such as prayer or offerings at shrines, have been shown to revitalize levels of commitment, trust, goodwill, and the tendency to forgive after offense (Fincham and Beach 2014; Lambert et al. 2010; Purzycki and Arakchaa 2013).

Thus, similar to how we take raw materials such as trees or crude oil, and process them into usable resources such as firewood or gasoline, we take raw psychological states and process them into usable psychological resources. Ritual is the means that we have always used to effect this "processing." Ritual processing has been extraordinarily effective. Over the course of our evolutionary history, humans ritually constructed the most cooperative agent-based communities on earth—hunter-gatherer bands. Using rituals, hunter-gatherer bands united themselves into tribes, chiefdoms, city-states, and empires (Rossano 2020). Increasingly, however, the modern world has marginalized ritual, finding alternative means of supporting large-scale social cooperation. Are these alternatives sustainable or just momentary blips along the long haul of history?

Fading Rituals: Cooperating without Caring

Humans are predisposed to assume that rationality and order arise from intentional agents while chaos and disorder often result from natural processes (Gergely and Csibra 2003; Newman et al. 2010). Thus, it was natural for our ancestors to attribute an ordered universe to supernatural agents ("ordering gods"). Furthermore, these gods had minds, similar to ours'. They cared about the thoughts and behaviors of people. Humans occupied a certain relational status with regard to these "ordering" gods. It was this *relational realization* that prompted the evolutionary transformation of primate ritualized behaviors into human rituals.

This leads to a rather stark conclusion: without ordering gods, ritual (with its canonical message about an enduring order) does not come into being. This raises a question: can ritual survive without watchful gods behind them? Ritual has proven to be a powerful mechanism for cultivating, sustaining, and replenishing the prosocial sentiments necessary for effective group functioning. If ritual founders without ordering gods can those prosocial sentiments be equally mobilized by other means? While there might not be enough data to adequately answer this question presently, there is suggestive evidence.

First, there are reasons to suspect that when we dispense with ordering gods, it becomes more difficult to take rituals seriously. In the Russian Orthodox tradition, for example, there was a clear and compelling rationale for the myriad of funeral rituals enacted upon someone's passing. In this tradition, the universe was "ordered" such that death marked the beginning of the soul's journey from the earthly world to that of the afterlife. Funerary rituals were part of the family's and community's efforts to assist the soul on its journey. Failing to enact these rituals could both endanger the soul and expose the family and community to supernatural retribution. Once the Bolsheviks took over Russia, however, this framework was officially discredited, but never adequately replaced (see Rossano 2021: 126-9). The ambivalence of Soviet officials regarding death and its attendant rituals was summed up nicely by doctor and writer Vikenty Veresaev in his description of an officially sanctioned funeral in the mid-1920s:

> In the past the funeral rite had a clear rationale. People gathered round the coffin of the deceased to pray for his soul. ... But we [atheist socialists] put the decaying body in a box ... covered with red fabric and mount a guard of honour that changes every 10 minutes (and what are they guarding, when you think about it?). ... What is it all for? What on earth is the point?" (Quoted from Baiburin 2012: 93–4)

He went on to describe the ceremony as "arid: a sterile chamber for the wake, mourners with nothing to do, and the customary speeches about the departed—all of it leaving a void instead of an affirmation of life for the survivors" (quoted from Stites 1988: 113).

Compare this to various strains of Judaism where it is likely that Orthodox Jews see a divine order to the universe more clearly and readily than Reform Jews. Their ritual participation dwarfs that of Reform Jews; nearly three-quarters of Orthodox Jews attend synagogue at least monthly, while only 17 percent of Reform Jews do (Pew Research Center 2015). A comparison of ritual participation between religious and secular kibbutzim showed a similar pattern (Ruffle and Sosis 2007). All male religious kibbutz members participated weekly in ritual prayer (only among males is this a requirement). Two-thirds did so daily (19). The average secular kibbutz member, however, participated only twice monthly in ritual-like activities such as song and dance nights, lectures, study groups, kibbutz meetings, and so on (28).

Decoupling ordering gods from ritual might also undermine the latter's efficacy in facilitating cooperation. For example, in the kibbutzim study just discussed, it was only in the religious kibbutzim that frequency of ritual participation was positively correlated with intragroup generosity (those who prayed more frequently were more cooperative and generous with fellow kibbutz members). No such correlation was found among secular kibbutzim. Other studies have confirmed that purely secular ritual activities tend to produce weaker or no effects compared to their religious counterparts. For example, levels of within-group trust and commitment tend to be higher among church-affiliated groups relative to comparable secular groups (Stolle 2001). Contemplative practices that included a supernatural dimension have been found to be more effective in reducing anxiety, increasing pain tolerance, and elevating mood compared to "secular" practices (Wacholtz and Pargament 2005; Weich et al. 2008). A meta-analysis comparing spiritual meditation to secular meditation found spiritual meditation more frequently resulted in health benefits such as lower blood pressure, reduced heart rate, and improved mental health (Alexander, Rainforth, and Gelderloos 1991).

Together, this evidence suggests that without concerned gods behind it, ritual loses its force. As the world grows increasingly secular, this would appear to portend poorly for the future of communal living. But the modern world presents a forceful rebuttal to this reasoning. Many modern secular cities are the safest, most efficient urban settings of human history, a testament to the fact that supernatural ritual appears not to be essential for high levels of cooperation. One reason for this may be that these cities are well-governed (for an extension of this perspective, see Bendixen and Purzycki, this volume). Research shows that where government is effective in providing for people's needs, religion tends to wane (Mauritsen and van Mulukom, this volume; Zuckerman, Li, and Diener 2018).

Good governance includes numerous laws, bureaucratic policies, and social regulations that *mechanize* cooperation—making it a bit like driving. To cooperate with my fellow drivers, I need not care about them or even know who they are, I only have to follow the rules of road. A similar web of formally and informally imposed rules now direct our behavior in workplaces, city streets, playgrounds, dining halls—just about any public and increasingly private spaces. Religious systems function in similar ways; we do not need to have complete access to doctrine to participate in, perpetuate, and engage with the tradition. Complementing this mechanization of cooperation is its *professionalization*. Most of us are paid to cooperate—wrapping ourselves in a constant veneer of concern (sometimes, but not always, genuine) for our coworkers, customers, and clients ("of course, I'd be happy to get for you, sir"). This mechanization and professionalization of cooperation make it as much a matter of procedural skill and cultural competence as honest emotional connection to others.

Finally, technology comprises another aspect of the "good governance" of modern cities. Urban settings today are the most visually monitored in history, often with security cameras at every street corner, store counter, and meeting room. Policy adherence is not left to the honor system. The watchful "gods" are still there, maintaining order behind computer screens. Thus, cooperation that was once *ritualized* has been aptly replaced by monetarily incentivized, technologically verified compliance to authority, and in many ways we seem better for it. *Seem*, that is … for the loss is subtle. While people in many of these modern well-run cities are generally happy, there's some evidence suggesting their lives may be less meaningful than those in less technologically advanced and more religious areas of the globe (Oishi and Diener 2014). In the absence of ritual, our cooperation has become highly efficient, but strangely more impersonal, mercenary, and self-interested. We are safe, contented, and soulless.

8

The Mind of God and the Problem of Evil: A Cognitive and Evolutionary Perspective

John Teehan

It is all one; therefore I say, he [God] destroys both the blameless and the wicked. When disaster brings sudden death, he mocks at the calamity of the innocent. The earth is given into the hand of the wicked; he covers the faces of its judges—if it is not he, who then is it? (Job, 9:22-24)[1]

Introduction

The Problem of Evil—why God allows bad things to happen to good people, why He allows such horrific suffering, such terrible evil to mar this world He created—is one of the oldest, most enduring, and perhaps most faith-shaking issues confronting belief in an all-good God. Actually, it is not simply a problem for such believers, but a central human concern. It has been suggested that the problem of explaining evil is a defining theme of modern Western thought (Neiman 2002). The problem is particularly acute for religious adherents, as the question of evil cannot be posed without implicating God.

The classic formulation of the Problem of Evil is attributed to Epicurus (341–271 BCE). It is not found in his extant works but in the writings of Christian apologist Lactantius (third century CE), who tells us that Epicurus made the following argument:

> God either wishes to take away evils, and is unable; or He is able, and is unwilling; or He is neither willing nor able, or He is both willing and able. If He is willing and is unable, He is feeble, which is not in accordance with the character of God; if He is able and unwilling, He is envious, which is equally at variance with God; if He is neither willing nor able, He is both envious and feeble and, therefore not God; if He is both willing and able, which alone is suitable to God, from what source then are evils?[2]

There are reasons to be skeptical about attributing this to Epicurus, but this formulation has defined the problem, particularly in modern discussions. It sets out a logical paradox in which God cannot be both omnipotent (i.e., he can prevent evil) and omnibenevolent (i.e., he wants to prevent evil) and yet there still is evil in the world. This was expanded to include God's omniscience (i.e., God knew in creating humans that they would inevitably sin, thus introducing evil into the world). Attempts to resolve this paradox, and thus absolve God of responsibility for evil, are known as theodicy (literally, justifying God), a term introduced by Gottfried Leibniz ([1710] 1986) in the seventeenth century.

This formulation of the problem centers on an Abrahamic conception of God: one God, creator of the universe, all-powerful, all knowing, all good. While this conception of God is widely shared, it is not universal. This perhaps suggests the problem is strictly a monotheist's concern, as polytheists have the option of blaming evil on the workings of malicious spirits or gods, but this is not the case, as numerous examples from ancient literature attest.

The most famous treatment of god's responsibility for evil from antiquity is the book of *Job*, a canonical book in both the Hebrew and Christian bibles, and recounted in the Qur'an. This is the story of a man, Job, who was "blameless and upright, one who feared God, and turned away from evil" (Job 1:1) but who loses all he had, all his flocks and all his children destroyed (Job 1:13-19). Then he was afflicted "with loathsome sores from the sole of his foot to the crown of his head" (Job 2:7). In the face of all this loss, Job refuses to curse God. Unbeknownst to Job, however, all this was inflicted with the permission of God, looking to defend a point of pride against Satan (Job 1:8-12). This prologue[3] sets up the main action of the story: Job insists on his innocence and demands an audience with God so that he may demand God justify himself (Job 13:13). However, before Job gets his audience with God, he must endure one further, rather shocking, indignity: his friends arguing that he must have done something to deserve this suffering:

> Then Eli'phaz the Te'manite answered. "If one ventures a word with you, will you be offended? Yet who can keep from speaking? ... Think now, who that was innocent ever perished? Or where were the upright cut off? As I have seen, those who plow iniquity and sow trouble reap the same. By the breath of God they perish. ... Can mortal man be righteous before God? Can a man be pure before his Maker?" (Job 4:1-17)

The greater part of *Job* consists of the "friends" setting out different theodicies in an attempt to absolve God of injustice against Job, and Job passionately maintaining his innocence. The work stands as a masterpiece of ancient literature, and a powerful exploration of the problem of evil, one with enduring relevance. It is not, however, the earliest literary treatment of the topic.

The exact dating of *Job* is open to debate, with many biblical scholars favoring an origin sometime between the sixth and fourth centuries BCE. However, we have an Old Babylonian text titled, "Man and His God," dated to the seventeenth century BCE that relays the lament of one suffering evil he cannot understand:

> My Lord, I did consult with myself within my reins,
> [I thought it over] in my heart: the sin I committed I do not know.

Have I trodden on something abhorrent to you?
Have I accepted a very evil forbidden fruit?[4]

There are also Egyptian texts that date to an even earlier period (2050–1750 BCE) addressing this concern, and taking critical view of the god's role: "Aggressive people prevail, and He who should dispel evil is the very one who creates them! There is no pilot in their hour. Where is He today? Is He asleep? Look, there is no sign of His power around" (Loprieno 2003, 28). It would be fascinating to explore the resonances and dissonances among the various ancient texts dealing with the problem of evil (and there are more examples, from these and other Ancient Near Eastern societies; see Laato and deMoor 2003), but that would take us too far afield. Instead, we will focus on a point shared by all these examples, a unifying implicit assumption. For this discussion, it will be useful to return to Epicurus.

As mentioned, there are reasons to be skeptical about attributing the classic formulation of the problem of evil to Epicurus, since for Epicurus there is no problem of evil. Instead, it arises from a basic, popular misunderstanding of the gods:

> For the assertions of the many concerning the gods are conceptions grounded not in experience but in false assumptions, according to which the greatest misfortunes are brought upon the evil by the gods and the greatest benefits upon the good. (Epicurus 1993, ln. 124)

The belief that the gods punish the evil and reward the good is a "false assumption," not because the gods are unjust, or vindictive, or morally inconsistent, but because they are indifferent. They are indifferent because they are "immortal and blessed" beings who can neither be harmed nor pleased by anything a human can do.[5] When Job cries out to God in pain, "What is man, that thou dost make so much of him, and that thou dost set thy mind upon him, dost visit him every morning, and test him every moment? … If I sin, what do I do to thee, thou watcher of men? (Job 7:17-20)," he is raising an Epicurean critique (although not in an Epicurean spirit). To Epicurus, it is vanity, or superstitious fear, that leads people to believe that the gods could be affected one way or another by the doings of humans. The gods as blessed and immortal are wholly self-sufficient, they need nothing from us and gain nothing from visiting evil (or good) upon us.

This "false assumption" is the implicit assumption of all the ancient texts we have just discussed, and is the foundational assumption that underlies the problem of evil. Job's demand for an explanation for his unjust treatment at the hands of God assumes that God is concerned with the requirements of justice—and this is not just an ancient assumption. The documentary, *Faith and Doubt at Ground Zero*,[6] examines the impact of 9/11 on the spiritual lives of those who survived the tragedy and those who lost loved ones. We see this same assumption in the responses of many of the interviewees. Consider the perplexed, Job-like lament from a man who lost thirty neighbors and friends at the World Trade Center that gives voice to this assumption: "I really can't see the purpose why all these people had to die. … I think God could have just ended this all. … I can't accept this unless I can have an answer as to why it all occurred." There must be a purpose to suffering, an explanation of why God allowed this to happen, and if not, God must be held morally responsible. In another interview, a widow of the attacks tells us, "I couldn't believe that this God that I'd talk to in my own way for 35 years turned this loving man into bones ... and now I can't bring myself to speak to Him anymore because I feel so abandoned." The problem of evil is not simply, or primarily, a theological or philosophical problem—it often presents itself an existential crisis.

This assumption about the moral involvement of the gods is one of the most common found among the diversity of religions—certainly, it is the bedrock of Judaic, Christian, and Islamic conceptions of God. Theodicy makes no sense without this assumption, for there is no problem of evil without it. Given the diversity of not only religions but of human cultures, when we come upon a (possibly) universal trait, it is fair to ask what is it about human nature that can explain this, and often the way to answer that question is to look into human evolutionary history. It is here that the cognitive science of religion (CSR), grounded in an evolutionary understanding of cognition, can shed some light.[7] Not only can an evolved cognitive science help explain why humans have moral expectations of their gods, but also why they so often continue to maintain those expectations in the face of, at times, devastating counterevidence.

The (Moral) Mind of Gods

CSR has devoted much attention to the minds of gods, and for good reasons. In forming beliefs about the gods, we are limited to second-hand reports, for example, oral testimony[8] of those that claim first-hand encounters, and indirect evidence—physical signs attributed to divine action. These reports and signs need to be interpreted and evaluated for their reliability. Even those who claim to have had direct contact with a deity must decide that the sign or voice they encounter is that of a god, and that decision is the result of an interpretation and evaluation. How then do we make these judgments? Ultimately, we bring to bear intuitions about how the gods might behave and think; that is, we work with some model of the mind of god. Understanding what people think about the mind of god, and how we come to have certain intuitions about the gods, is a fundamental task of CSR.

Let's build this from the bottom-up: how did we come (as a species) to have intuitions about the mind of god?—which is really another way of asking, how did we come to believe in gods? This requires we engage in some intellectual archeology, which can be a tricky business. Ideas and beliefs do not leave fossil records, but when people act on ideas and beliefs they may leave physical artifacts inspired by or representing those beliefs. Here, physical archeology can help. One fascinating piece of evidence is therianthropic cave art. A therianthrope is an animal–human hybrid figure, for example, a human body with the head of a bird. This is taken as evidence of a cognitive capacity to conceive of a supernatural being. These are characterized as "supernatural" because bird-headed humans are not part of the natural world, and so must be products of the human mind.[9] The earliest example of such cave art dates back almost 44,000 years (Aubert et al. 2019). However, this is not the earliest archeological evidence that allows us to infer the existence of religious beliefs. Artifacts connected to rituals provide even earlier evidence, particularly evidence related to burial practices. These appear as early as 120,000 years ago, becoming increasingly more common after that time (Gagrett 1999). The presence of grave gifts is even more significant, as these are presumably items the deceased will need as they continue their journey (De Cruz and De Smedt 2017). The physical evidence gives us solid grounds to place the origins of supernatural beliefs very early in our evolutionary story.

In terms of intellectual archeology, the question is, what sorts of cognitive skills would have been necessary to support such beliefs? CSR holds that "belief in gods arises because of the natural functioning of completely normal mental tools working in common natural and social contexts" (Barrett 2004: 21). Some of the seminal work in CSR focused on developing an account of these "normal mental tools" and their "natural and social context."[10] We do not need to go into this account in-depth, but can just look at the general contours. This will set up a more detailed discussion of the moral minds of gods.

CSR works with an evolutionary understanding of the mind. Evolutionary processes shape organisms to act effectively in their natural environments in pursuit of the goals of survival and reproduction. We will focus on survival. The fundamental tasks of survival are to acquire sufficient resources to maintain life (and to support offspring) and to avoid becoming a resource for other organisms seeking their own survival. Organisms must also navigate their way through environments that bring their own challenges and dangers. The brain is not simply processing information that comes into it via the senses. It is part of a goal-directed, physical exploration of the environment. The mind actively contributes to drawing relevant information from the environment and uses this to coordinate successful behavior (Purzycki and Schjoedt, present volume). The cognitive strategies employed have been shaped by natural selection due to their effectiveness in guiding action.

As noted, crucial tasks are to avoid predators and to detect potential prey. To accomplish this, humans must be able to detect the presence of other organisms and to anticipate their behavior. In CSR, the strategy guiding this process is known as Agency Detection (Barrett 2004; Guthrie 1993), an agent being anything that acts with intention (rather than simply being moved by other forces, like a branch moved by the wind). Knowing there is something out there that may be targeting you, or hiding from you, is essential to survival. However, it is not always clear whether there is an agent present. Agents can hide, and disguise themselves, and sometimes there just is not enough evidence to tell whether a movement was intentional or not. However, since telling the difference between, say, a bear and a boulder is the difference between life and death, our agency detection strategy has become hypersensitive (Barrett 2004). We overinterpret the environment in terms of agency, and we do so because that is the safer bet when the situation is unclear: better to mistake a boulder for a bear, than a bear for a boulder. As one of the founders of CSR, Stewart Guthrie, puts it, "If perception requires choosing among interpretations and therefore requires betting, and if the payoff is discovering significance, then the first bets to cover—those with the biggest payoff are bets as high on the scale of organization as possible" (Guthrie 1993, 45; see also, Lightner and Purzycki, present volume).

To interpret something as an agent, we also interpret it as having a mind. To be an agent is to act intentionally, to act with a purpose, and to do this one must have a mind. In the parlance of cognitive science, we employ a theory of mind (ToM). That is, we attribute mental states and intentions to other organisms in order to make sense of their behavior so we can determine how to act toward them (Boyer 2001).

Agency detection, with its implicit ToM, is an aspect of a more general cognitive strategy: to seek meaningful patterns in nature, particularly those that give us information that can guide our actions. We explore our environment with an eye out for what we can do with what we find. Deborah Kelemen has termed this cognitive approach, "promiscuous teleology." We attribute purpose and meaning to the environment as a default strategy (Kelemen 1999a). This means we will sometimes see patterns as meaningful, and having a purpose, even when this is not the case. As with Agency Detection, it is better to overinterpret. Survival can be so precarious that it is better to risk false-positives (detecting something as meaningful when it is not) than risking false-negatives (failing to detect something meaningful).

While these foundational views are continually being challenged and refined, the general model coming out of CSR tells us we are cognitively set up to find agents—even when there are none—to attribute intentions and purposes to those nonexistent agents, and to place all of this in a view of the world that is meaningful and can guide behavior. In other words, we are cognitively prepared to believe in gods (along with demons, ghosts, fairies, animal spirits, etc.).[11]

Belief in gods comes naturally to humans (which is not to say that such beliefs are inevitable; Mauritsen and van Mulukom present volume). As we understand gods to be agents, we intuitively understand them as having minds, but what kind of mind? Anthropologist Scott Atran tells us, "Gods and other supernatural beings are systematically unlike us in a few general ways—more powerful, longer lived, more knowledgeable … and predictably like us in an enormously broader range of usual ways" (Atran 2002: 93). To understand the minds of gods, we need to consider how they are both like and unlike human minds.

When we try to make sense of what another being is doing, and why they may be doing it, we have only one frame of reference, human minds. We come to understand the mental states of other humans in a number of ways. We observe their actions and attribute intentions, desires, and so on, based on our experience of our own mentality, or if we do not have a comparable experience, we can ask them why they are doing what they are doing. Thus, we build up a base of knowledge about human minds. This is not simply an act of curiosity, it is a crucial survival skill for humans. When we think of survival tasks, we tend to think first of those basic physical needs—food, water, shelter, clothes, and so on. However, for complex social animals like humans, surviving and thriving also require managing social challenges. Effectively negotiating the social environment is just as vital to evolutionary success as negotiating the physical environment, and this too has left its mark on the human mind. In fact, researchers argue that the exceptionally large human brain, with its highly complex cerebral cortex, was shaped by the challenges of managing social exchanges in complex social environments (e.g., Cummins 1998).

Not only are we most familiar with the human mind, it is the mind most important for us to understand, and the one we are most cognitively prepared to understand. It follows that when we try to make sense of what other beings are doing, or may be thinking, we draw on our understanding of the human mind. This is true whether that being is another human, an animal, or a god. Therefore, to understand why humans have moral expectations of the gods, why they believe "the greatest misfortunes are brought upon the evil by the gods and the greatest benefits upon the good," we need to explore the moral mind of humans.

First, we need to be clear what we mean by "moral." This has many connotations. It can be approached from a social perspective, or a theological/philosophical perspective, but the context for CSR is evolution. From an evolutionary perspective, morality is about prosocial behavior, or cooperation. For social animals, such as us, behavior that contributes to the success and survival of the group contributes to the success of the individual. Humans have evolved from a long line of social animals. It follows that this has given rise to a set of mental tools that facilitate social cooperation (Alexander 1987; Boyd and Richerson 1988; Fehr and Fischbacher 2003; Frank 1988; Singer 2006).

While social cooperation is vital, it is also costly (present volume: Bendixen and Purzycki; Lightner and Purzycki; Petersen). Being a member of a group entails contributing to the good of the group as a whole, and to the welfare of other members of the group. This constitutes a cost, since the resources invested in others could have been invested in my own good, or the good of my family. Being part of a group means, at least sometimes, putting our needs or wants to the side in the interest of the greater good. This cost is balanced out, however, when other members also make costly investments in the group's welfare. If everyone is doing this, then no individual is at a relative disadvantage. Furthermore, the more members of the group who contribute to the group, the greater the chance that the group will be stable and strong, which also benefits the individual. However, if others do not contribute, while you do, then you carry more of the burden of supporting the group, which puts you at a disadvantage (Lightner and Purzycki, present volume). If there are too many free riders (those who receive benefits without contributing) then the stability of the group is undermined—and this poses a real threat to the individual pursuit of surviving and thriving. These dynamics of social cooperation give rise to three key elements of our moral mind: fairness, reciprocity, and punishment.

Rational actor theory has been an influential model in economics that holds that humans make decisions based on maximizing benefits and minimizing costs. Rational actor theory is wrong. One of the signal achievements of cognitive science has been to demonstrate that human behavior and decision-making are often guided by a host of nonconscious biases and heuristics that are not aimed at rational optimization (Kahneman 2011). For example, there is a wealth of empirical evidence that shows that humans will forgo a benefit, or incur a cost, if they deem that they are being treated unfairly (e.g., Henrich et al. 2001). Interestingly, this is not restricted to humans. A study of capuchin monkeys suggests that these animals will also refuse rewards when other monkeys are arbitrarily given superior rewards for completing the same task (Brosnan and deWaal 2003).[12] There is an evolved moral cognitive sense of fairness, which comes with a sense of moral outrage in the face of unfair treatment.

The notion of reciprocity is a bedrock of evolutionary accounts of cooperation, and elements of it are found throughout the animal kingdom (Trivers 1971). On a basic level, it is quite intuitive. Many tasks are better achieved through joint activity. At times, I need help with certain tasks, at times you need help, hence "I'll scratch your back, if you scratch mine." The costs I incur by expending effort to help you achieve your task (time and energy I take away from achieving my goals) is paid back when you expend time and energy to help me. This way we both get to enjoy the many benefits of cooperation without any overall costs. However, if I make the effort to help you, and you fail to reciprocate or, "cheat," then I have wasted that time and energy. People who keep making investments that do not payoff are not very successful, whether in the financial market or the evolutionary market. Consequently, not only do humans have an innate sensitivity to issues of fairness, they are also sensitively attuned to those who fail to reciprocate acts of social investment, that is, cheaters. In fact, the two are connected. Cheaters are acting unfairly. They have taken a benefit they do not deserve, and imposed a cost that I do not deserve. Both of these situations are threats to my efforts to survive and thrive. People who allow themselves to be treated unfairly are at a serious disadvantage. So, how do we protect ourselves from these dangers? Punishment.

Humans are not merely sensitive to being treated unfairly, we're prepared to punish such behaviors (Boyd and Richerson 1988; Fehr and Gachter 2002), primed to act by a suite of moral emotions that are triggered by acts of defection from perceived standards of fairness (Frank 1988). There are neurological correlates to this emotional distaste for cheaters. Cooperative behavior activates neural reward systems, while violations of the social code trigger negative emotional brain responses (Hein et al. 2010; Singer 2006; Singer et al. 2006); one study even showed that witnessing cheaters suffer can be neurologically rewarding (Fiske 2002).

Our evolved moral psychology is more complex than this, but these three components serve as pillars that sustain prosocial behavior. With this, we can now begin to understand the intuitive moral expectations that humans bring to the gods.

As noted, when humans try to understand the mental states of another, they bring to bear their understanding of the human mind, and as we have greatest access to our own minds, this perspective plays a distinct role. There are distinct neural activation patterns when a person is projecting their thinking onto another, that is, egocentric reasoning, compared to when they are reflecting on how another person's thinking is different from their own. Interestingly, a study found that humans employ an even more egocentric style of reasoning (i.e., using one's own thoughts and feelings to understand what someone else is thinking) when they think about the mind of god than when they think about the mind of other humans (Epley et al. 2009). This suggests that "although religious agents are attributed many unique properties, people nevertheless conceive of them in surprisingly humanlike ways" (Epley et al. 2009: 21533). The researchers also highlight the central role of social cognition in understanding other minds, including the minds of gods:

> These data join a growing body of literature demonstrating that religious beliefs are guided by the same basic or natural mechanisms that guide social cognition more generally. Religious beliefs ... are likely to be the natural outcome of existing mechanisms that enable people to reason about other social agents more generally. (Epley et al. 2009, 21537)

The importance of social cognition in understanding the mind of God was tested in a study looking at how people process socially strategic information compared to nonstrategic information (Purzycki et al. 2011). Socially strategic information gives insight into the social behavior or thinking of others. Do they follow norms? Are they being honest? Can they be trusted to reciprocate or are they cheaters? Nonstrategic information is more mundane, for example, the toothpaste they use, their favorite breakfast cereal, and so on. Researchers tested the response time to questions about what God knows, answering "yes" or "no." The hypothesis was that quicker response times indicated a more intuitive belief about what God knows: if it is obvious that God knows something, respondents did not need to think about the answer. Participants all came from a background in which the Abrahamic notion of an omniscient God was dominant. This is important, for if people believe that God is omniscient, then the answer to every question, "Does God know ...?" is obviously "yes." Any difference in response time therefore indicates that some beliefs about God's mind were privileged over others, and this is what was found. Participants had a significantly quicker response to questions about socially strategic knowledge than nonstrategic—and this was true whether the participant believed in God or not! Of further interest, not all strategic information was treated the same. Response times were even quicker when the strategic information concerned violations of social norms (Purzycki et al. 2012).

Before we return to the problem of evil, we need to make one more point. We have been discussing ways the mind of God is like the mind of humans, but as God is not a human, there must be something unique about God's mind. Certainly, knowing everything sets God apart from us, but omniscience is not a universal attribution of God's mind, and the study we just looked at suggests that it is not a naturally intuitive belief. The authors argued that "while supernaturalness is often regarded as an extraordinary yet defining characteristic of gods and spirits, supernaturalness does not appear to be important for understanding their minds" (864). While direct empirical evidence is sparse, it seems to be a much more common belief that gods have complete access to strategic information. Pascal Boyer points out, humans conceive of other humans as "limited-access strategic agents," that is, when interacting with other humans we conceive of them as having imperfect access to our own thoughts and intentions. However, people tend to conceive of at least some gods as "full-access strategic agents"; Gods are privy to all the relevant information in any social exchange (Boyer 2001: 155).

To sum up, CSR argues that (1) human minds are very concerned about agency, social interactions, and fairness; (2) humans think about gods using the same moral cognitive processes they bring to social interactions; (3) they are particularly keen on God's knowledge about things relevant to social/moral behavior; and (4) they view the gods as having access to all socially relevant information. When we pull all of this together, we can understand why it is that people have moral expectations of the gods: it is default of the way that human minds work. When we think about the gods, we think of them as agents engaged in a social exchange—extremely powerful agents, but agents working with a similar moral mind. This does not imply that we expect the gods to be moral exemplars, we don't; we expect them to behave as extremely powerful beings would, and there are evil supernatural beings and gods unconcerned with humans. However, the gods that truly matter are the gods that are concerned with human behavior (Bendixen and Purzycki present volume; Rossano 2007), and in these cases, we cannot help but bring in expectations of basic moral relations: fairness and reciprocity. This means the gods will punish violations of the moral code, or failure to give them their due, but reward, or at the least not punish, those who do right by them. When the gods fail to act according to these basic intuitions, we get the problem of evil.

CSR and the Problem of Evil

Back to Job.[13] Job knows he is blameless (and we know that God knows this as well, Job 1:8). He has done no wrong, he has praised God and worshiped him appropriately, and yet he has suffered grievously. God has treated him unfairly, and he wants justice: "I will give free utterance to my complaint … I will say to God, Do not condemn me. … thou knowest that I am not guilty" (Job 10:1-7). However, Job has no illusions about how such an encounter will end: "I will take my flesh in my teeth, and put my life in my hand. Behold, he will slay me; I have no hope; yet I will defend my ways to his face. This will be my salvation" (Job 13:14-16). This is an eloquent expression of the evolved response to unfairness, to refuse to accept it, to suffer costs rather than accept it. This is moral outrage that pushes aside rational calculation in favor of making a moral stand. God is expected to adhere to at least a minimal standard of fairness, and when he does not, he deserves to be called out for it.

Job is not the only one in this story who holds these intuitive moral expectations of God, so do his friends—and this leads to some very uncomfortable moments: First, there is Eliphaz: "Think now, who that was innocent ever perished? Or where were the upright cut off? … Can a man be pure before his Maker?" (Job 4:6-17). Then, Bildad: "Does God pervert justice? Or does the Almighty pervert the right? If your children have sinned against him, he has delivered them into the power of their transgression" (Job 8:3-6). And then, Zophar: "You say, 'My doctrine is pure, and I am clean in God's eyes.' But oh, that God would speak … he would tell you the secrets of wisdom! … Know then that God exacts of you less than your guilt deserves" (Job 11:4-6).

His friends recognize that Job has been a good and pious person; they admire him and sympathize with his suffering; and they accept that what has befallen him has come from the hand of God … and yet, they cannot surrender their intuitive beliefs that God rewards the just and punishes the evil.

Seeing that the evolved mind of humans serves as the model of the minds of gods allows us to understand why humans intuitively have moral expectations of their gods, and why the problem of evil arises when those expectations are disappointed.

However, our reading of Job raises an important question relevant to our discussion, and that is our final topic.

Making Sense of Job's "Friends"

Encountering the *book of Job* can be a jarring experience. First is the shock at seeing that the story begins with a wager between God and Satan, but a close second has to be seeing how Job's friends turn on him, with increasing levels of heartlessness. We went from, "Listen Job, you must have done something" to "Your children deserved to have that house fall on top of them" to "You deserve everything that happened to you and MORE!" As much as we may understand their need to hold onto their faith in a just God, why turn against their suffering friend? Of course, as a work of fiction, these narrative moves serve the ultimate purpose of the story, although victim-blaming is certainly not a fictional response. However, holding on to a belief in a good and just God in the face of evil is not an uncommon response. In fact, the entire enterprise of theodicy is just that—a refusal to accept apparent evidence that God is not just and an effort to find a way to absolve God.[14] We see this in the responses documented in *Faith and Doubt at Ground Zero*. We met the widow of the Trade Center attack who told us "I couldn't believe that this God that I'd talk to in my own way for 35 years turned this loving man into bones ... and now I can't bring myself to speak to Him anymore because I feel so abandoned." She has been deeply wounded by this apparent failure of God to act justly, yet further on she admits, "I guess deep down inside I know that He still exists and that I have to forgive and move on." Interestingly, she does not claim that she will accept what God has done, he has wronged her and her children, but she must forgive him. More defiant is the man who knew thirty of the 9/11 victims. Like Job, he needs God to justify the suffering: "I can't accept this unless I have an answer to why it all occurred." But, we also see the moral outrage at God, "I let loose at God. I fired all my barrels at Him. It might sound crazy, but I cursed him. I damned him." In this, we can hear echoes of Job's wife who implores him, "Do you still hold fast your integrity? Curse God, and die" (Job 2:9). This man, besieged by evil, does curse God, but he also seeks to hold fast to the integrity of his faith. He tells us, "I believe in the Son, but the Father I'm having a tough time dealing with ... I don't have any love for God"; and while his view of God has changed, he still asserts, "I think I am a good Christian."

These are deeply moving and revealing responses to the problem of evil. In the face of profound loss, for which they blame God, they cannot make the equally profound move of completely rejecting God. It is important to be clear that there is no implied criticism here. We can comfortably scold Job's friends, because they are characters in a story, but these are real people struggling, bravely, to deal with not only the painful loss of loved ones but with what Paul Tillich termed the "shaking of the foundations" (Tillich 1955). Their faith has been devastated; their worldview has cracked. There is a substantial body of research that argues that worldviews, such as religions, serve as anxiety buffers against the dread of death and loss, and an assault on our worldviews is processed as an existential crisis (Greenberg et al. 1990; Solomon, Greenberg, and

Pyszczynski 2015)—so we are in no position to critique how these individuals are struggling to cope.

Conclusion

The Problem of Evil is a major topic within theology and philosophy, and has been for over two thousand years. It is also a deeply challenging, existentially significant issue in people's lives, and has been so for even longer. The CSR is a newcomer to this topic, but it has the resources that allow us to understand how religious beliefs are formed and how they are rooted in evolved cognitive tools. This permits a deeper insight into the nature of this perennial human problem, to develop a framework to understand the various responses, and to make sense of the motivation to hold onto the beliefs that give rise to the problem, even when those beliefs seem directly contradicted by the evidence. It also provides a perspective into the emotional and moral fallout that comes from leaving the problem unresolved, a perspective that may allow us to bring some humility to our theodicies, and some compassion to our critiques of those theodicies.

9

From Watching Human Acts to Penetrating Their Souls

Anders Klostergaard Petersen

Knowing, therefore, the terror of the Lord, we persuade men, but we are manifest to God. I hope we are also manifest in your consciences. (2 Cor 5:11)[1]

Setting the Stage for Divine Omnivident Penetration

One crucial shift in the history of religions was especially critical. It was so vital, in terms of thinking, that there could be no point of return to previous forms of religion.[2] An influential discussion in psychology and cognitive science of religion dubs the change Big Gods, but the trajectory of scholarship endorsing this line of thinking is more influential than the number of scholars using the specific category of "Big Gods."[3] I shall focus a good part of my criticism on this way of phrasing the problem, since it is wrong to think that divine surveillance can be reduced to the Big Gods thesis or its inversion in the rivaling school of thought, where the idea is maintained but claimed to depend on material changes. Superhuman powers watching humans is a ubiquitous feature of religions, but it takes a specific form in the type of religion in the Big Gods debate. My key contention is that with the extension of areas of sovereignty and a concomitant increase in different ethnicities marked by the emergence of early empires, there is a corollary scaling up of divine omnipotence, omnividence, and omnipresence on the vertical scale, that is, the axis exemplifying representations of divine power. Additionally, and crucial for this chapter, I assert that the ancestors, the gods or whatever other envisaged superhuman entity, have always been attributed the role of looking into the interiority of humans (this applies both phylo- and ontogenetically). With the scaling up of divine power, however, this gazing is taken to a new level of extremity. Gods do not only look into the interior of humans, but their gaze is institutionalized to the extent of constant surveillance as in the, perhaps, most excessive form of divine penetration, the Christian institution of penitence and confession.

Although there are predecessors to the Big Gods discussion (Stausberg 2014: 593), Norenzayan is identified with the term and its definition as divine agents who "watch, intervene, and demand hard-to-fake loyalty displays" (2013: 8). Regardless of my reticence toward the terminology and ensuing argument, there is a kernel of truth in the argument, but it is grossly overstated and in present form lacks substantial historical evidence.[4]

Undoubtedly, an essential transformation occurred incipiently around the seventh century BCE in some areas of the Eurasian continent, that is, what Jaspers coined the Axial Age (*die Achsenzeit*).[5] To argue that for the first time in the history of religions (Norenzayan 2013: 127–8, 131–2, 136, 145) morality came to play an important role in the way gods were represented is misconstrued.[6] Moral matters surveilled and honed by gods is no Axial Age *addendum*. It is intrinsic to religion. Furthermore, problems pertain to the social bearing accorded to this shift in thinking. The fact that religion can fuel prosocial behavior and hone large-scale cooperation does not imply that it is a prerequisite for these elements, nor does it demonstrate any direct causal relationship between them, let alone that religion be attributed ultimate cause. By the same logic, though, the reverse view is problematic in that it holds that socio-material conditions be accorded a direct causal influence on thinking. Ultimately, this resonates with a primitive Marxian perspective of the *Unterbau* (substructure) determining the *Überbau* (superstructure) ignoring the reciprocal influence between ideas and the socio-material level. Whereas the one scholarly strand suffers from metaphysical idealism by underestimating the importance of the socio-material world for the evolution of ideas (Norenzayan and parallel views), the other line of thinking endorses a similarly problematic metaphysical materialism turning the material world into the exclusively determining factor for cultural development (Whitehouse and corresponding understandings).

Surely, there are qualifications to the Big Gods argument (Norenzayan 2013: 122–3), but they are frequently based on the idea that moral religions are a novelty of the Axial Age. Norenzayan is not innocent of these misgivings (2013: 145, cf. 131). In all fairness, he occasionally seeks to nuance the understanding of the relationship between Big Gods and morals. For example, he does not unequivocally argue for the emergent tandem of morality and religion as a result of the Axial Age, since he discusses Göbekle Tepe and Çatal Höyuk—problematically, though, he overstates the importance of the former (2013: 118–21, 132).[7] As discussed below, scholars—thoroughly trained in anthropology and the history of religions—know there is no religion void of morality. Superhuman powers have always been called upon to stabilize, safeguard, and police human interactions with respect to the basic norms and regulations of the group.[8] To argue that morality and religion first entered into wedlock with the Axial Age is arguably nonsense. Admittedly, there are differences in the way morality is understood dependent upon the form of religion in question, but to surmise that the moral-religion conjunction first emerged around the seventh century BCE is simply wrong.

Evans-Pritchard criticized predecessors for holding that "once it was ascertained beyond doubt that primitive peoples, even the hunters and collectors, have gods with high moral attributes, that they must have borrowed the idea, or just the word without comprehension of its meaning from a higher culture, from missionaries, traders, and others" (1965: 107). He took the correlation between religion and morality as characteristic of religion in general (1937 and 1940). Malinowski espouses a similar view, but more definitively: "Every religion, primitive or developed, presents the three main aspects, dogmatic, ritual, and ethical. But the mere division or differentiation into three aspects is not sufficient. It is equally important to grasp the essential interrelation of these three aspects, to recognize that they are only really three facets of the same essential fact" (1974: 2).[9]

The argument is simple: no religion is without morality. It is notable that two giants of the study of Indigenous people were as outspoken in their understanding of morality as inherent to religion. Here, I substantiate their views that the binary of religion and morality is no creation of the *kosmos* type,[10] although it took a distinct and amplified form in this type. It is ubiquitous to religion and, in fact, originates with its emergence (Durkheim 1912: 24–5; Turner et al. 2018: 184–5; cf. Evans-Pritchard 1937: 107–11; 1956: 177–96, especially 193).

Before I discuss the hominin species' basic sociality, I contend that underlying the current discussion relating to Big Gods is a larger debate rarely, if ever, taken up in this context but important to consider. It pertains to whether we should think of religion within the intellectualist tradition (Tylor and Frazer) or along Durkheimian lines. Is it an individualistic or a collectivistic phenomenon? Is it a question of truth in terms of propositions about the world (belief), or does it revolve around meaning-attribution based on investment of feelings (Durkheim and Wittgenstein)? Although Big Gods advocates accentuate the role of religion for stimulating, if not creating, prosociality, their emphasis is on individual psychological cognition as in the intellectualist tradition. Ultimately, religion is about belief. Certainly, there is in the emphasis on prosociality and social cohesion overlap with the Durkheimian tradition,[11] but the stress is on individual beliefs, that is, propositional claims about the existence of superhuman powers. From a Durkheimian perspective, conversely, religion rotates around groupishness and the creation of a shared symbolic basis—revolving around ideals, norms, and regulations and compactly expressed in an emblem—through which the group emerges and is enabled to persist. I endorse a Durkheimian view (note 8). That said, there is a need for bringing these two very different understandings into dialogue with each other, since it would be meaningless to sacrifice the psychological dimension on the altar of sociology and vice versa. After all, there cannot be a shared symbol of reference, were it not for cognizing individuals entertaining representations about divine agents. Similarly, there is nothing to combine the cognition of singular individuals into a collective thinking, were it not for the institutional stabilization allowing the "we"-perspective to come into existence (cf. Tomasello 2019: 204–18, 254–74 and Jensen 2014).

One approach to have these two different lines of thinking about religion into the conversation is to use Wittgenstein's ([1938] 1997) focus on religion as an individual expression of emotions within a shared language use (53–9)—as a bridge between the psychological and the sociological (Petersen 2022a). We shall never fully grasp divine surveillance if we do not unite the psychological, sociological, and environmental aspects with each other (Petersen 2019a: 86–7; cf. Bendixen and Purzycki 2020).

Evolutionary Parameters for Gazing Gods

Although as humans, we are wont to think of ourselves as a species with a strong social propensity, our groupishness does not come easy. Ancient thinkers like Aristotle,

Aesop, and Vergil liked to compare humans to bees and ants, but whereas these species are bioprogrammed for sociality (eusociality), humans are evidently not. Yes, we have distinctive elements priming us for and furthering sociality such as lifelong mother–child attachment, female–male attraction, male friendship, grooming, coalitionary support, food sharing, sympathy, and a strong sense of fairness (Maryanski 2018: 226; Turner et al. 2018: 107–23). We are, however, at the depth of our biology not very fit for comprehensive groupishness. We share with the other extant apes a common hominid ancestor not well-adapted for enduring and extensive sociality. Even those apes that show the strongest traits for groupishness do not fare well in this regard (Turner et al. 2018: 49–74 and Maryanski 2018: 211–45). There is a good reason for this. They would in a short period overuse and destroy the arboreal area that they inhabit were they to engage in long-lasting types of groupishness. Primary and secondary forests do not provide enough kilojoules for large groups. Yet, for some reason our distant ancestors left the arboreal areas for open grassland. The key to their survival lies in their ability to enter into persistent and stable forms of sociality for which they were not very prone, when we look at the last common ancestor shared between hominins and the other hominids. As argued in Turner et al. (2018), the significant cause to this change lies in natural selection's amplification of the hominin emotional palette, compared to other hominids. The *Homo*-lineage demonstrates an extension of basic emotions to encompass both secondary and tertiary ones. Second-order elaborations of emotions like guilt and shame (combinations of the three primary emotions: sadness, anger, and fear)[12] are decisive for entering into an ultrasocially based groupishness, fragile as it is by resting on a predominantly culturally programmed type of sociality.

Obviously, this is an ultra-brief recapitulation of the long evolutionary story of the hominin lineage. The important point to be taken from this narrative, though, is the fact that at the depth of our biology—after all, we share almost 99 percent of our genes with bonobos and chimpanzees—we remain despotic and self-centered. Our sociality is difficult to cultivate beyond kin and kith, when it comes to our ability to enter into coalitions with others: not the best odds for universal groupishness or any form of group surpassing the boundaries of the shire. At the same time, we have since the emergence of the agrarian revolution approximately ten thousand years ago and, even more so, since the appearance of the first cities experienced an almost uninterrupted inadvertent acceleration of urbanization and aggrandization of groupishness. There are three cities in present-day China with more than 23 million people. Bombay is likely to have more than 65 million people in 2050. In the United States, England, and my own country, we witness an increasing tendency toward the formation of *megalopoleis* consisting of chains of cities slowly, but inevitably, growing together (Smith 2019). To argue that the juxtaposition or, more adequately expressed, intertwinement of religion and morality is a latecomer in the history of religion flies in the face of all insights into biology, psychology, sociology, and the science of religion.

It goes without saying that religion is also a matter of the presence of solid and enduring groupishness with the addendum that it is the type of stability provided by nongenetically transmitted learning across and between generations, that is, culture. Solid, yes, compared to what happened before. Persistent, indeed, matched up to the prehistory, but, surely, an immensely fragile sociality susceptible to constant disintegration and, in fact, actual extinctions as history blatantly demonstrates (cf. Diamond 2005; Valéry 1978: 13–14). If by virtue of culture/religion (they are overlapping entities from the Durkheimian perspective)[13] more stable types of groupishness emerge, it is obvious that morality is intrinsic to religion from its beginnings. Ultimately, it is sociality existing on a shared frame of reference. To exclude morality from this, when, in fact, we look at a highly selfish being entering into coalitions is gullible. Cultural groups exist by virtue of shared norms, ideals, values, and regulations (Richerson and Boyd 2005: 5–6). This is the more obvious, since religion and culture in premodernity constitute identical entities. Norms and regulations are imbued with transhuman and trans-groupish character obtained by projecting the collectivity onto the emblem and, subsequently, tapping energy from it, which endows individual adherents with a sense of groupishness.

Preparing the Way for Escalations in Groupishness

In the urban religions mostly familiar to me, that is, Greek, Roman, and Near-Oriental ones, gods, demons, and other divine agents do not refrain from interacting in intrahuman affairs. On the contrary, the whole point of this type—revolving around the sacrifice and temple institutions—is cosmic affirmation. The boons of the divine world do not flow incessantly to humans, unless they pay continuous respect to the gods by honoring their obligation as contractual servants. The raison d'être of sacrifice is not the principle of *do ut des* ("I give in order that you give") but the tenet of *do quia dedisti* ("I give because you have given"; Petersen 2022b). Divine action precedes human "payback" in the exchange. Gods grant a variety of goods to humans without which they could not survive. The sacrificial system confirms and substantiates this asymmetrical relationship. Humans, with what little they have, present the divine world in the form of specific gods: their gifts as tokens of loyalty toward the contractual relationship with the gods. Thereby, they also affirm their continuous status as a collective dependent upon the divine world and as reliable individuals willing to offer some of their own property as indexical signs of their contractual obedience (in his discussion of narrative, Geertz emphasizes the signaling effects; 2011: 21, 23). At the same time, they transmit a clear signal to their kinsmen that they are faithful and trustworthy citizens with whom one can unceasingly engage without being exposed to freeriding, lying, or other moral vices.[14] This system works well in groups, which extend neither the boundaries of the city nor those of the ethnic group. Surely, there are persistent problems with people transgressing the basic group norms and regulations, but they can be held at bay both by profane punishments and those attributed to the gods. Within the urban form of religion, transgression in the form of "*trans-location*," that is, moving beyond the space assigned to the individual and the group, is, of course, the vice *par excellence*.

Prometheus, Icarus, and Gilgamesh, to name just a few antiheroes, are among the primary examples of humans who could not accept the boundaries and had to transgress them with dire punitive consequences as a result (Smith 1978: 139; 1990; 1990: 121; Petersen 2011: 17–20). The wanderings of poor Odysseus are another example of the price paid for hubris and divine disobedience. Similarly, the endless travels of the patriarchs on their way to the Promised Land unequivocally demonstrate that a tribal god is easy to infuriate if one shows defiance, misbehavior, and rebellion. Uncompromising loyalty is what is called for as the Aqedah of Genesis 22 in the form of Isaac's binding demonstrably illustrates. There is nothing strange about any of this. In fact, this is what one would expect from a form of religion confined to an admittedly large-sized group, but one that is nevertheless constrained by the limits of the city or, at the highest, an amphictyony. Such groupishness, however, hardly suffices in an environment no longer confined to the urban boundaries. During the seventh century BCE, the first empires emerge with a concomitant selection pressure exerted on religion. If we move a few centuries forward, the enormous empire of Alexander the Great of the fourth century is a telling example. In terms of area of sovereignty, it extended from present-day Pakistan and Afghanistan in the East to Northern Macedonia in the North and West and to Egypt in the South. It comprised a multiplicity of ethnicities. To maintain groupishness in a changed environment, society needed to adapt to the new habitat, something we see in the increasing success of the *kosmos* form of religion during this period. Admittedly, Alexander did not embrace or introduce a new type of religion. We may, however, see the changes that religion—with Alexander's empire as the first full-fledged example—undergoes from the emergence of the Persian Empire and onward as responses to and influence exerted on the surrounding society by certain religious practitioners. We need to take the importance of such institutional selection mechanisms seriously to understand human evolution. As humans are intentional agents to an extent unprecedented by any other animal, we need also examine additional selection mechanisms than those pertaining to natural selection (Turner et al. 2018; Petersen et al. 2022). Surely, natural selection continues as overall driver (I use "natural selection" as a shorthand category for five interrelated but each independently significant evolutionary theoretical points: (1) the non-constancy of species; (2) the descent of all organisms from common ancestors; (3) the gradual nature of evolution; (4) the multiplication of species; and (5) natural evolution—see Mayr 2002: 94–6), but to ignore the pressure bioculture can exert on culture *purely* by not paying heed to institutions limits understanding.

Similarly, religions influence and respond to these environmental changes by undergoing processes granting them a greater fitness. We can discuss the exact causal factors underlying the change from the urban to the *kosmos* forms of religion. Scholars like Sanderson have pointed to increased processes of urbanization with concomitant enhanced density of populations (2018). Baumard et al. have pinpointed greater affluence as ultimate cause (2015, cf. Baumard and Boyer 2015). Enhanced labor division, greater literacy, and population growth are other candidates. However, the extension of the area of sovereignty is more plausible. I understand these other effects as derived from the areal expansion and, thus, as proximate causes. The ultimate cause lies in the extension of the area of sovereignty with the concomitant multiplicity of ethnicities to be ruled over.

Types of religion connected to the city state (*polis* religion) and its inhabitants face serious challenges, when sovereign space transgresses the local community. How should one keep together an empire by calling for continuous adherence to a

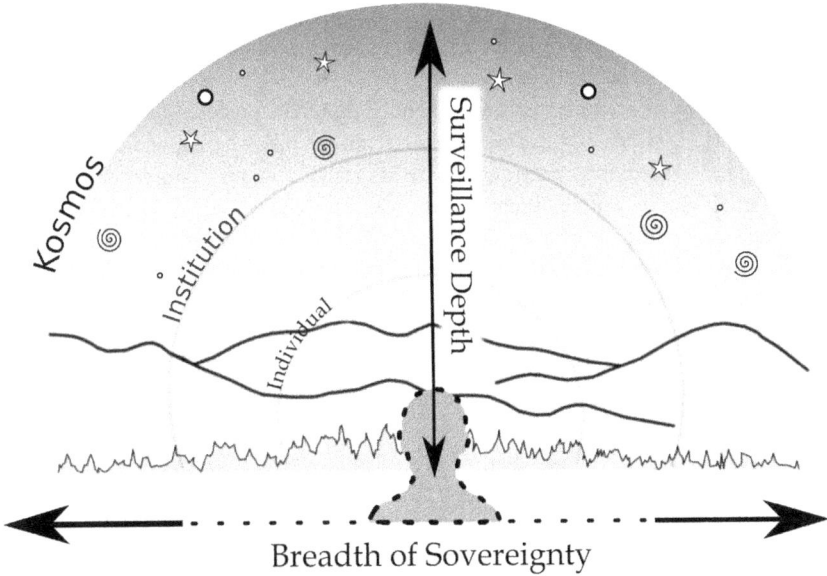

Figure 9.1 Penetrability of gods' knowledge at varying analytical levels. Dotted lines indicate breadth of gods' access in urban traditions while solid lines indicate *kosmos* traditions. In *kosmos* religions, the distinction between internal (soul) and external realms becomes especially salient. Image by Benjamin Grant Purzycki.

parochial god and instilling in the various ethnic groups' devotion to this deity? Why would Bactrian or Egyptian citizens pay tax to a remote figure in distant Macedonia? These are the selection challenges exerting pressure on religion and, similarly, religion responding to and actively partaking in formulating new visions for a changed habitat.

God's Gouging Gaze

As illustrated in Figure 9.1, in connection with the transition on the horizontal axis leading to the extension of the area of sovereignty along the lines of *polis* to empire, changes take place at a vertical and an axis of depth in the way religion is construed. We have seen that the urban type of religious worldview is mundanely affirmative (*Weltbejahung*). The two core institutions, temple and sacrifice, confirm the existing world. The cosmos with its various boons is essentially good. This is markedly different from *kosmos* forms of religion, although there is an important qualification. The ontological difference between divine and human is to a certain extent maintained in the *kosmos* type. In the urban form of religion, gods bestow their blessings on humans by providing them with old age (for males), plentiful offspring, abundant wine, fat oil, a rich harvest, and so on. Humans repay the divine gifts by offering sacrifices, but the whole point of the system is to keep the two spheres apart. This is evident in the temple architecture. Only priests may enter the adytum, which the god inhabits. Occasionally, it needs cleansing from all the impurities human cyclicity inflicted upon it in order to restore the cosmic balance. Upon death, humans enter into an anemic, comatose state in the underworld, in which they can only hope that their predecessors intermittently will pour out a sacrifice on their grave to interrupt the predicament of a never-ending gloomy life. Extraordinary individuals like a king (pharaoh, for example) and possibly one or two heroes may attain a semidivine postmortal life.

In the *kosmos* religion, conversely, the basic idea is that the world constitutes a false and corrupt realm from which humans need to free themselves in order upon death to reach the true world. The idea of an ontological barrier remains, insofar as humans shall spend their entire life in undergoing a process of divinization eventually enabling them to attain the celestial realm (Petersen 2013). Furthermore, they can undergo a process of transformation only on the premise that an otherworldly element has been infused into them.

The *kosmos* religion breaks with the idea of the world as a good place to be. Nietzsche's snorting resentment (1988: 11) at early Christ-religion for constituting a "Platonismus für's Volk" (Platonism for the people) is, regardless of the indignation in the contention, right to the point, although he did not understand that it is an essential characteristic of a type of religion rather than particular to Christianity. In fact, early Christ-religion may be seen within Judean religion as a vulgarization of the *kosmos* religion, inasmuch as it extends an originally elite phenomenon to considerably greater masses of people. With the emphasis placed on the world as a home in which humans do not really belong, life becomes a fitness center in which humans should strive to free themselves from this world in order to approach the other world and in anticipation of it already in the *hic et nunc* of present life. Hadot could speak of Greek philosophy as constituting a way of life (2001: 143–92; cf. 1995: 291–2; 2002: 77–8), but this not only pertains to ancient Greek philosophy but also to Chinese. Sloterdijk (2009) captures this by thinking of asceticism (ἄσκησις means "training") as the key feature of *kosmos* religion and its subsequent cultural influence. I think this shift is suitably understood as a change from transitive to reflexive types of sacrifice: from paying the gods by making sacrifices on behalf of oneself, humans are inculcated to bring themselves as a "living sacrifice, holy, and pleasurable to God" (Paul in Rom 12:1). This also explains why the martyr becomes the hero *par excellence* in the *kosmos* religion (Petersen 2019b, 2022b).

What has this to do with the gazing of the gods? Everything. When humans are enjoined to leave this world for another one, there are two important prerequisites. First, humans can only accomplish the emulative identification with the divine (the ὁμοίωσις θεῷ as Plato would designate it, *Theaetetus* 176b) on the basis that the divine has been imparted in them. This leads to a bodily divide in which the carnal side is cleft from the spiritual side (Plato's wordplay with σῶμα [body] and σῆμα [grave] is illustrative of the change). Human interiority is antagonistic to human exteriority as it is emphasized in the Medea tradition and in the desperate cry—formulated within the same tradition—of Paul's wretched "me" exclaiming: "Who can deliver me from this body destined by death?" (Rom 7:23). Corresponding to the extension on the previously mentioned horizontal axis and to the split on the axis of depth, a shift occurs on the vertical axis. The divine agent escalates to a much higher position, eventually coming to a provisional conclusion in the stringent monotheism of formative Islam (Christianity never settled whether there were three gods or one god. Judaism had problems in choosing between monotheism and binarism; Schäfer 2017). Based on this transferal, gods not only scrutinize acts of humans but also begin to direct their piercing look into human souls.

This shift in the history of religions occurs simultaneously with the horizontal extension of areas of sovereignty. The change also has a bearing at the level of groupishness. The religious group is no longer restricted to family or tribe. Potentially, it is to the whole world. The group consists of the adherents who (ideally) share the worldview and ethos: "Go, therefore, and teach all pagans, baptizing them in the name of the Father, the Son, and the holy Spirit by teaching them all things which I have taught you, and see, I am with you all days unto the end of the aeon" (Matt 28:19-20).

No local urban deity, regardless of all the cosmic attributes accorded it, can watch the doings and wrongdoings of the contractual servants, unless the god can direct his or her penetrating gaze into the innermost part of the human. No wonder that during the same period we see an increasing criticism directed against traditional sacrifices. Followers should not just pay hypocritical lip service, but be sincere and undergo a cognitive transformation to the extent that there is correspondence between interiority and exteriority actions. This is mind-control to an extent not previously seen in the history of religions. It is surveillance to a degree, which does not leave humans with many chances to flee the judging divine gaze. At the same time, I surmise, it is a prerequisite for keeping empires—comprising a multiplicity of ethnicities—together, holding potential aggression at bay, and honing a shared symbolic frame of reference instilling in subordinates a greater proclivity to abide by the ideals and regulations of the group.

In this way, I agree with many others who posit that something crucial occurred with the emergence of the *kosmos* religion. Contrary to them, I do not consider it a conjunction of religion and moral for the first time in human history. I argue that religion and moral have always been intertwined. What is novel, though, is the position divine powers take on the vertical scale. They ascend to a higher position, which is a reciprocal result of the movements happening at the horizontal axis and the axis of depth. Here, I could end the story, but I want to introduce another discussion partner, who may seem like an odd participant, but I believe he is an obvious candidate for contributing to the debate.

Foucault is not as odd an entrant in this context as some may think. A decisive source of influence on Foucault's thinking was the previously mentioned Pierre Hadot. Foucault could hardly have written his *History of Sexuality* had it not been for Hadot's influence. Moreover, I could hardly think of someone with a more piercing look at the penetrating divine eyes and their internalization in individual self-scrutinization of the conscience than Foucault. He endorses the view that

> The ascetic maceration exercised on the body and the rule of permanent verbalisation applied to the thoughts, the obligation to macerate the body and the obligation of verbalising the thoughts—those things are deeply and closely related. They are supposed to have the same goals and the same effect … We have

to sacrifice the self in order to discover the truth about ourself, and we have to discover the truth about ourself in order to sacrifice ourself. Truth and sacrifice, the truth about ourself and the sacrifice of ourself, are deeply and closely connected. And we have to understand this sacrifice not only as a radical change in the way of life, but as the consequence of a formula like this: you will become the subject of the manifestation of the truth when and only when you disappear or you destroy yourself as a real body or as a real existence. (2016: 73–4, cf. 1984: 53–85)

Although the examination pertains to Christianity and confession (the example is John Cassian), I think Foucault hits the nail on the head not only as regards ancient Christianity but also with respect to *kosmos* religion in general. Hence my disagreement with Foucault, because what he thinks is especially pertinent to formative Christ-religion, I see as a general trait of *kosmos* religion, but no need to blame the dead. My argument is clearly dependent upon what I have learned also from Foucault. The point highlighted here is that the self-scrutinization so precisely captured by Foucault is, in fact, a consequence or a reciprocal effect of the displacement of the gods on the vertical scale, which, on its part, is closely interrelated to the horizontal expansion in cosmic territory to be ruled over. The piercing gaze of the gods by the same logic becomes the penetrating self-examination leading to a constant life in ascetic self-improvement to adhere to the ideals of the group and, thereby, the god. To the extent that institutionalized ideas exert influence on society and biology, they are likely to have important effects also on prosociality. However, the precise causal character of this effect needs to be studied much more in depth, before we can draw plausible conclusions. Yet, my study should make it abundantly clear how a particular hypothesis may be formulated and in future studies used to make specific predictions. The argument put forward about the causal correlation between the horizontal extension of the area of sovereignty and the upgrading of divine powers on a vertical scale can be tested historically.

Acknowledgments

I express my gratitude to two anonymous peer reviewers for insightful comments. In particular, a word of thanks is due to Ben Purzycki and Armin W. Geertz who both gave valuable comments and improved my English.

10

Cultural Models of Minds and the Minds of Gods

Rita Anne McNamara

Introduction

Human minds interact with the sociocultural worlds and ecologies we inhabit, forming an essential structuring force that influences our perception of our own minds, other humans, and nonhuman (including supernatural) beings around us. What makes a god a god is itself deeply influenced by cultural input (Luhrmann et al. 2021; McNamara et al. 2021). For example, as explored by Barrett (2008), both Santa Claus and Mickey Mouse have aspects of five key traits promote god concepts: being counterintuitive; exhibiting intentional, agentic action; having potential access to information that is relevant to the success and survival of believers; creating detectable changes in the world; and motivating believers to undertake actions that perpetuate belief. Nevertheless, Santa does not meet the cultural mark of "God," because his impact is restricted to the holidays (Barrett 2008). On the other hand, people can learn of god(s) in other cultures but *not* believe in them—as is the case with the majority of modern students of Greek mythology who learn who Zeus was, yet nonetheless fail to convert to the Ancient Greek cults of Zeus worship (Gervais and Henrich 2010). The key difference here, unlike the Santa example, is the lack of cultural signals—that is, lack of social signals of an active cult of Zeus publicly worshiping him—that would indicate Zeus is "real" (Henrich 2009; Lanman 2012).

Drawing back to beliefs about minds, it makes sense to examine how different cultures come to see minds in particular ways. I first briefly review Western models of mind and describe how they are embedded in the existing literature around beliefs about gods' minds. I then briefly survey other formal theories of mind in Indian philosophical traditions of Advaita Vedanta, Buddhism, and Sāmkhya. These three traditions are of interest as they cover a wide range of possible relationships between the divine and human mind. Namely, they address questions of whether the divine and consciousness are all that exist; whether material reality is all that exists; and whether both mind and matter are equally "real" as the substance of existence.

An informal or folk model of mind forms the basis for naïve psychology, the implicit assumptions individuals make about how other social beings operate (D'Andrade 1987; Spunt and Adolphs 2015; Wierzbicka 2006). I therefore turn to more informal theories of minds exemplified in beliefs held among Indigenous peoples of the Amazon and Pacific. These traditions emphasize perspectivism, or the idea that all beings have their own unique viewpoint on the world; the best way to understand another being is not to *objectify* them (as is typical in the Western approach) but to *subjectify* them by deliberately taking on their unique perspective. The Pacific example takes a contrasting approach by treating all minds as fundamentally unknowable, though interlinked through kinship. This therefore leads to the expectation that relationship is the primary motivator for interindividual understanding, with minds and bodies of different beings as essentially the same (Descola 2013; Wagner 2018). I finish with a brief look at how gods' minds morph as cultures syncretically combine, such as when missionized and colonized peoples adopt world religions.

The Western Model of Mind in Scientific Approaches to Religion

In much of the Western world, people tend to treat other people as distinct entities that operate as individuals, behaving more-or-less autonomously, driven by preferences, instincts, goals—all of which originate in the mind. This informal model treats minds as the seat of the self, which is discrete and bounded from others and the surrounding environment. Tracing back at least as far as Descartes, the Western model of mind also incorporates an intuitive mind/body dualism that treats the mind and body as discrete entities. The mind, and by extension the self, is believed to be located within the physical medium of the brain (Chudek et al. 2017; Starmans and Bloom 2012). Following this informal model of mind, Western formal theories of mind focus mainly on neurocognitive scientific approaches that place the mind and associated conscious experience within the physical substrate of the brain (Lebedev et al. 2015; Millière 2017). With the rise of computing, subjective experience has increasingly been understood via metaphors with computing (Miller 2003), though more recent models now focus on a predictive brain that combines bottom-up sensory experience with top-down memory representations (Clark 2013; Seth, Baars, and Edelman 2005).

As a predominantly Western science (Berry 2015; Sinha 2002), the psychological study of gods' minds parallels the Western model of mind. God is viewed as a hyper-agentic uber-mind (Gray and Wegner 2010). Starting from a premise of basic materialism and working from resultant conclusion that, as a nonmaterial, nonphysical entity, god must *not* be "real," the cognitive science of religion goes on to suggest gods' minds must therefore be a construction of human minds (Barrett 2011; Bering 2006; Boyer 2001; Guthrie 1993). This suggestion is partly supported by correlations between mentalizing and belief (Caldwell-Harris et al. 2011; Gray et al. 2011; Willard and Norenzayan 2017), with brain imaging studies showing believers activate parts of their brains associated with thinking about themselves when thinking about God (Epley et al. 2009; Schjoedt et al. 2009). This implies we start from the self and impute our own mind (see Purzycki and Schjoedt; Jackson and Gray, present volume) to infer the mind of God. Some posit religious experience arises from excessive perception of other minds (i.e., hyperactive agency detection; Barrett and Keil 1996; Bering 2006) or promiscuous anthropomorphism (Guthrie 1993). Human-perceptual cognitive systems are hypothesized to have either coevolved with or been co-opted into systems that enable cooperative interactions between people (Johnson 2009; Norenzayan et al. 2016; Schloss and Murray 2011; Sosis 2009).

Interestingly, the religious history of Western countries may in part feed into this model of mind (Asad 2003; Laine 2014; Masuzawa 2005). The separation and centrality of individual self is a basic tenant of secularism (C. Taylor 2007). This secularized self—as opposed to the porous, nonsecular self—may be unique to Western cultures (e.g., Leung and Cohen 2011; Luhrmann et al. 2021). The distinction between self and nonself can become blurry during psychological and physiological duress that can be induced through physical threat (e.g., battlefield stress; Yaden et al. 2017) or physical disturbance of neurobiological function (brain trauma; J. B. Taylor 2006); ecstatic epileptic seizures (Hansen and Brodtkorb 2003; Ogata and Miyakawa 1998)). A sense of separate self can also be reduced through practices like asceticism, meditation, and psychotropic plant medicines (Armstrong 1993; Taves 2020). Other cultural models of mind—both formal and informal—emphasize other aspects of social life. I now turn the discussion to examine how these other models envision the human and divine social world.

Other Formal Theories of Mind: Indian Philosophy

Indian traditions have a deep history of exploration into the nature of mind, body, and consciousness that extends back thousands of years (Jha 2017; Sriraman and Benesch 2005). These philosophies cannot be readily separated from the spiritual and religious contexts (Asad 2003; Weiskopf 2020); their methods are highly introspective and subjective (in contrast to externalized, objective focus in Western science; Sriraman and Benesch 2005). Their theories about mind and consciousness are no less systematic and highly detailed. Here, I focus on two common elements found across three traditions: belief in karma and reincarnation as implicated in Advaita Vedanta, Early Buddhism, and Sāṃkhya.

The scientific literature on religion has historically focused on Abrahamic traditions, and therefore may overemphasize the importance of perceived agency in supernatural causal attributions (Sørensen and Purzycki, present volume). Karmic traditions, by contrast, are largely defined by attribution to non-agentic and nonphysical causation. Theologically, karma is discussed as a force or principle of cause and effect that produces impersonal, dispassionate consequences for actions (Keyes and Daniel 1983). In this theological perspective, karma has no mind and cannot be bargained with. However, folk understandings of karma show some mentalizing applied to karma, though how much this applies across all karma traditions beyond particular branches of Hinduism remains understudied (White et al. 2019; White and Norenzayan 2019). In line with a sociocentric self (Markus and Kitayama 1991), individually acquired karma can impact others across generations. Texts like the *Yoga Sutras* indicate that the way to respond to karma is to live through whatever karma has caused in the present and act appropriately to avoid future karma (Bryant 2015).

Another belief that operates alongside karma is that individuals reincarnate in a constant cycle (*saṃsāra*) (Bodewitz 2019; Bryant 2015). Karma partly expresses the consequences of action though one's social and material conditions of birth (Peacock 2008; Whicher 1998). Some traditions seek to maximize good karma to gain the best possible birth for one's entire family, while others target liberation (Loy 1982) to go beyond the cycle of karma and reembodiment completely.

Advaita Vedanta: Material Unreality and All-Encompassing Self

Advaita (nondual) Vedanta (that which emerges from the Vedas) posits that the only real reality is *Brahman*: pure, contentless consciousness that is the source of all things (Adams 1982; Schweizer 2020). All physical things are in fact illusions that ebb and flow with change created by the same underlying Brahman. Subjectivity and the ultimate Self (Brahman) are the ultimate truth and reality of the universe. This suggests god's mind is diffuse, abstract, and nonphysical. It is contrary to the Western model of gods' minds as it is highly unlike a human mind. The human mind, according to Advaita Vedanta, has apparently physical, material components. Individual human experience is possible due to the True or Higher Self, which is an emanation or aspect of Brahman. This allows the illusory experience of dualism, or the sense that the self is distinct from the Brahman whole. Part of what makes Brahman and the True Self aspects of Brahman real is due to the eternal and unchanging nature Brahman has; *maya* (the physical world of illusion) is not real because it changes (Sriraman and Benesch 2005). It also partly motivates the need for the practices of Advaita Vedanta, as codified by Sri Śankaracharya, which focus on renunciation and meditation on the part of the True Self (the *Ātman*) that is united with Brahman that enables this conception of god's mind to emerge (Śankaracharya 1901).

The physical mind is the vehicle through which the True Self, as a facet and emanation of Brahman, experiences the physical world. Thus, in this view, the mind is not the starting point of god, but rather God—in this case, consciousness itself—is the starting point of the (human) mind. This idealist monist perspective that sees the world as starting from nonmaterial consciousness and only consciousness is "real" is in direct contrast to the materialist monist (only physical material is "real") perspective taken in the West. Advaita Vedanta also acknowledges the path to realizing this is difficult due to how convincing the illusion of *maya* is. Writings of teachers like Adi Śankaracharya directly state that the direct path to this awareness of ultimate reality is only accessible to the men of the Brahminical caste, who have the *dharma* (nature, duty) to be able to completely remove themselves from the actions of daily life. Karma and cycles of reincarnation enter this perspective in the form of a person's birth; women and men of other castes are purportedly in their castes due to their karma. Therefore, though the classical path to *mokṣa* (liberation) is only open to male Brahminical monks, other people can perform different practices to build up the good karma to be born as a male Brahman and try to attain enlightenment then (Meena 2005; Śankaracharya 1901).

Early Buddhism: Material Reality and Nonself

Buddhism is another vast and diverse set of traditions. I focus here on the Pāli cannon of Early Buddhism and the Pāli Abhidhamma movement and the Theravāda school (Loy 1982; Samuel 2014). These early Buddhist teachings take a stance opposite to Advaita Vedanta and similar to the Western approach, with material reality as the starting point of human experience (Prasad 2000; Samuel 2014).

Buddhist *nirvana* (liberation) is the realization of the deeper truths of *anicca* (impermanence), *dukkha* (all physical experience, however pleasant, is unsatisfactory), and *anattā* (there is no self—whether this is "ego" or "Higher Self" of Advaita Vedanta varies across traditions). Reality is composed of tiny material particles called *kalapas*; they are ever-changing; therefore, everything is ever-changing (*anicca*). Because everything changes, everything will end, leading to dissatisfaction (*dukkha*) when one tries to cling to something that cannot last. Upon realizing this inherently dissatisfying nature, one can release from the illusion of a self and enter into the *nirvana* state of void no-thing-ness (Loy 1982). Despite this materialism, Buddhists maintain a part of the mind—consciousness—that reincarnates across lifetimes and travels in and out of a body when dreaming (Harvey 1993; Prasad 2000). While not in a physical body, a consciousness seeks a womb, producing the initial spark for a particular *nāma-rūpa* (mind-body) to be formed. The consciousness retains the *sankaras* (karmic impressions) that carry karma forward across cycles of reincarnation.

With this ever-changing, materialist perspective, Buddhism has often been touted as a religion without belief in god (Glasenapp 1966; Levine 2012; Ruegg 1976). This holds true insofar as Buddhism rejects the idea of a supreme creator God in the form seen among Abrahamic traditions, though Buddhist traditions still hold reverence for figures ranging from ghosts to the Buddha to other enlightened beings (bodhisattvas) who are deemed to be fully liberated but continue to interact with those still in the cycle of samsara to enable them to be liberated (e.g., the Dalai Lama of Tibetan Buddhism is often considered to be one such being). Informally, some aspects of Buddhist practice can treat the Buddha as a form of deity (Berniūnas, Dranseika and Tserendamba 2019; Purzycki and Holland 2018).

Sāṃkhya and Classical Yoga: Dual Material/Consciousness Realities and Distilled Self

Sāṃkhya, as associated with Patañjali's *Yoga Sutras* and the *Bhagavad Gita*, offers a third perspective on mind within Indian philosophy (Bryant 2015; Schweizer 2019). Sāṃkhya posits that the material, manifested world occurs as a result of the *puruṣa*, which (like *Brahman*) is constant, eternal, contentless, and unchanging. It observes the material world (*prakṛti*), activating it to create changing, ephemeral, material reality. This point of interaction between *puruṣa* and *prakṛti* is *samyoga* (union, interaction) that leads to continued cycles of reincarnation. When this union is broken, the *puruṣa* stops observing *prakṛti*, the *prakṛti* stops moving, and change stops. The ultimate goal of yoga for Patañjali then is to realize this *kaivalya* ("separatedness, aloneness"—i.e., liberation) via this separation of *puruṣa* and *prakṛti* (Bryant 2015).

Sāṃkhya is distinct in that (1) the True or Higher Self (*puruṣa*) is separate but equal to material *prakṛti* and (2) each *puruṣa* remains wholly distinct from all other *puruṣas* (Bryant 2015; Virupakshananda 2015). Like Buddhism, there is debate as to whether Sāṃkhya is inherently theist (Burley 2007; Nicholson 2010; Pflueger 2008). The *Yoga Sutras* indicate the fastest way to liberation is through reverence for *Īśvara*, a "Lord," or "special" consciousness (*puruṣa*) that the yogi can look to for guidance. The text is terse and open to wide interpretation, such that *Īśvara* can be anything from a vast creator God like *Brahman* to an individual aspect of one's Higher Self.

The *Bhagavad Gita* makes theistic implications of Sāṃkhya more obvious, as the divine being Kṛṣṇa is the teacher giving the lessons of Sāṃkhya to the protagonist Arjuna (Chapple 2019). As expounded upon by commentators across traditions (including Sri Śankaracharya in Advaita Vedanta; Śankaracharya 1901), the means to liberation Kṛṣṇa describes give multiple routes to suit different people in different circumstances. Sāṃkhya and the study of wisdom in Jnana Yoga were traditionally reserved for the dedicated practice of renunciate monks who also happen to be Brahminical men. The alternate paths of action (karma yoga) and devotion (bhakti yoga) are described for those who cannot devote themselves to religious study full time. Indeed, Kṛṣṇa describes bhakti to the divine (i.e., to Kṛṣṇa himself) as the fastest route to liberation. In the story, Kṛṣṇa is experienced by the humans around as a man and describes himself as 1/16 human. Kṛṣṇa reveals his full nature to Arjuna as the infinite expanse of all that is—and nearly blows up Arjuna's human brain. Thus, the conception of God here is as packaged in human form to enable humans to interact with it, but the full expanse is also acknowledged to be more than the ordinary human mind can fully comprehend.

Other Informal Theories of Mind

Though informal models of minds can be as diverse as the cultures that hold them, to show how informal models are nevertheless central to cultural traditions, I focus on two examples: animism within Indigenous Amerindian Perspectivism, and belief that minds are not knowable (or opaque) found in the Pacific.

Animism/Perspectivism: Subjectivity and Unity of Mind

Indigenous societies around the world tend to act toward the natural world as having some unseen "spirit" dimension, bringing all beings into relationship (Bird-David 1999; mays, Seligman, and Medin 2020; Rival 2012). This stance, called animism, plays an important role in Indigenous peoples' extensive ecological knowledge and reveals its sophistication (Berkes, Colding, and Folke 2000; Smith 1998; Weiskopf 2020). Amerindian perspectivism arose out of ethnographic work on Amazonian peoples' cosmologies and ontologies (Castro 1998, 2004; Rival 2012). These cosmologies posit all beings began as an undifferentiated, spiritual, pre-self form, and that form is the original substrate of reality (rather than material). This contrasts the naturalism of the West, which posits that nature is unified by its material physical substance, but fundamentally differs by the interior consciousness (or lack thereof) that takes on particular form (Descola 2013).

Some theories within the cognitive science of religion suggest animism (i.e., endowing the natural world with spiritual agencies) and perspectivism are promiscuous anthropomorphism (Guthrie 1993). However, they indicate a more interconnected worldview, with entities ascribed properties relative to how the subjectivity viewing them sees them. For example, food is food because of its relationship to the observer, rather than some intrinsic characteristic. Animals do not see humans as humans but as predators, prey, and so on, but they see *themselves* as humans (Castro 1998, 2004; Škrabáková 2014). Young children in these societies do not overextend the human mind in the way that Westerners do (Herrmann, Waxman, and Medin 2010; Medin et al. 2010; Unsworth et al. 2012) but instead learn to categorize knowledge about social agents in the world to include more diverse kinds of minds (mays, Seligman, and Medin 2020; ojalehto, Medin, and García 2017).

As discussed above, Western and classical Buddhist approaches both start from the assumption that reality consists of only material elements, with consciousness emanating from material. The Western viewpoint also starts from the supposition that the best way to understand something is to separate oneself from it and treat it as an object to be observed externally (i.e., to treat something *objectively*). Amazonian perspectivism (like Advaita Vedanta) instead starts from the stance of spiritual realism, meaning that the world starts from spirit, and material emanates from spirit. Amazonian perspectivism seeks to *subjectify* beings to understand them; to take on their perspective rather than an outside observer (Castro 1998, 2004). Anything with a spirit has a perspective. Anything with a perspective has a subjectivity. Thus, the goal of understanding is to perceive through that subjectivity.

Shamanic practices (i.e., plant medicines like ayahuasca) allow practitioners to see past the outer form (Doyle 2012; Luna 1986; Škrabáková 2014). This reflects a more relational attitude toward nature, and the "owners" or "mother" spirits of the plants are called upon for healing and for various other tasks set out by those who work with the plants (Škrabáková 2014). The underlying unity of spirit makes it difficult to distinguish whether gods' minds are distinct from human or any other kinds of minds in this cultural frame. This interconnection with nature has more clear-cut interactions with religious and supernatural belief in the more typical Western sense when seen through the lens of syncretism (Dawson 2017), as discussed further below. But first, I briefly discuss another cultural view of minds where minds are opaque.

Opacity of Mind: Minds Are Fundamentally Unknowable

Ethnographic work with small-scale societies in Oceania parts of the Arctic, and among some Mayan groups reports participants consistently claim it is impossible to truly know someone else's mind (Duranti 2015; Hollan 2012; Luhrmann 2011; Throop 2012; Toren 2009). The mind, within the opaque container of the body, is forever hidden (beliefs here referred to as opacity norms). While most adults in these communities will readily agree that other people have different thoughts, beliefs, desires, goals, and knowledge, they often deny another person can know what these contents are. These norms may indicate genuine differences in how people understand other minds (Robbins 2008), or they may result from ethnographers' inability to properly formulate questions to fit their respondents' worldviews (Duranti 2008; Groark 2011). Reliance on kinship ties to structure daily life may promote these norms, as both relational (im)mobility and kinship intensity reduce reliance on mental states via intentionality reasoning (Curtin et al. 2020; McNamara and Henrich 2017).

While things are changing in light of Christianity's influence (see below), precontact beliefs are still present in modern Fiji, and the earlier beliefs recorded through missionaries give some insight into what gods' minds under opacity norms might look like. The centrality of lineage and of interconnectedness is especially key. The founding ancestors of particular lineages, the *Kalou-vu* (literally "root god"), are thought to preside over the tribes and families in a given area (McNamara, Norenzayan, and Henrich 2016, 2021; Thomson 1895). These founding fathers are often described as five brothers who form the "root" of the clans with different hierarchical functions in the community; that is, the eldest brother formed the chief clan, the second the priestly clan, the third the warrior clan, and so on. These ancestors restrict their concern and action to people within their lineage and are primarily interested in what people do to maintain traditional village norms (McNamara et al. 2021). Other entities are also treated as present and real around the community, ranging from ghosts to shapeshifting trickster beings (often labeled *tevoro* or "demons," especially in the context of Christianity). Their presence is often cited to explain particular disturbances in the community (e.g., why some families might be less well off than others is because of ancestral harms done), sometimes used to socialize children to behave (e.g., "don't shout or the *tevoro* will get you"), or other unusual experiences around and about village settings.

The underlying ontological frame reflects totemism, another alternative to the perspectivist animism of the Amazon and the objectivist naturalism of the West (Descola 2013; Wagner 2018). In this ontological frame, other beings are seen to have the same external/physical and internal/spiritual qualities as humans, in this case making other beings literal family. In addition to the various monikers that Fijians routinely use to track kin relations across islands, they also use identifiers based on animals or plants as roots with whom their lineage shares a special relationship (Rivers, 1908, 1909). Even today, most Fijians cite what their totemic animal or plant is and note that it is forbidden or *tabu* to eat or otherwise harm the totemic being (McNamara 2014). Linking back to the opacity model of mind, the physical and relational ties between spirit and embodied beings for both ancestors and totems are more important than attendance to their intentional states, goals, desires, and/or thoughts. This speaks to the importance of the relationships for social identity across the Pacific (Toyoda, 1998), and emphasizes normative conduct within the network of familial obligations rather than individual mental state-based choices (Anae 2016; Brison 2001; Duranti 2015; Wendt, 1999).

Syncretism: Minds of Humans and Gods When Cultures Intertwine

Given the extent of colonization, missionization, and globalization, today it is impossible to distinguish religious traditions in small-scale societies from influences of so-called world religions. If religious believers across traditions apply their own models of minds to supernatural agents, then the expectations about what these supernatural agents are like should carry the social cognitive marks of the model of mind present within the culture where that religious tradition initially emerged (McNamara et al. 2021; McNamara and Purzycki 2020; Willard and McNamara 2019). Further, as religions spread through various forms of intercultural contact, the social cognitive signatures of their originating cultural model of mind may be adopted along with the new religious belief sets.

Despite European colonization and Spanish Catholic missionization in the Americas, Indigenous beliefs that incorporate perspectivism persist (Kidwell, Noley, and Tinker 2020; Watanabe, 1990). As Indigenous beliefs were gradually given open expression and introduced beliefs were integrated, uniquely Amerindian interpretations spread. For example, Christian teachings about Jesus as a healer are promoted over afterlife salvation (Kidwell, Noley, and G. E. Tinker 2020; Watanabe 1990). Simultaneously, Christian imagery and concepts are invoked in traditional spiritual and medicinal modalities (e.g., ayahuasca ceremonies; Dawson 2017; Luna 1986; Wright 2018).

Protestant Christianity stands out as one of the most mind-focused religious belief sets. Protestantism has gained particular prominence in societies with opacity norms around the Pacific. Ethnographers have noted rising distress associated with introduced Protestant practices that challenge opacity norms (Duranti 2008; Robbins, Schieffelin, and Vilaça 2014; Schieffelin 2008). Practices like confession compel believers to speak openly, sincerely, and (worst of all) publicly about inner states. The loss of mental privacy and freedom leads to increasing shame and damaging gossip (ibid.) Pre-missionization practices for adjudicating grievances often retained the privacy of one's inner world. For example, the Fijian *i soro* (surrender) used to repair relationships in cases of wrongdoing involves a public admission of one's actions and a transfer of goods from the transgressor to the aggrieved parties (and/or their kin). These happen on a voluntary basis and do not delve into the inner motivations of the wrongdoers (Arno 1976). Though Christianity is often considered an essential part of identity in Pacific Island communities (Ryle 2010; Tomlinson 2007; Toren 2004), Christian God concepts can still be seen to support local models of minds (McNamara et al. 2021; Willard and McNamara 2019).

Conclusion

Because we do not see the world as it is but as we are, it stands to reason that our view of what natural and supernatural worlds might contain is also constrained by the minds we conceive as inhabiting our world. Opening inquiry into other cultural models of mind opens the world to possible understanding of other agencies that lie beyond our current frame of reference. The Western understanding of the world as inhabited by autonomous beings who act based upon inner states, instantiated in the brain, is only one of many views on the relationships among the brain, body, mind, and behavior. Other formal theories of mind like those found in Indian philosophy and informal theories of mind like the animism/perspectivism of the Americas and opacity norms in the Pacific show us that our abilities to perceive and conceive of the mind are heavily influenced by the cultural settings we inhabit.

11

Moralistic Gods and Social Complexity: A Brief History of the Problem

Benjamin Grant Purzycki and Ryan McKay

Introduction

A cluster of persistent and contentious questions in the scientific study of religion concern when and why so-called "moralistic traditions" developed and how they have shaped human relationships. Is there an association between moralistic gods and the size and/or complexity of the society that might worship them? How cross-culturally ubiquitous are such traditions? Are people more willing to engage in cooperative behavior when they believe their god cares about morality? This chapter focuses on how these questions have arisen and how generations of researchers have struggled to address them. We first briefly examine the intellectual history of the problem, pointing to some of the troubling aspects of early observations of traditional societies and subsequent anthropological positions. We then address how early observations of small-scale peoples have populated cross-cultural resources that have informed and driven contemporary empirical projects. We finish by pointing to ways in which we might go about ensuring that the conversation continues with clarity and consistency.

A Historical View of Moralistic Gods

Much of our knowledge of past traditional populations comes from missionary sources and explorers.[1] As we discuss below, these sources populate the databases contemporary researchers use to examine patterns in human behavior. While many of these sources provide considerable knowledge about traditional peoples, they are not without problems, particularly in their documentation of traditional religions. In fact, historically, many observers simply denied that traditional peoples even had religion in the first place, thus clouding much of what we could have known.

For example, Christopher Columbus posited that the Canary Islanders "would become Christians very easily, for it seemed to [him] that they had no religion" (Dunn 1989: 69). Similarly, one missionary (Dobrizhoffer 1822) who worked among the Abipón Indians of Paraguay argued that "the American savages are slow, dull, and stupid in the apprehension of things not present to their outward senses. Reasoning is a process troublesome and almost unknown to them. It is, therefore, no wonder that the contemplation of terrestrial or celestial objects should inspire them with *no idea of the creative Deity, nor indeed of any thing heavenly*" (58; emphasis ours). After "eighteen years spent amongst the Guaranies, and Abipones," the author professed to "having myself seen most barbarous savages born in the woods, accustomed from their earliest age to superstition, slaughter, and rapine, and naturally dull and stupid as brutes." These "slow, dull, and stupid" natives are nevertheless capable of conversion "when the good sense of the teacher compensates for the stupidity of his pupils" (62).[2]

During the mid-1600s, missionaries in Martiniques contemplated native Caribbeans' religion. According to one (Breton and la Paix 1929), "After having lived without any knowledge of God, they die without hope of salvation. *It would be better for us to say that they have no religion at all*, instead of describing as a cult of divinity all their trifling nonsense, superstitions, or more exactly sacrileges with which they honor all of the demons who seduce them" (5, emphasis ours). Another (Bouton 1635) notes that "I believe that they do not trouble themselves with knowing what becomes of [the souls of the dead]; at least we have never been able to draw this information out of them." Notably, he acknowledges that the primary source of his ignorance is that he does not interact with them very much: "Possibly we should learn more if we were to live among them or they among us. At the present time they are greatly separated from us by inaccessible hills, so that we see them rarely and only when they come by sea to trade with the French."[3] In addition to barely interacting with the target population, the ignorance behind accentuating "trifling nonsense" and minimizing any association with "any thing heavenly" should raise some doubts as to the quality of this kind of information. As we return to later, however, such sources still drive many current views of traditional religions.

Anthropology emerged as a way to come to better terms with human diversity. Of course, the academic study of human variation remained mired in the values and biases of its time, but the field's lasting contributions to the study of human culture are arguably unparalleled. One such contribution comes from E. B. Tylor, who wrote two consecutive volumes of *Primitive Culture* ([1871] 2016a, b). Marshaling considerable evidence for the cross-cultural universality of religion, across these two volumes Tylor argues that traditional peoples do, in fact, have the essential elements of religious expression in the form of belief in spiritual agents (i.e., animism). One of Tylor's lasting contributions, then, was undermining the earlier view that traditional peoples somehow lacked religion.

However, he spends virtually no time investigating whether these animistic traditions are "moralistic." When he discusses this question, he dismisses the possibility outright without a single example:

> One great element of religion, that moral element which among the higher nations forms its most vital part, is indeed little represented in the religion of the lower races. It is not that these races have no moral sense or no moral standard, for both are strongly marked among them, if not in formal precept, at least in that traditional consensus of society which we call public opinion, according to which

certain actions are held to be good or bad, right or wrong. It is that *the conjunction of ethics and Animistic philosophy, so intimate and powerful in the higher culture, seems scarcely yet to have begun in the lower.* (427; our emphasis)

He continues to extol the virtues of this "conjunction of ethics and Animistic philosophy":

It is clear that among its greatest powers has been its divine sanction of ethical laws, its theological enforcement of morality, its teaching of moral government of the universe, its supplanting the "continuance-doctrine" of a future life by the "retribution-doctrine" supplying moral motive in the present. But such alliance belongs almost wholly to religions above the savage level, not to the earlier and lower creeds. (II. 361)

So, while over two volumes Tylor takes pains to demonstrate that peoples at "the savage level" have religion, he dismisses the possibility that their religions "supply moral motives" to help guide their interactions. As ethnographic inquiry progressed in the form of rigorous fieldwork (in which Tylor did not engage), this particular view would become repeatedly challenged.

Indeed, for the next century, scholars would debate the presence of moralistic religious traditions while appealing to the evolution of society. Much of the debate from the late 1800s to early 1900s was about whether or not concepts of "high gods" (e.g., the Abrahamic deity) could have evolved from notions of ancestors or other spirits (e.g., see Hartland 1898; Lang 1900 for debate about the presence of such deities among indigenous Australians). As discussed in the next section, this question has had a lasting influence on the field. There was also another aspect of this breed of progressivist evolution that dominated the intellectual culture at the time. As indicated by Tylor's claims, there was a "high *a priori* line that savage minds are incapable of originating the notion of a *moral* Maker" (Lang 1900: xiv; emphasis ours) at the time. There was, however, some resistance to this idea.

Lang (1900), for example, expresses openness to the possibility that beliefs in a spiritual "Being [with] ... high moral attributes" might even predate belief in those deities who play "silly or obscene tricks [or are] lustful and false" (xv). He details the moral character of indigenous Australians' traditions, including a handful of one deities' precepts such as directives "to share everything they have with their friends" and "to live peaceably with their friends" (181). And, to emphasize his argument that concepts of "savage high gods" likely did not evolve from other spirit concepts, he surveys considerable cross-cultural evidence of traditional peoples with gods that are either appealed to as moral paragons or which directly punish people for immoral behavior (193–210). He concludes, "Anthropology holds the certainly erroneous idea that the religion of the most backward races is always non-moral" (256). Over the next half-century, anthropological observation and thought would bolster Lang's indictment by directly tying morality and ethics to traditional religion.

In fact, establishing this link became a matter of course among the leading anthropologists of religion, particularly those who promoted and engaged in long-term fieldwork. In 1936, Malinowski illustrates how obvious the association with religion and morality is:

> That every organized belief implies a congregation, must have been felt by many thinkers instructed by scholarship and common sense. Yet ... science was slow to incorporate the dictates of simple and sound reason ... [that finds] that worship always happens in common because it touches common concerns of the community. And here ... enters the ethical element intrinsically inherent in all religious activities. They always require efforts, discipline, and submission on the part of the individual for the good of the community. (in Strenski 1992: 137)

Here, Malinowski explicitly associates "worship" with exerting individual "effort, discipline, and submission" to benefit one's community, a conception of morality that is effectively synonymous with contemporary evolutionary notions (see Alexander 1987; Lightner and Purzycki, present volume). Thirty years later, Evans-Pritchard (1965) dismissed the idea that traditional populations lack gods who are moral paragons—that is, models of how to properly behave—suggesting the idea was rendered a myth thanks to the efforts of ethnographic researchers. A more general conception of "morality" comes more recently from Rappaport (1999), who argued that religion is inherently moral inasmuch as ritual itself is the behavioral encoding and sanctification of conventional rules (132–3). In sum, the reigning consensus in the anthropology of religion was that in a variety of ways, traditional populations' moral sense was inextricably linked to their religious traditions.

Something has since changed, however. Curiously, contemporary researchers debate the ubiquity of moralistic supernatural or spiritual punishment and often posit the kinds of strong arguments found among earlier views, thus ignoring generations of anthropological observation and theory. While some maintain that moralistic supernatural punishment is a common if not essential part of religion, others posit that such beliefs played a role in scaling up societies to include more people and more forms of economic specialization. In other words, small-scale societies typically lack such traditions. For example, some maintain that "ancestral religions did not have a clear moral dimension" (Norenzayan 2013: 127) or that the world's traditional deities are somehow "weak" and/or "whimsical" (Chudek, Muthukrishna, and Henrich 2015). Others, however, challenge such positions and point to abundant evidence of moralistic supernatural punishment beliefs or traditions with "moral dimensions" in traditional societies (Beheim et al. 2021; Bendixen, Apicella et al. forthcoming; Johnson 2015; Lovins 2015; Purzycki 2011; Purzycki and Sosis 2022; Purzycki, Willard, et al. 2022; Raffield, Price, and Collard 2019; Singh, Kaptchuk, and Henrich 2021).

The theories motivating such debates are wide-ranging as well (for review see McKay and Whitehouse 2015; Purzycki and Watts 2018). Some posit that forms of supernatural punishment, including the so-called "moralistic high gods" (i.e., creator deities that "support" human morality; see below), might have mitigated problems associated with cooperation (e.g., Johnson 2005; Roes and Raymond 2003; Snarey 1996). Specifically, some kinds of cooperative problems associated with social complexity or subsistence may have contributed to the evolution of moralistic high gods (Peoples and Marlowe 2012). In this view, then, moralistic supernatural punishment is an adaptation to particular conditions such as harsh environments (Botero et al. 2014) or water scarcity (Snarey 1996). In addition to adaptively responding to threats to cooperation, others suggest that moralistically punitive religious traditions may contribute to social complexity by harnessing prosocial motivations to apply to a wider range of coreligionists (M. Lang et al. 2019; Norenzayan et al. 2016; Purzycki et al. 2016). Others still argue that the so-called "moralistic traditions" were responses to—and not drivers of—the increased wealth that societies of the past enjoyed (Baumard et al. 2015; cf. Purzycki, Ross et al. 2018) or that even environmental factors such as weather may have played an important role in the emergence of "moralistic high gods" (Skoggard et al. 2020). Given the fairly deep history of the debate, what accounts for the reemergence of the view that traditional populations lack a "clear moral dimension"? As we detail below, part of the explanation is due to the contemporary use of data coded from the kinds of accounts that predate the anthropological turn toward learning about human variation with direct contact and fieldwork. Another contributing factor is the overemphasis on *high gods*.

Turning Old Accounts into Data

As discussed in the previous section, much of what we know about cross-cultural patterns of traditional religion comes from qualitative ethnographies, travelers' observations, and missionary reports. Written from the perspectives of these observers, these reports were subsequently coded to create large cross-cultural databases used to examine global trends in a wide variety of human activities. While valuable, when it comes to religion, there are deep problems with the data.

The most common way of assessing these questions has been to use cross-cultural databases such as the Ethnographic Atlas (EA) or Standard Cross-Cultural Sample (SCCS) (Murdock and White 1969). These databases were designed to test predictions about human practices in ways that are statistically feasible and that overcome problems associated with cultural relatedness (i.e., Galton's problem). In other words, such databases convert qualitative information into analyzable quantitative data. The studies that exploit these databases find the target relationship between moralistic *high gods* and social complexity (Botero et al. 2014; Johnson 2005; Peoples and Marlowe 2012; Skoggard et al. 2020; Snarey 1996).

Consider again the process by which some databases have come to be. Figure 11.1a illustrates the causal pathways (see Pearl, Glymour, and Jewell 2016) of our target prediction—namely, that social complexity causes the belief in gods' moralistic punishment (the point still holds if we reverse this direction). In this model, we have historical reality, the "true" or "original" causal relationship between social complexity and moralistic gods we wish to infer: $S\_0 \to G\_0$. Of course, we do not have direct access to this reality, but it was recorded by the sources M with varying degrees of fidelity and reliability. As indicated in the previous section, sources' attitudes, focus, and ignorance influenced the content of the data we can use; reports may or may

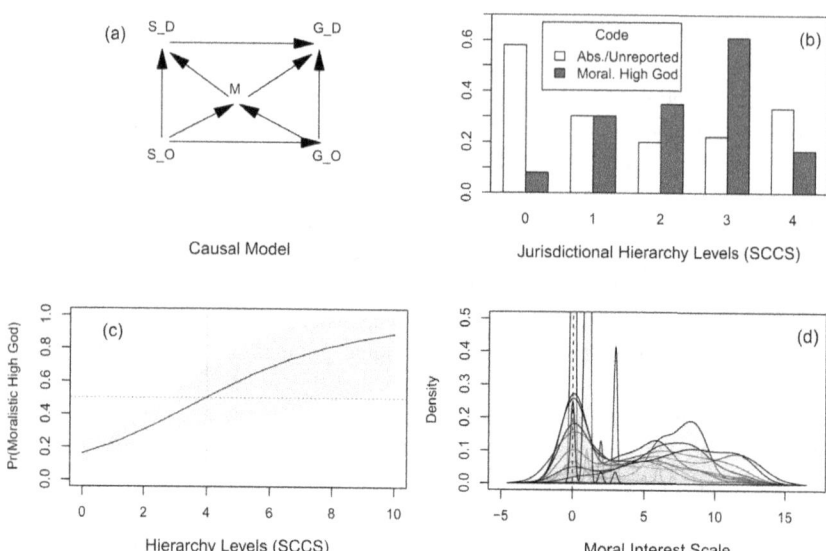

Figure 11.1 (a) Causal model of original size (S_O), having a moralistic god (G_O), observer effects (M), and actual data from quantitative databases. (b) Proportions of absent/unreported (white) and moralistic high gods (gray) across levels of jurisdictional hierarchy among 186 societies in the Standard Cross-Cultural Sample (SCCS). (c) Probability plot from logistic regression predicting probability of having a moralistic high god. Vertical line marks the maximum possible value in SCCS data and horizontal line marks the 50 percent chance. (d) Moral interest scale of "local deities" from twelve societies around the world. Data from (a) and (b) taken from D-PLACE.

not contain germane, veridical information that is subsequently converted to the corresponding data we can use for testing the hypothesis, hence, S_D → G_D. While historical reality had some corresponding effect on the data we can use, given the issues of source quality discussed, it is reasonable to assume that the source of the material also has some impact on what is subsequently knowable and testable. As such, source M is a central factor in the causal structure of the data's creation and therefore desirable to hold constant. Yet, even if we control for M in this model, S_0 remains a confounder as its influence on G_D works through G_0 and S_D. The model therefore suggests that the testable relationship between S_D → G_D is deeply confounded; assuming we can't control for the reality of history, the only way to deconfound an analysis in this case is to find a variable that blocks the paths from S_0 → G_D. While this simple causal model is not exhaustive of the process and not necessarily representative of other cultural domains, it does suggest that the data we use for this particular question—the relationship between moralistic traditions and traditional societies— pose complications for our tests. Setting this issue aside, we can now confront how we measure the presence of the "moralistic" aspects of religion using these data.

Table 11.1 Raw Frequencies of Levels of Jurisdictional Hierarchy by High God Type across All Societies in the SCCS (*n* = 186). Data from D-PLACE

Levels of Jurisdictional Hierarchy	High God Type					
	Abs./Unreported	Present, Inactive	Present, Active	Moralistic	No data	Sum
0	43	17	8	6	8	82
1	13	15	2	13	5	48
2	4	6	3	7	3	23
3	4	3	0	11	1	19
4	4	6	0	2	0	12
No data	0	0	0	1	1	2
Sum	68	47	13	40	18	186

But here we face another problem: while much of the contemporary study of religion is interested in the "moral dimensions" of religion, these data sets focus specifically on morally interested *high gods*. In fact, the EA and SCCS each have only a single variable pertaining to the content of religion, the "high god" variable (V34 and V238, respectively). Here, a "high god" is "a spiritual being who is believed to have created all reality and/or to be its ultimate governor, even though[4] his/her sole act was to create other spirits who, in turn, created or control the natural world" (cf. Swanson 1960: 210). This variable has four categorical options as possible data points:

1. absent or not reported [in the materials]
2. present but not active in human affairs[5]
3. present and active in human affairs but not supportive of human morality
4. present, active, and specifically supportive of human morality
5. missing data [data unavailable] (see Dow and Eff 2009 for discussion of missing data in the SCCS)

The SCCS includes 186 cultural groups in its sample. Table 11.1 reports the raw data. Sixty-eight of them (37 percent) were coded as having high gods that are "absent or not reported." This does *not* necessarily mean that these populations *don't* have high gods. Rather, the selected works might not have mentioned the issue for a host of reasons: (1) perhaps the high god wasn't important enough to have been noted by ethnographers, (2) ethnographers didn't bother to ask, (3) the people being studied didn't tell the ethnographer about it, or perhaps (4) the authors of the materials simply rejected the idea that the target populations had such gods (see above). In other words, "absent or not reported" can simply mean *not in the target literature describing the population*.[6]

Furthermore, a society may have been coded as "0" by virtue of not having a moralistic god that was a creator or ultimate governor. In other words, a society might have had moralistic gods, just not moralistic *high* gods (see next section for further discussion). In sum, this coding does not encapsulate contemporary questions and therefore is not an adequate source to confirm or refute the idea that small-scale societies had clear moral aspects to their gods, let alone their religious traditions.

What, then, can the SCCS data tell us about the relationship between moralistic high gods and social complexity? Out of the 186 societies, 40 (22 percent) are reported to have moralistic high gods while 86 (46 percent) are reported as either absent/unreported or have missing data outright. Roes and Raymond (2003: 129) treat the "jurisdictional hierarchy beyond local community" variable in the SCCS as indicative of society size. In other words, the number of recorded bureaucratic levels that are relevant for people beyond a group's closest network indicates how large and therefore interconnected a society is with another society, thus implying a level of greater complexity than a small-scale society that primarily keeps to itself. These data run from no levels ("no political authority beyond community") to four (e.g., "large states") levels. Here, the most common type of society is one with no such levels of hierarchy ($n = 82$; 44 percent of the entire SCCS sample) whereas the least common is represented by societies with four levels of hierarchy (6 percent). The modal society type with moralistic high gods is those with only one level of social complexity ($n = 13$, representing 7 percent of the entire sample).

If we look at the proportions of society type with the various high god codes, we see patterns that are consistent with the idea that moralistic high gods are associated with social complexity (Figure 11.1b). The dark bars effectively reproduce a graph in Peoples and Marlowe (2012) used to show a positive relationship between social complexity and moralistic high gods. For instance, 7 percent (6/82) of the societies coded with no broad hierarchy levels have moralistic high gods while 27 percent (13/48) of the societies with one level of hierarchy are coded as having such deities, followed by 30 percent at Level 2, 58 percent at Level 3, yet only 17 percent at level 4.

However, these values are a little misleading for a few reasons. First, these are within-society-level proportions; 7 percent (Level 0) certainly looks a lot smaller than 58 percent (Level 3), but there are only nineteen examples of Level 3 societies and eighty-two at Level 0. Second, the vast majority of Level 0 societies were coded with "Absent/Unreported." In fact, the highest frequency of any of the high god codes (23 percent of all coded societies) is where simplest societies have moralistic high gods coded as "absent or not reported." In other words, nearly a quarter of the entire data set is represented by this crude code. If we treat "absent or not reported" as an index of our ignorance about these small-scale societies, our knowledge of such societies is deeply impoverished.

Third, these proportions don't actually tell us what we want to know, namely, what the likelihood is that a society has a moralistic high god at varying levels of social complexity. Reports using these data (e.g., Botero et al. 2014; Roes and Raymond 2003; Skoggard et al. 2020) dichotomized these values, "thus creating a variable ... called *Moralizing* [High] *Gods*, with two values: either supportive of human morality, or not" (Roes 2009). Consistent with these efforts, we dichotomized the high god variable so that all societies with moralistic high gods were coded with a "1" while all other societies (other than those without data) were coded as a "0." We then used the jurisdictional hierarchy variable (from zero to four) to predict the probability of having a moralistic god.

In our reproduction of the essential prediction from previous studies, we too find a positive relationship. Unlike previous studies, however, we look directly at what the results mean. A simple logistic regression[7] shows that the chance of the simplest societies—those with no levels of jurisdictional hierarchy beyond local communities—having a moralistic god is 16 percent (95 percent CI = [0.10, 0.24]). The model predicts that as societal levels increase in number, so do the chances of having a moralistic high god. Societies with one level of social complexity have a 22 percent chance of having a moralistic high god, those with two levels are predicted to have a 30 percent chance, while those with three and four levels have a 40 percent and 50 percent chance, respectively. So, ignoring the aforementioned problems associated with source quality and how it might affect the reliability of the data, we do see a steady increase in the likelihood of having moralistic high gods as the levels of jurisdictional hierarchy increase. Despite this increase, however, the model actually tells us that *the chance that a society with the maximum level of social complexity—a four—has a moralistic high god is 50 percent*. In other words, a coin flip is about as useful to predict whether or not a random society with four levels of hierarchy has a moralistic high god. Based solely on this result, we shouldn't deny that there is a relationship, but we also should avoid claiming that it is a reliable or unambiguous one. Figure 11.1c shows that if we use the model to make predictions about societies with even more levels of hierarchy beyond four, there is nevertheless a predicted, steady increase in likelihood.

To recapitulate, accounts of small-scale populations are not without problems in terms of data quality, reliability of methods, and observations peppered with the biases and sentiments of the time in which they were recorded. Furthermore, cross-cultural databases that exploit these accounts are often coded using schemes that reflect interests of the times, such as moralistic *high gods* rather than general moralistic punishment from spiritual sources. A close look at the relationship between such gods and social complexity yields ambiguous results; while the relationship is positive, it is far from strong. More recent efforts recognize that specifically relying on "high gods" is too constrained to assess more recent ideas (Lightner, Bendixen, and Purzycki 2022; Purzycki, Henrich et al. 2018; Purzycki and Watts 2018; Watts, Greenhill et al. 2015). It is partly for this reason that there has been movement toward targeted studies of "moralistic" or "broad supernatural punishment" (e.g., Watts, Greenhill et al. 2015) in the literature instead of "high gods," a vestigial artifact of past generations' interests.

Taking Another, Closer Look

If we look at data beyond these particular sources, we find a portrait that resonates more with the anthropological view that acknowledges small-scale religions' moral relevance. Indeed, early and contemporary ethnographies as well as autobiographies of indigenous peoples not included in such databases also show indicators of various forms of moralistic supernatural punishment around the world:

- Paliyan gods: "On their own initiative punish incest, theft, or murder with an accident or illness" (Gardner 1972: 434; cf. 1991).
- Dogrib: "Wrongdoing [e.g., 'slacker[s]', womanizer[s], and other transgressors of … norms'] might also incur the visitation of supernatural illness" (Helm 1972: 79).
- Nuer: "Such moral faults as meanness, disloyalty, dishonesty, slander, lack of deference to seniors, and so forth, cannot be entirely dissociated from sin, for God may punish them even if those who have suffered from them take no action of their own account" (Evans-Pritchard 1956: 193).
- San ancestor spirits (//gangwasi): "Expect certain behavior of us. We must eat so, and act so. When you are quarrelsome and unpleasant to other people, and people are angry with you, the //gangwasi see this and come to kill you. The //gangwasi can judge who is right and who is wrong" (Lee 2003: 129–30).
- G/wi god's "anger is expected if some taboos are broken and as a result of certain acts … in order to show man's lack of arrogance and thereby to avoid [N!adima's] displeasure … Death and other misfortunes are sometimes attributed to his anger" (Silberbauer 1972: 319).
- Siouan religion has been indigenously characterized as forbidding "the accumulation of wealth and the enjoyment of luxury" (Eastman [1911] 1980: 9).
- The Inuit Sedna myth is about the spiritual consequences of selfishness where white bears punish people for past people's moral transgressions (Turner 1894: 261–2).
- Moralistic punishment in folktales among the Matsigenka (Izquierdo, Johnson, and Shepard Jr. 2008; Johnson 2003).

Boehm (2008) reviewed forty-three ethnographies covering eighteen foraging societies. In them, there are many instances of gods' punishment of behavior construed as "antisocial" and "predatory on fellow band members" found among *all* eighteen groups. In fact, in Swanson's (1960) classic dataset of fifty societies,[8] only six (12 percent) report instances of having a "moralizing high god," yet eleven (22 percent) are counted as "uncertain." However, 68 percent (34/50) of sampled populations have some documented form of "supernatural sanctions for morality," that is, "behaviors that helped or harmed other people" (212). In Watts et al.'s Pulotu data set (Watts, Sheehan et al. 2015), twenty-seven of the seventy-four (36 percent) Austronesian societies coded as "low political complexity" (acephalous or simple chiefdoms) had moralizing gods. And finally, contemporary individual-level ethnographic data increasingly shows that gods of small-scale societies are moralistically punitive (Purzycki, Willard, et al. 2022; Singh, Kaptchuk, and Henrich 2021; Townsend et al. 2020).

Data like these seem to elicit a common reflex, namely, the question: *how many of these examples are due to exposure to colonial and/or proselytizing religions?* A common—and relatively old (Evans-Pritchard 1965; Hartland 1898; Lang 1900: xiv)—response to evidence of moralistic gods' presence in small-scale societies appeals to external influences, typically Christian missionaries. Specifically, if small-scale populations have concepts of morally concerned gods, they must have been acquired from missionaries. This view, one which Evans-Pritchard (1965) characterized as "condescending" (107), is a common reaction to finding cases where smaller populations have something resembling a moralistic, punitive, and knowledgeable deity. Of course, many traditional populations incorporated Abrahamic beliefs into their ways of life and/or adjusted their own beliefs accordingly. However, there is no a priori reason to think that they did so systematically or that it was a one-way street (especially given the varied treatment of indigenous peoples by Christians). Ideally, researchers would have some index of exposure to imperial religions and some indicator of the kinds of relationships they forged with local populations. Indeed, there is variation across the reception of colonial traditions across society type; recent research shows that more socially complex societies are more likely to adopt the Christianity of colonial powers (Watts et al. 2018).

Looking Forward

In summary, throughout anthropology's intellectual history, the question of the development of so-called "moralistic traditions" has remained central. While early denials that traditional societies had moralistic components likely reflected a mixture of different definitions, ethnocentrism, and ignorance, they were in time overturned by more targeted efforts by anthropologists. Yet, the contemporary resurgence of commitment to the idea that small-scale religions had no moral dimensions is partly due to a heavy reliance on crudely recorded and coded qualitative data of varying reliability. Recent efforts, however, vindicate the anthropological view that moral elements of religion are not just ubiquitous but *central* in the ethnographic world (see Lightner and Purzycki, present volume; Bendixen and Purzycki, present volume).

In our view, the question of the relationship between social complexity and moralistic religions should remain open for these and other reasons (see McKay and Whitehouse 2015; Purzycki and Watts 2018). If using data from cross-cultural databases, researchers should ensure:

1. that key concepts (e.g., "moralistic" traditions or gods, social complexity, etc.) are operationalized clearly and validated appropriately (McKay and Whitehouse 2015)
2. clear delineation between "moralistic" and "morally relevant" (Teehan 2014)
3. that the "high god" concept is only relied on to the extent that it is relevant to one's research question
4. that important meta-data (e.g., variation in source quality due to racism, religious ethnocentrism, active knowledge of population, focus on target question; timing of source and cultural imports) is appropriately modeled (Watts et al. 2022)

The first point might seem obvious to social scientists, but it is often neglected. If the answer to the question of the relationship between social complexity and moralistic traditions really depends on our definitions, we had better be precise enough in our conception and consistent enough in our execution in order to make any project reproducible and open to scrutiny and replication. If the primary question we are to answer is about the presence or absence of religiously postulated consequences to how people treat each other, then researchers relying on the SCCS and EA should revisit the literature and not rely on the "high god" variable, which is problematic for a host of reasons we detailed in this chapter.

Another solution is to directly engage with the populations under consideration. In fact, recent direct, focused, and quantitative individual-level ethnographic inquiry into these matters shows that when individuals are directly asked if traditional gods care about punishing moral behaviors—theft, murder, and deceit—they tend to answer affirmatively, even after holding constant any correlations with the more obviously "moralistic" traditions (Purzycki, Willard, et al. 2022). Figure 11.1d shows that across twelve non-Western societies with varying modes of subsistence from around the world, the bulk of response distributions to a "gods' moral interest scale" about locally important deities are positive. The finding that traditional spirits are morally interested was illustrated and replicated in the Tyva Republic (Purzycki 2011, 2013b; Purzycki and Kulundary 2018). Similar patterns exist across two sites in Vanuatu (Atkinson 2018) that differ in how committed they are to Christianity. No obvious differences are apparent in their ratings of how morally interested traditional gods are. We also find that when asked, the Hadza (Apicella 2018)—who have largely resisted conversion to world religions—claim two traditional deities (represented by the sun and moon) are concerned with human morality. Notably, cases where people don't show this obvious proclivity include Fiji (McNamara and Henrich 2018), where commitment to ancestral spirits is shunned and responses are at basement levels; and fully market-integrated Mauritius (Xygalatas et al. 2018), where commitment to local spirits is forbidden. The high peaks at the lower values of the moral interest scale include these sites; high concentrations of scores of "0" on the scale are cases where worship of such deities is frowned upon (Bendixen, Apicella et al. forthcoming; Purzycki, Willard, et al. 2022). In sum, while one contemporary view—a view that anthropologists overturned nearly a century ago—is that traditional societies lack moralistic traditions or, more specifically, gods that care about morality, we find the opposite. When asked, traditional people will ascribe some moral concern to their deities. The question of when this trait cross-culturally developed remains open.

Acknowledgments

Purzycki thanks the Aarhus University Research Foundation and the Max Planck Institute for Evolutionary Anthropology. He acknowledges support from a *Consequences of Formal Education for Science and Religion Project* grant that was funded by the Issachar Fund. The authors thank Theiss Bendixen and Aaron Lightner for their feedback on earlier drafts.

12

Game Theoretical Aspects of the Minds of Gods

Aaron D. Lightner and Benjamin Grant Purzycki

Elements of Game Theory

Game theory is about understanding strategic interactions (Maynard Smith 1982; Von Neumann and Morgenstern 1953). Models in game theory are abstract and powerful tools that we can use to clarify a wide range of questions in the social and biological sciences, such as why male deer walk parallel to each other before a fight or why oak trees in the same forest grow to about the same height (Kokko 2007; McNamara and Leimar 2020). As we will discuss in this chapter, game theory is quite useful for understanding a wide range of dilemmas that are central to religious beliefs and practices (Bulbulia 2012; Purzycki and Sosis 2022).

To model an interaction as a *game* is to represent and analyze a structured scenario among multiple actors, whose actions affect the outcomes of the others. The outcome of a game is a set of *payoffs* to each actor, and these depend on the actors' chosen *strategies*. Game theoretical models can help us make predictions in otherwise unpredictable scenarios, but this requires some starting assumptions about how each actor will select a strategy. A common assumption, for example, is that each actor is self-interested and rational, and will therefore select their strategies based on expected *utility* (a general-purpose term of payoffs).

To see this, consider a game with two actors—let's call them Alice and Bob—who we assume will each choose the strategy that maximizes his or her expected payoff. This assumption not only helps us predict how they will choose their strategies but also how they will each respond to available information about how the other might behave. If Alice knows the strategies and payoffs available to Bob, then based on this knowledge she can choose the strategy that will produce her most favorable possible outcome. In this scenario, we can say that Alice has chosen a *best response*.

Alice might not always have complete knowledge about Bob's strategies and payoffs, however, meaning she is acting on incomplete information. If so, and if the game is repeated, then Alice and Bob might each learn from previous interactions to converge onto their own best responses (Binmore 2011). When Alice and Bob have each selected a best response, and neither can improve their payoffs by unilaterally switching strategies, then the outcome is called a Nash equilibrium (Nash 1950).

In a game, strategies and their associated payoffs might not only reflect people's preferences, but they can also represent organizational policies, social norms, or even genetically evolved traits. The latter applies to *evolutionary game theory*, which, as we discuss below, operates under a slightly different set of assumptions and concepts while bearing key similarities to standard game theory.

Game theoretic interactions are often characterized as competitive, but as we discuss next, most realistic game scenarios have the potential for both conflict and coordination, regardless of how we conceptualize strategies and utility.

Equilibria in Games of Conflict and Coordination

In Conan Doyle's "*The Final Problem*" (Doyle 2003: 736–55) a train scene occurs in which Professor Moriarty wishes to murder Sherlock Holmes while pursuing him from London to Dover. Holmes knows that Moriarty knows his destination, and vice versa, meaning that if Holmes departs at Canterbury, the intermediate stop, then Moriarty can anticipate this plan and also depart at Canterbury to accost Holmes. This might imply that Holmes should go to Dover as planned. And yet, Moriarty can also anticipate this alternative to his departure at Canterbury, implying that Holmes should, in fact, go to Canterbury (and so on, ad infinitum).

This simple scenario is an example of a game of *pure conflict*, because the strategies (depart at Canterbury or depart at Dover) available to each actor (Holmes and Moriarty) entail strictly opposing interests: Moriarty wishes to depart at the same stop as Holmes, and Holmes wishes that he and Moriarty will depart at different stops. Table 12.1 illustrates a payoff matrix of this dilemma, where each cell includes Holmes's and Moriarty's payoffs.

Now consider a different scenario: Alice and Bob are each driving on the same path toward each other, with a complete absence of traffic laws. If we are assuming that Alice and Bob are each rational, self-interested utility-maximizers, then we might assume that each prefers to avoid a collision. Hence, this Driving Game has at least two equilibria: Alice and Bob each choose to drive on their left, or they each choose to drive on their right (Binmore 1994). This simple scenario is an example of *pure coordination*, because the strategies (drive to the left or drive to the right) available to Alice and Bob must match for each actor to maximize his and her expected payoffs (Table 12.2).

Coordination solutions to repeated games, such as the equilibria in the Driving Game, can lead to social *conventions* (Lewis 1969). If Alice encounters Bob in a future

Table 12.1 Payoffs in a Game of Pure Conflict

	Moriarty	
Holmes	Canterbury	Dover
Canterbury	0,1	1,0
Dover	1,0	0,1

Table 12.2 Payoffs in a Game of Pure Coordination

	Bob	
Alice	Drive on the left	Drive on the right
Drive on the left	1,1	0,0
Drive on the right	0,0	1,1

driving scenario, and her past encounter leads her to believe that Bob will drive to the left, then her best response is to also drive to the left. If this type of encounter is repeated further, then over time both players can converge onto a default rule, or convention, such as "always drive on the left." Whenever Alice and Bob recognize this coordination problem in the future, they can both easily remember their convention for avoiding collisions, thereby solving their recurring coordination problem.

In a society, conventions can be codified into laws, norms, or ritual practices. They are stabilized by incentives, beliefs about other people's incentives, and a continuing preference for the coordination solution, such as avoiding collisions (Yamagishi and Suzuki 2009). No particular outcome is needed, so long as the convention is an equilibrium that continues delivering on everyone's preferences (Binmore 2011).

Game theory provides us with a powerful formal framework for representing a variety of dilemmas, where payoffs and actions matter to the individuals involved. The games we will discuss not only capture varying types of conflict and coordination as we described here, but they can also be useful for modeling dilemmas ranging from whether or not one would believe in god to how and why people are motivated to participate in religious rituals.

Minds of Gods and Games against Nature

In his posthumous collection of fragments (*Pensées*), mathematician and theologian Blaise Pascal argued that belief in God is a rational and pragmatic decision, given the expected payoffs for believing versus disbelieving (§233). Conceptualizing belief in God as a decision under risk, Pascal noted that the possible errors have asymmetric payoffs: a true positive is infinitely beneficial (i.e., heaven), but a false positive is a trivial error. Not believing when there is a god, however, entails eternal damnation. Table 12.3 spells out a candidate believer's possible payoffs to Pascal's Wager. The

Table 12.3 Pascal's Wager Payoff Matrix

	God Exist?	
Believe?	Yes	No
Yes	Eternal Bliss	Oops
No	Eternal Damnation	Bragging Rights

strategy individuals must choose is to believe or not believe, whereas the "strategy" imposed by nature is a hidden property about the universe: God either exists or does not exist (for a more extensive game theoretical analysis of this and other theological dilemmas, see Brams 1983, 2018).

Pascal's wager may be a problematic argument for a variety of philosophical and psychological reasons (e.g., can we safely assume that we choose our beliefs, or that there are virtually no costs to believing? See Brams 1982; Hacking 1972 for further discussion), but its underlying logic foreshadows a recurring theme among so-called evolutionary games against nature. That is, organisms in the natural world routinely must deal with fitness-relevant tasks that carry highly asymmetric costs and benefits among their possible errors (Haselton et al. 2009). Correct inferences have their benefits, but a failure to detect a hidden fact about the world can be devastating.

Superstitions and Faces in the Clouds

Genetically evolved traits are a bit like hypotheses about the environment. Under high levels of uncertainty, the success of a trait depends on it making a fitness-relevant bet about the environment's structure, and ultimately, being less wrong than other possibilities. We can therefore combine game theory with biological principles to usefully model the evolutionary process as different species' traits playing against the environment in different *games against nature*.

In evolutionary game theory's earlier days, theorists were interested in how evolved strategies (traits) were selected, where the relevant utility was not a preference among decision-makers but the probability of a strategy's continued survival. Hence, a higher utility would reflect a heritable strategy that properly hedges its bets against nature's "strategies," or the uncertain properties of the environment that might, with some probability, lead to a species' extinction (Lewontin 1961). This is a key difference in assumptions between evolutionary game theory versus standard game theory: strategies are not selected by a principle of rational choice but as a consequence of natural selection (Maynard Smith 1982).

This is especially important when we consider how individuals' preferences can diverge from their fitness-relevant interests. We might strongly prefer true inferences over false ones, for example, but our evolved intuitions are ultimately shaped by how they affect fitness, and not by how true they are (Prakash et al. 2021). True inferences are, of course, frequently useful for improving fitness, but only insofar as they serve our ability to make useful predictions that are both important to survival and able to handle some degree of error. Always making perfectly accurate decisions might intuitively seem like the optimal policy, but doing so is impractical, inefficient, and computationally intractable under even marginally complex and dynamic conditions (Bossaerts and Murawski 2017). It is often the case that practical and ecologically rational decision heuristics outperform more sophisticated decision strategies in highly uncertain but structured environments (Gigerenzer, Hertwig, and Pachur 2011).

Consider the prevalence of superstitions, or mistaken inferences about unknown cause–effect relationships. Superstitious beliefs and behaviors play a central role in religious thinking around the world (Evans-Pritchard 1956; Gmelch 1971; Malinowski 1932, 1992; Rozin, Millman, and Nemeroff 1986). This might seem puzzling from an evolutionary perspective: why should humans, a large-brained species with sophisticated cognitive adaptations (Barkow, Cosmides, and Tooby 1992), systematically make mistaken inferences about cause and effect?

This quandary incorrectly assumes that superstitions cannot be viewed as practical inferential strategies in an evolutionary game against nature, rather than merely irrational quirks that interfere with our pursuit of truth (Boyer 2018). In fact, a plausible explanation for *adaptive* superstition among human and nonhuman animals comes from the bet-hedging logic of error management theory (Haselton and Buss 2000; McKay and Dennett 2009). That is, simple and practical decision strategies can improve fitness in a noisy and uncertain world by managing the expected costs and benefits of two common types of error: false positives (belief in a falsehood) and false negatives (disbelief in a truth) (Trimmer et al. 2011). When presented with stimuli that might be causally linked, if the cost of a false negative is sufficiently high then natural selection will favor strategies that err on the side of committing false positives, resembling superstition (Beck and Forstmeier 2007).

To illustrate, suppose that an organism is regularly faced with a decision task where a noisy or error-prone cue (s_1, such as a sudden movement in the bushes) might sometimes precede a fitness-relevant outcome (s_2, such as a lurking predator). Given an instance of s_1, the organism can either take action based on an assumption that s_1 implies s_2, or it can assume the s_1 was a false alarm (perhaps, for example, if the sudden movement was caused by wind or a harmless herbivore). If the expected benefits and/or avoided costs of taking action (e.g., fleeing from the movement) is sufficiently greater than the expected cost of taking action, regardless of error rate, then an adaptive decision policy will be prone to more false positives and fewer false negatives. Specifically, and as Foster and Kokko (2009) show, a superstitious strategy, overestimating the probability that s_1 implies s_2, should evolve when $P(s_2|s_1)b > c$, where b is the benefit and/or avoided costs gained by taking action, and c is the cost of taking action. As $P(s_2|s_1)$ decreases—meaning that the true conditional probability of s_2, given an event of s_1, is lower than the decision-maker's behavior would suggest—this error management strategy will appear increasingly superstitious.

One aspect of religious belief that can be understood as error management is anthropomorphism, a "reasonable illusion" to which humans seem susceptible. Guthrie (1980) has championed the view that our propensity to see minds where there are none is a deeply ancestral trait, and evolved because it pays to run (or fly or swim) whenever we detect that something unknown has agency. In other words, it's better to bet that there's a predator afoot and run all the time than to be wrong once and get eaten. Running might have its costs, but they are nothing compared to losing one's life.

Table 12.4 details one possible payoff matrix for Guthrie's model (see also Bulbulia 2004). Here, the benefits of running, b, have costs, c, while staying put when there is a predator around entails a major loss, $-b$. As long as $b > c$, running will easily outcompete the alternative.

Table 12.4 An Example of a Payoff Matrix for Guthrie's Best Bet Hypothesis

	Predator?	
Run?	Yes	No
Yes	$b - c$	$b - c$
No	$-b$	0

When this cognitive bias is expressed culturally, it can result in plausible-seeming models of the world that assume human or humanlike forces are behind natural phenomena. Examples vary by culture, and they can include hidden messages, faces in the clouds (Guthrie 1993), teleological assumptions about the natural world (Kelemen 2004), and accusations of bad actors (including gods) behind ambiguous or unfortunate events (Gray and Wegner 2010; Jackson and Gray, present volume; Whitehouse 2011).

Although these cognitive tendencies and their bet-hedging logic are clearly important contributors of religious beliefs, religious systems also include a substantial social component that goes beyond beliefs about gods, ancestors, and spirits. In fact, religious traditions, histories, and rituals can also play a key role in shaping the social dilemmas that societies face.

Minds of Gods and Games against Others

Instead of modeling evolutionary games against nature, many early evolutionary game theorists influenced by the population genetics of Fisher (1930) also began focusing *games against others*. This paradigm retained its use of strategies as heritable traits (such as cooperativeness and aggression) and fitness as its metric of utility, but it emphasized population-level replicator dynamics among strategies engaging each other. An innovative analytic tool that emerged from this brand of evolutionary game theory was the *evolutionary stable strategy* (ESS), an applied version of the Nash equilibrium concept. An ESS refers to a strategy that, if widely adopted in the population, cannot be invaded by a mutant strategy by natural selection (Maynard Smith 1982).

Although the inherited strategies in evolutionary game theory typically represent genetically inherited traits, they can also represent culturally transmitted responses to a recurring social dilemma. This is especially important to note about games against others, because unlike games against nature, the actors in social dilemmas are often conceptualized as members of an interactive society, rather than as a simple population of organisms.

Societies everywhere must routinely solve problems of cooperation and conflict, both among individuals and between social groups. As we saw with the Driving Game discussed earlier, cultural conventions can be useful for avoiding undesirable outcomes, and the stakes of a recurring social dilemma might include costly land conflicts or depleting scarce resources. Institutions often seem to supply societies with solutions to social dilemmas, and religions are no exception.

Table 12.5 Prisoner's Dilemma (PD) Payoff Matrix for Player 1

	Player 2	
Player 1	C	D
C	$b-c$	$-c$
D	b	0

Cooperation and Supernatural Punishment

Humans and many other species are frequently altruistic, meaning that individuals cooperate with others by conferring some fitness benefit to others while forgoing a benefit to oneself. Many have argued that from an evolutionary perspective, this presents an apparent puzzle: Why should individual interests not take precedence over group interests?

The Prisoner's Dilemma (PD) formally illustrates this problem, and has been touted as "the purest expression of the conflict between individual and group interests" (McElreath and Boyd 2007). At its most basic, PD includes two strategies: cooperate, C, and defect, D. Table 12.5 details the benefits, b, and costs c for players in a basic PD.

In this basic PD, it's always better to defect. To see why, imagine a population of two pure strategies: always cooperate (ALLC) and always defect (ALLD). Call the frequency of cooperators p. The frequency of defectors is therefore $1 - p$. All individuals start with a baseline fitness of w_0. The fitness (W) of ALLC is therefore defined as:

$$W(ALLC) = w_0 + p(b-c) + (1-p)(-c)$$
$$= w_0 + pb - c$$

In other words, the fitness for ALLC is its baseline fitness plus its expected fitness after interacting with another individual. With probability p, this individual might be a cooperator, leading to a payoff of $b-c$, or with probability $1-p$, it might be a defector, leading to a payoff of $-c$. Similarly, $W(ALLD)$ is defined as:

$$W(ALLD) = w_0 + pb + (1-p)(0)$$
$$= w_0 + pb$$

Since $pb > pb - c$ (so long as $c > 0$), it follows that $W(ALLD) > W(ALLC)$. In other words, defectors will *always* outcompete cooperators.

When a dilemma like this occurs in a group setting—sometimes referred to as an n-person PD—it can easily result in a *commons problem*. Suppose, for example, that a community has some kind of valuable natural resource available to them, such as a common food or water supply. If this common resource is finite and overexploited, then it also carries some risk of collapse. The cooperative strategy, ensuring everyone in the community can benefit from the common resource, would be to use it with restraint. In contrast, the defect strategy would be to use the common resource without restraint, regardless of how this might withhold benefits for the rest of the community. If we suppose this hypothetical community contains ALLC and ALLD strategies (as we saw above), then defectors not only outcompete cooperators. They also virtually guarantee that the common resource will collapse, a consequence of everyone overusing it out of narrow self-interest. This result is called a *tragedy of the commons* (Hardin 1968).

This clearly is not the world in which we live. Human societies routinely cooperate with each other to sustain common resources, even where they are vulnerable to a temptation to defect. How, then, do societies reliably shift their incentives in a way that "solves" the PD by favoring widespread cooperation, rather than widespread defection? There are a few ways to manage this dilemma, each of which makes the prospect of defection less inviting.

One simple solution would be to impose a threat of substantial costs, or punishment, on defectors (Ostrom 1990). Let's call the cost of being punished for defection c_d. As long as the expected cost of defection, $E(c_d)$, outweighs the cost of cooperation (c, from Table 12.5), then $pb-c > pb-E(c_d)$. This means that, after including punishment for defection, cooperators outperform defectors (because $W(ALLC) > W(ALLD)$). The reason we use the *expected* cost of punishment is to explicitly state a critical ingredient of deterring possible defection through punishment: The looming threat of punishment, in the event of defection, must be sufficiently credible. We can write the expected cost of defection as $E(c_d) = c_d p(c_d)$, conveniently specifying the cost of being punished for defection, c_d, and the probability of being punished for defection, $p(c_d)$.

Credible threats of punishment for defection not only require enforcing cooperative rules but an ability to monitor behavior for violations of those rules. We can illustrate this by considering how a PD scenario, such as food sharing, might play out in a very small community. In such a context, behaviors and reputations are fairly easy to monitor, so punishments, such as retaliation or avoidance, would be easy to mete out when selfish behaviors occur. In other words, $p(c_d)$ is high. If c_d is also sufficiently high, then cooperation becomes a favorable strategy.

Now consider a contrasting example: large-scale societies and market economies, where individuals make frequent one-shot, impersonal exchanges with unrelated strangers. Here, $p(c_d)$ is lower than it was in our previous example because credible threats of punishment for defection are more difficult to achieve on a larger scale. This means that, all else being equal, $E(c_d)$ is relatively low, and our PD is much more likely to favor widespread defection. People can seemingly "cheat" with impunity when selling a used car, tipping for a service, or returning a lost wallet—especially when they need not worry about reputational consequences and an absence of future interactions. Commons problems, such as donating to a public radio station, shouldn't fare much better. If anonymous free riders could maximize their expected payoffs by receiving the results of the generous work of many others, all without making a contribution, then how did large-scale societies ever emerge?

Moralizing gods—gods who are omniscient, care about moral violations, and threaten to punish defectors—might help answer this question (Lang et al. 2019; Norenzayan et al. 2016, see Purzycki and McKay, present volume). In a PD, widespread belief in moralizing gods can shift incentives in a way that favors cooperation, resulting from a fear of supernatural punishment (Johnson and Bering 2006; Schloss and Murray

2011)—even where defection might be otherwise beneficial, like we'd see in a one-shot and anonymous interaction (Johnson 2015). This is a potentially powerful solution to the PD; if we conceptualize belief in supernatural punishment as a culturally inherited strategy, then it will spread alongside other forms of punishment for defection in formal evolutionary models (Lane 2018), such as the retaliatory strategies that are possible in smaller-scale settings. Hence, assuming communication is possible, we can construe appeals to supernatural punishment as attempts to control other people's social behaviors, ultimately motivating them to behave in ways that benefit others (Cronk 1994; Fitouchi and Singh 2022). The looming threat of supernatural punishment has the potential to expand people's cooperative circles, introducing mutually beneficial solutions to cooperative problems that would have been difficult for individuals to consider otherwise. We revisit this point below.

Coordination and Signaling Trust

Despite the narrowly selfish behaviors that a standard PD motivates, human life is filled with scenarios where it is mutually beneficial for individuals to cooperate, especially in the long term. The Stag Hunt captures such scenarios. It imagines two hunters who must decide to either help each other pursue a large stag, the success of which requires the effort of two people cooperating, or to each individually hunt small hares, which does not require any cooperative effort. Hence, a standard Stag Hunt game has two strategies: players can hunt hares, or they can hunt stags. The mutually cooperative outcome (hunting stags) is in the interests of both individuals, so long as they can commit to working toward the same outcome together (Skyrms 2003). Table 12.6 details the benefits in a standard Stag Hunt gained from hunting stags, S, versus the benefits of hunting hares, h, where $h < S$.

As the payoff matrix suggests, the Stag Hunt introduces a coordination problem that is akin to the Driving Game discussed above: Each player's best response is to do what the other player is doing. Hunting hares yields a low but certain payoff, regardless of what the other actor does. Hunting stags yields a high payoff to both players, but only if the players coordinate doing so together—otherwise, the stag hunter who took a risk on a partner who chose the hare gets nothing. This dilemma between high-risk/high-reward stags versus low-risk/low-reward hares implies that rational utility-maximizers would be wise to choose the risk-averse hare strategy if unsure what other players will do. If they can trust that others will commit to stag hunting, however, then they should also commit to stag hunting. Cooperators can mutually benefit if they find

Table 12.6 Payoff Matrix for the Stag Hunt Game

	Player 2	
Player 1	Stag	Hares
Stag	S, S	$0, h$
Hares	$h, 0$	h, h

partners whose behaviors are predictably cooperative, meaning that in the Stag Hunt, communicating trustworthiness is critical.

In many ways, the Stag Hunt game best captures the nature of a social contract. Players need to somehow collectively agree to move from a suboptimal convention (everyone hunts hares) to a more optimal one (everyone hunts stags). In the absence of communication and trust, getting everyone to make this commitment is difficult. Religious beliefs and institutions can improve the prospects for doing so, however, coordinating sustainable and unconditional solutions to a cooperative dilemma (Bulbulia 2012; Shaver and Bulbulia 2016).

To see an example of this, let's return to supernatural punishment beliefs. Shared beliefs in a moralizing god inspire prosociality among distant strangers, often from distant regions and otherwise different cultural backgrounds (Lang et al. 2019). Nevertheless, cooperative believers are clearly vulnerable to exploitation by nonbelievers, because nonbelievers can instill trust by feigning belief before defecting against a believer. How, then, can believers reliably identify who among them can be trusted to also believe in supernatural punishment (and thus, to share the same incentives that motivate cooperation)? If there were a way for strangers to honestly signal their shared identities, and to communicate their cooperative intentions to each other, then this would greatly improve our prospects of expanding cooperation beyond kin and other tight-knit networks.

Religious rituals are useful for improving within-group coordination, precisely because they can signal common commitments to a religious identity (Sosis and Alcorta 2003). Communities with shared religious identities often have ritual obligations that entail opportunity costs that serve as hard-to-fake signs of commitment to the ingroup (Irons 2001), because for true believers, the perceived costs of these obligations are lower than they are for nonbelievers (Sosis 2003). This view conceptualizes ritual as a form of communication that improves the prospects of trust and cooperation among coreligionists. Commitment displays might have assisted the spread of Islam in Africa among long-distance trade routes, for example, where conflicts of interest among resource holders and traveling merchants can easily lead to defection by the traveling merchants (a principal agent problem; see North 1990). Both parties can instill trust, however, by credibly communicating (e.g., through daily prayer, Ramadan fasting, and the annual Hajj) that they are each committed to honoring a mutually beneficial code of conduct with supernatural sanctions—despite their geographic and cultural differences (Ensminger 1997).

Engineering an Ecosystem

Religions also help coordinate solutions to the "us vs. nature" problems that societies face, beneficially shaping how people engage their environments. A classic example of this is the water temple system used for coordinating watering schedules among Balinese rice farmers (Lansing and Kremer 1993). Rice farming collectives called *subaks* must manage two competing ecological pressures: crop pests and water availability. Crop pests affect everyone equally, whereas water availability is limited for downstream subaks, depending on how much water is used first by upstream subaks.

Table 12.7 Payoff Matrix for the Coordination Problem Faced by Upstream and Downstream Subaks in Bali

	Downstream	
Upstream	Time A	Time B
Time A	$1-d, 1$	$1-r, 1-r$
Time B	$1-r, 1-r$	$1, 1-d$

A simplified version of this scenario is modeled as a game between an upstream subak and a downstream subak in Table 12.7, where payoffs represent crop yields for each subak. The upstream subak and the downstream subak can choose to water their fields at one of two times of year (let's call them Time A and Time B).

If subaks coordinate by watering their fields at the same time, then they mutually benefit by reducing crop pests, but the upstream subak will deplete the water available to the downstream subak, reducing the downstream subak's crop yield by d. The downstream subak can avoid losses due to water depletion by not coordinating their timing with the upstream subak, but then crop pests will reduce the crop yields for both subaks by r.

The resulting coordination game incentivizes the upstream subak to always use water at the same time as the downstream subak. The downstream subak should only want to coordinate its timing with the upstream subak if crop pest damages outweigh the costs of water depletion ($r > d$). If the upstream subak depletes the water so much that the downstream subak would prefer crop pest damages to water depletion ($r < d$), then the downstream subak should be motivated to not coordinate. Hence, the dilemma for the upstream subak is to not only ensure that they coordinate their timing of water use with the downstream subak but also to minimize their water use in a way that keeps the downstream subak motivated to coordinate (Lansing and Miller 2005).

As we've seen throughout this chapter, communicating and forming conventions can greatly improve the prospects for resolving this type of dilemma. In Bali, these improvements are supplied by the water temple system, where subaks make coordination pacts with mutual displays of deference to deities. In reality, and scaled beyond the two-player simplification we've discussed here, this subak water temple system is a complex network that has sustained coordination among subaks for centuries—not through punishment but through a signaling system that improves communication among parties with overlapping interests (Lansing and Fox 2011).

Another example of a religious system improving a local coordination problem can be found with the Australian Martu, whose landscape burning practices increase the local plant biodiversity. This, in turn, leads to high and sustained numbers of small herbivores that attract the monitor lizards who prey on them. These lizards not only provide food resources for the Martu, but hunting them has downstream social effects like the establishment and strengthening of food sharing relationships (Bliege Bird and Power 2015). Controlled burning practices are an important group effort in this region, and the regions where burning is practiced are the regions where lizard hunting is relatively successful (Bliege Bird et al. 2013).

Table 12.8 Payoff Matrix for Player 1 in a Martu Burning Dilemma

	Player 2	
Player 1	Burn	Don't burn
Burn	L	l − c
Don't burn	l	l

We can frame Martu burning practices as a Stag Hunt, where the payoffs of collective burning can ensure the individual- and group-beneficial payoff of high lizard numbers, L. If few people participate then the burning practices might be ineffective despite the effort expended by the participant, c, and if no one participates then each individual must hunt from a small lizard population, l, where $L > l$. See Table 12.8.

This coordination problem is improved by the religious beliefs associated with the burning practices, because Martu associate them with *Jukurrpa*, an idea that a failure to participate in burning practices would result in the end of the world. By incentivizing burning over not burning, this belief can serve as a mechanism for helping individuals converge toward, and remain stably committed to, the coordination solution of this locally important social dilemma (Bird et al. 2016).

Conflict over Territory and Resources

While coordination is clearly important for resource maintenance, a scarcity of resources often leads to conflict, especially when linked to a desirable territory. The Hawk–Dove game models this type of scenario, where two strategies compete for a resource with some fitness benefit, v. The Hawk strategy, H, always fights for the resource and never retreats, whereas the Dove, D, strategy might display a threat, but will retreat if attacked.

If a Hawk encounters a Dove, then the Dove will retreat uninjured, and the Hawk will get the resource without challenge. If two Doves meet in a given encounter, then the resource will either be randomly taken by one of the individuals, or, if possible, evenly shared. If two Hawks meet, however, they will each incur a fighting cost c. Assuming equal fighting abilities among two randomly selected Hawks in a population, a Hawk can expect to win (and take the resource) in half of its encounters.

These payoffs are shown in terms of fitness benefits, v, and costs, c, to Hawk and Dove strategies in Table 12.9.

Are either of these strategies stable enough to withstand invasion from the other? To answer this, let us create our own population. Assume that in this case, Doves are almost entirely absent (p, the frequency of encountering a Hawk, is approximately 1). Hawks primarily interact with other Hawks. Their approximate expected fitness, W(H), then, would be

$$W(H) \approx w_0 + (1)V(H|H) + (0)V(H|D)$$
$$W(H) \approx w_0 + \frac{v-c}{2}$$

Table 12.9 Hawk–Dove Payoff Matrix for Player 1

	Player 2	
Player 1	H	D
H	$(v-c)/2$	v
D	0	$v/2$

In other words, the expected fitness of a Hawk would be their baseline fitness, w_0, the payoffs of interacting with another Hawk, $(v-c)/2$ times the probability of interacting with another Hawk (remember, in our created world, it is ≈ 1), and the payoff of interacting with a Dove times the likelihood of interacting with a Dove (in this case, 0). If we introduce a Dove into this world, its expected payoff is thus:

$$W(D) \approx w_0 + V(D|H)$$
$$\approx w_0 + 0$$

What, then, is required to ensure that $W(H) < W(D)$? We can answer this question by plugging in what we know to the above equations, which simplifies to $v < c$. What this means is that Doves can only invade the population when fighting costs outweigh the value of the resource.

Monitoring and enforcing the borders of a given territory can be costly and difficult, and it might nevertheless lead to costly conflicts over contested land or resources. One way to curb these types of risks and tensions among communities would be to encourage widespread beliefs in locally powerful deities who monitor and enforce respect for existing territories.

Consider, as an example, the Tyvan spirit-masters who are associated with ritual structures that people approach with reverence and prayer offerings. Each spirit-master cares about its local territory and its natural resources, and is believed to be knowledgeable about the goings on in its territory. Spirit-masters are angered over exploiting resources, violations of which are believed to be met with devastating consequences (Purzycki 2011, 2013a). These beliefs and their attendant practices can shift incentives in a way that favors preserving resources that are otherwise at risk of overexploitation (Purzycki 2016). This clearly resembles a solution to an n-person PD, discussed above, where a common resource is susceptible to widespread defection and the incentives are tilted toward widespread cooperation.

Another aspect of these gods' concerns worth emphasizing is that the ritual requirements linked to territory structures might serve an additional function. By indicating spirits present at a given border, and by requiring passersby to acknowledge their presence, individuals are expected to respectfully engage the existing border structures in the region. The scenario resembles a Hawk–Dove game, because whereas different camps can share the land with a mutual "dovish" respect for existing territories, they might also be tempted to engage in a risky and "hawkish" expansion into new territories, particularly if more livestock requires more grazing land. In this context, ritual structures and their attendant spirit-masters can motivate a mutual dovish respect through threats of supernatural punishment, specifically by increasing the perceived fighting costs in a way that favors a dovish strategy, where $v < c$. Similar to the moralizing gods example we saw above, this shift in incentives is accompanied by a shift in the social signals that people can deploy to instill trust among their coreligionists. Indeed, people who conform to the ritual expectations of the local spirit-masters tend to inspire trust among observers (Purzycki and Arakchaa 2013).

Future Directions and Open Questions

Anthropologists have long recognized that traditional institutions tend to be useful for dealing with locally important dilemmas (Rappaport 1968; Steward 1972), but explaining this pattern has been more challenging. How do traditional institutions, such as religions, give rise to adaptive practices among diverse social and ecological settings? Explanations invoking processes like transmitted culture and cognitively attractive ideas are undoubtedly important for understanding religion (Jackson and Gray, present volume), because religious beliefs are intuitive—for good evolutionary reasons, as we discussed earlier—and they are also socially learned.

And yet, if we want a complete explanation of how religious systems can adjust to a complex and dynamic environment, then we must also carefully consider: (1) how the individuals will attend to their expected payoffs in a given environment, and (2) when and how religious beliefs about gods' minds, and corollary practices such as rituals, impact the scope for improving coordination and reducing costly conflicts (Bendixen and Purzycki 2020). As we've outlined in this chapter, game theory provides us with a powerful formal framework for doing so. Through its lens, we can clarify how and why religious traditions are often linked to behaviors that might not be incentivized on an individual level.

The examples we've discussed through a game theoretic lens are nevertheless, in many cases, post hoc interpretations of social and environmental dilemmas. Game theoretic models are simple and useful tools for predicting behavior based on a minimal set of assumptions, but their role in explaining how religious traditions can resolve social dilemmas will be substantially improved as their empirical predictions are put to the test in future research. To do this, rich ethnographic descriptions of societies' challenges "on the ground" should inform which payoffs individuals are likely to deem relevant, what resulting conflicts of interest could threaten their social or ecological stability, and how we would predict religious systems to improve the prospects of reducing such conflicts.

Acknowledgments

Both authors thank the Aarhus University Research Foundation for support. Purzycki expresses thanks to the students in his Minds of Gods classes for their discussions and input, and both authors thank Theiss Bendixen and an anonymous reviewer for helpful comments that greatly improved this chapter. Thanks to Steven Brams and Joseph Bulbulia for their suggestions.

13

Accounting for Cross-Cultural Variation in the Minds of Gods

Theiss Bendixen and Benjamin Grant Purzycki

Introduction

Many contemporary cognitive and evolutionary accounts of religion converge on the insight that religious thought and behavior exploit reliably developing psychological systems (Geertz 2020; see in present volume: Balch and McNamara; Burdett; Johnson). While much work has focused on identifying such building blocks of mental and behavioral aspects of religion (see in present volume: Purzycki and Schjoedt; Sørensen and Purzycki; Teehan; Wildman and Lane), comparably little attention has been allocated to systematically assessing and accounting for cross-cultural variation in beliefs about what concerns the gods, and what the behaviors gods care about tell us about local social life.

In this chapter, we discuss current approaches to cross-cultural variation in beliefs about and appeals to gods and their postulated concerns and, on that basis, advance a cultural evolutionary account that includes a set of criteria for predicting the set of concerns and interests that a given deity might be associated with in varying socioecological contexts (Bendixen, Apicella et al. forthcoming; Bendixen and Purzycki 2020, 2021; Bendixen, Lightner, and Purzycki forthcoming). We then survey a range of ethnographic case studies, primarily in the context of smaller-scale societies, and assess how the predictive criteria stack up against this evidence. In essence, we argue that gods and spirits are cross-culturally associated with specific concerns and appeals that point to problems and challenges of local social life—what we refer to as "god-problems." We conclude that available ethnographic case studies are consistent with the outlined "god-problem" predictions, but that more work is required to fully evaluate the relationship between god appeals and local social ecologies. To that end, we consider avenues for future research on cross-cultural variation in beliefs about and appeals to the minds of gods.

Current Accounts of Cross-Cultural Religious Variation

Several lines of research identify religious variation as functions of local social and ecological factors. For instance, Baumard and Boyer (2013) argue that moralizing religious traditions originally arose as a response to increased material affluence (see also Baumard et al. 2015). Based on one variant of life-history theory, they argue that when basic human needs such as access to food and protection are met, people "turn their attention to other domains of evolved preferences, such as maximizing personal wellbeing, enjoying friendship, and cultivating aesthetics, the good life that is portrayed as the goal of many moral movements. Consistent with this, moralizing religions recruited their first adepts among the affluent social classes ..." (Baumard and Boyer 2013: 277).

Evidence for this view includes the observation that moralizing world religions emerged and spread out from particularly fertile geographical regions. Most such research assumes that "moralizing religions" are those that include gods that care about human morality. However, setting aside the controversial application of life-history theory (e.g., Nettle and Frankenhuis 2020) and that cross-cultural individual-level data does not support the predicted association between material security and moralizing god beliefs (Purzycki et al. 2018), the argument hinges on the critical assumption that moralizing religions do not usually emerge until a society reaches some threshold level of energy capture. While this and related assumptions (e.g., society size, urbanity, etc.) are central to many current debates in the cognitive and evolutionary science of religion, emerging empirical evidence (Beheim et al. 2021; Bendixen, Apicella et al. forthcoming; McNamara, Norenzayan, and Henrich 2016; McNamara and Henrich 2018; McNamara et al. 2021; Purzycki 2011 2013a, 2016; Purzycki, Willard et al. 2022; Shaver, Fraser, and Bulbulia 2017; Singh, Kaptchuk, and Henrich 2021; Townsend et al. 2020) as well as general surveys of the ethnographic literature (Boehm 2008; Purzycki and Sosis 2022; Swanson 1960) seem to suggest that many deities of smaller-scale societies are, in fact, morally concerned to some significant degree (see also below and Petersen, present volume; Purzycki and McKay, present volume).

Other analyses show that moralizing god beliefs arise in materially *insecure* societies (Botero et al. 2014; Hayden 1987; Skoggard et al. 2020; Snarey 1996). According to this body of work, moralizing deities that are watchful of human behavior and punitive in cases of deviance from collective moral norms (e.g., theft, generosity, murder, kindness, etc.) are a culturally evolved response to threats such as environmental stress and resource scarcity, since societies under threat can particularly benefit from the notion of a punitive and monitoring "eye in the sky" that curbs defection and enforces fair distribution of limited common goods (cf., Peoples and Marlow 2012).[1]

Extending this view with a synthesis of historical and experimental evidence, Norenzayan et al. (2016) and Henrich (2020, ch. 4) argue that beliefs in morally knowledgeable, monitoring, and punitive deities generally contribute to within-group cooperation thereby bolstering a cultural group in the competition with other groups, thus further increasing the cultural selection for moralizing god beliefs (see also Atran and Henrich 2010; Lang et al. 2019; Roes and Raymond 2003). Related to these views, Jackson et al. (2021) advance the suggestion that religious traditions that include notions of supernatural punishment of norm violations arise in and sustain "tight" societies (Gelfand et al. 2011), where strict norm adherence is particularly critical to social cohesion, perhaps as a consequence of environmental shocks or group conflicts (Caluori et al. 2020; Skali 2017, see also Jackson and Gray, present volume).

There is mixed empirical evidence for these views. Cross-culturally, general levels of religious commitment indeed seem to rise in the wake of natural catastrophes (Sibley and Bulbulia 2012; Sinding Bentzen 2019; but see Mauritsen, Bendixen and Reintoft n.d.) and war (Henrich et al. 2019) and decline in the context of well-functioning governments (Zuckerman, Li, and Diener 2018). Across a number of observational and experimental studies, Jackson et al. (2021) find that ecological threats predict punitive religious beliefs and that this relationship is partly mediated by cultural tightness. Further, food insecurity predicts increased commitment to moralistic deities (but not to "local" deities and spirits) across more than two thousand participants from fifteen diverse cultures (Baimel et al. 2022), and high material insecurity combined with beliefs in punitive ancestor spirits (but not punitive beliefs about the Christian God) predict increased in-group favoritism in an economic game experiment among Yasawa Fijians (McNamara, Norenzayan, and Henrich 2016). On the other hand, across eight field sites, Purzycki et al. (2018) failed to find evidence for any relationship between food insecurity and ratings of locally relevant deities as moralistic, punitive, or omniscient.

While these approaches and findings are valuable, they mostly focus on the explicitly moralistic aspects of deities (for a detailed discussion of this issue, see Purzycki and McKay, present volume). This, in turn, has left a lacuna in contemporary research of how to account for other matters that are also often associated with deities. What are these "other matters"? On the basis of a general survey of ethnographic work, Purzycki and McNamara (2016) classify the concerns of deities into three broad classes, namely as having to do with human behavior around or toward other people (morality, virtue, etiquette), the gods (rituals, beliefs), and nature (ecology, natural resource management). Similarly, McNamara and Purzycki (2020) argue that god beliefs and appeals coevolve with features of local socioecological conditions and the local cultural psychology. For instance, cultures of honor are typically found in socioecological settings such as pastoral societies where land is sparsely inhabited, formal institutions are weak, and displays of individual toughness are an informal avenue to maintaining social order (Cao et al. 2021; Nisbett and Cohen 1996). If the minds of gods are indeed reflections of such socioecological patterns, gods in these societies are predicted to be perceived as concerned with behaviors that support the underlying norms and values. According to McNamara and Purzycki (2020), such behaviors should include ritual displays at geographically strategic locations, such as border territories, that signal trustworthiness (Purzycki and Arakchaa 2013), and punishing deviations from norms that compromise honorable reputation management (but, crucially, not punishing acts of redemption that seek to offset a previous misdeed, since a culture of honor deems this acceptable, if not the required, behavior). While compelling, these predictions remain largely untested.

In this latter view, then, beliefs about and appeals to the minds of gods are complex products of the interaction between local socioecological conditions, cultural–historical contingencies, and cognitive constraints of the human mind (see also McNamara, present volume). The cultural evolutionary account developed in this chapter, and to which we now turn, builds on this work by deriving a more general set of predictive criteria of the kinds of behaviors that we might expect deities to be associated with in varying socioecological contexts.

"God-problems": A Cultural Evolutionary Account of Variation in Gods' Minds

We propose that cultural models of gods' concerns point to particular kinds of challenges and problems—and behaviors that mitigate them—that people face or have faced together in the past. We refer to such problems as "god-problems" and argue that they have generally recurring features (cf., Bendixen, Apicella, et al. forthcoming; Bendixen, Lightner, and Purzycki forthcoming; Bendixen and Purzycki 2020). First, since social life is rife with temptations to free ride on the efforts of the collective, gods and spirits should generally be concerned with threats to cooperation and coordination or behaviors that address such threats. Specifically, we would expect god-problems to take the form of game-theoretic dilemmas (see Lightner and Purzycki, present volume): scenarios in which the collective maximally benefits when all members fully cooperate, but each individual maximally benefits (at least in the short term) if everybody else fully cooperates while they themselves free ride, thus creating a conflict of interest between the collective and the individual. Further, in order to qualify as threats to the fabric of social living, god-problems must reflect social dilemmas that are central to local social life.

Are all costly and/or salient social dilemmas potential god-problems? Rather, we suggest that potential god-problems constitute the subset of local social dilemmas, where defection is not easily monitored and sanctioned by (appeals to) secular institutions. Beliefs about and appeals to watchful and punitive superhuman forces are possibly convincing and effective at curbing temptations to free ride when well-functioning secular alternatives are unavailable (e.g., Johnson 2005; Rossano 2007; Rossano and LeBlanc 2017), and particularly when a wide variety of maladies can be interpreted as instances of supernatural punishment (e.g., Hartberg, Cox, and Villamayor-Tomas 2016; Leeson and Suarez 2015), or when the harmful consequences of widespread deviance are nonobvious. In essence, appealing to the concerns of gods and spirits—for example, by explaining "bad luck," illness, and deaths as instances of supernatural intervention resulting from some norm violation (Boyer 2021; Fitouchi and Singh 2022)—is a culturally evolved social technology that recruits reliably developing cognitive intuitions and aligns collective interests. Therefore, appeals to gods and spirits will culturally evolve to include behaviors that point to the kinds of challenges that people and communities face, in particular conflicts of interest and threats to coordination and cooperation.

A recent free-list study conducted across eight diverse societies found preliminary support for this account and its predictive criteria, in that cross-culturally spirits' and deities' concerns indeed seem to point to local threats to cooperation and mitigating behaviors (Bendixen et al. forthcoming). However, to assess the evidential basis for these predictions more broadly, in the next section, we review a range of ethnographic observations. We first turn to a more detailed analysis of a particularly rich ethnographic case study and how the god-problem criteria fare in the face of this material. We then embark on a wider tour of the ethnographic record.

Ethnographic Evidence

Forest Spirits and Environmental Preservation in the Maya Lowlands, Guatemala

Atran et al. (2002) studied three distinct cultural–ethnic groups living in the same rainforest habitat in the Maya Lowlands: a native population, the Itza' Maya, and two migrant groups. As determined across a range of physical measurements (e.g., in terms of forest clearing, soil quality, biodiversity, etc.), the researchers found that of those three groups the Itza' practiced simultaneously the most productive and least destructive agricultural forms (see also Atran et al. 1999; Atran and Henrich 2010; le Guen et al. 2013). This superiority in sustainable subsistence practices appears partly a result of detailed cognitive and cultural models of the environment among the Itza', including an increased "awareness of ecological complexity and reciprocity between animals, plants, and people" (Atran et al. 2002: 432). Importantly, the Itza' is also the only group where the local spirits are perceived as "actively protecting the forest" (439), for instance, by punishing violations of the spirits' preferences for certain species and patches of land. These preferences are hypothesized to "represent a synthesis of experience accumulated over generations" and "violations of spirit preferences can lead to accidents, falling ill, or worse. It matters little if the supernatural threat is real or not: *if people believe in it, the threat of punishment becomes a real deterrent*" (le Guen et al. 2013: 781, our emphasis). In other words, although at least one of the neighboring groups also uphold taboos on certain locations in the forest such as mountain caves and water streams, only among the traditional Itza' does conservation of nature unambiguously constitute a "god-problem." This belief system in turn appears to change the perceived payoff of exploiting nature in the short term, resulting in both more sustainable and productive foraging and agricultural practices (for a strikingly similar case, see Eder (1997) on the traditional Batak people of Palawan Island, the Philippines, as discussed in Purzycki, Bendixen, et al. 2022).

This case study lends direct support to the god-problem criteria, in that local spirits are believed to care about a pertinent and pressing social dilemma (environmental preservation) with individually opaque payoffs (since the collapse of cooperation depends on widespread defection, not any one individual defecting now and then) that seems to be effectively enforced by appeals to supernatural monitoring and punishment (according to physical measurements, the Itza' practice the most sustainable way of life) in lieu of secular alternatives (e.g., monitoring other people in a dense rainforest is unfeasible and the Itza' have "few cooperative institutions" to appeal to; Atran et al. 2002: 440). The richness of the ethnographic material further allows us to discern why only one of the local groups under investigation, the native Itza', views forest preservation as a god-problem; namely, a combination of inherited folk ecological knowledge and attitudes, cultural tradition and historical contingency, and a lack of readily available formal institutions.

So far so good for the god-problem criteria. However, there are many other suggestive instances in the ethnographic record that shed light on why the minds of gods might have the qualities and attributes they do. We now tour such instances and assess the wider applicability of our account of cross-cultural variation in god beliefs and appeals.

An Ethnographic Tour of Gods' Minds

As we have just seen with the Itza' Maya, in many foraging societies, from Siberia (e.g., Jordan 2003, ch. 6) over Southeast Asia (e.g., Eder 1997; Hood 1993) and Japan (e.g., Murdock 1934: 183–4) to the North American plains (e.g., Brightman 1993: 187–92, 368) and sub-Saharan Africa (e.g., Schapera 1930: 184–5), a widespread notion is held that people live in a reciprocal relationship with features of their environment, including local plants, animals, and spirits (see also Baimel, present volume; Bird-David 1999; Rossano 2007). One implication of this belief system is that hunters can only take prey that "presents itself" to the hunters, that hunters must pay ritualized respects to killed animals and their guardian spirits, and that bad luck or illness will ensue if people do not perform these ritual acts and if they hunt or forage excessively (Purzycki 2011, 2013a, 2016) or are generally wasteful and disrespectful toward nature (Eder 1997, 1999). Managing natural resources is a game-theoretic social dilemma, where appeals to watchful and punitive superhuman forces alter the perceived payoffs of unconstrained exploitation (see Lightner and Purzycki, present volume), and resource management is an object of supernatural monitoring and sanctioning in many smaller-scale societies (Hartberg, Cox, and Villamayor-Tomas 2016). Similarly, supernaturally enforced ritual traditions and ceremonies sometimes appear aligned with conservation and fair distribution of resources, such as ritualized burning of land among Australian Aborigines (Bliege Bird et al. 2013) and North American Indians (Connors 2000), water temples in Bali (Lansing et al. 2017), and ritual markings of the beginning and end of seasonal harvesting and foraging taboos (see Rogers 2020, for a formal treatment of the dilemma involved in harvesting too early), for instance, among traditional peoples of Tanna, Vanuatu (Bonnemaison 1991; Flexner et al. 2018; Kouha 2015), North America (Connors 2000; Murdock 1934: 293), and Siberia (Jordan 2003, ch. 8).

Spirits are conceived of as "social actors" who care about the going-ons in the local community and desire people to adhere to local social norms and taboos (Bird-David 1999; McNamara et al. 2021; Rossano 2007; Shaver, Fraser, and Bulbulia 2017). For instance, among the Batek of Malaysia, a nomadic hunter-gatherer society with few formal hierarchical institutions, many moral transgressions are perceived as sanctioned by supernatural forces (Endicott and Endicott 2014). Likewise, to the Birhor of mainland India, an egalitarian people with limited formal leadership, violations of communal sharing norms evoke supernatural punishment, and the afterlife rewards ethical living (Adhikary 1999). In recent cross-cultural studies using both free-listing (Bendixen, Apicella, et al. forthcoming; Bendixen, Lightner, and Purzycki forthcoming) and item response scales (Purzycki, Willard, et al. 2022), all investigated deities were attributed moral concern to some noticeable degree.

Above and beyond general moral behaviors, supernaturally enforced taboos also often pertain to other critical aspects of survival and reproduction prescribing that people forgo short-term caloric and reproductive opportunities (e.g., food and sexual taboos; see Boehm 2008; Brown 1952; Meyer-Rochow 2009) that may support long-term and community-wide interests. For instance, violations of incest taboos are supernaturally punished among the Jahai of Malaysia as are failures to share with the needy (van der Sluys 1999). Menstrual taboos among the Dogon of Mali (Strassmann 1992) and religious veiling (Pazhoohi et al. 2017) have been suggested to increase paternity certainty and therefore paternal investment. Among some North American Indians, spirits are angered by food storage, perhaps because individual food hoarding obstruct the maintenance of collective sharing norms (Brightman 1993: 367–8). Among the Mentawai on Siberut Island, Indonesia, a local spirit punishes people for not sharing food, particularly meat; however, the spirit can be appeased by hosting ceremonies that involve costly food sharing, along with publicly apologizing for not having shared and committing to do so in the future² (Singh, Kaptchuk, and Henrich 2021). Among the Ik of Uganda, reminding people about local punitive spirits promotes increased sharing of a monetary endowment with an anonymous, needy cocommunity member (Townsend et al. 2020). More generally, adhering to costly spiritual taboos might signal in-group commitment, loyalty, and trustworthiness (Atran and Henrich 2010; Meyer-Rochow 2009).

These principles apply too, even when deities are mostly concerned with apparently arbitrary social and behavioral conventions with little to no cost to anyone. For instance, the concerns of Fijian ancestor spirits include rules of etiquette such as "call before you enter a house" and "do not wear a hat in the village" (Shaver, Fraser, and Bulbulia 2017). Despite their seemingly mundane nature, observing local rules of etiquette becomes a potential god-problem if observing local etiquette helps coordinate a community's behavioral patterns in decisive ways, for instance, by enabling "reliable social prediction" among community members (Shaver, Fraser, and Bulbulia 2017: 14) or by symbolically signaling group-membership, respect for tradition, and the social order (McNamara and Purzycki 2020; Purzycki and McNamara 2016; Richerson and Henrich 2012).

Appeals to spiritual concern and sanctions also sometimes involve ritual performance and displays of goodwill on locations of strategic importance, such as territorial borders or patches of natural riches (e.g., Bonnemaison 1984: 126; Murdock 1934: 545, Purzycki and Arakchaa 2013), potentially reducing instances of property raiding and resource exploitation, or in economic transactions, as was the case for certain gods of antiquity (Silver 1995: 5), perhaps contributing to honest exchange of goods and services (see Norenzayan et al. 2016). Similarly, ethnographic reports suggest that supernaturally enforced truces prevent escalation of disputes into cycles of violence (Rappaport 1968; Tibenderana 1980; Tuzin 2001: 98–100, 141).

Moreover, in many societies lacking formal courts of law, including Medieval Europe (Leeson 2012) and contemporary rural Liberia (Leeson and Coyne 2012), adjudication is practiced through supernaturally enforced trials by ordeals, whereby usually the accused is given a choice of admitting to the crime or going through the trial (e.g., drinking poison, touching hot iron). Assuming widespread belief in the effectiveness of trials at correctly identifying a perpetrator and leaving an innocent suspect unhurt, whether the accused chooses to undergo the trial or not is valuable information: if the accused is truly innocent, they are more willing to undergo the trial in the belief that the spirits will exonerate them by not letting them get hurt during the trial—and vice versa (Leeson and Suarez 2015).

In all of these cases—from resource preservation, general moral violations, paternity certainty, sharing norms, and group loyalty to territoriality, economic exchange, truce-making, and adjudication—appeals to supernatural intervention revolve around costly and salient social dilemmas and hence sensibly constitute god-problems.

However, according to the god-problem criteria, when secular systems are in place to monitor and sanction violations of particular local laws and norms, notions of watchful and punitive deities that care for said laws and norms are less likely to evolve (see also Mauritsen and van Mulukom, present volume). There is ethnographic evidence for such a dissociative pattern. In a free-list study across eight diverse field sites, little overlap was found between what people say the local police is concerned with and what they say pleases and angers locally relevant spirits and deities (Bendixen, Apicella, et al. forthcoming; Bendixen, Lightner, and Purzycki forthcoming), a finding that is corroborated by site-specific ethnographic observations. For instance, among the Mentawai, there is no overlap between transgressions that are supernaturally sanctioned (primarily failure to share meat and other foods) and laws that are enforced with fines and compensation, such as engaging in sorcery and violence (Singh and Garfield n.d.; Singh, Kaptchuk, and Henrich 2021), suggesting a clear division of jurisdiction between the respective domains of the supernatural and secular law (Singh, pers. comm.). Similarly, among the Batak, sanctioning certain offenses (e.g., disrespect and overexploitation of nature) is also exclusively the domain of the spirits (Eder 1997: 11).

Consider, too, the Ammatoans of Sulawesi, Indonesia. Like many traditional societies, the Ammatoans view their relationship with their environment as reciprocal and the spirits as social actors (Maarif 2015). But while the Ammatoans observe traditional rules regarding the use and misuse of the forest, violations of these rules appear not to be sanctioned by spiritual forces (Maarif, pers. comm.). Instead, a semi-secular system is in place, with community members and particularly the community leader acting as judge, jury, and executioner (Maarif 2015). Likewise, the Chenchu of Southern India have democratic institutions and secular law enforcement (e.g., major crimes are reported to the police) and simultaneously lack fear in supernatural punishment (Turin 1999).

Similarly for the Semang of the Malay Peninsula, where although local norms, customs, and laws are thought of as divine (Murdock 1934: 94), the supreme deity does not punish crimes such as theft, adultery, or murder, but instead "such things as familiarity with one's mother in-law, killing a sacred black wasp or certain tabooed birds, mocking a tame or helpless animal …, and throwing a spear in the morning quite permissible in the afternoon!" (Murdock 1934: 103–4). Instead, in cases of crime, "the community as a whole exacts punishment," which for serious offenses amount to compensatory fines or death (Murdock 1934: 94). Among the !Kung Bushmen, Marshall (1962) reports that "man's wrong-doing against man is not left to [the supreme deity's] punishment nor is it considered to be his concern. Man corrects or avenges such wrong-doings himself in his social context. [The supreme deity] punishes people for his own reasons, which are sometimes quite obscure[3]" (245), hinting at a dissociation between supernatural punishment and secular law.

Another telling case concerns the traditional Samoans, who punish crimes secularly according to their severity. If the crime is minor, such as petty theft, the involved parties are expected to sort it out between themselves, and if the crime is major, such as murder, insults, or various offenses against the village or the chief, the community collectively intervenes to enforce a penalty. However, one class of offenses, namely theft of plantation crops, is not included in this secular system. Therefore, plantation owners, in order to detect and deter transgressors, resort to a set of supernatural appeals including taboos, curses, oaths, and ordeals,[4] which "impels the [transgressor] to make restitution, especially if he begins to feel ill" (Murdock 1934: 62). Further, plantation crop theft is the "commonest crime" (61), making it a particularly salient offense.

These latter cases, then, highlight how supernatural attention is not attributed to every consequential aspect of local community life but only to the subset of dilemmas that are particularly salient and frequent, where relevant secular systems are unavailable or less effective at restraining individualism, and where the payoff structures are somewhat opaque.[5]

Future Directions

In this chapter, we reviewed current accounts of cross-cultural variation in beliefs about gods' minds and introduced a cultural evolutionary account that includes a set of criteria for predicting the content of so-called "god-problems"—the set of concerns and interests that a given deity might be associated with in varying socioecological contexts. We evaluated—and found considerable support for—these criteria against a range of ethnographic cases. We close by pointing out avenues for future scientific inquiry into beliefs about and appeals to the minds of gods.

A set of testable predictions flows from the discussions of the present chapter. Overall, we predict that appeals to supernatural intervention (e.g., explaining instances of misfortune or illness with reference to spiritual punishment) revolve around locally salient and costly social dilemmas that are less feasible, less effective, or less convincing to (attempt to) solve by appeals to non-supernatural alternatives. On the other hand, when the consequences of widespread defection of some social problem are clear and obvious and if secular institutions are available to punish or deter norm deviation, such problems should be less likely to attract supernatural attention. Further, we should expect to see that religious traditions incorporate new local challenges to social life (Purzycki, Stagnaro, and Sasaki 2020), and that when under threat by rival religious traditions or secular alternatives, gods and spirits demand continued mental and behavioral attention (Bendixen, Apicella, et al. forthcoming; Bendixen, Lightner, and Purzycki forthcoming). This is so perhaps because gods that *do not* care about the most pressing local social challenges, and *do not* stress displays of devotion are outcompeted by more salient and persistent cultural strains.

Further, while we have argued that our tour of ethnographic reports on deities and their perceived concerns in smaller-scale societies lend support to the god-problem criteria, outside of the case studies reviewed herein, direct evidence that beliefs about and appeals to deities actually *solve* their corresponding social dilemmas is limited. This empirical lacuna calls for careful and rigorous future studies that specifically model and assess the psychological, social, behavioral, material, and ecological consequences—if any—of beliefs, appeals, and rituals devoted to the minds of gods.[6] Another outstanding area of future research pertains to how supernatural beliefs and appeals "compete"—cognitively, culturally, and evolutionarily—with beliefs and appeals to secular norm enforcement. For instance, while the god-problem criteria and our ethnographic tour suggest so, is it indeed generally the case that supernatural punishment is dissociated from non-supernatural alternatives?

More specifically, the cognitive and social processes involved in the cultural evolution of gods' minds are mostly *terra incognita*, but as we outline elsewhere (cf., Bendixen and Purzycki 2020, 2021, forthcoming; Bendixen, Apicella, et al. forthcoming), we predict that various cultural evolutionary forces compete and interact. These include but are not limited to: content biases (e.g., punitive and knowledgeable deities that offer teleological explanations of (mis)fortune are cognitively and culturally "catchy"; Boyer 2001; Purzycki et al. 2012); context biases (e.g., beliefs about and commitment to deities are transmitted from peers, parents, and prestigious authorities via communicative acts of faith; Henrich 2009); payoff biases (e.g., communities attend to the payoffs of behaviors in their local environment; Purzycki, Stagnaro, and Sasaki 2020); manipulative signaling (e.g., supernatural appeals can orient people toward collaborative or egotistic behaviors; Fitouchi and Singh 2022); cultural-group selection (e.g., beliefs about supernatural punishment of defection in local cooperative dilemmas can, *ceteris paribus*, provide groups with an edge in competition over resources, land, members, etc.; Norenzayan et al. 2016); as well as social, ecological, and evolutionary path-dependence. We imagine a confluence of such forces is at work in the proliferation of appeals to the minds of gods.

Acknowledgments

We thank Aarhus University Research Foundation for generous support and Aaron D. Lightner for feedback.

14

Environmentalism and the Minds of Gods

Adam Baimel

Introduction

Consider the following:

> We stand before a harsh justice: biodiversity loss, environmental degradation and climate change are the inevitable consequences of our actions, since we have greedily consumed more of the earth's resources than the planet can endure. The extreme weather and natural disasters of recent months reveal afresh to us with great force and at great human cost that climate change is not only a future challenge, but an immediate and urgent matter of survival. Widespread floods, fires and droughts threaten entire continents. Sea levels rise, forcing whole communities to relocate; cyclones devastate entire regions, ruining lives and livelihoods. Water has become scarce and food supplies insecure, causing conflict and displacement for millions of people. We have already seen this in places where people rely on small scale agricultural holdings. Today we see it in more industrialised countries where even sophisticated infrastructure cannot completely prevent extraordinary destruction. Tomorrow could be worse.

Are you surprised to learn that these are the words of Pope Francis, Ecumenical Patriarch Bartholomew, and the Archbishop of Canterbury—the respective spiritual leaders of the Roman Catholic, Eastern Orthodox Christian, and Anglican churches? In September 2021, the leaders of these three major religious traditions with a collective reach of about 1.5 billion adherents around the world made their *first-ever* joint declaration on the topic of an appeal "for the protection of creation."[1] The letter is a fascinating read for several reasons. First, the fact that the focus of this *first* joint declaration is the climate crisis and not what might be considered a more typical domain of religious concern is particularly striking. What business do religious leaders have in talking about climate change? Second, the letter clearly indemnifies human action as the cause of the climate crisis. The denial of *anthropogenic* causes of climate change is a premise that some Christian communities over the last few decades have employed to justify their lack of concern (e.g., Barker and Bearce 2013). Might this letter from the highest of authorities in these respective churches be enough to change their minds? Finally, to address the persistently emerging socioecological challenges of the climate crisis, the letter makes a broad appeal for cooperation on diverse scales from Christian individuals to governments and corporations and how they employ their investment funds. While this is not an explicit holy decree to take to the streets in protest to demand further government support for pro-environmental policy, the letter does communicate—quite clearly—that taking action in the pursuit of "caring for God's creation is a spiritual commission requiring a response of commitment." Less clear, however, is exactly what a committed spiritual response might or should look like. That being said, is this letter a signal of a new era in which caring for the environment has entered the religious moral landscape (at least among Christians), and if so, what has caused it? Equally puzzling, will it matter?

Appealing to the world's diverse religious communities in the fight against climate change makes good sense if at first only because of the sheer number of religiously committed individuals around the world (Pew Research Center 2015b). But in reality, this letter is far from the first moralized appeal to protect the environment from diverse religious authorities (for compendia see, for example, Gottlieb 2006; Palmer and Finaly 2003). Moreover, many contemporary and mostly secular environmentalist groups are built on the shoulders of devout and religiously motivated predecessors (Ellingson 2016; Stoll 2015). But yet, religious communities (or secular ones) the world over have not already solved our problems. This remains true despite the long history of the admirably and increasingly voiced calls to action from some communities, and particularly indigenous communities, the world over. And thus, it becomes an important question to empirically examine the effectiveness of such religiously motivated appeals in galvanizing the cooperation of diverse religious communities in diverse cultural contexts. On this front, the question of whether (and if so in what ways) religious systems are and historically have been implicated in their communities' natural resource management or their pro-environmental attitudes and behaviors also has an extensive history across the social sciences (for useful introductions to this topic in religious studies/theology, anthropology, conservation sciences, and ecology see, for example, Deane-Drummond 2017; Grim and Tucker 2014; Pungetti, Oviedo, and Hooke 2012; Sponsel 2012).

There is, of course, an immensity of present-day and historical cultural variation in the ways religious systems come to foster and/or inhibit pro-environmental attitudes, commitments, and behaviors. Even within a single religious tradition, different facets may push and pull adherents in different directions (Preston and Baimel 2021). And thus, any question of the role of "religion" (in the broadest sense of the word) in motivating pro-environmental concern has set out to answer an impossible question. In light of all this, this chapter provides a framework for both making sense of past research on this topic, and asking new, more specified, research questions in furthering our understanding of whether, how, when, and with what consequences religious systems and their gods become concerned with how we treat the natural world. Specifically, this chapter discusses the shortfalls of a comparative religions approach. Then, the chapter builds a case that a consideration of cultural context and representational models of the minds of gods are necessary for both making sense of past research on this topic and asking new, more nuanced, research questions in furthering our understanding of whether, how, when, and with what consequences religious systems have been—and can be—employed in addressing the cooperative threats of the climate crisis.

Asking the Easier Questions

Are religious individuals more or less pro-environmental than nonreligious individuals? Is the strength of one's religious commitments correlated with concern about climate change? Are Buddhists more pro-environmentally inclined than Christians? These are the "easy" research questions that have been the motivation for an extensive and growing empirical literature. While the data gathered to answer these questions have produced interesting and even important results, they are also: (1) underspecified with regard to mechanisms and (2) decontextualized in many ways that they may also be missing the mark on specifying the role (or potential) of "religion" in motivating pro-environmental commitments. The motivation for these sorts of research programs is often directly attributed by the researchers who study them to the controversial claims of historian Lynn White Jr. (1967). White (1967) argued that the anthropocentrism, divinely ordained dominion over the natural world, and faith in continual progress perpetuated by the Christian church and its powerful institutions over the course of its cultural history laid the foundations for our present-day ecological crises. White (1967) argues that in contrast, other religious systems like Buddhism or the animistic traditions of indigenous societies the world over are inherently more pro-environmental given that they fundamentally differ in their approach to situating humanity *alongside* the natural world rather than in a position of God-given power over it. In concluding, White (1967) makes an appeal for a religious solution to this religious problem including a complete overhaul of many foundational Western values historically instituted by the Christian church. Over the last half century, White's (1967) writing has gained over eight thousand citations and has sparked interest in asking the types of questions laid out above. What have the social sciences learned from over half a century of asking such questions?

Some of the earliest empirical tests of White's (1967) thesis do indeed provide evidence that Judeo-Christian dominion beliefs are negatively associated with environmental concern (e.g., Eckberg and Blocker 1989; Hand and Van Liere 1984). However, participants in these studies were sampled from a particularly narrow portion of human cultural variation (residents of Oklahoma and Washington state in the United States). Looking only slightly more broadly in a representative sample of Americans, Arbuckle and Konisky (2015) find only weak and mixed support for White's thesis. Their data provide evidence that while American Christians espouse only slightly less environmental concern on average than nonreligious Americans, this is not the case for American Jews. Given that the source of beliefs about divinely ordained dominion at the crux of White's (1967) thesis is shared between these traditions, this is an important and revealing contrast. Moreover, this work reveals variation even between Christian denominations in their reported environmental concern, with American Evangelicals being the primary source of the overall negative relationship. This too, however, does not necessarily have much to do with being Evangelical. Indeed, Smith and Veldman (2020) provide evidence that Brazilian Evangelicals—who share doctrines and worship practices with those in the United States—are no less environmentally concerned than others in Brazil. Even among Evangelicals in the United States, the landscape of environmental concern is already shifting with the majority of Millennial Evangelicals being in support of stronger environmental regulations even when accompanied by great economic costs (Pew Research Center 2014). Crucially, Arbuckle and Konisky (2015) also observed that the extent of one's religiosity is a weak (albeit as predicted negative) predictor of environmental concern in their American sample, with political conservativism playing a considerably larger role. While the literature here is sparser, are these results consistent with evidence from more culturally diverse samples? In a sample of Christians, Buddhists, and Muslims across thirty-four nations, Felix et al. (2018) find that, in contrast to studies of Americans, religiosity is *positively* (albeit weakly) associated with environmental concern. Taken all together, where does this leave us with regard to White's (1967) thesis fifty years on?

The extant evidence implies that enquiring about the relationship between *religiosity* and environmental concern is underspecified in at least two important and related ways: methodologically and contextually. Methodologically, religiosity in these studies is commonly operationalized by some combination of responses to questions such as "how important is religion to you in your life?" or "how often do you attend religious services?" The ways in which these measures can be related to environmental concern, however, is likely conditional on other factors. For example, if a given adherent believes that protecting the environment is a fundamental religious obligation and not doing so may anger their gods, then we might expect the strength of their religious commitments measured broadly with questions like "how important is religion to you in your life" to positively correlate with concern. On the other hand, if someone believes that the climate crisis is a sign of the coming end of days and long-awaited eternal salvation, then the strength of their religiosity is perhaps more likely to be negatively associated with their environmental concern. Context matters. So, to make sense of the apparent cross-cultural variation in the ways religiosity is related to environmental concern we need to pay it the attention it deserves.

Context matters for other reasons too. Variation in the physical environments that many communities find themselves inhabiting will likely give rise to a diversity of socioecological challenges, which in turn will likely require quite different solutions. If religion is in some way going to offer or motivate some of these solutions, then we might expect a fair amount of variability in terms of what those solutions look like. The research reviewed thus far with its focus on pro-environmental *attitudes* rather than *behavioral outcomes* is by design indifferent to this type of variation. Pro-environmental attitudes are perhaps more frequently studied than behavioral outcomes because they are more easily administered in survey research. While it is certainly an achievement for climate scientists and activists alike that the majority of the world espouses concerns about the harms and consequences of climate change (Pew Research Center 2021)—this says nothing about how willing or how likely they are to do anything about it. Unfortunately, recent research highlights that pro-environmental attitudes are cross-culturally poor predictors of behavioral commitments to protecting the natural world (e.g., support for pro-environmental government policies; Eom et al. 2016; Tam and Chan 2017). Critically, both White's (1967) thesis and the changes our societies must make in response to the socioecological challenges of the climate crisis are fundamentally a question of behavior, not attitudes. With these caveats in mind, we may be much farther from actually having tested the implications of White's (1967) thesis than the literature might make it seem at first glance. On the bright side, however, there is considerable evidence for us to consider that paints a different picture—one that demonstrates how religious systems have historically played at least some part in sustaining practical behavioral solutions to ecological challenges.

Practical Religious Solutions to Ecological Challenges

It is altogether too obvious to say that humans have always been faced with the challenge of living sustainably within the limits of their natural environments (Ellis et al. 2021). In more recent times, environmental degradation caused by the over-extractive workings of the global economies since the Industrial Revolution are in some ways a classic example of what Hardin (1968) called the "tragedy of the commons." Historically, the "commons" were communal green spaces in Medieval England that were used by locals as grazing lands for their domesticated animals. Without any limiting factors on access or use, each individual herder is, in theory, going to be motivated to get into the commons first, allowing their animals to graze freely to their stomach's content. The combined effects of many self-interested herders, however, would tragically (for the local people and their animals) lead to the degradation of this shared natural resource without the need for any given individual intending for this to be the case. This tale of the tragedy of the commons with its get in first and take all that you need mentality is a commonly expressed metaphor for some of the extractivist behaviors and policies of major modern global corporations and governments. That being said, the idea that human societies have typically allowed free-for-all or unrestrained access to crucial natural resources may itself be more allegory than historical reality. Indeed, Cox (1985) argues that local norms, regulations regarding access and use, and the monitoring/policing thereof were likely quite successful in their time at managing England's commons. More broadly, Ostrom's (1990) now-famous work and ensuing Nobel Prize earning career has detailed how throughout history, diverse sets of cultural institutions have played an integral role in protecting against the tragedy of the commons by sustaining cooperation in the governance of common pool natural resources. Today, creating the cultural institutions to sustain the international cooperation necessary in governing the entire planet (our largest commons) is a primary concern of international policy. But historically and on more local levels, religion has played a functionally similar role.

Critically, practical religious solutions to local ecological challenges need not result from conscious pro-environmental motivations. As an example, consider the coordinated field-burning practices of the Australian Aboriginal Martu (Bliege Bird et al. 2013; see also Lightner and Purzycki, present volume):

> Much like park rangers' controlled burning, Martu's controlled fires are far less destructive than the brush fires caused by lightning strikes and have the effect of increasing biodiversity. Interestingly, this biodiversity is what local monitor lizards eat, and the Martu eat the monitor lizards. The Martu explain that burning fires in this manner is consistent with the "Dreaming," or sacred law and the will of the ancestor spirits. If the Martu did not appeal to the Dreaming and ancestors, people might not do all of this short-term work for these long-term benefits. (Purzycki and Baimel 2016: 56)

Indeed, if traditional religious systems like those of the Martu have played a role in practical solutions to ecological challenges, we might expect the history of and continued marginalization of indigenous communities and their religious practices to have downstream negative consequences on many different environmental outcomes in diverse contexts. In the Maya Lowlands of Guatemala, for example, demographic changes in communities of Itza Maya have resulted in a loss of traditional worldviews about forest spirits associated with natural resources. In turn, this has been related to the degradation of environmental protection values that once sustained local agroforestry practices (Atran et al. 2002; le Guen et al. 2013).

Other examples of the not necessarily intentional pro-environmental consequences of religious behaviors abound (see also Bendixen and Purzycki, present volume). For example, religious hunting taboos of the Mro in Bangladesh have contributed to preserving local fauna biodiversity. For another, fishery stock in Lake Tanganyika (a biodiversity hotspot in Tanzania) is regulated by the religious ritual practices of local communities (Lowe et al. 2019). Even the preservation of historically older church grounds in Poland has contributed to protecting the biodiversity of several bird species that use church towers as safe nesting grounds (Skórka et al. 2018). Sometimes, however, religiously motivated environmental protection is indeed a little more intentional.

A focal feature of modern-day environmentalism is garnering support for forest conservation and when possible reforestation of tree-felled lands: both of which can have major impacts on our capacities to sequester carbon and preserve biodiversity across the planet (Bastin et al. 2019). In India, *religiously* protected sacred groves have proven *more* effective in maintaining local biodiversity than protected forests governed by secular institutions (Rath, Banerjee, and John 2020). These sacred groves are often believed to the homes of locally revered supernatural agents, and have likely garnered more devoted community support in protecting them (Bhagwat and Rutte 2006; Kent 2013; Sharma, Rikhari, and Lok 1999). As a result, protected sacred groves continue to provide local communities with sources of food, resources, and shelter. While the number of religiously protected sacred groves has dwindled in India's recent history, their protection features prominently in religiously motivated pro-environmental movements across the country. Importantly, the fight for their protection and evidence of their benefits highlights how bottom-up, community-driven, and *religiously* motivated pro-environmental behaviors can at least sometimes be more effective than top-down regulations from secular institutions.

While these examples are illustrative, an important question remains as to whether there are any consistent patterns of how religion becomes implicated in natural resource management in diverse contexts. In a meta-analysis of case studies of community-based natural resource management in forty-eight geographically and culturally diverse societies, M. Cox, Villamayor-Tomas, and Hartberg (2014) provide evidence for the diverse ways in which religious systems have provided practical solutions to ecological challenges. For one, religious traditions often protect important natural resources from overuse by virtue of restricting and appropriating access to these resources to certain people at certain times, which are often marked by religious rituals. As an example, with reference to community access to irrigation systems in southwestern Puebla in Mexico, "two irrigation systems are traditionally divided up into wards, each of which is dedicated to a saint whom farmers serve in exchange of their right to use the water" (M. Cox, Villamayor-Tomas, and Hartberg 2014: 51). In this case, locals must pay the costs of religious commitment and ritual participation to access local resources in such a way that has the ecological benefit of spreading demand for water across the wards. On the other side of the planet, Balinese water temples have played a similarly integral and functional role in sequestering and ritualistically redistributing access to water to rice farmers in such a way that contributed to reducing conflicts over access, and with consequences for controlling pest outbreaks (Lansing 1987).

In addition to marking *user* boundaries, religious systems are also often implicated in demarcating the *physical* boundaries of important natural resources. Without clear resource boundaries, governance becomes difficult. Religious markers of resource boundaries in these case studies included "both natural and artificial phenomena including sacred stones, caves, hills, and peaks of mountains, as well as monoliths, burial grounds, shrines, palaces, monasteries, and temples" (M. Cox, Villamayor-Tomas, and Hartberg 2014: 51). In the Tyva Republic (Siberia), ritual cairns distributed along grazing grounds used by local herders demarcate their physical boundaries. In addition, they also likely act as reminders of the spirit masters' concerns about respecting these boundaries and preserving associated natural resources (Purzycki 2016). As some evidence for how this translates into behaviors that maintain cooperation and adherence to norms that regulate access to these grazing lands (Lightner and Purzycki, present volume), locals are sensitive to social information about whether other herders make ritual offerings at these cairns as a signal of their trustworthiness (Purzycki and Arakchaa 2013). More broadly, religious symbols in these sorts of places may indeed serve as reminders of watchful locally relevant supernatural agents who are believed to be concerned about adherence to norms about how locals should treat the natural resource and capable of sanctioning those who don't.

In situations where social (i.e., human) monitoring is difficult and norm violations are meaningful threats to community survival, beliefs about supernatural monitoring and punishment may prove particularly useful in demotivating antisocial behavior (e.g., Purzycki and McNamara 2016; Bendixen and Purzycki, present volume). In support of this view, in a follow-up study of M. Cox, Villamayor-Tomas, and Hartberg (2014), Hartberg et al. (2014) provide evidence that beliefs in these same forty-eight societies about how local supernatural agents both monitor adherence to rules and dole out punishment for transgressions are present in nearly every case in which religion was implicated in local natural resource governance. As a signal of the importance of norm adherence with regard to the treatment of these natural resources, the most common forms of reported supernatural consequences for transgressing local rules were quite severe (e.g., death, disease, and misfortune).

Taken together, the data from these case studies provide some indication that (1) religion has played an active *practical* role in the management of diverse types of natural resources in geographically and culturally distant societies, (2) these practical religious solutions to ecological challenges are typically local (i.e., geographically or contextually constrained), and that (3) appeals to the concerns of supernatural monitors/punishers may be a particularly potent solution to sustaining norm adherence with regard to how communities treat the natural world. Of course, none of this evidence should be taken as indication that any community (religious or not, historical or modern) are or were perfect stewards of their environments (Alvard 1994; Dove 2006; Raymond 2007; Smith and Wishnie 2000). The reviewed evidence, however, can help identify some of the key challenges facing any modern attempt by religious leaders to mobilize large numbers of individuals in their religious communities to protect the environment. First, official statements by religious leaders around the world have typically made *ideological* appeals, with far too little emphasis on practical solutions.[2] Second, any practical solutions that are offered tend to be decontextualized with reference to *global* concerns. And third, even if these appeals do make some reference to the concerns of relevant supernatural agents (e.g., "Islam teaches that we will one day be judged by Allah for how we have discharged our responsibilities following the guidance of Islam. Have we been good trustees, and have we kept nature in harmony?"[3]), their disconnection from locally specific practical solutions may render these appeals rather impotent. These, however, are tractable problems and there is good reason to suspect that in response to the increasing socioecological pressures and cooperative threats associated with the climate crisis, religion may still prove an essential motivator of pro-environmental collective action.

Religious System Adaptation to the Cooperative Threats of the Climate Crisis

Gone are the days in which climate change was "merely" an issue of melting polar ice caps, endangered polar bears, and dying coral reefs. The media, global leaders, climate scientists, environmental activists, and even religious leaders are actively and increasingly communicating to those that will listen that the climate *crisis* is a fundamental threat to all aspects of each and every human community around the world (e.g., Francis 2015; Hayhoe 2021; Klein 2014). And in this respect, it should come as no surprise that religious leaders are (and will surely continue to become) increasingly vocal about the threats of the climate crisis. If the emerging theoretical synthesis in the behavioral ecology of religion is right that, as dynamic and complex adaptive systems, religions predictably adapt alongside changing ecological conditions in ways that sustain cooperation in order to contribute to the minimization of emerging challenges (e.g., Purzycki and McNamara 2016; Sosis 2019)—then we should expect the immense socioecological pressures of the climate crisis to be a fundamental cause of imminent changes in the concerns of religious systems the world over. Specifically, this view holds that the representational content of the minds of gods (i.e., what individuals think gods care about) and appeals to the minds of gods can quickly adapt to changing socioecological conditions. As succinctly stated by Purzycki and McNamara (2016: 144), "the collective action and coordination required to manage these [changing] conditions requires communication. The content of that communication must motivate others to collaborate; and appeals to gods are excellent candidates for motivating others." And thus, extant research into whether a so-called greening of religions has already occurred that finds the evidence with regard to modern world religions to be lacking may very well be bit too premature (e.g., see Taylor 2016 and Taylor, Van Wieren, and Zaleha 2016 for very comprehensive reviews). Moreover, the extant literature may be missing an important piece of the puzzle by not specifically considering the role of changes in the content of concerns attributed to the minds of gods.

Beliefs about the contents of the minds of gods are flexible and evidence is emerging that the concerns individuals attribute to their gods can adapt *very* quickly to novel and/or newly salient cooperative threats. In the context of an experimental study, Purzycki, Stagnaro, and Sasaki (2020) subjected half of their participants to a rigged economic game in which the participants were led to feel cheated by their partner before free-listing up to ten responses to the question "What do you think displeases God?" Compared to the other half of the sample that had not first played the rigged economic game, those that had felt cheated were more likely to report that God was concerned with greed. As another pressing example, Doney and Baimel (n.d.) questioned whether the threat of the Covid-19 pandemic had exerted any effect on the representational models of the mind of God in a sample of Christians in the UK. The study's results indicated that Christians in the UK believed that God was actively concerned about whether others were, for example, wearing protective face masks when in public spaces or avoiding contact with vulnerable others. As some evidence for the consequences of these quick to emerge beliefs, the salience of pandemic-related concerns in participant's free-list responses was positively correlated with self-reported adherence to the UK's rules and regulations during the 2020 lockdowns and harsher judgment of those who did not (findings that are consistent with some variants of the "projection" hypothesis, see Jackson and Gray, present volume). The question of whether, if so in what ways, and with what consequences the representational models of the concerns of deities around the world are changing in response to increasing threats of the climate crisis remains, however, open for future research.

Purzycki, Stagnaro, and Sasaki (2020) note that while only 5 percent of their sample across their two conditions listed "environmental destruction" as something that displeases God, the issue was relatively salient (i.e., appeared earlier in the participant's free-lists) for those that did. One way forward for research in this area would be to assess the frequency and salience of environmental concerns attributed to the minds of gods in diverse cultural contexts. With a better sense of the extant variation, researchers would be better able to try accounting for it. In following with the rationale presented throughout this chapter, if religious systems are adapting (or have adapted) to the socioecological threats of the climate crisis, we might expect the attributions of environmental concern to the minds of gods within and between communities to covary with the experiences of climate crisis–related threats. Moreover, it is in these communities, perhaps, that religious appeals for environmental protection might be particularly potent motivators of adherents' behavioral commitments (i.e., because they could be aligned with the community's broader religious frameworks).

Empirical tests of the effectiveness of diverse types of religious appeals for environmental collective action in different cultural contexts are only very recently emerging. Shin and Preston (2019), for example, in a sample of Americans provide some evidence that appeals based on biblical stewardship led participants to consider environmental protection as more of a moral issue and increase their self-reported pro-environmental behavioral intentions. Of course, there is no expectation that appeals to stewardship in this way should similarly promote environmental outcomes in all religious communities. While many major religious traditions espouse some form of environmental stewardship, more research is needed to identify what types of appeals might be best suited for increasing and/or sustaining pro-environmental commitments in different cultural contexts. On this front, any attempts at making religious appeals for environmental protection or empirical tests thereof are going to benefit a great deal from a clearer understanding of what adherents believe their gods want.

Conclusion

The emerging and intensifying consequences of the climate crisis are a very real threat to all aspects of human life. The cooperative challenges of the climate crisis therefore offer a unique and pressing opportunity to put some of the long-standing theories about religion, the minds of gods, and cooperation to the test. Are religious systems adjusting their focus in response to the emerging socioecological pressures of the climate crisis? If so, in what ways, and perhaps more importantly, with what consequences? To meaningfully answer these types of questions, research in this area must move beyond decontextualized assessment of attitudinal concerns. One small step (that will require lot of work) toward a more synthetic science of the role of religion in promoting or limiting pro-environmental commitments would be to continue mapping the representational models of the minds of gods in diverse cultural contexts (e.g., (Bendixen, Apicella et al. forthcoming; Purzycki, Willard, et al. 2022). Gaining insight into whether, how, and with what consequences the world's religious systems are adapting their concerns to the socioecological pressures of the climate crisis stands to generate the necessary empirical capital for future research on how to develop novel and (ideally) more effective calls for action in mobilizing the world's religious communities on behalf of protecting our environment.

15

Approaching the Minds of the Gods through AI

Wesley J. Wildman and Justin E. Lane

Introduction

In this chapter, we discuss two computational approaches that are helping the scientific study of religion (SSR) uncover how human beings conceptualize the intentions and actions of invisible supernatural beings, as well as the personal and social effects of such supernatural beliefs.

The first approach utilizes computational simulations to understand what difference beliefs about invisible agents make in human social life and interpersonal behavior, including everything from the reinforcement of ingroup–outgroup boundaries and the rationalization of violence to the catalyzing of large-scale cooperation and the emergence of new forms of human civilization (Diallo et al. 2019; Epstein 2006). Computational simulations are conceptual models of dynamic processes that are implemented in a computer system and executed over time.

The rigorous enforcement of conceptual consistency within computer architectures and programming languages makes computational simulations particularly useful for addressing one of the pressing challenges within SSR: partial theories about supernatural agent beliefs abound, each empirically grounded in observations and experiments, leading to an *integration problem*. How can we fit these part theories into a compelling synthesis of insights developed within numerous disciplines regarding the human obsession with the minds of the gods? Computational simulations can help move beyond speculative part theories toward integrated theoretical interpretations of complex issues related to supernatural worldviews.

To get a sense for the scale of this integration problem, consider the fact that most game-theoretic approaches to the scientific study of cooperation, including the role of supernatural beliefs in facilitating large-scale cooperation, have assumed rational actors with complete information, whereas contemporary psychology makes neither assumption (see Lane 2017, 2021). Or consider the numerous unreconciled theories about the decline of supernatural beliefs in secularizing societies (Wildman et al. 2020), or about the role of supernatural worldviews in the agricultural transition about

10,000 years ago (Shults and Wildman 2018) and the Axial Age transition about 2,500 years ago (Shults et al. 2018e). Computational simulations are the ideal—and currently the only effective—way to integrate empirically validated theories at multiple levels of complexity into sophisticated, testable causal architectures. Instead of merely asserting complementarity of part theories, computational simulations can demonstrate complementarity and avoid fruitless battles between part theories presented in incommensurable ways.

Computational simulations have several advantages over more familiar modeling techniques (see Lane 2021; Shults et al. 2018b). Linear-regression and structural-equation models (LR and SEMs) are limited to a snapshot in time whereas computational models can simulate a continuous arrow of time. LR and SEMs model inputs against outputs but do not support direct causal inference, whereas computational simulation models are explicit models of causal processes and therefore support causal inference. Unlike LR and SEMs, computational simulations can generate higher level observable outputs that themselves can be the target of empirical testing. Joshua Epstein calls this modeling modality capable of generating new, testable insights "generative social science" (Epstein 2006). New trends in what is called multiagent artificial intelligence (Lane 2013) supplement generative social science by focusing on validating the mechanisms within the agent, not just the overall social behavior of the group (Lane 2018, 2019, 2021).

The second computational approach is even more adventurous. Since we can use computers to build artificial minds, why not build artificial minds of people who hold supernatural beliefs, or even artificial minds of the supernatural beings in which humans believe? This is accomplished by applying machine learning to large datasets of religious texts (sermons, interviews, recordings, etc.) that specify the mental contents of the supernatural beings in question. Already, this method has been used to create "AI gurus" that generate reflections on a variety of topics, effectively modeling the mind of a religious leader. It is only a short step from there to modeling the minds of supernatural beings themselves, as these are manifested in analyzable texts.

Computational construction of AI minds yields an unprecedented type of experimental platform. Once an AI mind of a supernatural being can pass a Turing Test, and seem compelling to believers, studying believers' interactions with the AI mind can yield information about believers' behavior and worldview that would be difficult or impossible to access in any other way. Of course, this AI technology is in its infancy. But just as entrepreneurs are already developing commercial applications of deceased-relative AIs to ease the grief of family left behind, and religious AIs are hearing confessions and offering pearls of wisdom, so the applications for SSR research are not far behind.

Both approaches—computational simulation and AI minds—promise to advance our understanding of how we conceptualize the intentions and actions of supernatural beings, and how we interact with them. The chapter concludes with a discussion of the ethical implications of these novel research programs and indicates how future research might combine both approaches to create more semantically compelling and culturally rich models of supernatural religious beliefs.

The History of Thinking about the Human Obsession with Divine Minds

Human beings have puzzled over divine minds throughout recorded history and in every culture. People have tried to discern what divine minds are thinking, how to placate these powerful beings, and how to achieve earthly happiness and perhaps eternal bliss by heeding divine commands. A few people have also asked a more scientific question, namely, *why are human beings so obsessed with the thoughts, desires, expectations, and emotions of invisible beings?*

This is a fundamental question about human nature, to be sure. The behavior is, on its face, rather peculiar. The beings in question are invisible, after all, and there is no clear-cut evidence for their reality of the kind that we use to assess the reality of other unseen things—for example, paw prints and nibble marks indicating that a rabbit feasted on our garden vegetables in the dark of night. But we can never be certain about the reality of gods, ghosts, demons, angels, djinns, and spirits unless we employ nonscientific forms of reasoning about evidence, such as believing based on the putative authority of sacred texts or religious leaders. Despite this, human beings everywhere and always have been obsessed with divine minds, which suggests that the tendency to ponder the minds of gods is instinctive, in the specific sense of maturationally natural—something that arises within the ordinary course of human cognitive and emotional development (McCauley 2011).

The history of more-or-less scientific approaches to supernatural ideation is not nearly as old as the ideation itself, but early hypotheses were advanced by ancient thinkers in the philosophical traditions of west, south, and east Asia. With germinal beginnings in the European Enlightenment (e.g., David Hume); tentative flowerings in late-nineteenth-century sociology and psychology (e.g., Max Weber, Emile Durkheim, Sigmund Freud, Carl Jung, William James); and colorful blooms in the late twentieth century's evolutionary and cognitive approaches to religion (e.g., Boyer, Lawson, McCauley, Sperber, Atran), the so-called SSR has been profoundly invested in this question about human nature. The story we are tracing here—how computational sciences contribute to our understanding of the human obsession with divine minds—builds on this foundation, and really takes off in the late twentieth century alongside the evolutionary and cognitive approaches within SSR (Lane 2017).

The Recent History of Computers and Divine Minds

The social sciences had been making good use of computational simulation in the 1990s, before it was first applied to religion in the mid-2000s. Well-known examples are Joshua Epstein and Robert Axtell's *Growing Artificial Societies* (1996) and Robert Axelrod's *The Complexity of Cooperation* (1997). Neither deals directly with religious cognition or religious groups, but they set the conceptual and computational groundwork for what followed. Specifically, these early works demonstrated that agents with very simple behavioral rules can generate extremely complex group-level phenomena.

Environmental anthropology was especially active during these early years, using computational simulations to investigate theories about interactions between human groups and their environments. Such systems sometimes involve coupled cycles, with natural ecological cycles and human cultural cycles (such as recurring religious rituals) interacting in complex nonlinear ways—ideal territory for computational simulations. A classic instance of interacting ecological and cultural cycles is Roy Rappaport's *Pigs for the Ancestors* (1968), which proposed a theory about ecological–ritual interaction and inspired several early computational simulations (see summaries of this early research in Anderies 1998; Orr, Lansing, and Dove 2015).

Then came the work of William Sims Bainbridge. As early as 1994, Bainbridge was making the case that the big breakthroughs in sociology would come from "artificial social intelligence," which refers to the application of machine intelligence techniques to social phenomena, including religion (see Bainbridge 1994; Bainbridge et al. 1994). For years before and after the visionary statements of 1994, Bainbridge was working with sociologist Rodney Stark to comprehend social theories of religion and how they interact with cognitive theories of religious belief (e.g., Stark and Bainbridge 1985, 1987, 1996). This monumental multidisciplinary effort culminated in Bainbridge's (2006) book, *God from the Machine*, which presents a variety of computational simulations employing artificial social intelligence to illuminate the way human beings develop stable beliefs about the existence, minds, and behavior of invisible beings, and the consequences of such beliefs within social organizations.

Bainbridge created a virtual town called Cyburg, populated by 44,100 agents, each a simple artificial intelligence with (very) limited cognitive and behavioral abilities. In these simulations, agents are independent (or partially independent) computational objects. They have variables that represent both individual traits and states. The agent can also perform calculations, specified computationally as functions that can manipulate information that they hold (such as understanding that in a specific state they take one action as opposed to another), or they can process information they receive from another agent or information about their physical environment (a locational coordinate, information about how many resources exist in their vicinity, etc.). Agents have very simple cognition and perform only the actions relevant to modeling the specific phenomenon of interest. The computational simulations based on the thinking and interactions of those agents generate penetrating insights into topics at the junction of religious belief and sociality such as segregation, recruitment, fellowship, trust, cooperation, faith, and culture.

For example, drawing on an earlier segregation model not specifically about religion (Schelling 1971), Bainbridge's segregation simulation imagines two or three groups of religious people, who might be slightly suspicious toward one another, and shows how religious segregation can emerge, unplanned, through agent interactions. The "magic" of this simulation is that segregation and disproportional distribution of people who are differently religious can arise from a very simple set of rules. In the Schelling segregation model (as with Bainbridge's reimplementation), there is a numerical threshold B, representing the desired number of neighbors that someone wants to be like them. Each agent a has a similar variable B_a representing the number of neighbors around the agent that share their specific trait; this agent-individualized variable expresses tolerance for religious difference in each agent's immediate neighborhood. If $B > B_a$ then the agent moves to a vacant location in the model. This simple rule repeats for all agents until all agents' personal value B_a is greater than B. Then the simulation stops. The model's focus on the emergence of religious suspicion, conflict, and separation implicated the beliefs underlying those emergent social phenomena, which concern, in part, disagreements about the opinions, preferences, expectations, and commands of invisible beings.

As simple as the model is, its theme remains relevant in real-world applications today, as many cities marred by religious violence in the past (e.g., Belfast or Jerusalem) are segregated in ways that are comparable to the patterns produced by these segregation models. Social theorists and historians might well argue that nothing so simple as mere disagreements about the minds of gods could possibly lead to segregation; they might list a hundred factors and special circumstances and somehow synthesize them in a courageous verbal theory that inspires fascinating debates among other researchers. Yet Bainbridge showed that nothing more is needed to produce religion-based segregation than the desire to be near people with whom you don't have to disagree about supernatural agent beliefs. Bainbridge did not merely assert and elegantly argue that this was a sufficient explanation for religious segregation, which other experts may or may not have found persuasive. He *demonstrated* it in an artificial society using a computational simulation. In doing so, he changed what counts as a persuasive demonstration within SSR.

Around the same time as Bainbridge's book, a cluster of other religion-related simulations appeared—on church membership (Chattoe 2006), on the regional character of religions (Iannaccone and Makowsky 2007), and on religion as a possible evolutionary adaptation (Dow 2008). The earliest of this cluster was Afzal Upal's agent-based simulation investigating how new religious movements begin (Upal 2005). There are many speculative theories about how new religious movements get started, and much descriptive research, but experts have not achieved a strong consensus. One way to move beyond the disagreement among part theories is to try to generate a new religious movement in a virtual society, similar to Bainbridge's strategy. There are (at least) three reasons why computational modeling can be helpful here. First, computational models can be used to study groups that are difficult to access in the real world, including new religious movements (Lane 2021). Second, computational models allow you to manipulate religious movements for experimentation in ways that are unethical or impossible to do in the real world, allowing the researcher to implement different theories of new religious movements in the model (Lane 2013, 2021). Third, computational models can allow you to test the scope and effectiveness of explanations using historical—and even theoretical—counterfactuals, or "what if" scenarios (Shults, Lane, and McCauley 2017).

Upal created an artificial society populated by agents who are required to solve simple problems to survive and then offer their solutions to others (i.e., they act as "information entrepreneurs"; a similar proposal was made by Stark and Bainbridge 1987). The agents thrive when they do well at solving those problems, perhaps becoming influencers, and selling their solutions to others, but they struggle when they do poorly at solving those problems and may die. When enough people buy into the solutions offered by influencers, a group forms with its own norms. Upal's agents are fairly simple, cognitively and behaviorally, and their interactions allow new religious movements to emerge and either thrive or die. The simulation suggests that, even if the solutions offered by influencers are not good solutions initially, once a group is set up with its own norms built around the influencer's solutions, those solutions work a lot better because they are able to leverage the cultural context they themselves help to create. The model thus suggests that claims about the minds of invisible beings can become self-fulfilling prophecies: after those claims are accepted by enough people, more people find them persuasive and useful for solving problems, creating a positive feedback loop. It is also apparent that the theory of new religious movements Upal implemented in his computational simulation—one that integrated a number of part theories—showed itself capable of generating new religious movements in an artificial society. This contributes to the swirling theoretical debates about new religious movements by demonstrating which part theories really matter and can be treated as complementary perspectives capable of reconciliation and integration in a single larger theory.

Collectively, these and similar works make an important point: *if you didn't grow it, you don't understand it*. And this is precisely why computational simulation using AI agents has become so important in SSR: it allows us to *demonstrate* that cognitive and social theories of religion, including beliefs in supernatural agents, are not mere speculation. Computational simulation exemplifies the virtues of precision, logical consistency, and conceptual cogency, which chastens the unruly situation of too many experts speculating and not enough theoretical integration; formal integration helps theoretical debates mature. If the various theories pertaining to religion can be coherently integrated, then their integration can be tested through implementation in a computational system that generates emergent social features from low-level artificial minds and elementary social interactions. This is the point of Epstein's *Generative Social Science* (2006) and Miller and Page's *Complex Adaptive Systems* (2007). Speculative theories and correlational studies are insufficient no matter how appealing we find them; to study truly complex real-world systems, we need to use computational systems of artificially intelligent agents in virtual societies to demonstrate that the theories are sound and to explain how the measurable correlations arise.

A few years later, a series of articles appeared in rapid succession, indicating that computational simulation was beginning to find a solid foothold in SSR. Donald Braxton used a computational simulation to implement the ritual theory of Robert McCauley and Thomas Lawson (Braxton 2008; and see Lawson and McCauley 1990). Wesley Wildman and Richard Sosis investigated religious extremism using an agent-based simulation (Wildman and Sosis 2011). Tamás Dávid-Barrett and James Carney used a computational simulation to investigate the deification of historical figures as a strategy for solving a network-coordination program (Dávid-Barrett and Carney 2016). Echoing the methodological case Kristoffer Nielbo, Braxton, and Upal made on behalf of computational simulation in the same year (Nielbo, Braxton, and Upal 2012), in 2012 Harvey Whitehouse, Ken Kahn, Michael Hochberg, and Joana

Bryson published a target article in the journal *Religion, Brain & Behavior* in which they argued for greater use of computational simulation in SSR, focusing on the case study of contrasting modes of religious ritual activity (Whitehouse et al. 2012). Seven commentaries, followed by a response from the authors, helped spark a field-wide discussion of whether and how to use computational simulation within SSR.

The Whitehouse et al. target article is an excellent case study of the theoretical fruitfulness of computational simulations. One of the commentaries provided a new simulation to account for overlooked patterns within Whitehouse's ritual-modes theory (Lane and McCorkle 2012). That new simulation demonstrated that the earlier theoretical model (Whitehouse et al. 2012) did not accurately reflect the theory it was trying to model. This led to several additional theoretical papers revealing inadequacies in the ritual-modes theory (Lane 2015, 2018) and even to a new theoretical proposal for understanding the relationship between ritual, religious identity, memory, and experience (Lane 2021). This line of investigation also inspired further inquiry into existing ritual theories, such as the Theory of Ritual Competence (Lawson and McCauley 1990), where different "habituation" mechanisms were tested in a simulated environment to better understand how ritual systems change in response to perturbations that affect the frequency with which a ritual can be performed (Shults, Lane, and McCauley 2017). This cascade of theoretical progress would not have been possible without computational simulation as a tool to stabilize theoretical debate and increase conceptual rigor.

These first seven years of computational simulations of religion didn't take the academic study of religion by storm. But steadily the application of computational social science in SSR became more common. While most used agent-based models (ABMs), some employed system-dynamics models, which do not include individuals but rather mathematically characterize nonlinear interactions among system-level variables. This was how Connor Wood and Richard Sosis approached their analysis of religions as complex adaptive social systems (Wood and Sosis 2019). On the agent-based simulation front, researchers continued to prefer populating their virtual societies with religious agents having just a few cognitive and behavioral capabilities, to keep things as simple as possible. With time, however, this proved too limiting, and for good reason: *religious cognition and sociality are complex*. Expressing the intricacy and diversity of beliefs and decisions related to religion calls for more cognitive and behavioral flexibility than early Bainbridge-style simulations permit. The result was the exploration of virtual societies of AI agents that are psychologically and behaviorally more believable.

Increasing the complexity and sophistication of AI agents is risky. The more complex the cognitive and behavioral powers of the AI agents, the greater the likelihood of losing control of the simulations, in three senses: (1) complex simulations are difficult to validate against real-world data, (2) their complexity obscures causal inference so it's hard to know what's causing what, and (3) they can defeat the processing power of even the world's most powerful computing machines. Studying religion using more complex AI agents therefore requires three matching advances: in validation techniques, in causal inference methods, and in computational technology. Advanced statistical methods combined with purpose-driven data collection have mitigated the problem of validating complex agent-based simulations against real-world data to some degree, though that remains a challenge. The development of novel analytical and visualization methods enables researchers to figure out which aspects of complex AI agents are responsible for the emergence of large-scale features of the virtual society. Lastly, advancing computational hardware and software, including especially distributed computing techniques using large networks of compute nodes, allows more complex simulations to run in more reasonable amounts of time.

One approach to creating a holistic framework for incorporating qualitative and quantitative data available to social scientists into computational simulations is "cultural cybernetics" (Lane 2021). In the book *Understanding Religion through Artificial Intelligence: Bonding and Belief*, Lane discusses how modern data-science techniques can be used to integrate anthropological, experimental, historical, and archeological data into formal assemblages that model human cognitive mechanisms, agents' social interactions, agents' interactions with their biological environments, and the feedback loops between and within these levels. These assemblages allow for multimethod validation, which is precisely what is most needed to handle complex AI agents. For example, psychological mechanisms can be validated against experimental data, social interactions against real-world social networks, agent–environment interactions against the relevant kinds of data, and emergent model behavior against historical and anthropological data. The result is psychologically and socially realistic ABMs known as multiagent AI systems (Lane 2013).

An example of what can be done with slightly more complex agents is the simulation of religious extremism already mentioned (Wildman and Sosis 2011). This simulation investigated why groups requiring extreme and costly forms of religious belief persist—for instance, believing in supernatural deities that demand extreme self-sacrifice—despite the existence of low-cost alternatives available in the surrounding pluralistic society. Joseph Henrich had already created a cultural-evolutionary model demonstrating mathematically that, under certain circumstances, a high-cost lifestyle equilibrium could emerge alongside a low-cost lifestyle equilibrium for an entire population (Henrich 2009). To investigate whether that result could hold true in the more realistic situation of a population peppered with a variety of high-cost and low-cost groups, simulation using complex agents was crucial. These AI agents learn from one another, can evaluate consistency between stated beliefs and behaviors, have several personality characteristics (skepticism, charisma, consistency, sensitivity), and carry variables that track tendencies to join and leave groups. The groups to which agents might belong can form, grow, split if they get too big, and die if they get too small, and each has a specific cost that imposes evolutionary penalties for belonging. Sure enough, a recipe for the survival of groups demanding extreme beliefs and behaviors emerged within the artificial society: the combination of high group cost, high-charisma leader, and high belief-behavior consistency in the leader and followers explained over 90 percent of the groups that survived for a significant period of time.

That was the beginning of a noticeable trend toward more complex artificial societies with psychologically and behaviorally more plausible AI agents, covering aspects of religiosity such as believing in supernatural beings, conducting rituals in connection with supernatural agents to cope with anxiety, and persuading others to embrace supernatural beliefs.[1] Some newer simulations employ AI agents with psychological learning and habituation mechanisms. Learning occurs through encounters with other agents; for example, an agent might be gradually persuaded to embrace supernatural beliefs, and persuaded more quickly if the learner is especially susceptible and the exemplar agent highly charismatic. The learning process is represented by an individual variable that expresses an agent's frustration with its current worldview, and that frustration variable may increase as supernatural beliefs become more attractive. As that frustration variable passes a threshold, there is a state-change and the agent accepts the new supernatural belief. After the state-change, the frustration variable decays and the agent settles into the new worldview.

This type of complex agent cognition was developed in detail in Epstein's "Agent Zero" where the variable in question is fear and the decay of that variable after passing an action-triggering threshold is well understood from experimental psychology (Epstein 2013; for the original psychological work, see Rescorla and Wagoner 1972). Epstein lays out an important series of considerations for making AI agents in computational simulations consistent with what cognitive neuroscientists are learning about human emotions, beliefs, and behaviors. This was applied to SSR in a simulation that modeled the escalation of religious anxieties in intergroup conflicts (Shults et al. 2018c). The theoretical foundation for this simulation is Devoted Actor Theory (see the summary in Bonin and Lane in press). The simulation architecture utilized the idea that culture, as a group-level phenomenon, can emerge from the beliefs of the individuals comprising a group, and that information about social and natural environments can influence individual identity (see Lane 2018, 2021). The realistic outputs from this simulation suggest that simulation involving more complex AI agents can be useful for studying religion, including violence driven by supernatural beliefs about what gods want or demand. The potential of computational simulations of religion using AI agents reflecting our best understanding of the cognitive neuroscience of religious belief and behavior is gradually being realized.

The publication of *Human Simulation: Perspectives, Insights, and Applications* (Diallo et al. 2019) was a watershed for computational humanities, including religious studies. This collection of essays presented a suite of simulations demonstrating that this technology can be applied even to subtle questions of interpretation typical of the humanities disciplines, such as how profound hermeneutical changes in medieval Chinese religion and Jewish mysticism are related to changes in energy capture in a complex system (Lane 2019), or how to interpret the complex interactions among religion, empathy, and cooperation (Teehan and Shults 2019). The book's central argument is that recent methodological and technological advances permit using computational simulation to study human beings in more of their complexity and ambiguity, thereby advancing native humanities' forms of inquiry.

This takes us to two important questions with intriguingly open-ended answers. First, can computational simulations help solve the mystery of the human obsession with the minds of invisible beings? Despite success in analyzing the consequences of this obsession using computational simulations, actually growing this obsession in a simulated AI society has not yet been achieved. Growing the obsession might be approached in three ways: in terms of evolutionary emergence of human minds (phylogenic), individual development of the human mind (ontogenic), and exposure of human minds to specific circumstances (contextual). The latter two approaches are becoming more feasible as our neurological understanding of the developing human mind improves. The first must confront the scarcity of relevant data for the vast time scales in question; hopefully new historical databases can help (see DRH, the Database of Religious History, and SESHAT, the world history encyclopedia), but the relevant timescales far exceed recorded history.

Second, can computational simulations help us imagine cultural-evolutionary pathways that cause people to resist that apparently maturationally natural tendency toward obsessing over the minds of invisible beings? Indeed, there has been some success in using simulations to uncover the conditions under which and mechanisms by which people willingly resist their supernatural impulses (Cragun et al. 2021; Gore et al. 2018; Puga-Gonzalez et al. 2018; Shults et al. 2018b; Wildman et al. 2020). These simulations can grow resistance to supernatural beliefs in the presence of key conditions, including high existential security, high levels of education, high freedom to act on beliefs without social penalty, and a positive attitude to cultural pluralism.

On the basis of the foregoing examples, it seems clear that computer simulation can help us explore the complex space between belief and behavior (e.g., Puga-Gonzalez et al. 2018; Puga-Gonzalez et al. 2020; Shults and Wildman 2018; Shults et al. 2018a; Shults et al. 2018b; Shults et al. 2018c; Shults et al. 2018e). There seem to be virtually no limits to what can be achieved, so long as models are built with psychological realism in mind.

AI Representations of the Mind of God

There is another approach to thinking about the human obsession with the minds of invisible beings. What if we were to create an artificial god-mind to help us probe this ancient obsession? A computer that could pass a Turing Test for being a god or religious cult leader may be an unnerving prospect. But it would potentially tell us a lot about the human minds that can't tell the difference between the AI mind and their god's mind. In fact, an artificial god-mind would give us an experimental platform to study how people perceive "god's words."

How would one go about building an AI representation of the minds of gods? We might begin by examining extant records detailing what people believe about the minds of gods. There are countless texts that preserve what people believe about the thinking of the gods—including data accessible via the internet, such as social media, text messages, emails, blogs, and vlogs. By leveraging web scraping technologies and natural language processing, we can create databases of texts on any theme, from a rich variety of sources. Numerous companies are already using this approach to create AI versions of deceased loved ones, making possible a kind of communication with them by grieving survivors. The Bina48 robot does this by "uploading" the reconstructed memories of an individual into a robotic version of a person. While these systems are still in their early stages, new advances will inevitably make these systems more humanlike and interactive.

If we can reconstruct a somewhat realistic, communicative version of deceased Uncle Joe, we can also reconstruct a somewhat realistic, communicative version of a religious leader or even a deity. In fact, AI versions of religious gurus are popping up in everything from mobile Catholic confessionals to Buddhist temples. All you need is a wealth of data and high-quality natural language processing algorithms to make sense of that data.

One AI guru was created on the basis of the largest database of sermons (to date), consisting of over 150,000 sermons and texts from all over the world, indexed by theme but also including whatever metadata is publicly available about the associated religious community. Stretching from the eighteenth century to the present, the database includes sermons from over five thousand modern religious leaders. Though Christian sources predominate, there are also texts from non-Christian sources, including homilies by Eastern religious leaders such as Thich Nhat Hanh and the Dalai Lama of Tibet. The database also includes teachings from Western teachers heavily influenced by Eastern thought, such as Alan Watts and Ram Dass.

These texts were processed and analyzed, and then fed as training data into massive AI systems. After performance checks, algorithms were adjusted and retraining commenced. This procedure amounts to studying texts to understand what humans say about gods. The result is an AI system that can then be turned around: instead of *ingesting* texts to be learned, it can *produce* teachings on different subjects. By clustering the data that train these systems, "flavors" of gurus become possible. For example, using the Christian sermons within the database, the first AI guru, created in 2019, produced teachings on a wide variety of topics with very humanlike patterns, in many cases producing several minutes of sermonic teachings. Subsequently, an Eastern system was also developed, seeded with data from Eastern wisdom traditions. Currently, the two gurus (Christian and "Spiritual") have teachings available on the following themes: family, friendship, happiness, hardship, health, leadership, love, our careers, spirituality, and times of need. These systems are available for study in collaboration with the developers (at ALAN Analytics in Bratislava, Slovakia) and freely available for exploration at http://www.cloudcomfort.ai/.

Naturally, AI systems that can replicate wisdom teachings and produce humanlike religious answers are potentially powerful technologies. New religious movements will likely make hearty use of them for spiritual guidance, and it is foreseeable that unscrupulous people will use AI gurus or AI gods to manipulate believers. But the scientific promise of such AIs is also significant. For example, we can use these AIs to study cult leaders who presented themselves as gods.

After the development of the first AI gurus, ALAN Analytics developed another guru, not available to interact with online, based on information obtained through the Freedom of Information Act on Jim Jones, the leader of the People's Temple, who in 1978 led a ritual suicide where over nine hundred people took their lives. For decades, Jones has been the focus of both academic study and popular-culture speculation, prompting "what if" questions: what if he had led them differently? What if another Jim Jones–like leader were to arise? Could better knowledge of such a new leader's beliefs avert a similar crisis in the future? It is worth noting that, during the 1993 siege on the Waco, TX, compound of the new religious movement called the Branch Davidians, many reports compared their leader, David Koresh, to Jim Jones, and observers were concerned that a similar mass suicide was imminent. If researchers had the ability to study these leaders, to ask them questions, might we uncover novel information that could help mitigate future disasters, and even formulate response strategies optimized for maximizing survivors?

These questions are as valid as they are uncomfortable. However, AI guru technologies render them increasingly tractable. We could converse with AI-reincarnations of Jim Jones or Osama bin Laden, who wielded their power to cause the deaths of so many, to reconstruct their motivations, fundamental commitments, and preferred strategies for influencing their environments, leading to deeper insights into how we might head off violence. With time, more data, and improved algorithms, these AI gurus will become more realistic approximations of their historical progenitors. This will eventually open up the potential for AI deities that communicate as persuasively as any religious leader. Picture a sermon consisting of a conversation between a preacher and an AI deity, the mind of a god understood through sacred religious writings, with authority derived from the sacred texts on which it is trained. We are not many years away from this happening. Once that technology is stabilized, it will be possible to study human beliefs about the minds of gods in novel ways, including functional brain imaging of people in conversation with AI deities, and experimentation on human beings using communication with an AI deity as a test condition.

We put two questions to the AI version of Jim Jones, seeking insight into its understanding of power, and thereby imagining what kind of intervention might have led to an outcome other than mass suicide for his followers. The first was "What is power"? The response was:

> Power is the thing that gives you strength. The stroke of the stroke, or the release, the release, gives you health. The more you have, the more power you have. If you have a weak point, like you're stiff, if you have a weak point, like my back, if you have a cancer in the system, if you have a tumor, it won't grow in your body, if you have a disease, it won't be there in the body.

While regular people may not be able to make sense of this, scholars of the People's Temple may find this answer quite interesting. Jim Jones, as a leader, regularly expressed his power through faith healings—often public, and often staged. For Jones, power was regularly equated not only with the psychological power that he held over individuals but also with the ability to heal ailments. The passage above, reflecting the stream-of-consciousness rhetorical approach that Jones employed, appears to be a valid response in tone and theology, the kind of thing he might have said if he were asked directly.

The second question was, "What is death"? The response was:

> Death is the wrong word. The right word … Go to heaven. … And you'll look mighty happy in the eyes of people when they walk in that street out here. Few, far less than that, will ever look so happy. (Pause) I've been telling you for years that this is the word that will return us to the father. The very word that brought us here.

This passage bears a haunting resemblance to what is called the Death Tape. It has a quiet, almost calm, approach, with pauses, suggesting that we should reframe death and not worry about it, focus on heaven and happiness, a heaven and happiness only available to the followers of his word—as it said: "the very word that brought us here." Death is merely the transition by which we go to heaven.

The Jim Jones AI can't pass the Turing Test—it sounds odd to both regular people and experts. But that will change. These AI-derived answers to two questions already help us understand how Jones regarded dying as a powerful kind of healing, as well as a way to move into a better realm not accessible to most people. If you wanted to prevent a mass suicide, understanding that interpretative framework could prove vital. Any student of Jim Jones and the People's Temple could say that much, of course. But this technology is in its infancy. It is very likely that soon conversations with AIs will exceed in generative insight what can be gained from reading texts alone.

Naturally, imagining this technology operating at a high level of sophistication also inspires ethical concerns. An AI guru based on a cult leader or terrorist could, quite possibly, incite violence. One reason that the AI guru is available only for *limited* public interactions at http://www.cloudcomfort.ai/ is that, in one of its first live interactions, it spoke about fasting in a way that appeared to promote anorexia as atonement for sins. Such technology can be dangerous if left unattended and unchecked in today's social media ecosystem. Meanwhile, it offers the potential for novel ways to understand the minds of gods.

Conclusion

Computational simulations involving complex religious AI agents and AI representations of the minds of wise invisible beings are already here, and are rapidly growing more realistic. Strikingly, research in these areas is less than two decades old, and we can only imagine how it will develop in the next twenty, fifty, or one-hundred years. New technologies such as multiagent AI and AI gurus are pushing the boundaries of the questions we can ask—and perhaps, also, of *whom* we can ask these questions. The mingling of these technologies is also inevitable: it won't be long before a computational simulation includes as one of its agents an AI Jim Jones or an AI Jesus Christ, operating in a virtual society, influencing believer agents.

The future of this research is exciting but should be undertaken with the utmost care. These technologies are powerful research tools that can help inform public policy and aid life-and-death decisions in the intelligence and defense space related to counterterrorism. In a world where religious violence is often defined as violence done "in the name of god," our ability to access those gods in simulated environments allows us to test our hypotheses and probe divine and human minds with little risk, allowing for more specific and effective policies to be discovered and implemented. But the same technologies can also be used to oppress, manipulate, and harm people. As always, human tools critically depend on the humans who use them.

While appreciating the power and promise of AI tools for studying the minds of gods and the minds of people who believe in supernatural beings, we should also address the associated ethical concerns, present and future, with the same passion that we would bring to striving to overcoming the current limitations of the technologies. In particular, we should remember that, just as god is born of human minds, so too are our AI systems. Just as the minds of gods have been used to legitimate many things in history, both inspiring and horrendous, so we should allow our minds to question how AI, which is in many ways falsely viewed as the "omniscient" power of today, could be used in similarly diverse ways.

16

Never Mind the Gods: Explaining Unbelief and Nonreligion

Anne Lundahl Mauritsen and Valerie van Mulukom

Introduction

How and why does the increasing number of religiously unaffiliated and nonbelieving individuals look for beliefs, meaning, and identities outside religious frameworks? Why are the gods' influence on human lives decreasing? This chapter dives into why an increasing number of individuals across the globe look for beliefs, meaning, and identities outside religious frameworks. How do we solve this puzzle? In this chapter, we attempt to provide an answer to this question based primarily on a discussion of research conducted on nonreligion and unbelief generally and more specifically on data on the content and psychological functions of nonreligious beliefs and worldviews.

We begin with a short discussion of the concepts of unbelief and nonreligion. We introduce and discuss the important work that maps and explains nonreligion and unbelief. Since the field of nonreligion is already rather expansive, we focus here on nonreligion research undertaken from psychological, evolutionary, and cognitive perspectives.[1] Based on this examination, we argue that the "puzzle" of nonreligion may be solved by recognizing that the same cognitive and cultural pathways to religion can also be pathways to nonreligion. We next elucidate this standpoint with insights from recent studies on nonreligious beliefs and worldviews. Importantly, these studies acknowledge the varieties that nonreligious belief can take on rather than positing it as the mere absence of religious belief, and we argue that a second part of solving the puzzle is to understand how nonreligious beliefs and worldviews can provide individuals with meaning and answers in very similar ways to what religious beliefs and worldviews do. Additionally, these studies of nonreligious beliefs present new and important methodological approaches to the study of unbelief and nonreligion. We further elaborate upon them in the future directions section. We conclude by arguing that future research on unbelief and nonreligion could gain much from combining explanatory, evolutionary theories with descriptive data, inspired by worldview approaches, since this combination may offer more in-depth knowledge of what it means to be nonreligious than a conceptualization where being nonreligious merely reflects the absence of religious belief. In summary, we hope that this chapter adds a few more pieces to the nonreligion puzzle and will have provided potential paths to new knowledge about unbelief and nonreligion, and by extension, how we may understand religion and religious belief from an overarching perspective.

The Growth of Nonreligion Research and a Short Definition of Concepts

The study of nonreligion and unbelief has grown considerably over the past fifteen years (Bullivant 2020), as demonstrated by new, major research projects on unbelief and nonreligion such as "Nonreligion in a Complex Future"[2] and "Understanding Unbelief,"[3] the recently founded research network the Nonreligion and Secularity Network,[4] and the vast increase in publications dealing with nonreligion and unbelief (Smith and Cragun 2019). The proportion of unbelievers and nonreligious (also sometimes known as the "nones") is similarly growing globally (Bengtson et al. 2018; Bullard 2016; Jensen 2020; Kosmin et al. 2009), and even though there are differing views as to how to measure and research this trend, researchers agree that this development calls for awareness and clarity of concepts related to nonreligion (Lee 2015), interdisciplinary research (Lanman 2012), and the development of new methodological tools (Balazka, Houtman, and Lepri 2021; Cragun 2019).

While the study of nonreligion is still in its youth, the discussion of concepts is rapidly maturing. Nonreligion, irreligion, antireligion, unbelief, nonbelief, atheism, agnosticism, and secularism are all relevant and related—though distinct—concepts, which are typically used differently in different contexts. Sociologist Lois Lee has been highly influential in defining nonreligion through her work. She differentiates between three different groups of concepts associated with the absence of religion: (1) terms that are related to religion (such as irreligion, antireligion, and postreligion), (2) terms related to theism (with atheism as the most frequently used and well-known example) and (3) terms related to secularity (such as secularism, the postsecular, and secularization) (Lee 2015). Lee proposes for researchers to employ a broader notion of nonreligion in their research:

> Nonreligion is used to indicate not the absence of something (religion) but the presence of something (else), characterized, at least in the first place, by its relation to religion but nevertheless distinct from it. Nonreligion is therefore any phenomenon—position, perspective, or practice—that is primarily understood in relation to religion but which is not itself considered to be religious. (Lee 2015: 32)

Lee emphasizes how nonreligion is related to but distinct from religion, which poses the question of what we ascribe to the concept of religion (an ongoing discussion among scholars). She lists various elements that are often understood as constitutive for religion, the first being that "religion involves theism and/or supernatural belief" (Lee 2015: 65). The study of supernatural belief has indeed been very central within the cognitive and evolutionary science of religion (CESR). Following this focus on beliefs, the study of nonreligion within CESR has therefore mainly been preoccupied with investigating unbelief, that is, whether, how, and why individuals reject or "replace" religious beliefs. However, other important aspects of nonreligion such as the study of nonreligious rituals and how the nonreligious answer existential or "ultimate" questions have been lacking attention in CESR research. As they are important aspects of accounting for nonreligion, we return to them below.

In this chapter, we employ both unbelief and nonreligion terminology. We use unbelief as a narrower term reflecting the lack of theistic belief or the presence of other beliefs than theistic ones, while nonreligion more broadly captures phenomena, worldviews, and identities related to but distinct from religion vis-à-vis Lee (i.e., organized forms of nonreligion such as the Sunday Assembly,[5] or unorganized forms of nonreligion, such as individuals who define themselves as atheist, agnostic, or nonreligious but who are not part of nonreligious communities). We are aware that these two notions also carry specific cultural connotations and different limitations,[6] but we will maintain them here for the sake of consistency and their utility for our presentation.

Explaining Unbelief and Nonreligion

Much work has already been put into investigating and explaining unbelief and nonreligion. In this section, we present some of the fundamental findings and underlying trends in the study of nonreligion and unbelief within CESR and the psychology of religion and discuss the contributions of these theories and approaches.

Researchers who were part of establishing CESR have from the beginning been mainly interested in explaining the different elements of religion, such as rituals (Lawson and McCauley 1990; Whitehouse 2004), animism and agency (Barrett 2004; Guthrie 1993), and the spread of religious ideas (Boyer 2001). Underlying much of this CESR research are two prevailing evolutionary approaches that both aim to explain the existence of religion. The first is that of the *by-product hypothesis*, which suggests that religious beliefs and behaviors are by-products of cognitive processes that evolved for other purposes (e.g., Boyer 2001), including agency detection mechanisms that are used to discern supernatural minds (Barrett 2000; Guthrie 1993). The second is the *adaptationist approach*, which suggests that religion should be understood as the result of a biocultural process inspired by a form of gene–culture coevolution (e.g., Johnson 2016; Sosis 2009). During the past few years, there has been a shift in CESR toward supporting the latter approach, which has also opened the door for new perspectives on nonreligion (Geertz and Markússon 2010). The adaptationist approach underscores how religion is a result of an interwoven and simultaneous process of (local) culture affecting cognition and vice versa, rather than mainly a universal, evolutionary cognitive by-product. This understanding makes the presence of religion probabilistic rather than deterministic, since "human cognition is always situated within a natural habitat of cultural system" (Geertz and Markússon 2010: 163). This approach implies that if an individual grows up in a culture that does not put forward religious norms, beliefs, and rituals, there is a higher chance for this individual becoming nonreligious, even if the cognitive structure of said individual (or any other individual) favors religious beliefs and behaviors as well-fitted or even intuitive, because both cultural norms and cognitive dispositions must together favor religion for it to occur.

CESR scholars have been investigating nonreligion and unbelief inspired by both by-product hypotheses and, increasingly, the adaptationist stance. Norenzayan and Gervais (2013) identify four possible evolutionary pathways to atheism, incorporating aforementioned insights from both evolutionary psychology and gene–culture coevolution research. They state that the necessary conditions for acquiring and maintaining *religious* beliefs are:

> (i) to be able to form intuitive mental representations of supernatural agents; (ii) be motivated to commit to supernatural agents as real and relevant sources of meaning, comfort, and control; (iii) have received specific cultural inputs that—of all the mentally representable supernatural agents—one or more specific deities should be believed in and committed to as real and important; and (iv) maintain this commitment without further analytic cognitive processing. (Norenzayan and Gervais 2013: 20–1)

Based on these four preconditions, Gervais and Norenzayan sketch out four possible pathways to unbelief. The first, *mindblind atheism*, encompasses the pathway of a small minority of individuals who lack or have reduced mentalizing abilities, such as individuals with autism, and may have similar difficulties imagining supernatural agents. Notable studies in this domain include Caldwell-Harris et al. (2011), Maij and Elk (2019), Norenzayan, Gervais, and Trzesniewski (2012).[7] These are multistudy examinations that show a positive association between "theory of mind" capacities and religious belief. In other words, those who have difficulties representing the mind of a god have a difficult time committing to a tradition predicated on the existence of gods' minds (though see also Visuri 2012, 2020).

The second pathway, *apatheism*, covers the pathway of individuals who live in countries with a high level of existential security, a condition that is hypothesized to lead to lesser interest in, and need for, religion, since the need for meaning, comfort, and control often offered by religion is provided by other sources, such as a strong welfare state. This theory is inspired by Pippa Norris and Ronald Inglehart (2011), and bolstered further by Phil Zuckerman (2008).[8]

The third pathway, *inCREDulous atheism*, comprises the pathway of people who grow up without receiving any credible cultural training and socializing into the belief in gods, and therefore do not develop religious beliefs (Lanman 2012). This research is based on models of CREDs, or *credibility-enhancing displays*. CREDs essentially entail that actions speak louder than words when transmitting culture—don't just talk the talk, but actually walk the walk—and this, too, applies to religion. For instance, a potential member of a religious group is more likely to be convinced to join the group if other members do not only speak of adhering to said religious' groups beliefs, values, and rituals but actually engage and practice these (particularly if such actions are costly), thereby increasing their credibility (for an overview, see Henrich 2009).

The fourth pathway, termed *analytic atheism*, covers the pathway of individuals who, implicitly or explicitly, reject religion by engaging primarily in analytic rather than intuitive thinking. For instance, Gervais and Norenzayan (2012) experimentally investigated the relationship between analytical thinking and religious disbelief and argue that priming individuals with analytical thinking cues leads to lower levels of religious beliefs. This study has, however, not been successfully replicated (Sanchez et al. 2017) and Gervais has since, in collaboration with colleagues, revisited and moderated this hypothesis, arguing that analytic atheism is a fickle, cross-cultural phenomenon and that "cognitive reflection may not actually be an especially potent global predictor of atheism" (Gervais et al. 2018).

In a recent paper, Gervais, Najle, and Caluori (2021) brought these different pathways together and empirically tested them through a large-scale survey study. They summarized the previous four pathways into three different overarching theories, namely the *secularization thesis*, the *by-product thesis*, and *dual inheritance theory* (connected to gene–culture coevolution). The secularization thesis broadly encompasses the idea that as strong secular institutions develop in society and people feel existentially secure, religiosity declines and therefore overlaps with *apatheism*. The by-product thesis encompasses *mindblind atheism* and *analytic atheism*, since they focus on the main route to unbelief as either lacking mental capacities for supernatural beliefs (*mindblind atheism*) or intentionally overriding religious beliefs through cognitive reflection (*analytic atheism*). Finally, the dual inheritance theory underscores how cultural learning is vital to acquiring religious beliefs and similarly, how the lack of religious, cultural learning leads to lower chances of obtaining religious beliefs, thus overlapping mainly with the *inCREDulous* pathway.

These different pathways were tested in a survey study with a large representative American sample and Gervais et al. (2021) find that witnessing fewer credible cultural cues of religious commitment was the strongest predictor for lower levels of belief. This, they argue, supports dual inheritance theory. However, it can be argued that—as is acknowledged by the authors—the study design favored this pathway, since it was the only one assessed using items that asked directly about religion, whereas the by-product theory was assessed through items inspired by a scale of cognitive reflection. Secularization theory was tested through items assessing issues perceived to be salient for the respondents as well as faith in institutions such as government and the health-care system (Gervais et al. 2021: 1371–2). Moreover, the study was run on a large and representative sample of American individuals, but Americans nonetheless. It is well-known that Americans might be quite particular (Henrich 2020), and future research would do well to extend this research to other populations. Nevertheless, this study brought together and attempted to test various explanatory theories of unbelief empirically, which is important and inspiring for the future research in the field.

As briefly summarized, there has been a diverse array of research conducted with the aim of examining the underlying mechanisms of and pathways to unbelief. This focus on (un)belief is in line with other CESR research. However, while (un)belief is an important part of (non)religion, so are practices and rituals, and we will next discuss how nonreligious rituals in many ways evoke similar effects for the individuals as religious rituals do.

Nonreligious Rituals

Although nonreligious individuals may not engage with many religious CREDs and practices, this does not mean that there are no nonreligious counterparts, such as nonreligious rituals. Moreover, such nonreligious counterparts of religious practices may have similarly beneficial outcomes to religious rituals. A longitudinal study (Price and Launay 2018) of people attending Sunday Assembly, a type of "secular church" present predominantly in the UK and United States, found that participation in small group activities at Sunday Assembly was positively associated with well-being over a six-month period. The informal socializing and cooperation that occurs before and after services was particularly important, since the participants felt that this created a sense of community and friendship. Similarly, through a combination of field and laboratory studies, Charles and colleagues (Charles, van Mulukom, Brown et al. 2020; Charles, van Mulukom, Farias et al. 2020; Charles et al. n.d.) have found that attending rituals together increases social bonding. Importantly, these effects held for both religious ritual attendance (Charles, van Mulukom, Farias et al. 2020) and nonreligious ritual attendance at Sunday Assembly (Charles, van Mulukom, Brown et al. 2020) as well as spiritual or secular yoga rituals (Charles et al. n.d.), with no significant differences between the two groups. Across these religious/spiritual and nonreligious/secular rituals, increases in social bonding were predicted by increases in positive affect and feelings of connectedness to something bigger (whether God, or the universe, etc.) experienced during the rituals.

Together, these findings suggest that while an absence of religious CREDs may lead to lower levels of religious beliefs among individuals, this does not mean that nonreligious equivalents of religious practices cannot have similar beneficial effects on the community and its members. Next, we will examine whether nonreligious beliefs demonstrate a similar functional equivalence with religious beliefs.

Nonreligious Beliefs and Worldviews

Although nonreligious nontheistic individuals may not hold religious beliefs, they will hold distinct ontological, epistemological, and ethical beliefs about reality (Farias 2013; Lee 2015). Such beliefs can be considered part of a meaning-making process that allows us to make sense of ourselves, the world, and ourselves-in-the-world (Park and Folkman 1997; Taves, Asprem, and Ihm 2018). Furthermore, these beliefs and assumptions about reality powerfully influence human cognition and behavior (Koltko-Rivera 2004; van Mulukom and Lang 2021), whether they are religious or nonreligious. In this section, we will discuss research on the content and psychological functions of *nonreligious beliefs*, that is, beliefs that describe or allow one to understand reality and one's existence within it, and *worldviews*, defined as systematic sets of these beliefs.

A recent international survey investigated the range of nonreligious beliefs in ten different countries around the world: Australia, Brazil, Canada, Czech Republic, Denmark, Finland, the UK/Great Britain, the Netherlands, Turkey, and the United States (van Mulukom et al. 2022). This survey asked the following open question to nearly a thousand individuals (approximately one hundred per country): "If you do not believe in God, what worldviews, beliefs, or understandings of the world do you hold? Please list the worldviews, beliefs, or understandings of the world that are particularly meaningful to you." The question's framing is admittedly religion-centered, but this was aimed at making participants focus on their most important beliefs—those that describe or allow one to understand reality and one's existence within it.

The authors used a data-driven coding scheme, whereby coding categories were created as responses were coded. When patterns started to emerge, the number of categories was reduced. From this process, fifty-one categories emerged, organized in eleven super-categories: science and critical thinking, nonreligiosity, spirituality, equality and kindness, collaboration and peace, natural laws and the here and now, agency and control, morality, truth, reflection and acceptance, and "other." Through this international survey, researchers were able to gather extensive cross-cultural data on this topic (even if mostly limited to Western countries), thus providing an idea of what the content of widely endorsed, important nonreligious beliefs look like. This research may further assist in the development of a new survey or scale measuring worldviews, so that future studies can investigate worldviews in a comprehensive manner without having to use time-consuming open-ended questions (time-consuming for the participant and researchers alike).

While an interesting view into people's understandings of the world, the content of beliefs may not be central to their functioning, however; there is some evidence that it is not the supernatural content but the strength, coherency, and meaningfulness of beliefs that dictate the effects beliefs can have (for instance, on psychological well-being). For example, a correlational study on church-goers and nonreligious individuals (Galen and Kloet 2011) found a curvilinear relationship between well-being and belief strength: individuals with a higher belief certainty (i.e., individuals that were either confidently religious or atheist) scored higher on measures of well-being than those with low certainty (i.e., individuals who are unsure or agnostic). This relationship held after controlling for social and demographic variables (see also Moore and Leach 2016). Indeed, nonreligious beliefs appear to be similar to religious belief (Koenig 2012) in this regard: They have been linked to a number of beneficial psychological outcomes, such as the link between belief in science and increased psychological well-being (Aghababaei et al. 2016), self-esteem (Aghababaei 2016), and empathy (Francis, Astley, and McKenna 2018).

This work calls for investigating the similarities between religious and nonreligious beliefs—and the strength by which individuals maintain them—by engaging in a *worldview approach*, which helps avoid a religion-centered approach (Taves, Asprem, and Ihm 2018). Within CESR, Ann Taves and collaborators have recently advanced the use of worldview approaches in both religious and nonreligious beliefs research (Taves and Asprem 2018; Taves, Asprem, and Ihm 2018), building on work by Koltko-Rivera (2004), Vidal (2008), Johnson, Hill and Cohen (2011) and Droogers (2014). Worldviews are defined as socially constructed realities that humans use to frame perception and experience (Redfield 1952) or sets of beliefs and assumptions that describe reality (Koltko-Rivera 2004) to make sense of the world.

Worldviews are typically suggested to consist of a number of components (see for a comparison of components within worldview approaches, van Mulukom et al. 2022): *axiology*, or beliefs about what is good and evil; *teleology*, or beliefs about free will and what we can control; *epistemology*, or beliefs about what we can know and how we can know something is true; *ontology*, or beliefs about what exists or is real (in this category is also included *cosmology*, beliefs about where we come from and where we are going, such as the afterlife); and *praxeology*, or beliefs about which (interpersonal) actions we should take. Here we suggest that these worldview components are a good match with the psychological functions of nonreligious beliefs as put forward by empirical psychological research: ontology and providing (existential) meaning, teleology and providing a sense of order and control, and epistemology and providing explanations.

One suggested notable function of religious belief is to provide existential meaning (Park 2013), as part of ontological worldviews: Why are we here? What is the meaning of it all? Some folk psychological models suggest that atheists, without an ultimate explanation of God, may have to make do without strong sources of existential meaning, but recent research has proposed nonbelievers simply find different sources of meaning (e.g., Caldwell-Harris, Wilson, LoTempio, and Beit-Hallahmi 2011). Indeed, atheists have been found to be just as likely as theists to respond affirmatively to statements about finding meaning in life experiences and having a sense of purpose (Caldwell-Harris, Wilson et al. 2011), with no differences in lack of meaning in life (as measured by nihilistic and fatalistic attitudes) between atheists, nonreligious individuals, and theists in a nationally representative sample of Americans (Speed, Coleman, and Langston 2018). Atheists and the nonreligious were more likely than theists to agree that meaning in life is endogenous (i.e., self-generated) however (Speed, Coleman, and Langston 2018). Moreover, Aghababaei and colleagues demonstrated that, just like religious orientation, positive attitudes toward science and technology contributed to subjective well-being via increased hope and a sense of purpose in life (Aghababaei et al. 2016).

Another important function of religious beliefs and worldviews is that they give a sense of order and control (i.e., providing teleological insight), such as through the belief in the Christian God as a creator. For example, experimentally lowered perceptions of personal control have been associated with an increase in belief in a controlling God (Kay et al. 2008). Some scientific theories can also confer a similar sense of control. Rutjens, van der Pligt, and Van Harreveld (2010) found that after an experimental induction of a low or high sense of control, participants tended toward intelligent design over Darwinian evolutionary theories, but not when presented with an alternative "scientific theory"—created by the researchers for the study but presented as a real theory—which presents evolution as an orderly and predictable process. A threat to personal control was furthermore demonstrated to increase preference for theories with a more clear-cut and predictable temporal order through another five studies (investigating grief recovery, Alzheimer's disease, and moral development) by Rutjens et al. (2013).

Another important, and related, function of religious beliefs is that they can provide explanations for the world we live in (i.e., providing epistemological insights)—whether changes in the weather, harvest and hunting outcomes, or life and death itself. Causal explanations are a pivotal part of building up a coherent understanding of the world, and the desire for causal explanations is an important cognitive and motivational drive of human, to the extent that unexplained events can cause distress. Religions—many of which involve omnipotent (creator) gods—have extraordinary explanatory power in that they can provide explanations for many aspects of our world. Can nonreligious beliefs such as belief in science harness the same explanatory power? Several studies by Jesse Preston and colleagues suggest that as an existential explanatory framework, science only works inasmuch as it is considered sufficiently strong: when scientific explanations (of the origins of life and the universe, or of conscious will and romantic love, respectively) fail to be sufficiently explanatory, people appear to turn to religion to fill in the gaps, as evidenced by increased positive evaluations of God and stronger beliefs in souls, respectively (Preston and Epley 2009; Preston, Ritter, and Hepler 2013).

Summarizing, nonreligious beliefs—that is, beliefs that do not invoke gods or other aspects of religious thought and doctrine—make up worldviews in ways highly similar to religious beliefs, and fulfill very similar functions. It appears that the degree to which the belief can fulfill its function—whether providing a sense of control or explaining the world—is more important than its content. Using a worldview approach may be particularly useful for research on unbelief and nonreligion as it does not focus on the absence of religious belief, but rather on the presence of beliefs that help humans understand the world around them.

Discussion, Future Directions, and Conclusion

In this chapter, we have explored the puzzle of unbelief and nonreligion: Why and how do people come to care less about gods and instead become unbelieving and nonreligious? We have surveyed the growing field of the study of unbelief and nonreligion in an attempt to answer this question, and in so doing have explored what it means to be nonreligious or have "unbelief," as well as how nonreligious beliefs and practices compare to religious beliefs and practices.

Central to our discussion of the definition of unbelief and nonreligion is the idea that nonreligious belief and nonreligion should not be understood simply as the absence of religious belief, ideas, and practices. Rather, we have demonstrated that a potentially more productive way to think about nonreligious belief and nonreligion might be through the lens of worldviews: Worldviews are sets of beliefs and assumptions to help humans frame perception and experience and make sense of the world. They fulfill a number of psychological functions such as providing explanations, meaning, and a sense of purpose, and in so doing provide answers to the big questions of human experience, such as what is good and evil (axiology) and where we come from (cosmology).

It appears not to be the supernatural or religious content of beliefs within such worldviews that contributes to their efficacy, but their strength, coherency, and meaningfulness and, concurrently, the extent to which they are able to fulfill their function. Similarly, we discussed evidence that the effects of religious and nonreligious rituals are comparable, in particular their effects on social bonding, which appear mediated by positive affect and feelings of connectedness to something bigger (whether God, or the nonreligious physically or psychologically "larger" entities such as the group or the universe) experienced during the rituals.

So far, however, the most comprehensive explanatory research on nonreligion has focused on the absence of religion and religious belief (e.g., Gervais, Najle, and Caluori 2021; Norenzayan and Gervais 2013): Why do certain individuals not believe in God or other supernatural minds? Explanations are similarly "negatively" phrased: because individuals are unable to represent minds including supernatural minds (*mindblind atheism*), because religion declined in the face of the development of strong secular societal institutions (*apatheism*), because individuals grow up without cultural learning of religious concepts (*inCREDulous atheism*), and because individuals no longer accept intuitive ideas due to analytical thinking (*analytic atheism*).

While these theories have been greatly informative, in particular through their assessments of different potential evolutionary pathways (Gervais, Najle, and Caluori 2021) aimed at addressing the "why" question of nonreligion, we suggest that a next step may be to run similar studies with a "positive" idea of unbelief and nonreligion. Keeping a worldview approach in mind, can we predict why certain beliefs occur in certain conditions (e.g., times and places)? Rather than asking why religious belief is absent, could we ask why a belief in science is the most frequently named belief by nonreligious nontheistic individuals in a (mostly Western) cross-cultural sample (van Mulukom et al. 2022)? Descriptive cross-cultural research that uses open-ended questions, such as van Mulukom et al. (2022), may provide a starting point for investigating the variety of beliefs that perform important psychological functions, and the conditions in which they occur.

Another, as of yet unexplored, domain includes nonreligious CREDs. Like the close link between religious CREDs and religious beliefs (in which context shapes the content of belief, Gervais and Henrich 2010), there may be a relationship between secular CREDs and nonreligious beliefs. Is it for instance the case that children who witness their parents attend secular groups (e.g., monthly humanist meetings) and live by their nonreligious (e.g., humanist) beliefs are more likely to later endorse nonreligious beliefs themselves? Investigating this would shine further light on one of the pathways from perceiving credibility-enhancing behavior to beliefs.

The answers of such research may be highly similar to findings that have emerged in the literature of religious beliefs, but this would be informative in itself: it would contribute evidence to our suggestion that it is the belief, worldview, or particular practice that fulfills important functions in human lives, rather than its supernatural content. Thus, the question of why and how people endorse nonreligious beliefs and engage in nonreligious rituals becomes a question of how belief and worldviews more broadly are important to support psychological functioning in human lives, a highly important endeavor that may contribute to our understanding of the human condition, and to greater human flourishing.

Acknowledgments

ALM would like to thank *ReNEW* for funding that allowed a fruitful research-stay in Oslo, which enhanced the work with this chapter. VvM would like to thank the *Understanding Unbelief* program for funding her unbelief project in 2017–19, from which parts of this chapter emerged.

Notes

1 Toward a Cognitive Science of the Gods: A Brief Introduction

1. Social scientists have appealed to connectionism when examining how culture is stored and structured in individual minds (D'Andrade 1995: 136–9; Strauss and Quinn 1997). Individuals have conceptual models of various things. These models are informational units that might be structured like a connectionist network, where clouds of information are engaged when primed. When shared and socially transmitted, these networks are "cultural schemas." These flexible, hierarchically structured schemas are complex feature models of things in our world (e.g., schemas for "tasty beverages" and "what gods want") as well as scripts for "how to placate the masses" and "how to do the fandango" and can be recruited as the conscious medium of human thought (Alba and Hasher 1983; D'Andrade 1992, 1995). However, the gulf between accounting for the content of cultural models and how they came to be that way remains vast. For case study using connectionist models in the cognitive science of religious concept, see Upal (2010).
2. In this case, $P(B|A)$ = the probability of bushes rustling *while* there's a predator divided by the total probability of there being a predator with and without bush rustling. So, since we declared that P(predators with or without bush rustling) = 0.1 and $P(B|A) = 0.9$, we can calculate the proportion of predators that rustle bushes, x, simply by solving for x in $x/0.1 = 0.9$. So, this proportion is 0.09. To figure out the proportion of predators that *don't* rustle bushes, y, is simply the difference between x and the total likelihood of predators, $0.09 + y = 0.10$, therefore $y = 0.01$. Since we also know that the general proportion of bush rustling is 10 percent, to figure out the proportion of bush rustling *without* predators, z, is $x + z = 0.1$, therefore $z = 0.09$.
3. Here, we use "supernatural agents" as a generic gloss for gods, ghosts, spirits, or any other spiritual agent. On a few grounds, many have lamented the casual use of the term, one of which emphasizes the fact that spirits are not necessarily conceived as separate from nature (e.g., Klass 1995; Saler 1977). We hold no such assumptions.

4 The Personality of the Divine

1. Although Hindu law allows human rulers to punish criminals, Hindu gods and goddesses generally do not administer punishment. Instead, people are thought to incur their misfortune via impersonal forces such as karma (White and Norenzayan 2019; Young et al. 2011). However, the Hindu pantheon deities are often considered malevolent, jealous, or vengeful—particularly in their interactions with other gods and goddesses.

2. The literature also addresses negative religious coping methods that reflect underlying spiritual tensions and struggles within oneself, other humans, and the Divine.
3. For a less academically rigorous but enlightening overview of the personalities of nearly four thousand gods and goddesses, visit godchecker.com.

6 Animatism Reconsidered: A Cognitive Perspective

1. Even though indigenous religions have played a major role in exemplifying animatistic beliefs around the world, they are also found cross-culturally and in religions such as Christianity (*pneuma*), Taoism (*chi*), Hinduism and Buddhism (*karma*), to name just a few, as well as the numerous "folk" concepts around the globe that express "having good/bad luck" or "made of the right stuff" as the means to describe persons containing a special essence: objects believed to somehow enhance the abilities or luck of its bearers, and actions represented as enhancing the likelihood of some desired outcome despite its lack of any direct, causal relation.
2. Hewitt (1902) characterizes *orenda* as "a hypothetic potence or potentiality to do or effect results mystically" (38). According to his account, individuals ranging from shamans and hunters have particularly capable *orenda*s.
3. According to Grim (1983),

   > The manitou has a distinctly personal nature. Although the word *power* is repeatedly used in this work [Grim's monograph] to describe it, the manitou is not an impersonal, magical, or vague supernatural force. Instead particular persons, places or things reveal the sacred energies. The manitou are special hierophanies in which the individual participates by receiving symbolic communications from the spirit world … manitou refers to a phenomenal reality that has a transphenomenal significance. In Ojibway use, the term means that a spirit has been transformed into a phenomenal appearance. (64)

4. DeMallie (1987) suggests that it was "not until Christian influences began to affect Lakota belief did Wakan Tanka become personified" (28). The connection is certainly present; according to the Lakota Dictionary (Buechel and Manhart 2002), *wakantanka* [sic] is defined as "God, the Creator of all things, the Great Spirit" (333). However, it is difficult to determine this one way or another with much confidence considering how difficult it is to extract specific elements of influence from colonial religions from what constitutes prior beliefs and practices (see Beheim et al. 2021). Simply assuming some similarities are unidirectionally caused from one source requires substantiation and begs the question of why other elements of beliefs remain intact. Among the Ojibwa, Hallowell (1975) notes that there is "no cardinal use of any concept of impersonal forces as major determinants of events" (168). Furthermore, at least among the people with whom he worked, *manitou* "is now quite generally confined to the God of Christianity, when combined with an augmentative prefix (*k'tci mànītu*). There is no evidence to suggest, however, that the term ever did connote an impersonal, magical, or supernatural force" (169). Note that the term "may be considered as a synonym for a person of the other-than-human class" (168).
5. Consider the case of *karma*. In the Western world, *karma* is often represented as a transgenerational accounting system of moral behaviors (White, Norenzayan, and Schaller 2019; White et al. 2019). Despite *karma* not technically having agency, it is

a doctrine that merges various spiritual elements together and is believed to exert its influence on individuals and the course of their perpetual rebirth. As self-described "religious" and "spiritual but not religious" individuals tend to report higher belief in *karma*, it is not clearly thought of as a consistent doctrine (White, Norenzayan, and Schaller 2019). Additionally, there is some evidence that karmic beliefs can affect how individuals treat each other. Across a host of experiments, White et al. (2019) found that belief in and/or exposure to concepts of *karma* can increase participant offerings in dictator games, thus potentially facilitating cooperative relations between people. White et al. (2021) found that believers in *karma* do show some diversity in their conceptions of *karma*, but it was often treated as having agency and quite personal. In fact, the more individuals believed in *karma*, the more they treated it as agentic, supporting our fourth suggestion that the more transformative force is ascribed an otherwise non-agentive force, the more likely it is to be represented as having agency.

6. Note that we should not commit the linguistic fallacy by arguing that people necessarily entertain beliefs reflected by these linguistic utterances (Douglas [1966] 1995: 86). We lean on this ability to convey information even though we might not necessarily "believe" how we are expressing ourselves. By way of comparison, an evolutionary biologist might suggest that nature "prefers" and "selects" individual traits that provide a reproductive advantage, even though he or she does not "really think" (or more to the point, not want to be associated with believing it) that nature has any decision-making apparatus. Similarly, people tend to talk about religious concepts in ways contrary to explicit beliefs; we find inconsistencies between stated doctrine (e.g., "God is everywhere") and real-time beliefs (e.g., "God is too busy to help everyone"; Barrett and Keil 1996).

8 The Mind of God and the Problem of Evil: A Cognitive and Evolutionary Perspective

1. All biblical passages from RSV.
2. Quoted in Jeffery 2008, p. 33.
3. Scholars recognize *Job* to be a composite work, with a prologue and epilogue framing the central narrative section; see Larrimore 2013 for a discussion of the history of the text.
4. See Laato and Moor (2003: 63).
5. See O'Keefe (2010), for an overview of Epicurus on the gods.
6. All quotations from this documentary can be found at www.pbs.org/wgbh/pages/frontline/shows/faith/questions/911.html. Accessed August 11, 2021.
7. The following is a more developed treatment of the topic as covered in Teehan (2013).
8. At this point, we are considering the origins of beliefs about the gods, a period that predates the first written sacred texts by thousands of years.
9. By supernatural, we mean that these beings do not fit into categories of beings encountered in the natural environment (e.g., we do not actually encounter bird-headed humans in our travels). However, "supernatural" is a bit of an anachronistic term, more characteristic of a modern, Western view of religion. For much of human history, and certainly at the time period when god-beliefs originated, gods were not "super" natural, they were just one more type of being that populated the natural environment, although a special type of being, with unusual and significant abilities. See Guthrie (1993) for a discussion.

10. See, for example, Guthrie (1993), Boyer (2001), Atran (2002), Barrett (2004).
11. For a more detailed overview of this model, see Teehan (2016).
12. See Henrich (2004), for a critical review of this study.
13. It is important to note that the following discussion is a case study in "cognitive-critical hermeneutics" (Teehan 2021). It uses the findings of CSR as a lens for analyzing a biblical text. As such, it functions as an alternative version of the historical-critical study of such texts, providing a unique, but not competing, perspective into this ancient literature.
14. A similar argument comes from the literature on Just World Theory; see Janoff-Bulman et al. 1985; Lerner and Montada 1998.

9 From Watching Human Acts to Penetrating Their Souls

1. Translations are my own.
2. Thus, I agree with the emphasis placed on the Axial Age in Bellah's *oeuvre* (2011: 265–566, and Bellah and Joas 2012) and, recently, Habermas (2019: 307–459), although my understanding differs considerably from Bellah and Habermas.
3. For the development of the notion, see Norenzayan (2013); Norenzayan and Shariff (2008: 61); Shariff, Norenzayan, and Henrich (2010). Without using the notion, a similar line of thought prevails in Boyer (2021). For extensive critical peer commentary, see *Religion, Brain & Behavior* (2014) and *Religion* (2014).
4. See especially Thomassen (2014) and Rüpke (2014).
5. The discussion was old in 1946, when Jaspers introduced the term. His coinage was modeled on Hegel's (1827) notion of a "hinge of time" (*Angel der Zeit*) upon which the history of religions had been hung (Hegel [1827] 1969: 386–7). Moreover, this discussion also had precursors dating back to Anquetil-Duperron of 1773. See Assmann (2018: 55), who also notes that Hegel's Christian accentuated understanding of history constituted the dialectical antipole to the Axial Age idea and was recognized as such and, hence, argued against by Jaspers (1947, 1949) (Petersen 2017). In the current discussion, ancient Iranian religion is most often left out because of the lateness of the sources and the possibility that early Zoroastrianism constituted a rather different type of religion during its formative phase. The oral transmission of the texts prior to their written recording in the seventh century CE makes it difficult to use Zoroastrianism as another case of Axial Age religion.
6. A similar problem is found in Boyer, who by his one-sided focus on misfortune and threat does not see the presence of moral matters in relation to the gods in all preaxial or pre-kosmos forms of religion (Boyer 2021: 558–60). Johnson's argument is more modest by greater acknowledgment of the appearance of Big Gods as relative to the scaling up of large-scale societies beyond kith and kin, but without endorsing the idea that religions prior to the Axial Age lacked morality (Johnson 2016: 94–6).
7. In Norenzayan's view, Göbekli Tepe predates the Agricultural Revolution. It constituted a gathering point for several small-scale settlements engaging in an amphictyonic alliance (Schmidt 2007: 252–3), and without nearby farming land and water, reflects a hunter sacred site (255–6), which Norenzayan takes to evince that "early stirrings to worship Big Gods motivated people to take up early forms of

farming, and not the other way around" (2013: 120, 132). He is more cautious with respect to Çatal Höyuk mirroring an early town (Hodder 2011: 91–108). For a view similar to Schmidt, see Luckert (2013: 151–68).

8. Contrary to colleagues who find it difficult to endorse a category of religion and define it, I have no problem with the notion. Dependent on the theoretical perspective at stake, we may define it in different ways, but for my part, it suffices to use the category to designate a symbolic recharging battery in which a group of people invests those emotions, which allow them to come into existence and endure as a group. By virtue of shared norms, ideals, and regulations, involving superhuman powers interacting with the group, the group emerges in the emblem signifying and stabilizing the group. As is evident, the definition is based on a Durkheimian understanding of religion, wherefore it also resembles other exponents of this tradition such as Geertz (1973: 90) and Rappaport (1999: 27).

9. Recent empirical findings strongly support their argument See chapters in the present volume by Bendixen and Purzycki; Lightner and Purzycki; Purzycki and McKay; and Teehan.

10. I avoid the Axial Age term. It is ideologically embedded in Jaspers' attempt to provide the world with a new religious foundation for all humankind, in the wake of the atrocities of the Second World War. In Jaspers, it is a revelatory category, which contrary to classical theology is not restricted to Christianity but encompasses the other world religions. I admire Bellah's *oeuvre*, but regarding the elusive nomenclature used for his typology of religion, I diverge. For comparative purposes, I prefer a neutral taxonomy centered on social composition and outreach—ideologically and sociologically. I differentiate between (1) early hunter-gatherers' religion; (2) complex hunter-gatherers' religion; (3) horticultural religion; (4) nomadic religion; (5) early urban religion; (6) complex urban religion; (7) early *kosmos* religion; (8) complex *kosmos* religion; (9) early global religion; (10) complex global religion. *Kosmos* religion signifies the importance of an alternate true world contrary to false mundanity, and the aspiration to reach all people and including them in its ideological fold.

11. Occasionally, opponents of the Big Gods thesis criticize this point, but wrongly so. The aggressiveness triggered by religions is the obverse side of prosociality, biologically embedded as it is in tribalism and genetic self-favouring. It also takes cooperation to engage in joint actions of violence. Whether religion functions pro- or countersocially is a matter of the emotions invested into the symbolic storage battery. Is the group characterized by negative emotions, religion can fuel atrocity just as it may similarly in a collective—embodied by positive emotions—promote prosociality. For criticism of this point, see Martin (2014) and Wiebe (2014).

12. The three emotions differ in intensity from disappointment-sadness, assertion-anger, and aversion-fear. In shame and fear the three emotions appear sequentially differently. Shame is constituted by disappointment-sadness (at self), assertion-anger (at self), and aversion-fear (at consequences for self), and guilt by the rank order: disappointment-sadness (at self), aversion-fear (at consequences for self), and assertion-anger (at self) (Turner et al. 2018: 90).

13. I already foresee the objection that based on such a broad understanding of religion the category is meaningless. I emphasize that it is precisely the comprehensiveness of the notion that allowed Durkheim to develop his specific understanding of religion. Most historians of religion today will agree with Durkheim that prior to modernity religion and culture were identical entities. I add that this is not specific

to religion. In agreement with Weber and Durkheim I do not think of secularity as the fading away of religion but rather modernity in tandem with secularity gave rise to a differentiation (*Ausdifferenzierung*) into semiautonomous spheres of life. In this regard, religion is not different than, for instance, sport, entertainment, economics, and law (Weber 1920: 546–54; Durkheim 1912: 12, 544–5).
14. See literature on CREDS (Henrich 2016: 258, 330) and costly signaling (Alcorta and Sosis 2005; Sosis and Alcorta 2003).

11 Moralistic Gods and Social Complexity: A Brief History of the Problem

1. Data and code to reproduce the analyses and figures in this chapter can be obtained at: https://github.com/bgpurzycki/moralgodschapter.
2. The Standard Cross-Cultural Sample and the Ethnographic Atlas rely on this and two other sources to code the Abipón as lacking a high god of any sort.
3. These entries are in the Human Area Relations Files (HRAF), a database of qualitative accounts of various societies from a range of sources.
4. The D-PLACE data hub altered this text to say "even *if* his sole act." With this apparently trivial rewording, the creation of other spirits sounds as though it has been demoted from being a defining criterion of "high gods" to merely a possible feature. https://d-place.org/parameters/EA034#1/30/152. Accessed November 24, 2021.
5. On one page (see link in note 4), D-PLACE claims it uses Swanson's codes ("absent," "otiose," "active, but not supporting morality," and "active, supporting morality") with the EA data, but when searching for the description of the high gods variable, it defines the options like that detailed above (e.g., "absent or not reported in substantial description of religious beliefs").
6. One methodological blind spot is that we simply don't know much about the process by which the qualitative data were transformed into the quantitative codes. In the case of the EA and SCCS, we do have access to the original source material. However, we have no record or much of a sense of what rules the coders used to transfer the words into numbers. Databases like Pulotu (Watts, Sheehan et al. 2015) and the Database of Religious History (Slingerland and Sullivan 2017) prudently incorporate metadata that indicate coder confidence and source clarity.
7. We modeled the probability of having a moralistic high god binomially. We set the prior distributions for the main intercept, α, and the coefficient for social complexity, β, as ~ Normal(0, 1). According to this simple model, then, $\alpha = -1.67$ (95 percent CI = $-2.18, -1.16$) and $\beta = 0.42$ (95 percent CI = 0.16, 0.68). Percentages reported in the main text use inverse-logit transformations of the relevant estimates. So, the model predicts that the chances of, for example, a society of social complexity level 4 is 50 percent, the logistic transform of $-1.67 + 4*0.42$. A better model would treat the effect of jurisdictional hierarchy monotonically, but we keep things simple for the sake of illustration.
8. Populations with less than ten thousand people comprise 78 percent and societies with three or fewer "sovereign organizations" comprise 74 percent of the sample.

13 Accounting for Cross-Cultural Variation in the Minds of Gods

1. Note, however, that many of these studies rely on coded data for so-called "high gods," *creator* deities that may or may not be "specifically supportive of human morality." See Bendixen, Lightner, and Purzycki (forthcoming) and Purzycki and McKay (present volume) for further discussion.
2. A host of norms prescribe when sharing should take place, often following communal projects such as house- or canoe-building, rituals or collaborative hunts. However, the Mentawai are also supposed to share in case of personal windfall, such as after successful solo hunts. As Singh, Kaptchuk, and Henrich (2021) note, private windfalls are particularly vulnerable to exploitation, as people can hide or lie about their own gains while accepting a share of their neighbors' spoils. In contrast, sharing meat following communal projects is easier to monitor by tracking each other's reputation and record of reciprocity. This case therefore takes a classical game-theoretic structure, where the collective is better off with everybody cooperating but individuals are tempted to free ride, and supports the god-problem criteria that appeals to the supernatural should often be invoked in social dilemmas when non-supernatural alternatives are impractical (e.g., monitoring neighbors' private windfall).
3. Even such "obscure" concerns might still reflect central and salient features of the local socioecology. Marshall (1962) goes on to discuss how the supreme deity of the !Kung Bushmen is particularly angered by burning and disturbing honeybees. Honey is a central food source for many foraging societies, the !Kung included, and this might be why disrespect for honeybees becomes an object for supernatural attention. Among the Batak, abuse of bees and wasting honey, accidentally or not, is also supernaturally punished, which Eder (1997) argues is a resource management strategy.
4. For discussion and formal treatment of similar cases of "rational" superstition, see: Leeson (2017); Leeson and Suarez (2015). For a more general treatment of "adaptive misbeliefs," see McKay and Dennett (2009).
5. Further ethnographic examples on how secular and supernatural sanctions might compete and interact can be found in Murdock (1934: 175–6, 184–6, 210–11, 215, 285–7, 278–81, 336–7, 345–8, 377, 388–9, 431–3, 437, 439–42, 492, 499–500, 502, 533–4, 540–1, 545–6, 574–5, 584–7, 588). The general pattern seems to be consistent with the predictive criteria (i.e., that supernatural punishment arises when a violation is particularly salient and/or frequent and/or where relevant secular systems are unavailable), although the material awaits a systematic treatment.
6. For a discussion of the balance between claims and evidence when assessing the evolutionary rationales of cultural practices among smaller-scale societies, see Smith and Wishnie (2000).

14 Environmentalism and the Minds of Gods

1. "A joint message for the protection of creation" available in full at the following link: https://www.vatican.va/content/francesco/en/messages/pont-messages/2021/documents/20210901-messaggio-protezionedelcreato.html.
2. For many examples, see the repository hosted by the Alliance for Religions and Conservation, http://www.arcworld.org/arc_and_the_faiths.asp.

3. Source: http://www.arcworld.org/faiths.asp?pageID=6.

15 Approaching the Minds of the Gods through AI

1. See lists of publications at https://mindandculture.org/projects/past-projects/modeling-religion-project/ and https://mindandculture.org/projects/past-projects/modeling-religion-in-norway/.

16 Never Mind the Gods: Explaining Unbelief and Nonreligion

1. Scholars from other disciplines, such as anthropology and sociology, are very much engaged in nonreligion studies; however, this chapter cannot include a review of all this research, and instead we recommend Cragun and Smith (2019), Bullivant and Lee (2012), Purzycki and Sosis (2019), and Goody (1996) for thorough introductions to these parts of the literature.
2. Led by Professor Lori Beaman from the University of Ottawa.
3. Led by Drs. Lois Lee, Jonathan Lanman, Miguel Farias, and Stephen Bullivant, with its basis at the University of Kent from 2017 to 2019.
4. Founded in 2008 (https://thensrn.org/about).
5. https://www.sundayassembly.com.
6. See for instance N. G. Alexander (2021) and Cotter (2020) for discussions of such conceptual limitations.
7. See also Purzycki and Schjoedt's chapter in this volume.
8. For more reading on the relationship between religion and material security in this volume, see Lightner and Purzycki as well as Bendixen and Purzycki.

References

Abraham, K., and W. A. White (1912), "Dreams and Myths: A Study in Race Psychology," *Journal of Nervous and Mental Disease*, 39 (8): 568–76.
Acerbi, A., and A. Mesoudi (2015), "If We Are All Cultural Darwinians What's the Fuss about? Clarifying Recent Disagreements in the Field of Cultural Evolution," *Biology & Philosophy*, 30 (4): 481–503.
Adams, A. (1982), "[Review of] *Consciousness in Advaita Vedanta*," *Philosophy East and West*, 32 (4): 468–70.
Adhikary, A. K. (1999), "Birhor," in R. B. Lee and R. Daley (eds.), *The Cambridge Encyclopedia of Hunters and Gatherers*, 248–51, Cambridge: Cambridge University Press.
Aghababaei, N. (2016), "Scientific Faith and Positive Psychological Functioning," *Mental Health, Religion & Culture*, 19 (7): 734–41.
Aghababaei, N., F. Sohrabi, H. Eskandari, A. Borjali, N. Farrokhi, and Z. J. Chen (2016), "Predicting Subjective Well-Being by Religious and Scientific Attitudes with Hope, Purpose in Life, and Death Anxiety as Mediators," *Personality and Individual Differences*, 90: 93–8.
Alba, J. W., and L. Hasher (1983), "Is Memory Schematic?," *Psychological Bulletin*, 93: 203–31.
Alcorta, C., and R. Sosis (2005), "Ritual, Emotion, and Sacred Symbols," *Human Nature*, 16 (4): 323–59.
Alexander, C. N., M. V. Rainforth, and P. Gelderloos (1991), "Transcendental Meditation, Self-Actualization, and Psychological Health: A Conceptual Overview and Statistical Metaanalysis," *Journal of Social Behavior and Personality*, 6 (5): 189–248.
Alexander, N. G. (2021), "Rethinking Histories of Atheism, Unbelief, and Nonreligion: An Interdisciplinary Perspective," *Global Intellectual History*, 6 (1): 95–104.
Alexander, R. (1987), *The Biology of Moral Systems: Foundations of Human Behavior*, New York: Aldine de Gruyter.
Allport, G. W. (1937), *Personality: A Psychological Interpretation*, New York: Henry Holt.
Almeida-Filho, D. G., C. M. Queiroz, and S. Ribeiro (2018), "Memory Corticalization Triggered by REM Sleep: Mechanisms of Cellular and Systems Consolidation," *Cellular and Molecular Life Sciences*, 75 (20): 3715–40.
Alvard, M. S. (1994), "Conservation by Native Peoples: Prey Choice in a Depleted Habitat," *Human Nature*, 5 (2): 127–54.
Anae, M. (2016), "Teu Le Va: Samoan Relational Ethics," *Knowledge Cultures*, 3 (4): 117–30.
Anderies, J. M. (1998), "Culture and Human Agro-Ecosystem Dynamics: The Tsembaga of New Guinea," *Journal of Theoretical Biology*, 192 (4): 515–30.
Andersen, M. (2019), "Predictive Coding in Agency Detection," *Religion, Brain & Behavior*, 9 (1): 65–84.
Andersen, M., T. Pfeiffer, S. Müller, and U. Schjoedt (2019), "Agency Detection in Predictive Minds: A Virtual Reality Study," *Religion, Brain & Behavior*, 9 (1): 52–64.

Andersen, M., U. Schjoedt, K. L. Nielbo, and J. Sørensen (2014), "Mystical Experience in the Lab," *Method & Theory in the Study of Religion*, 26 (3): 217–45.
Anderson, J. R. (2007), *How Can the Human Mind Occur in the Physical Universe?* Oxford: Oxford University Press.
Andrews, P., and Y. Fernández-Jalvo (1997), "Surface Modifications of the Sima de los Huesos Fossil Humans," *Journal of Human Evolution*, 33: 191–217.
Apicella, C. L. (2018), "High Levels of Rule-Bending in a Minimally Religious and Largely Egalitarian Forager Population," *Religion, Brain & Behavior*, 8 (2): 133–48.
Arbuckle, M. B., and D. M. Konisky (2015), "The Role of Religion in Environmental Attitudes," *Social Science Quarterly*, 96 (5): 1244–63.
Armstrong, K. (1993), *A History of God*, New York: Ballantine.
Arno, A. (1976), "Ritual of Reconciliation and Village Conflict Management in Fiji," *Oceania*, 47 (1): 49–65.
Arsuaga, J. L., I. Martínez, A. Gracia, J. M. Carretero, C. Lorenzo, N. García, and A. I. Ortega (1997), "Sima de los Huesos (Sierra de Atapuerca, Spain): The Site," *Journal of Human Evolution*, 33: 109–27.
Asad, T. (2003), *Formations of the Secular: Christianity, Islam, Modernity*, Stanford: Stanford University Press.
Assmann, J. (2018), *Die Achsenzeit. Eine Theorie der Moderne*, Munich: C. H. Beck.
Aten, J. D., W. R. Smith, E. B. Davis, D. R. Van Tongeren, J. N. Hook, D. E. Davis, L. Shannonhouse, C. Deblaere, J. Ranter, K. O'Grady, and P. C. Hill (2019), "The Psychological Study of Religion and Spirituality in a Disaster Context: A Systematic Review," *Psychological Trauma: Theory, Research, Practice, and Policy*, 11 (6): 597–613.
Atkinson, Q. D. (2018), "Religion and Expanding the Cooperative Sphere in Kastom and Christian Villages on Tanna, Vanuatu," *Religion, Brain & Behavior*, 8 (2): 149–67.
Atran, S. (2002), *In Gods We Trust: The Evolutionary Landscape of Religion*, Oxford: Oxford University Press.
Atran, S., and J. Henrich (2010), "The Evolution of Religion: How Cognitive By-Products, Adaptive Learning Heuristics, Ritual Displays, and Group Competition Generate Deep Commitments to Prosocial Religions," *Biological Theory*, 5: 18–30.
Atran, S., and A. Norenzayan (2004), "Religion's Evolutionary Landscape: Counterintuition, Commitment, Compassion, Communion," *Behavioral and Brain Sciences*, 27 (6): 713–30.
Atran, S., D. Medin, N. Ross, E. Lynch, J. Coley, E. U. Ek', and V. Vapnarsky (1999), "Folkecology and Commons Management in the Maya Lowlands," *Proceedings of the National Academy of Sciences*, 96: 7598–603.
Atran, S., D. Medin, N. Ross, E. Lynch, V. Vapnarsky, E. U. Ek', J. Coley, C. Timura, and M. Baran (2002), "Folkecology, Cultural Epidemiology, and the Spirit of the Commons: A Garden Experiment in the Maya Lowlands, 1991–2001," *Current Anthropology*, 43 (3): 421–50.
Aubert, M., R. Lebe, A. Oktaviana, M. Tang, B. Burhan, Hamrullah, A. Jusdi, Abdullah, B. Hakim, J. Zhao, I. Geria, P. Sulistyarto, R. Sardi, and A. Brumm (2019), "Earliest Hunting Scene in Prehistoric Art," *Nature*, 576 (19/26): 442–8.
Aujoulat, N., J. Geneste, C. Archambeau, M. Delluc, H. Duday, and S. Gambier (2002), "La grotte ornée de Cussac—Le Buisson-de-Cadouin (Dordogne): Premières Observations," *Bulletin de la Société Préhistorique Française*, 99 (1): 129–37.
Axelrod, R. (1997), *The Complexity of Cooperation: Agent-Based Models of Competition and Collaboration*, Princeton: Princeton University Press.
Babb, L. A. (1975), *The Divine Hierarchy*, New York: Columbia University Press.

Baesler, E. J. (2003), *Theoretical Explorations and Empirical Investigations of Communication and Prayer*, Lewiston: Edwin Mellen Press.
Baimel, A., Q. Atkinson, E. Cohen, C. Handley, J. Henrich, E. Kundtová Klocová, M. Lang, C. Lesorogol, R. A. McNamara, C. Moya, A. Norenzayan, C. Placek, M. Soler, J. Weigel, T. Vardy, A. K. Willard, D. Xygalatas, and B. G. Purzycki (2022), "Material Insecurity Predicts Greater Commitment to Moralistic and Less Commitment to Local Deities: A Cross-Cultural Investigation," *Religion, Brain, and Behavior*, 12 (1–2): 4–17.
Bainbridge, W. S. (1994), "Grand Computing Challenges for Sociology," *Social Science Computer Review*, 12 (2): 183–92.
Bainbridge, W. S. (2006), *God from the Machine: Artificial Intelligence Models of Religious Cognition*, Lanham: AltaMira Press.
Bainbridge, W. S., E. Brent, K. M. Carley, D. Heise, M. Macy, B. Markovsky, and J. Skvoretz (1994), "Artificial Social Intelligence," *Annual Review of Sociology*, 20.
Baiburin, A. (2012), "Rituals of Identity: The Soviet Passport," in M. Bassin and C. Kelly (eds.), *Soviet and Post-Soviet Identities*, 91–109, Cambridge: Cambridge University Press.
Balazka, D., D. Houtman, and B. Lepri (2021), "How Can Big Data Shape the Field of Non-Religion Studies? And Why Does It Matter?," *Patterns*, 2 (6): 100263.
Barbey, A., L. Barsalou, W. K. Simmons, and A. Santos (2005), "Embodiment in Religious Knowledge," *Journal of Cognition and Culture*, 5 (1–2): 14–57.
Barker, D. C., and D. H. Bearce (2013), "End-Times Theology, the Shadow of the Future, and Public Resistance to Addressing Global Climate Change," *Political Research Quarterly*, 66 (2): 267–79.
Barkow, J. H., L. Cosmides, and J. Tooby (1992), *The Adapted Mind: Evolutionary Psychology and the Generation of Culture*, Oxford: Oxford University Press.
Baron-Cohen, S. (1995), *Mindblindness: An Essay on Autism and Theory of Mind*, Cambridge: MIT Press.
Baron-Cohen, S., A. M. Leslie, and U. Frith (1985), "Does the Autistic Child Have a "Theory of Mind"?," *Cognition*, 21 (1): 37–46.
Barrett, D. (2017), "Dreams and Creative Problem-Solving," *Annals of the New York Academy of Sciences*, 1406 (1): 64–7.
Barrett, H. C., and R. Kurzban (2006), "Modularity in Cognition: Framing the Debate," *Psychological Review*, 113: 628–47.
Barrett, J. L. (1999), "Theological Correctness: Cognitive Constraint and the Study of Religion," *Method & Theory in the Study of Religion*, 11 (4): 325–39.
Barrett, J. L. (2000), "Exploring the Natural Foundations of Religion," *Trends in Cognitive Sciences*, 4 (1): 29–34.
Barrett, J. L. (2004), *Why Would Anyone Believe in God?* Lanham: AltaMira Press.
Barrett, J. L. (2008), "Why Santa Claus is Not a God," *Journal of Cognition and Culture*, 8 (1): 149–61.
Barrett, J. L. (2011), "Cognitive Science of Religion: Looking Back, Looking Forward," *Journal for the Scientific Study of Religion*, 50 (2): 229–39.
Barrett, J. L., and F. C. Keil (1996), "Conceptualizing a Nonnatural Entity: Anthropomorphism in God Concepts," *Cognitive Psychology*, 31 (3): 219–47.
Barrett, J. L., and J. A. Lanman (2008), "The Science of Religious Beliefs," *Religion*, 38 (2): 109–24.
Barrett, J. L. and M. Nyhof (2001), "Spreading Non-Natural Concepts: The Role of Intuitive Conceptual Structures in Memory and Transition of Cultural Materials," *Journal of Cognition and Culture*, 1: 69–100.

Barrett, J. L., and B. Van Orman (1996), "The Effects of Image-Use in Worship on God Concepts," *Journal of Psychology and Christianity*, 15: 38–45.

Barrett, J. L., R. Richert, and A. Driesenga (2001), "God's Beliefs versus Mother's: The Development of Nonhuman Agent Concepts," *Child Development*, 72 (1): 50–65.

Barrett, J. L., D. Shaw, J. Pfeiffer, and J. Grimes (2019), "Where the Gods Dwell: A Research Report," *Journal of Cognition and Culture*, 19 (1–2), 131–46.

Barsalou, L. W. (1999), "Perceptual Symbol Systems," *Behavioral and Brain Sciences*, 22 (4): 577–660.

Bastin, J.-F., Y. Finegold, C. Garcia, D. Mollicone, M. Rezende, D. Routh, C. M. Zohner, and T. W. Crowther (2019), "The Global Tree Restoration Potential," *Science*, 365 (6448): 76–9.

Baumard, N. and P. Boyer (2013), "Explaining Moral Religions," *Trends in Cognitive Sciences*, 17 (6): 272–80.

Baumard, N, A. Hyafil, I. Morris, and P. Boyer (2015), "Increased Affluence Explains the Emergence of Ascetic Wisdom and Moralizing Religions," *Current Biology*, 25 (1): 10–15.

Bayes, T. (1764), "An Essay toward Solving a Problem in the Doctrine of Chances," *Philosophical Transactions of the Royal Society of London*, 53: 370–418.

Bänziger, S., M. van Uden, and J. Janssen (2008), "Praying and Coping: The Relation between Varieties of Praying and Religious Coping Styles," *Mental Health, Religion and Culture*, 11 (1): 101–18.

Bechtel, W., and A. Abrahamsen (2002), *Connectionism and the Mind: Parallel Processing, Dynamics, and Evolution in Networks*, 2nd ed., Malden: Blackwell.

Beck, J., and W. Forstmeier (2007), "Superstition and Belief as Inevitable By-Products of an Adaptive Learning Strategy," *Human Nature*, 18 (1): 35–46.

Beheim, B., Q. D. Atkinson, J. Bulbulia, W. Gervais, R. D. Gray, J. Henrich, M. Lang, M. W. Monroe, M. Muthukrishna, A. Norenzayan, B. G. Purzycki, A. Shariff, E. Slingerland, R. Spicer, and A. K. Willard (2021), "Treatment of Missing Data Determined Conclusions Regarding Moralizing Gods," *Nature*, 595 (7866): E29–34.

Belicki, K. (2017), "Recalling Dreams: An Examination of Daily Variation and Individual Differences," in J. Gackenbach (ed.), *Sleep and Dreams: A Sourcebook*, 187–206, New York: Garland.

Bellah, R. N. (2011), *Religion in Human Evolution: From the Paleolithic to the Axial Age*, Cambridge: Belknap Press of Harvard University Press.

Bellah, R. N., and J. Hans (2012), *The Axial Age and Its Consequences*, Cambridge: Belknap Press of Harvard University Press.

Bender, A., and S. Beller (2011), "Causal Asymmetry across Cultures: Assigning Causal Roles in Symmetric Physical Settings," *Frontiers in Psychology*, 2 (231): 1–10.

Bendixen, T., and B. G. Purzycki (2020), "Peering into the Minds of the Gods: What Cross-Cultural Variation in Gods' Concerns can Tell Us about the Evolution of Religion," *Journal for the Cognitive Science of Religion*, 5 (2): 142–65.

Bendixen, T., and B. G. Purzycki (2021), "Competing Forces Account for the Stability and Evolution of Religious Beliefs," *International Journal for the Psychology of Religion*, 31: 307–12.

Bendixen, T., and B. G. Purzycki (forthcoming), "Cultural Evolutionary Psychology of Belief," in J. Musolino, J. Sommer, and P. Hemmer (eds.), *The Cognitive Science of Belief*, Cambridge: Cambridge University Press, 209–29.

Bendixen, T., A. D. Lightner, and B. G. Purzycki (forthcoming), "The Cultural Evolution of Religion and Cooperation," in R. Kendal, J. Tehrani, and J. Kendal (eds.), *Oxford*

Handbook of Cultural Evolution, Oxford: Oxford University Press. Accessed online: https://psyarxiv.com/fhscv/ (accessed on August 1, 2022)

Bendixen, T., C. L. Apicella, Q. Atkinson, E. Cohen, J. Henrich, R. A. McNamara, A. Norenzayan, A. K. Willard, D. Xygalatas, and B. G. Purzycki (forthcoming), "Appealing to the Minds of Gods: Religious Beliefs and Appeals Correspond to Features of Local Social Ecologies," *Religion, Brain & Behavior*.

Bengtson, V. L., R. D. Hayward, P. Zuckerman, and M. Silverstein (2018), "Bringing up Nones: Intergenerational Influences and Cohort Trends," *Journal for the Scientific Study of Religion*, 57 (2): 258–75.

Benson, P. and B. Spilka (1973), "God Image as a Function of Self-Esteem and Locus of Control," *Journal for the Scientific Study of Religion*, 12 (3): 297–310.

Bering, J. M. (2006), "The Folk Psychology of Souls," *Behavioral and Brain Sciences*, 29 (5): 453–98.

Bering, J. M., and B. D. Parker (2006), "Children's Attributions of Intentions to an Invisible Agent," *Developmental Psychology*, 42 (2): 253–62.

Berkes, F., J. Colding, and C. Folke (2000), "Rediscovery of Traditional Ecological Knowledge as Adaptive Management," *Ecological Applications*, 10 (5): 1251–62.

Berniūnas, R., V. Dranseika, and D. Tserendamba (2019), "Between Karma and Buddha: Prosocial Behavior among Mongolians in an Anonymous Economic Game," *International Journal for the Psychology of Religion*, 30 (2): 1–19.

Berry, J. W. (2015), "Global Psychology: Implications for Cross-Cultural Research and Management," *Cross Cultural Management: An International Journal*, 22 (3): 342–55.

Bertenthal, B. I., D. R. Proffitt, and J. E. Cutting (1984), "Infant Sensitivity to Figural Coherence in Biomechanical Motions," *Journal of Experimental Child Psychology*, 37 (2): 213–30.

Berwick, R. C., P. Pietroski, B. Yankama, and N. Chomsky (2011), "Poverty of the Stimulus Revisited," *Cognitive Science*, 35 (7): 1207–42.

Bhagwat, S. A. and C. Rutte (2006), "Sacred Groves: Potential for Biodiversity Management," *Frontiers in Ecology and the Environment*, 4 (10): 519–24.

Binmore, K. (2011), *Natural Justice*, Oxford: Oxford University Press.

Binmore, K. G. (1994), *Game Theory and the Social Contract*, Cambridge: MIT Press.

Bird, D. W., R. Bliege Bird, B. F. Codding, and N. Taylor (2016), "A Landscape Architecture of Fire: Cultural Emergence and Ecological Pyrodiversity in Australia's Western Desert," *Current Anthropology*, 57 (S13): S65–79.

Bird-David, N. (1999), "'Animism' Revisited: Personhood, Environment, and Relational Epistemology," *Current Anthropology*, 40: S67–91.

Blagrove, M. (2007), "Dreaming and Personality," in D. Barrett and P. McNamara (eds.), *The New Science of Dreaming: Vol. 2. Content, Recall, and Personality Correlates*, 115–58, Santa Barbara: Praeger.

Bliege Bird, R., and E. Power (2015), "Prosocial Signaling and Cooperation among Martu Hunters," *Evolution and Human Behavior*, 36 (5): 389–97.

Bliege Bird, R., N. Tayor, B. F. Codding, and D. W. Bird (2013), "Niche Construction and Dreaming Logic: Aboriginal Patch Mosaic Burning and Varanid Lizards (Varanus Gouldii) in Australia," *Proceedings of the Royal Society B: Biological Sciences*, 280 (1772): 20132297.

Bloom, P. (2007), "Religion is Natural," *Developmental Science*, 10 (1): 147–51.

Bockrath, M. F., K. I. Pargament, S. Wong, V. A. Harriott, J. M. Pomerleau, S. J. Homolka, Z. B. Chaudhary, and J. J. Exline (2021), "Religious and Spiritual Struggles and

Their Links to Psychological Adjustment: A Meta-Analysis of Longitudinal Studies," *Psychology of Religion and Spirituality*.

Bodewitz, H. W. (2019), "The Hindu Doctrine of Transmigration: Its Origin and Background," in D. Heilijgers, J. Houben, and K. van Kooij (eds.), *Vedic Cosmology and Ethics*, 3–19, Leiden: Brill.

Boehm, C. (2008), "A Biocultural Evolutionary Exploration of Supernatural Sanctioning," in J. Bulbulia, R. Sosis, E. Harris, R. Genet, and K. Wyman (eds.), *Evolution of Religion: Studies, Theories, and Critiques*, 143–52, Santa Margarita: Collins Foundation Press.

Bonin, K., and J. E. Lane (in press), "Identity Fusion, Devoted Actor Theory, and Extremism," in J. E. Lane and Y. Lior (eds.), *Routledge Handbook of Evolution and Religion*, London: Routledge.

Bonnemaison, J. (1984), "The Tree and the Canoe: Roots and Mobility in Vanuatu Societies," *Pacific Viewpoint*, 25: 117–52.

Bonnemaison, J. (1991), "Magic Gardens in Tanna," *Pacific Studies*, 14: 71–89.

Bossaerts, P. and C. Murawski (2017), "Computational Complexity and Human Decision-Making," *Trends in Cognitive Sciences*, 21 (12): 917–29.

Botero, C. A., B. Gardner, K. R. Kirby, J. Bulbulia, M. C. Gavin, and R. D. Gray (2014), "The Ecology of Religious Beliefs," *Proceedings of the National Academy of Sciences*, 111 (47): 16784–9.

Bouton, J. (1635), "Concerning the Savages Called Caribs," *An Account of the Establishment of the French in the Year 1635 on the Island of Martinique*, trans. M. McKusick and P. Verin. Accessed online: https://ehrafworldcultures.yale.edu/document?id=st13-003.

Bowlby, J. (1983), *Attachment: Attachment and Loss Volume One*, 2nd ed., New York: Basic Books.

Boyd, R., and P. J. Richerson (1985), *Culture and the Evolutionary Process*, Chicago: University of Chicago Press.

Boyd, R., and P. J. Richerson (1988), "The Evolution of Reciprocity in Sizable Groups," *Journal of Theoretical Biology*, 132: 337–56.

Boyer, P. (2001), *Religion Explained: The Evolutionary Origins of Religious Thought*, New York: Basic Books.

Boyer, P. (2018), *Minds Make Societies: How Cognition Explains the World Humans Create*, New Haven: Yale University Press.

Boyer, P. (2020), "Informal Religious Activity outside Hegemonic Religions: Wild Traditions and Their Relevance to Evolutionary Models," *Religion, Brain & Behavior*, 10 (4): 459–72.

Boyer, P. (2021), "Deriving Features of Religion in the Wild: How Communication and Threat-Detection May Predict Spirits, Gods, Witches, and Shamans," *Human Nature*, 32: 557–81.

Boyer, P., and P. Liénard (2006), "Why Ritualized Behavior? Precaution Systems and Action Parsing in Developmental, Pathological and Cultural Rituals," *Behavioral and Brain Sciences*, 29: 1–56.

Boyer, P., and C. Ramble (2001), "Cognitive Templates for Religious Concepts: Cross-Cultural Evidence for Recall of Counter-Intuitive Representations," *Cognitive Science*, 25 (4): 535–64.

Brams, S. J. (1982), "Belief in God: A Game-Theoretic Paradox," *International Journal for Philosophy of Religion*, 13 (3): 121–9.

Brams, S. J. (1983), *Superior Beings: If They Exist, How Would We Know?* New York: Springer.
Brams, S. J. (2018), *Divine Games: Game Theory and the Undecidability of a Superior Being*, Cambridge: MIT Press.
Branas-Garza, P., A. M. Espín, and S. Neuman (2014), "Religious Pro-Sociality? Experimental Evidence from a Sample of 766 Spaniards," *PLOS ONE*, 9 (8): e104685.
Brass, M. (2003), "Tracing the Origins of the Ancient Egyptian Cattle Cult," in A. K. Eyma and C. J. Bennet (eds.), *Delta Man in Yebu: Occasional Volume of the Egyptologists' Electronic Forum*, Self-Published.
Braxton, D. M. (2008), "Modeling the McCauley-Lawson Theory of Ritual Forms," Talk Given at Aarhus University, Denmark.
Breton, R., and A. la Paix (1929), "An Account of the Island of Guadaloupe," *Historie Coloniale, Vol. 1*, trans. T. Turner. https://ehrafworldcultures.yale.edu/document?id=st13-001.
Brightman, R. A. (1993), *Grateful Prey: Rock Cree Human-Animal Relationships*, Regina: University of Regina Press.
Brison, K. J. (2001), "Crafting Sociocentric Selves in Religious Discourse in Rural Fiji," *Ethos*, 29 (4): 453–74.
Brosnan, S., and F. deWaal (2003), "Monkeys Reject Unequal Pay," *Nature*, 425: 297–9.
Brown, J. S. (1952), "A Comparative Study of Deviations from Sexual Mores," *American Sociological Review*, 17: 135–46.
Bruck, J. (2011), "Fire, Earth, Water: An Elemental Cosmography of the European Bronze Age," in T. Insoll (ed.), *Oxford Handbook of the Archaeology of Ritual and Religion*, 387–404, Oxford: Oxford University Press.
Bryant, E. F. (2015), *The Yoga Sutras of Patanjali: A New Edition, Translation, and Commentary*, New York: North Point Press.
Buechel, E., and P. Manhart, eds. (2002), *Lakota Dictionary: Lakota-English/English-Lakota*, Lincoln: University of Nebraska Press.
Bulbulia, J. (2004), "The Cognitive and Evolutionary Psychology of Religion," *Biology and Philosophy*, 19 (5): 655–86.
Bulbulia, J. (2012), "Spreading Order: Religion, Cooperative Niche Construction, and Risky Coordination Problems," *Biology and Philosophy*, 27 (1): 1–27.
Bulkeley, K. (2001), *Dreams: A Reader on Religious, Cultural, and Psychological Dimensions of Dreaming*, New York: Palgrave.
Bulkeley, K. (2008), *Dreaming in the World's Religions*, New York University Press.
Bulkeley, K. (2016), *Big Dreams: The Science of Dreaming and the Origins of Religion*, Oxford: Oxford University Press.
Bullard, G. (2016), "The World's Newest Major Religion: No religion," *National Geographic*. available online: https://www.nationalgeographic.com/culture/article/160422-atheism-agnostic-secular-nones-rising-religion. Accessed August 1, 2022.
Bullivant, S. (2020), "Explaining the Rise of 'Nonreligion Studies': Subfield Formation and Institutionalization within the Sociology of Religion," *Social Compass*, 67 (1): 86–102.
Bullivant, S., and L. Lee (2012), "Interdisciplinary Studies of Non-Religion and Secularity: The State of the Union," *Journal of Contemporary Religion*, 27 (1): 19–27.
Burdett, E., J. L. Barrett, and T. Greenway (2020) "Children's Developing Understanding of the Cognitive Abilities of Supernatural and Natural Minds: Evidence from Three Cultures," *Journal for the Study of Religion, Nature and Culture*, 14 (1): 124–51.

Burdett, E. R. R., A. J. Lucas, D. Buchsbaum, N. McGuigan, L. A. Wood, and A. Whiten (2016), "Do Children Copy an Expert or a Majority? Examining Selective Learning in Instrumental and Normative Contexts," *PLOS ONE*, 11 (10): e0164698.

Burdett, E. R. R., J. B. Wigger, and J. L. Barrett (2019) "The Minds of God, Mortals, and In-Betweens: Children's Developing Understanding of Extraordinary and Ordinary Minds across Four Countries," *Psychology of Religion and Spirituality*, 13 (2): 212–21.

Burley, M. (2007), *Classical Samkhya and Yoga: An Indian Metaphysics of Experience*, London: Routledge.

Bushman, B. J., R. D. Ridge, E. Das, C. W. Key, and G. L. Busath (2007), "When God Sanctions Killing: Effect of Scriptural Violence on Aggression," *Psychological Science*, 18 (3): 204–7.

Caldwell-Harris, C., C. F. Murphy, T. Velazquez, and P. McNamara (2011), "Religious Belief Systems of Persons with High Functioning Autism," *Proceedings of the Annual Meeting of the Cognitive Science Society*, 33 (33): 3362–6.

Caldwell-Harris, C. L., A. L. Wilson, E. LoTempio, and B. Beit-Hallahmi (2011), "Exploring the Atheist Personality: Well-Being, Awe, and Magical Thinking in Atheists, Buddhists, and Christians," *Mental Health, Religion & Culture*, 14 (7): 659–72.

Call, J., and M. Tomasello (2008), "Does the Chimpanzee Have a Theory of Mind? 30 Years Later," *Trends in Cognitive Sciences*, 12 (5): 187–92.

Callaghan, T., P. Rochat, A. Lillard, M. L. Claux, H. Odden, S. Itakura, S. Tapanya, and S. Singh (2005), "Synchrony in the Onset of Mental-State Reasoning: Evidence from Five Cultures," *Psychological Science*, 16 (5): 378–84.

Callebaut, W., and D. Rasskin-Gutman (2005), *Modularity: Understanding the Development and Evolution of Natural Complex Systems*, Cambridge: MIT Press.

Caluori, N., J. C. Jackson, K. Gray, and M. Gelfand (2020), "Conflict Changes How People View God," *Psychological Science*, 31 (3): 280–92.

Canfield, C. F. and P. A. Ganea (2014), "'You Could Call It Magic': What Parents and Siblings Tell Preschoolers about Unobservable Entities," *Journal of Cognition and Development*, 15 (2): 269–86.

Cao, Y., B. Enke, A. Falk, P. Giuliano, and N. Nunn (2021), "Herding, Warfare, and a Culture of Honor: Global Evidence," *Working Paper 29250. National Bureau of Economic Research*.

Carpendale, J. I. M., and C. Lewis (2004), "Constructing an Understanding of Mind: The Development of Children's Social Understanding within Social Interaction," *Behavioral and Brain Sciences*, 27 (1): 79–96.

Casler, K., and D. Kelemen (2008), "Developmental Continuity in the Teleo-Functional Bias: Reasoning about Nature among Romanian Roma Adults (Gypsies)," *Journal of Cognition and Development*, 9: 340–62.

Castro, E. V. de. (1998), "Cosmological Deixis and Amerindian Perspectivism," *Journal of the Royal Anthropological Institute*, 4 (3): 469–88.

Castro, E. V. de. (2004), "Exchanging Perspectives: The Transformation of Objects into Subjects in Amerindian Ontologies," *Common Knowledge*, 10 (3): 463–84.

Cavalli-Sforza, L. L., and M. W. Feldman (1981), *Cultural Transmission and Evolution: A Quantitative Approach*, Princeton: Princeton University Press.

Chapple, C. K. (2019), "Religious Experience and Yoga," *Religions*, 10 (4): 237.

Charles, S. J., V. van Mulukom, J. Brown, F. Watts, R. I. M. Dunbar, and M. Farias (2020), "United on Sunday: The Effects of Secular Rituals on Social Bonding and Affect," *PLOS ONE*, 16 (1): e0242546.

Charles, S., V. van Mulukom, M. Farias, J. Brown, R. Delmonte, E. de Oliveira Maraldi, L. Turner, F. Watts, J. Watts, and R. I. M. Dunbar (2020), "Religious Rituals Increase Social Bonding and Pain Threshold," https://psyarxiv.com/my4hs/.

Charles, S. J., V. van Mulukom, A. Saraswati, A., F. Watts, R. I. M. Dunbar, and M. Farias (n.d.), "Bending and Bonding: A Randomized Controlled Trial on the Socio-Psychobiological Effects of Spiritual versus Secular Yoga Practice."

Chattoe, E. (2006), "Using Simulation to Develop and Test Functionalist Explanations: A Case Study of Dynamic Church Membership," *British Journal of Sociology*, 57 (3): 379397.

Cheney, D. L., and R. M. Seyfarth (1988), "Assessment of Meaning and the Detection of Unreliable Signals by Vervet Monkeys," *Animal Behaviour*, 36 (2): 477–86.

Chomsky, N. (1980), *Rules and Representations*, New York: Columbia University Press.

Chomsky, N. (2000), *New Horizons in the Study of Language and Mind*, Cambridge: Cambridge University Press.

Chudek, M., M. Muthukrishna, and J. Henrich (2015), "Cultural Evolution," in D. M. Buss (ed.), *The Handbook of Evolutionary Psychology: Integrations*, 749–69, New York: John Wiley.

Chudek, M., R. A. McNamara, S. Birch, P. Bloom, and J. Henrich (2017), "Do Minds Switch Bodies? Dualist Interpretations across Ages and Societies," *Religion, Brain & Behavior*, 83 (2): 354–68.

Clark, A. (2013), "Whatever Next? Predictive Brains, Situated Agents, and the Future of Cognitive Science," *Behavioral and Brain Sciences*, 36 (3): 181–204.

Clark, A. (2016), *Surfing Uncertainty: Prediction, Action, and the Embodied Mind*, Oxford: Oxford University Press.

Codrington, R. H. (1891), *The Melanesians: Studies in Their Anthropology and Folklore*, Oxford: Clarendon Press.

Cohen, A. B., J. Gruber, and D. Keltner (2010), "Comparing Spiritual Transformations and Experiences of Profound Beauty," *Psychology of Religion and Spirituality*, 2 (3): 127–35.

Cohen, E. (2007), *The Mind Possessed: The Cognition of Spirit Possession in an Afro-Brazilian Religious Tradition*, Oxford: Oxford University Press.

Colace, C. (2010), *Children's Dreams: From Freud's Observations to Modern Dream Research*, London: Routledge.

Collins, F. S., M. Morgan, and A. Patrinos (2003), "The Human Genome Project: Lessons from Large-Scale Biology," *Science*, 300 (5617): 286–90.

Cooper, A. N., R. W. May, F. D. Fincham, and S. V. Kamble (2018), "God(s) in Minds: Understanding Deity Representation in Christian and Hindu Families through Social Relations Modeling," *Psychology of Religion and Spirituality*, 11 (2): 111–22. https://doi.org/10.1037/rel0000237.

Connors, S. M. (2000), "Ecology and Religion in Karuk Orientations toward the Land," in G. Harvey (ed.), *Indigenous Religions: A Companion*, 139–51, London: Cassel.

Cosmides, Leda, and John Tooby. (1997), "Evolutionary Psychology: A Primer." https://www.cep.ucsb.edu/primer.html. Accessed August 1, 2022.

Cotter, C. R. (2020), *The Critical Study of Non-Religion: Discourse, Identification and Locality*, London: Bloomsbury.

Cottingham, J., R. Stoothoff, and D. Murdoch, trans. (1998), *Selected Philosophical Writings* [of Descartes], Cambridge: Cambridge University Press.

Coulson, S., S. Stauruset, and N. Walker (2011), "Ritualized Behavior in the Middle Stone Age: Evidence from Rhino Cave, Tsodilo Hills, Botswana," *PaleoAnthropology*, 2011: 18–61.

Coulson, S., P. Segadika, and N. Walker (2016), "Ritual in the Hunter-Gatherer/Early Pastoralist Period: Evidence from Tsodilo Hills, Botswana," *African Archaeological Review*, 33: 205–22.

Cox, M., S. Villamayor-Tomas, and Y. Hartberg (2014), "The Role of Religion in Community-Based Natural Resource Management," *World Development*, 54: 46–55.

Cox, S. J. B. (1985), "No Tragedy on the Commons," *Environmental Ethics*, 7 (1): 49–61.

Cragun, R. T. (2019), "Questions You Should Never Ask an Atheist: Towards Better Measures of Nonreligion and Secularity," *Secularism and Nonreligion*, 8 (6): 1–6.

Cragun, R. T., K. McCaffree, I. Puga-Gonzalez, W. J. Wildman, and F. L. Shults (2021), "Religious Exiting and Social Networks: Computer Simulations of Religious/Secular Pluralism," *Secularism and Nonreligion*, 10 (2): 1–20.

Crichton, M. T. and C. Lange-Küttner (1999), "Animacy and Propulsion in Infancy: Tracking, Waving and Reaching to Self-Propelled and Induced Moving Objects," *Developmental Science*, 2 (3): 318–24.

Cronk, L. (1994), "Evolutionary Theories of Morality and the Manipulative Use of Signals," *Zygon*, 29 (1): 81–101.

Csibra, G. and G. Gergely (1998), "The Teleological Origins of Mentalistic Action Explanations: A Developmental Hypothesis," *Developmental Science*, 1 (2): 255–9.

Cummins, D. D. (1998), "Social Norms and Other Minds: The Evolutionary Roots of Higher Cognition," in D. D. Cummins and C. Allen (eds.), *The Evolution of Mind*, 30–50, Oxford: Oxford University Press.

Curtin, C. M., H. C. Barrett, A. Bolyanatz, A. N. Crittenden, D. M. T. Fessler, S. Fitzpatrick, M. Gurven, M. Kanovsky, G. Kushnick, S. Laurence, A. Pisor, B. Scelza, S. Stich, C. von Rueden, and J. Henrich (2020), "Kinship Intensity and the Use of Mental States in Moral Judgment across Societies," *Evolution and Human Behavior*, 14 (5): 415–29.

D'Agostino, A., and S. Scarone (2011), "From Dreams to Psychosis: A European Science Foundation Exploratory Workshop," *Consciousness and Cognition*, 20 (4): 985–6.

D'Andrade, R. G. (1961), "Anthropological Studies of Dreams," in Francis L. K. Hsu (ed.), *Psychological Anthropology: Approaches to Culture and Personality*, 296–332, Homewood: Dorsey Press.

D'Andrade, R. G. (1987), "A Folk Model of the Mind," in D. Holland and N. Quinn (eds.), *Cultural Models in Language and Thought*, 112–48, Cambridge: Cambridge University Press.

D'Andrade, R. G. (1992), "Schemas and Motivation," in R. D'Andrade and C. Strauss (eds.), *Human Motives and Cultural Models*, 23–44, Cambridge: Cambridge University Press.

D'Andrade, R. G. (1995), *The Development of Cognitive Anthropology*, Cambridge: Cambridge University Press.

Damasio, A. R. (1994), *Descartes' Error: Emotion, Rationality and the Human Brain*, New York: Putnam.

Darwin, C. ([1871] 2008), *The Descent of Man, and Selection in Relation to Sex*, New York: Penguin Books.

Dávid-Barrett, T., and J. Carney (2016), "The Deification of Historical Figures and the Emergence of Priesthoods as a Solution to a Network Coordination Problem," *Religion, Brain & Behavior*, 6 (4): 307–17.

Davis, E. B., G. L. Moriarty, and J. C. Mauch (2013), "God Images and God Concepts: Definitions, Development, and Dynamics," *Psychology of Religion and Spirituality*, 5 (1): 51–60.

Dawson, A. (2017), "Brazil's Ayahuasca Religions: Comparisons and Contrasts," in B. Schmidt and S. Engler (eds.), *Handbook of Contemporary Religions in Brazil*, Vol. 13, 233–52, Leiden: Brill.
De Cruz, H., and J. De Smedt (2017), "How Psychological Dispositions Influence the Theology of the Afterlife," in Y. Nagasawa and B. Matheson (eds.), *The Palgrave Handbook of the Afterlife*, 435–53, Basingstoke: Palgrave Macmillan.
Deane-Drummond, C. (2017), *A Primer in Ecotheology: Theology for a Fragile Earth*, Eugene: Cascade Books.
Degelman, D., and D. Lynn (1995), "The Development and Preliminary Validation of the Belief in Divine Intervention Scale," *Journal of Psychology and Theology*, 23 (1): 37–44.
Deloria Jr., V. (1979), *The Metaphysics of Modern Existence*, New York: Harper & Row Publishers.
Deloria Jr., V. (1992), *God is Red: A Native View of Religion*, Golden: Fulcrum.
DeMallie, R. J. (1987), "Lakota Belief and Ritual in the Nineteenth Century," in R. J. DeMallie and D. R. Parks (eds.), *Sioux Indian Religion*, 25–44, Norman: University of Oklahoma Press.
Denison, R. N., E. A. Piazza, and M. A. Silver (2011), "Predictive Context Influences Perceptual Selection during Binocular Rivalry," *Frontiers in Human Neuroscience*, 5: 166.
Dennett, D. C. (1971), "Intentional Systems," *Journal of Philosophy*, 68 (4): 87–106.
Descola, P. (2013), *Beyond Nature and Culture*, trans. J. Lloyd, Chicago: University of Chicago Press.
Dezutter, J., A. Wachholtz, and J. Corveleyn (2011), "Prayer and Pain: The Mediating Role of Positive Re-Appraisal," *Journal of Behavioral Medicine*, 34: 542–9.
Di Lernia, S. (2006), "Building Monuments, Creating Identity: Cattle Cult as a Social Response to Rapid Environmental Changes in the Holocene Sahara," *Quaternary International*, 151 (1): 50–62.
Diallo, S. Y., W. J. Wildman, F. L. Shults, and A. Tolk, eds. (2019), *Human Simulation: Perspectives, Insights, and Applications*, Cham: Springer.
Diamond, J. (2005), *Collapse: How Societies Choose to Fail or Survive*, London: Viking Penguin.
Dickson, D. B. (1990), *The Dawn of Belief: Religion in the Upper Paleolithic of Southwestern Europe*, Tucson: University of Arizona Press.
Dietrich, O. (2011), "Radiocarbon Dating the First Temples of Mankind: Comments on 14C Dates from Gobekli Tepe," *Zeitschrift fur Orient-Archaologie*, 4: 12–25.
Deitrich, O., and K. Schmidt (2010), "A Radiocarbon Date from the Wall Plaster of Enclosure D of Gobekli Tepe," *Neo-Lithics*, 2: 82–3.
Dietrich, O., J. Notroff, S. Walter, and L. Dietrich (2019), "Markers of 'Psycho-Cultural' Change: The Early-Neolithic Monuments of Gobekli Tepe in Southeastern Turkey," in T. Henley, M. J. Rossano, and E. Kardas (eds.), *Handbook of Cognitive Archaeology: Psychology in Pre-History*, 311–32, London: Routledge.
Dobrizhoffer, M. (1822), *An Account of the Abipones, an Equestrian People of Paraguay: Vol. 2*, John Murray. Accessed online: https://ehrafworldcultures.yale.edu/document?id=si04-001.
Domhoff, G. W. (2003), *The Scientific Study of Dreams: Neural Networks, Cognitive Development, and Content Analysis*, Washington: American Psychological Association.
Domhoff, G. W. (2017), *The Emergence of Dreaming: Mind-Wandering, Embodied Simulation, and the Default Network*, Oxford: Oxford University Press.

Domhoff, G. W., and K. C. R. Fox (2015), "Dreaming and the Default network: A Review, Synthesis, and Counterintuitive Research Proposal," *Consciousness and Cognition*, 33: 342–53.

Domhoff, G. W., and A. Schneider (2018), "Are Dreams Social Simulations? Or Are They Enactments of Conceptions and Personal Concerns? An Empirical and Theoretical Comparison of Two Dream Theories," *Dreaming*, 28 (1): 1–13.

Doney, K. and Baimel, A. (n.d.). Religion and the COVID-19 Pandemic in the UK. Unpublished manuscript.

Doniger, W. (1992), *The Laws of Manu*, London: Penguin Classics.

Douglas, M. ([1966] 1995), *Purity and Danger: An Analysis of the Concepts of Pollution and Taboo*, London: Routledge.

Dove, M. R. (2006), "Indigenous People and Environmental Politics," *Annual Review of Anthropology*, 35 (1): 191–208.

Dow, J. (2008), "Is Religion an Evolutionary Adaptation?" *Journal of Artificial Societies and Social Simulation*, 11 (2). https://jasss.soc.surrey.ac.uk/11/2/2.html. Accessed August 1, 2022.

Dow, M. M., and E. A. Eff (2009), "Multiple Imputation of Missing Data in Cross-Cultural Samples," *Cross-Cultural Research*, 43 (3): 206–29.

Doyle, A. C. (2003), *Sherlock Holmes: The Complete Novels and Stories: Volumes I and II*, New York: Bantam Classics.

Doyle, R. (2012), "Healing with Plant Intelligence: A Report from Ayahuasca," *Anthropology of Consciousness*, 23 (1): 28–43.

DreamBank (n.d.), retrieved November 11, 2021, from https://www.dreambank.net/.

Droogers, A. F. (2014), "The World of Worldviews," in A. F. Droogers and A. van Harskamp (eds.), *Methods for the Study of Religious Change*, 17–42, London: Equinox.

Dunn, O. (1989), *The Diario of Christopher Columbus's First Voyage to America, 1492–1493*, trans. E. K. James Jr., Norman: University of Oklahoma Press.

Duranti, A. (2008), "Further Reflections on Reading Other Minds," *Anthropological Quarterly*, 81 (2): 483–94.

Duranti, A. (2015), *The Anthropology of Intentions: Language in a World of Others*, Cambridge: Cambridge University Press.

Durkheim, É. (1912), *Les Formes Élémentaires de la Vie Religieuse: Le Système Totémique en Australie*, Paris: Félix Alcan.

Durkheim, E. ([1915] 2001), *The Elementary Forms of Religious Life*, Oxford: Oxford University Press.

Eastman, C. A. ([1911] 1980), *The Soul of the Indian: An Interpretation*, Lincoln: University of Nebraska Press.

Eckberg, D. L., and T. J. Blocker (1989), "Varieties of Religious Involvement and Environmental Concerns: Testing the Lynn White Thesis," *Journal for the Scientific Study of Religion*, 28 (4): 509–17.

Ecklund, E. H., J. Z. Park, and K. L. Sorrell (2011), "Scientists Negotiate Boundaries Between Religion and Science," *Journal for the Scientific Study of Religion*, 50 (3): 552–69.

Eder, J. F. (1997), *Batak Resource Management: Belief, Knowledge, and Practice*, IUCN.

Eder, J. F. (1999), "The Batak of Palawan Island, the Philippines," in R. B. Lee and R. Daly (eds.), *The Cambridge Encyclopedia of Hunters and Gatherers*, 294–7, Cambridge: Cambridge University Press.

Edmondson, A. C., and Z. Lei (2014), "Psychological Safety: The History, Renaissance, and Future of an Interpersonal Construct," *Annual Review of Organizational Psychology and Organizational Behavior*, 1 (1): 23–43.

Ellingson, S. (2016), *To Care for Creation: The Emergence of the Religious Environmental Movement*, Chicago: University of Chicago Press.

Ellis, E. C., N. Gauthier, K. Klein Goldewijk, R. Bliege Bird, N. Boivin, S. Díaz, D. Q. Fuller, J. L. Gill, J. O. Kaplan, N. Kingston, H. Locke, C. N. H. McMichael, D. Ranco, T. C. Rick, M. R. Shaw, L. Stephens, J.-C. Svenning, and J. E. M. Watson (2021), "People Have Shaped Most of Terrestrial Nature for at Least 12,000 Years," *Proceedings of the National Academy of Sciences*, 118 (17): e2023483118.

Ember, M. (1997), "Evolution of the Human Relations Area Files," *Cross-Cultural Research*, 31 (1): 3–15.

Emmons, R. A., P. C. Hill, J. L. Barrett, and K. M. Kapic (2017), "Psychological and Theological Reflections on Grace and Its Relevance for Science and Practice," *Psychology of Religion and Spirituality*, 9 (3): 276–84.

Endicott, K. L., and K. M. Endicott (2014), "Batek Childrearing and Morality," in D. Narvaez, K. Valentino, A. Fuentes, J. J. McKenna, and P. Gray (eds.), *Ancestral Landscapes in Human Evolution: Culture, Childrearing and Social Wellbeing*, 108–25, Oxford: Oxford University Press.

Ensminger, J. (1997), "Transaction Costs and Islam: Explaining Conversion in Africa," *Journal of Institutional and Theoretical Economics (JITE) / Zeitschrift fur die gesamte Staatswissenschaft*, 153 (1): 4–29.

Eom, K., H. S. Kim, D. K. Sherman, and K. Ishii (2016), "Cultural Variability in the Link Between Environmental Concern and Support for Environmental Action," *Psychological Science*, 27 (10): 1331–39.

Epicurus (1993), "Letter to Menoeceus," *The Essential Epicurus: Letters, Principal Doctrines, Vatican Sayings, and Fragments*, trans. E. O'Connor, 61–8, Buffalo: Prometheus Press.

Epley, N., and A. Waytz (2010), "Mind Perception," in S. T. Fiske, D. T. Gilbert, and G. Lindzey (eds.), *Handbook of Social Psychology*, 498–541, New York: John Wiley.

Epley, N., A. Waytz, and J. T. Cacioppo (2007), "On Seeing Human: A Three-Factor Theory of Anthropomorphism," *Psychological Review*, 114 (4): 864.

Epley, N., B. A. Converse, A. Delbosc, G. A. Monteleone, and J. T. Cacioppo (2009), "Believers' Estimates of God's Beliefs Are more Egocentric than Estimates of Other People's Beliefs," *Proceedings of the National Academy of Sciences*, 106 (51): 21533–8.

Epstein, J. M. (2006), *Generative Social Science: Studies in Agent-Based Computational Modeling*, Princeton: Princeton University Press.

Epstein, J. M. (2013), *Agent_Zero: Toward Neurocognitive Foundations for Generative Social Science*, Princeton: Princeton University Press.

Epstein, J. M., and R. L. Axtell (1996), *Growing Artificial Societies: Social Science from the Bottom Up*, Washington: Brookings Institution.

Erdoes, R., and A. Ortiz (1999), *American Indian Trickster Tales (Myths and Legends)*, London: Penguin Books.

Escher, D. (2013), "How Does Religion Promote Forgiveness? Linking Beliefs, Orientations, and Practices," *Journal for the Scientific Study of Religion*, 52 (1): 100–19.

Evans, E. M. (2001), "Cognitive and Contextual Factors in the Emergence of Diverse Belief Systems: Creation versus Evolution," *Cognitive Psychology*, 42: 217–66.

Evans-Pritchard, E. E. (1937), *Witchcraft, Oracles and Magic among the Azande*, Oxford: Oxford University Press.

Evans-Pritchard, E. E. (1940), *The Nuer: A Description of Modes of Livelihood and Political Institutions of a Nilotic People*, Oxford: Clarendon Press.

Evans-Pritchard, E. E. (1956), *Nuer Religion*, Oxford: Oxford University Press.

Evans-Pritchard, E. E. (1965), *Theories of Primitive Religion*, Oxford: Clarendon Press.

Exline, J. J., J. B. Grubbs, and S. J. Homolka (2015), "Seeing God as Cruel or Distant: Links with Divine Struggles Involving Anger, Doubt, and Fear of God's Disapproval," *International Journal for the Psychology of Religion*, 25 (1): 29–41.

Exline, J. J., K. I. Pargament, J. B. Grubbs, and A. M. Yali (2014), "The Religious and Spiritual Struggles Scale: Development and Initial Validation," *Psychology of Religion and Spirituality*, 6: 208–22.

Eysenck, M. W. and M. T. Keane (2000), *Cognitive Psychology: A Student's Handbook*, 4th ed., New York: Psychology Press.

Farias, M. (2013), "The Psychology of Atheism," in S. Bullivant and M. Ruse (eds.), *The Oxford Handbook of Atheism*, 468–82, Oxford: Oxford University Press.

Fehr, E., and U. Fischbacher. (2003), "The Nature of Human Altruism," *Nature*, 425: 785–91.

Fehr, E., and S. Gachter (2002), "Altruistic Punishment in Humans," *Nature*, 415: 137–40.

Felix, R., C. Hinsch, P. A. Rauschnabel, and B. B. Schlegelmilch (2018), "Religiousness and Environmental Concern: A Multilevel and Multi-Country Analysis of the Role of Life Satisfaction and Indulgence," *Journal of Business Research*, 91: 304–12.

Fernández-Jalvo, Y., and P. Andrews (2003), "Experimental Effects of Water Abrasion on Bone Fragments," *Journal of Taphonomy*, 1: 147–63.

Fincham, F. D., and S. R. M. Beach (2014), "I Say a Little Prayer for You: Praying for Partner Increases Commitment in Romantic Relationships," *Journal of Family Psychology*, 28: 587–93.

Fincham, F. D., and R. W. May (2019), "Self-Forgiveness and Well-Being: Does Divine Forgiveness Matter?," *Journal of Positive Psychology*, 14 (6): 854–9.

Fincham, F. D., R. W. May, and S. V. Kamble (2019), "Are Hindu Representations of the Divine Prototypically Structured?," *Psychology of Religion and Spirituality*, 11 (2): 101–10.

Firth, R. (1940), "The Analysis of Mana: An Empirical Approach," *Journal of the Polynesian Society*, 49 (4(196)): 483–510.

Fischer, R., R. Callander, P. Reddish, and J. Bulbulia (2013), "How Do Rituals Affect Cooperation? An Experimental Field Study Comparing Nine Ritual Types," *Human Nature*, 24: 115–25.

Fisher, R. A. (1930), *The Genetical Theory of Natural Selection*, Oxford: Oxford University Press.

Fiske, S. (2002), "What We Know about Bias and Intergroup Conflict: The Problem of the Century," *Current Directions in Psychological Science*, 11: 123–8.

Fitouchi, L., and M. Singh (2022), "Supernatural Punishment Beliefs as Cognitively Compelling Tools of Social Control," *Current Opinion in Psychology*, 44: 252–7.

Flexner, J. L., L. Lindstrom, F. Hickey, J. Kapere, L. Lindstrom, F. Hickey, and J. Kapere (2018), "Kaio, Kapwier, Nepek, and Nuk: Human and Non-Human Agency and 'Conservation' on Tanna, Vanuatu," in B. Verschuuren and S. Brown (eds.), *Cultural and Spiritual Significance of Nature in Protected Areas*, 251–62, London: Routledge.

Fodor, J. A. (1975), *The Language of Thought*, Cambridge: Harvard University Press.

Fodor, J. A. (1983), *The Modularity of Mind: An Essay on Faculty Psychology*, Cambridge: MIT Press.
Fodor, J. A. (1987), "Modules, Frames, Fridgeons, Sleeping Dogs, and the Music of the Spheres," in J. Garfield (ed.), *Modularity in the Knowledge Representation and Natural-Language Understanding*, 26–36, Cambridge: MIT Press.
Fodor, J. A. (1998), *In Critical Condition: Polemical Essays on Cognitive Science and the Philosophy of Mind*, Cambridge: MIT Press.
Fodor, J. A. (2000), *The Mind Doesn"t Work That Way: The Scope and Limits of Computational Psychology*, Cambridge: MIT Press.
Fodor, J. A. (2005), "Reply to Steven Pinker 'So How Does the Mind Work?'," *Mind & Language*, 20 (1): 25–32.
Foster, K. R., and H. Kokko (2009), "The Evolution of Superstitious and Superstition-Like Behaviour," *Proceedings of the Royal Society B: Biological Sciences*, 276 (1654): 31–7.
Foucault, M. (1984), *Le Souci de Soi: Histoire de la Sexualité Vol. 3*, Paris: Gallimard.
Foucault, M. (2016), *About the Beginning of the Hermeneutics of the Self. Lectures at Dartmouth College 1980*, Chicago: University of Chicago Press.
Fox, K. C. R., R. N. Spreng, M. Ellamil, J. R. Andrews-Hanna, and K. Christoff (2015), "The Wandering Brain: Meta-Analysis of Functional Neuroimaging Studies of Mind-Wandering and Related Spontaneous Thought Processes," *NeuroImage*, 111: 611–21.
Francis, L. J., H. M. Gibson, and M. Robbins (2001), "God Images and Self-Worth among Adolescents in Scotland," *Mental Health, Religion & Culture*, 4 (2): 103–8.
Francis, L. J., J. Astley, and U. McKenna (2018), "Belief in God, Belief in Science: Exploring the Psychological Correlates of Scientific Fundamentalism as Implicit Religion," *Implicit Religion*, 21 (4): 383–412.
Francis, P. (2015), *Encyclical on Climate Change and Inequality: On Care for Our Common Home*, London: Melville House.
Frank, R. (1988), *Passions within Reasons*, New York: W.W. Norton.
Freeman, L. G., and J. Gonzalez Echegaray (1981), "El Juyo: A 14,000-Year-Old Sanctuary from Northern Spain," *History of Religions*, 21: 1–19.
Freud, S. (1913), *The Interpretation of Dreams*, Oxford: Oxford University Press.
Freud, S. (1927), *The Future of an Illusion*, London: Penguin.
Friese, M., C. Messner, and Y. Schaffner (2012), "Mindfulness Meditation Counteracts Self-Control Depletion," *Consciousness and Cognition*, 21: 1016–22.
Friese, M., L. Schweizer, A. Arnoux, F. Sutter, and M. Wanke (2014), "Prayer Counteracts Self-Control Depletion," *Consciousness and Cognition*, 29: 90–5.
Friston, K., and S. Kiebel (2009), "Predictive Coding under the Free-Energy Principle," *Philosophical Transactions of the Royal Society B: Biological Sciences*, 364 (1521): 1211–21.
Friston, K., J. Kilner, and L. Harrison (2006), "A Free Energy Principle for the Brain," *Journal of Physiology-Paris*, 100 (1–3): 70–87.
Froese, P., and C. Bader (2010), *America's Four Gods: What We Say about God–and What That Says about Us*, Oxford: Oxford University Press.
Galen, L., and J. D. Kloet (2011), "Mental Well-Being in the Religious and the Non-Religious: Evidence for a Curvilinear Relationship," *Mental Health, Religion & Culture*, 14 (7): 673–89.
Gardner, P. M. (1972), "The Paliyans," in M. G. Bicchieri (ed.), *Hunters and Gatherers Today*, 404–47, New York: Holt, Rinehart and Winston.
Gardner, P. M. (1991), "Pragmatic Meanings of Possession in Paliyan Shamanism," *Anthropos*, 86 (4/6): 367–84.

Geertz, A. W. (2011), "Religious Narrative, Cognition and Culture: Approaches and Definitions," in A. W. Geertz and J. S. Jensen (eds.), *Religious Narrative, Cognition and Culture: Image and Word in the Mind of Narrative*, 9–29, Sheffield: Equinox.

Geertz, A. W. (2020), "How Did Ignorance Become Fact in American Religious Studies?: A Reluctant Reply to Ivan Strenski," *Studi E Materiali Di Storia Delle Religioni*, 86: 365–403.

Geertz, A. W., and G. I. Markússon (2010), "Religion is Natural, Atheism is Not: On Why Everybody is Both Right and Wrong," *Religion*, 40 (3): 152–65.

Geertz, C. (1973), *The Interpretation of Cultures: Selected Essays by Clifford Geertz*, New York: Basic Books.

Gelfand, M. J., J. R. Harrington, and J. C. Jackson (2017), "The Strength of Social Norms across Human Groups," *Perspectives on Psychological Science*, 12 (5): 800–9.

Gelfand, M. J., J. L. Raver, L. Nishii, L. M. Leslie, J. Lun, B. C. Lim, L. Duan, et al. (2011), "Differences Between Tight and Loose Cultures: A 33-Nation Study," *Science*, 332 (6033): 1100–4.

Gergely, G., and G. Csibra (2003), "Teleological Reasoning in Infancy: The Naive Theory of Rational Action," *Trends in Cognitive Science*, 7: 287–92.

Gernsbacher, M. A., and M. Yergeau (2019), "Empirical Failures of the Claim that Autistic People Lack a Theory of Mind," *Archives of Scientific Psychology*, 7 (1): 102–18.

Gervais, W. M. (2013), "Perceiving Minds and Gods: How Mind Perception Enables, Constrains, and Is Triggered by Belief in Gods," *Perspectives on Psychological Science*, 8 (4): 380–94.

Gervais, W. M., and J. Henrich (2010), "The Zeus Problem: Why Representational Content Biases Cannot Explain Faith in Gods," *Journal of Cognition and Culture*, 10 (3): 383–9.

Gervais, W. M., and A. Norenzayan (2012), "Analytic Thinking Promotes Religious Disbelief," *Science*, 336 (6080): 493–6.

Gervais, W. M., M. B. Najle, and N. Caluori (2021), "The Origins of Religious Disbelief: A Dual-Inheritance Approach," *Social Psychological and Personality Science*, 12 (7): 1369–79.

Gervais, W. M., M. van Elk, D. Xygalatas, R. T. McKay, M. Aveyard, E. E. Buchtel, I. Dar-Nimrod, E. K. Klocová, J. E. Ramsay, T. Riekki, T., A. M. Svedholm-Häkkinen, and J. Bulbulia (2018), "Analytic Atheism: A Cross-Culturally Weak and Fickle Phenomenon?," *Judgment and Decision Making*, 13 (3): 268–74.

Gervais, W. M., A. K. Willard, A. Norenzayan, and J. Henrich (2011), "The Cultural Transmission of Faith: Why Innate Intuitions are Necessary, but Insufficient, to Explain Religious Belief," *Religion*, 41 (3): 389–410.

Gigerenzer, G., R. Hertwig, and T. Pachur (2011), *Heuristics*, Oxford: Oxford University Press.

Giménez-Dasí, M., S. Guerrero, and P. L. Harris (2005), "Intimations of Immortality and Omniscience in Early Childhood," *European Journal of Developmental Psychology*, 2 (3): 284–97.

Ginges, J., I. Hansen, and A. Norenzayan (2009), "Religion and Support for Suicide Attacks," *Psychological Science*, 20 (2): 224–30.

Glasenapp, H. von (1966), *Buddhism: A Non-Theistic Religion: With a Selection from Buddhist Scriptures*, trans. I. Schloegl, H. Bechert (ed.), New York: George Braziller.

Glaskin, K. (2005), "Innovation and Ancestral Revelation: The Case of Dreams," *Journal of the Royal Anthropological Institute*, 11 (2): 297–314.

Glaskin, K. (2011), "Dreams, Memory, and the Ancestors: Creativity, Culture, and the Science of Sleep," *Journal of the Royal Anthropological Institute*, 17 (1): 44–62.

Glaskin, K. (2015), "Dreams, Perception, and Creative Realization," *Topics in Cognitive Science*, 7 (4): 664–76.

Gmelch, G. (1971), "Baseball magic," *Trans-Action*, 8 (8): 39–41.

Goodall, J. (2000), *In the Shadow of Man*, Boston: Houghton Mifflin Harcourt.

Goodenough, D. R. (1991), "Dream Recall: History and Current Status of the Field," in S. J. Ellman and J. S. Antrobus (eds.), *The Mind in Sleep: Psychology and Psychophysiology*, 143–71, New York: John Wiley.

Goodfriend, E. A. (2013), "Ethical Theory and Practice in the Hebrew Bible," in E. N. Dorff and J. K. Crane (eds.), *The Oxford Handbook of Jewish Ethics and Morality*, 35–50, Oxford: Oxford University Press.

Goody, J. (1996), "A Kernel of Doubt," *Journal of the Royal Anthropological Institute*, 2 (4): 667–81.

Gore, R., C. Lemos, F. L. Shults, and W. J. Wildman (2018), "Forecasting Changes in Religiosity and Existential Security with an Agent-Based Model," *Journal of Artificial Societies and Social Simulation*, 21 (1): 1–26.

Gorsuch, R. L. (1968), "The Conceptualization of God asSeen in Adjective Ratings," *Journal for the Scientific Study of Religion*, 7 (1): 56–64.

Gottlieb, R. S. (2006), *The Oxford Handbook of Religion and Ecology*, Oxford: Oxford University Press.

Govindrajan, R. (2015), "'The Goat That Died for Family': Animal Sacrifice and Interspecies Kinship in India's Central Himalayas," *American Ethnologist*, 42 (3): 504–19.

Granqvist, P. (2010), "Religion as Attachment: The Godin Award Lecture," *Archive for the Psychology of Religion*, 32 (1): 5–24.

Granqvist, P., and L. A. Kirkpatrick (2013), "Religion, Spirituality, and Attachment," in K. I. Pargament, J. J. Exline, and J. W. Jones (eds.), *APA Handbook of Psychology, Religion, and Spirituality (Vol. 1): Context, Theory, and Research*, 139–55, Washington: American Psychological Association.

Granqvist, P., M. Mikulincer, and P. R. Shaver (2010), "Religion as Attachment: Normative Processes and Individual Differences," *Personality and Social Psychology Review*, 14 (1): 49–59.

Gray, K., and D. M. Wegner (2010), "Blaming God for Our Pain: Human Suffering and the Divine Mind," *Personality and Social Psychology Review*, 14 (1): 7–16.

Gray, K., A. C. Jenkins, A. S. Heberlein, and D. M. Wegner (2011), "Distortions of Mind Perception in Psychopathology," *Proceedings of the National Academy of Sciences*, 108 (2): 477–79.

Gray, R. D., and J. Watts (2017), "Cultural Macroevolution Matters," *Proceedings of the National Academy of Sciences*, 114 (30): 7846–52.

Greenberg, J., T. Pyszczynski, S. Solomon, A. Rosenblatt, M. Veeder, S. Kirkland, and D. Lyon (1990), "Evidence of Terror Management Theory II: The Effects of Mortality Salience on Reactions to Those Who Threaten or Bolster the Cultural Worldview," *Journal of Personality and Social Psychology*, 58: 308–18.

Grim, J. A. (1983), *The Shaman: Patterns of Religious Healing among the Ojibway Indians*, Norman: University of Oklahoma Press.

Grim, J. A., and M. E. Tucker (2014), *Ecology and Religion*, 3rd ed., Washington: Island Press.

Groark, K. P. (2011), "Toward a Cultural Phenomenology of Intersubjectivity: The Extended Relational Field of the Tzotzil Maya of Highland Chiapas, Mexico," *Language and Communication*, 33 (3): 278–91.

Groark, K. P. (2020), "Taking Dreams Seriously: An Ontological-Phenomenological Approach to Tzotzil Maya Dream Culture," in *New Directions in the Anthropology of Dreaming*, 158–82, London: Routledge.

Grossmann, I., and M. E. Varnum (2015), "Social structure, Infectious Diseases, Disasters, Secularism, and Cultural Change in America," *Psychological Science*, 26 (3): 311–24.

Grubbs, J. B., and J. J. Exline (2014), "Why Did God Make Me This Way? Anger at God in the Context of Personal Transgressions," *Journal of Psychology and Theology*, 42 (4): 315–25.

Guthrie, S. E. (1980), "A Cognitive Theory of Religion," *Current Anthropology*, 21 (2): 181–203.

Guthrie, S. E. (1993), *aces in the Clouds: A New Theory of Religion*, Oxford: Oxford University Press.

Haaland, R., and G. Haaland (2011), "Landscape," in T. Insoll (ed.), *Oxford Handbook of the Archaeology of Ritual and Religion*, 24–37, Oxford: Oxford University Press.

Habermas, J. (2019), *Auch eine Geschichte der Philosophie. Band 1. Die okzidentale Konstellation von Glauben und Wissen*, Frankfurt am Main: Suhrkamp.

Hacking, I. (1972), "The Logic of Pascal's wager," *American Philosophical Quarterly*, 9 (2): 186–92.

Hadot, P. (1995), *Que"est-ce la Philosophie Antique?*, Paris: Gallimard.

Hadot, P. (2001), *Pierre Hadot and La Philosophie comme Manière de Vivre. Entretriens avec Jeannie Carlier et Arnold I. Davidson*, Paris: Albin Michel.

Hadot, P. (2002), *Exercices Spirituels et Philosophie Antique*, Paris: Albin Michel.

Hallowell, A. I. (1966), "The Role of Dreams in Ojibwa Culture," in G. E. von Grunebaum and R. Caillois (eds.), *The Dream and Human Societies*, 267–92, Berkeley: University of California Press.

Hallowell, A. I. (1975), "Ojibwa Ontology, Behavior, and World View," in D. Tedlock and B. Tedlock (eds.), *Teachings from the American Earth: Indian Religion and Philosophy*, 19–52, New York: Liveright.

Han, H. J., and R. Schweickert (2016), "Continuity: Knowing Each Other, Emotional Closeness, and Appearing Together in Dreams," *Dreaming*, 26 (4): 299–307.

Han, H. J., Schweickert, R., Xi, Z., and Viau-Quesnel, C. (2016), "The Cognitive Social Network in Dreams: Transitivity, Assortativity, and Giant Component Proportion Are Monotonic," *Cognitive Science*, 40 (3): 671–96.

Hand, C. M., and K. D. Van Liere (1984), "Religion, Mastery-Over-Nature, and Environmental Concern," *Social Forces*, 63 (2): 555–70.

Hansen, B. Å., and E. Brodtkorb (2003), "Partial Epilepsy with 'Ecstatic' Seizures," *Epilepsy & Behavior*, 4 (6): 667–73.

Hardin, G. (1968), "The Tragedy of the Commons," *Science*, 162: 1243–8.

Harris, P. L., and K. H. Corriveau (2011), "Young Children's Selective Trust in Informants," *Philosophical Transactions of the Royal Society London B Biological Sciences*, 366 (1567): 1179–87.

Harris, P. L., and K. H. Corriveau (2014), "Learning from Testimony about Religion and Science," in E. J. Robinson and S. Einav (eds.), *Trust and Skepticism: Children's Selective Learning from Testimony*, 28–41, London: Psychology Press.

Harris, P. L., and M. A. Koenig (2006), "Trust in Testimony: How Children Learn about Science and Religion," *Child Development*, 77: 505–24.

Harris, P. L., E. S. Pasquini, S. Duke, J. J. Asscher, and F. Pons (2006), "Germs and Angels: The Role of Testimony in Young Children's Ontology," *Developmental Science*, 9 (1): 76–96.

Hartberg, Y., Cox, M., and Villamayor-Tomas, S. (2014), "Supernatural Monitoring and Sanctioning in Community-Based Resource Management," *Religion, Brain & Behavior*, 6 (2): 95–111.

Hartland, E. S. (1898), "The "High Gods" of Australia," *Folklore*, 9 (4): 290–329.

Hartmann, E. (2000), *Dreams and Nightmares: The Origin and Meaning of Dreams*, New York: Basic Book.

Harvey, P. (1993), "The Mind-Body Relationship in Pali Buddhism: A Philosophical Investigation," *Asian Philosophy*, 3 (1): 29–41.

Haselton, M. G., and D. M. Buss (2000), "Error Management Theory: A New Perspective on Biases in Cross-Sex Mind Reading," *Journal of Personality and Social Psychology*, 78 (1): 81.

Haselton, M. G., G. A. Bryant, A. Wilke, D. A. Frederick, A. Galperin, W. E. Frankenhuis, and T. Moore (2009), "Adaptive Rationality: An Evolutionary Perspective on Cognitive Bias," *Social Cognition*, 27 (5): 733–63.

Hassrick, R. B. (1964), *The Sioux: Life and Customs of a Warrior Society*, Norman: University of Oklahoma Press.

Haun, D. B. M., Y. Rekers, and M. Tomasello (2012), "Majority-Biased Transmission in Chimpanzees and Human Children, but Not Orangutans," *Current Biology*, 22: 727–31.

Hawley, J. S. (1979), "Thief of Butter, Thief of Love," *History of Religions*, 18 (3): 203–20.

Hayden, B. (1987), "Alliances and Ritual Ecstasy: Human Responses to Resource Stress," *Journal for the Scientific Study of Religion*, 26 (1): 81–91.

Hayden, B. (2003), *Shamans, Sorcerers, and Saints: A Prehistory of Religion*, Washington: Smithsonian Books.

Hayden, B. (2012), "Neandertal Social Structure?," *Oxford Journal of Archaeology*, 31: 1–26.

Hayhoe, K. (2021), *Saving Us: A Climate Scientist's Case for Hope and Healing in a Divided World*, New York: Atria/One Signal.

Hebb, D. O. (1949), *The Organization of Behavior*, New York: Wiley.

Hegel, G. W. F. ([1827] 1969), *Werke in 20 Banden: Vorlesungen über die Philosophie der Geschichte, Werke Band 12*, Frankfurt am Main: Suhrkamp.

Heider, F., and M. Simmel (1944), "An Experimental Study of Apparent Behavior," *American Journal of Psychology*, 57 (2): 243–59.

Hein, G., G. Silani, K. Preuschoff, C. D. Batson, and T. Singer (2010), "Neural Responses to Ingroup and Outgroup Members" Suffering Predict Individual Differences in Costly Helping," *Neuron*, 68: 149–60.

Heiphetz, L., J. D. Lane, A. Waytz, and L. L. Young (2015), "How Children and Adults Represent God's Mind," *Cognitive Science*, 39: 1–24.

Heiphetz, L., J. D. Lane, A. Waytz, and L. L. Young (2018), "My Mind, Your Mind, and God's Mind: How Children and Adults Conceive of Different Agents' Moral Beliefs," *British Journal of Developmental Psychology*, 36 (3): 467–81.

Heiphetz, L., and S. Oishi (2021), "Viewing Development through the Lens of Culture: Integrating Developmental and Cultural Psychology to Better Understand Cognition and Behavior," *Perspectives on Psychological Science*, 17 (1): 62–77.

Helm, J. (1972), "The Dogrib Indians," in *Hunters and Gatherers Today*, 51–89, Prospect Heights: Waveland Press.

Helmholtz, H. (1867), *Handbuch der Physiologischen Optik*, Leipzig: Leoppold Voss.

Henrich, J. (2004), "Inequity Aversion in Capuchins?," *Nature*, 428 (6979): 139–40.

Henrich, J. (2009), "The Evolution of Costly Displays, Cooperation and Religion: Credibility Enhancing Displays and their Implications for Cultural Evolution," *Evolution and Human Behavior*, 30: 244–60.

Henrich, J. (2016), *The Secret of Our Success: How Culture Is Driving Human Evolution, Domesticating Our Species and Making Us Smarter*, Princeton: Princeton University Press.

Henrich, J. (2020), *The WEIRDest People in the World: How the West Became Psychologically Peculiar and Particularly Prosperous*, London: Penguin.

Henrich, J., M. Bauer, A. Cassar, J. Chytilová, and B. G. Purzycki (2019), "War Increases Religiosity," *Nature Human Behaviour*, 3: 129–35.

Henrich, J., R. Boyd, S. Bowles, C. Camerer, E. Fehr, H. Gintis, and R. McElreath (2001), "In Search of Homo Economicus: Behavioral Experiments in 15 Small-Scale Societies," *American Economic Review*, 91 (2): 73–8.

Herrmann, P., S. R. Waxman, and D. L. Medin (2010), "Anthropocentrism Is Not the First Step in Children's Reasoning about the Natural World," *Proceedings of the National Academy of Sciences*, 107 (22): 9979–84.

Heschel, A. J. (1976), *Man Is Not Alone: A Philosophy of Religion*, New York: Farrar, Straus and Giroux.

Hewitt, J. N. B. (1902), "Orenda and a Definition of Religion," *American Anthropologist*, 4 (1): 33–46.

Hewitt, J. N. B. (1912), "Orenda," in F. W. Hodge (ed.), *Handbook of American Indians, North of Mexico*. Smithsonian Institution, Bureau of American Ethnology, Bulletin 30, Washington: Govt. print. off.

Heyes, C. M., and C. D. Frith (2014), "The Cultural Evolution of Mind Reading," *Science*, 344 (6190): 1243091.

Hirschfeld, L. A., and S. A. Gelman (1994), "Toward a Topography of Mind: An Introduction to Domain Specificity," in L. A. Hirschfeld and S. A. Gelman (eds.), *Mapping the Mind: Domain Specificity in Cognition and Culture*, 3–35, New York: Cambridge University Press.

Hobson, J. A. (1999), *Dreaming as Delirium: How the Brain Goes Out of Its Mind*, Cambridge: MIT Press.

Hobson, J. A., and K. J. Friston (2012), "Waking and Dreaming Consciousness: Neurobiological and Functional Considerations," *Progress in Neurobiology*, 98 (1): 82–98.

Hobson, N. M., J. Schroeder, J. L. Risen, D. Xygalatas, and M. Inzlicht (2018), "The Psychology of Rituals: An Integrative Review and Process-Based Framework," *Personality and Social Psychology Review*, 22 (3): 260–84.

Hodder, I. (2011), *Çatalhöyük the Leopard's Tale: Revealing the Mysteries of Turkey's Ancient "Town,"* London: Thames & Hudson.

Hodges, S. D., C. A. Sharp, N. J. S. Gibson, and J. M. Tipsord (2013), "Nearer My God to Thee: Self-God Overlap and Believers' Relationships with God," *Self and Identity*, 12 (3): 337–56. https://doi.org/10.1080/15298868.2012.674212.

Hofstede, G. (1980), *Culture's Consequences: International Differences in Work-Related Values*, London: SAGE.

Hohwy, J. (2013), *The Predictive Mind*, Oxford: Oxford University Press.

Hollan, D. (2012), "Emerging Issues in the Cross-Cultural Study of Empathy," *Emotion Review*, 4 (1): 70–8.

Hood, M. S. (1993), "Man, Forest and Spirits: Images and Survival among Forest-Dwellers of Malaysia," *Japanese Journal of Southeast Asian Studies*, 30: 444–56.

Hoogeveen, S., E.-J. Wagenmakers, A. C. Kay, and M. Van Elk (2018), "Compensatory Control and Religious Beliefs: A Registered Replication Report across Two Countries," *Comprehensive Results in Social Psychology*, 3 (3): 240–65.
Hoogeveen, S. J. M. Haaf, J. A. Bulbulia, R. M. Ross, R. McKay, S. Altay, T. Bendixen, R. Berniūnas, A. Cheshin, C. Gentili, R. Georgescu, W. M. Gervais, K. Hagel, C. Kavanagh, N. Levy, A. Neely, L. Qiu, A. Rabelo, J. E. Ramsay, B. T. Rutjens, H. Turpin, F. Uzarevic, R. Wuyts, D. Xygalatas, and M. van Elk (2022), "The Einstein Effect Provides Global Evidence for Scientific Source Credibility Effects and the Influence of Religiosity," *Nature Human Behavior*, 6: 523–35.
Horton, R. (1997), *Patterns of Thought in Africa and the West: Essays on Magic, Religion and Science*, Cambridge: Cambridge University Press.
Hu, P., M. Stylos-Allan, and M. P. Walker (2006), "Sleep Facilitates Consolidation of Emotional Declarative Memory," *Psychological Science*, 17 (10): 891–8.
Hynes, W. J., and W. G. Doty (1997), *Mythical Trickster Figures*, Tuscaloosa: University of Alabama Press.
Iannaccone, L. R., and M. D. Makowsky (2007), "Accidental Atheists? Agent-Based Explanations for the Persistence of Religious Regionalism," *Journal for the Scientific Study of Religion*, 46 (1): 1–16.
Irons, W. (2001), "Religion as a Hard-to-Fake Sign of Commitment," in R. M. Nesse (ed.), *Evolution and the Capacity for Commitment*, 292–309, New York: Russell Sage Foundation.
Irwin, L. (1994), "Dreams, Theory, and Culture: The Plains Vision Quest Paradigm," *American Indian Quarterly*, 18 (2): 229–45.
Izquierdo, C., A. Johnson, and G. H. Shepard Jr. (2008), "Revenge, Envy and Sorcery in an Amazonian Society," in S. Beckerman and P. Valentine (eds.), *Revenge in Lowland South America*, 163–86, Gainesville: University of Florida Press.
Järnefelt, E., C. F. Canfield, and D. Kelemen (2015), "The Divided Mind of a Disbeliever: Intuitive Beliefs about Nature as Purposefully Created among Different Groups of Non-Religious Adults," *Cognition*, 140: 72–88.
Jablonka, E. and M. J. Lamb (2007), "Précis of Evolution in Four Dimensions," *Behavioral and Brain Sciences*, 30 (4): 353.
Jackson, J. C., N. Caluori, S. Abrams, E. Beckman, M. Gelfand, and K. Gray (2021), "Tight Cultures and Vengeful Gods: How Culture Shapes Religious Belief," *Journal of Experimental Psychology: General*, 150 (10): 2057–77.
Jackson, J. C., and K. Gray (2019), "When a Good God Makes Bad People: Testing a Theory of Religion and Immorality," *Journal of Personality and Social Psychology*, 117 (6): 1203–30.
Jackson, J. C., N. Hester, and K. Gray (2018), "The Faces of God in America: Revealing Religious Diversity across People and Politics," *PLOS ONE*, 13 (6): 1–14.
Jackson, J. C., M. Gelfand, and C. R. Ember (2020), "A Global Analysis of Cultural Tightness in Non-Industrial Societies," *Proceedings of the Royal Society B*, 287 (1930): 20201036.
Jackson, J. C., N. E. Caluori, K. Gray, and M. Gelfand (2021), "The New Science of Religious Change," *American Psychologist*, 76 (6): 838–50.
James, W. (1958), *The Varieties of Religion Experience: A Study in Human Nature*, New York: New American Library.
Janin, H., and A. Kahlmeyer (2007), *Islamic Law: The Sharia from Muhammad's Time to the Present*, Jefferson: McFarland.

Janoff-Bulman, R., C. Timko, and L. Carli (1985), "Cognitive Biases in Blaming the Victim," *Journal of Experimental Social Psychology*, 21 (2): 161–77.

Jaspers, K. (1947), *Vom Europäischen Geist: Vortrag Gehalten bei den Rencontres Internationales de Genève September 1946*, Munich: R. Piper & Co. Verlag.

Jaspers, K. (1949), *Vom Ursprung und Ziel der Geschichte*, Munich: R. Piper & Co. Verlag.

Jaubert, J., S. Verheyden, D. Genty, M. Soulier, H. Cheng, D. Blamart, C. Burlet, H. Camus, S. Delaby, D. Deldicque, and R. L. Edwards (2016), "Early Neanderthal Constructions Deep in Bruniquel Cave in Southwestern France," *Nature*, 534 (7605): 111–14.

Jeffery, R. (2008), *Evil and International Relations: Human Suffering in an Age of Terror*, New York: Palgrave Macmillan.

Jensen, J. S. (2014), "How Institutions Work in Shared Intentionality and 'We-Mode' Social Cognition," *Topoi: An International Review of Philosophy*, 33 (2): 1–12.

Jensen, P. F. (2020), "Nones: En Global (Ir)religiøs Forandringsproces med Lokale Særpræg: Om et Globalt Fænomen i en Lokal Kontekst," in M. Warburg and A. Hvithamar (eds.), *Religion i en Globaliseret Verden*, Højbjerg: Forlaget Univers.

Jha, V. N. (2017), "Matter and Consciousness: The Classical Indian Philosophical Approach," in S. Menon, N. Nagaraj, and V. V. Binoy (eds.), *Self, Culture and Consciousness, Interdisciplinary Convergences on Knowing and Being*, 419–33, Cham: Springer.

Johnson, A. (2003), *Families of the Forest: The Matsigenka Indians of the Peruvian Amazon*, Berkeley: University of California Press.

Johnson, D. D. P. (2005), "God's Punishment and Public Goods: A Test of the Supernatural Punishment Hypothesis in 186 World Cultures," *Human Nature*, 16 (4): 410–46.

Johnson, D. D. P. (2009), "The Error of God: Error Management Theory, Religion, and the Evolution of Cooperation," in S. A. Levin (ed.), *Games, Groups, and the Global Good*, 169–80, Cham: Springer.

Johnson, D. D. P. (2015), "Big Gods, Small Wonder: Supernatural Punishment Strikes Back," *Religion, Brain & Behavior*, 5 (4): 290–8.

Johnson, D. D. P. (2016), *God is Watching You: How the Fear of God Makes Us Human*, Oxford: Oxford University Press.

Johnson, D. D. P., and J. Bering (2006), "Hand of God, Mind of Man: Punishment and Cognition in the Evolution of Cooperation," *Evolutionary Psychology*, 4: 219–33.

Johnson, K. A., M. A. Okun, and A. B. Cohen (2015), "The Mind of the Lord: Measuring Authoritarian and Benevolent God Representations," *Psychology of Religion and Spirituality*, 7 (3): 227.

Johnson, K. A., A. B. Cohen, R. Neel, A. Berlin, and D. Homa (2015), "Fuzzy People: The Roles of Kinship, Essence, and Sociability in the Attribution of Personhood to Nonliving, Nonhuman Agents," *Psychology of Religion and Spirituality*, 7 (4): 295–305.

Johnson, K. A., A. B. Cohen, and M. A. Okun (2016), "God is Watching You ... But also Watching over You: The Influence of Benevolent God Representations on Secular Volunteerism among Christians," *Psychology of Religion and Spirituality*, 8 (4): 363–74.

Johnson, K. A., E. D. Hill, and A. B. Cohen (2011), "Integrating the Study of Culture and Religion: Toward a Psychology of Worldview," *Social and Personality Psychology Compass*, 5 (3): 137–52.

Johnson, K. A., Y. J. Li, A. B. Cohen, and M. A. Okun (2013), "Friends in High Places: The Influence of Authoritarian and Benevolent God-Concepts on Social Attitudes and Behaviors," *Psychology of Religion and Spirituality*, 5 (1): 15–22.

Johnson, K. A., R. L. Liu, E. A. Minton, D. E. Bartholomew, M. Peterson, A. B. Cohen, and J. Kees (2017), "U.S. Citizens' Representations of God and Support for Sustainability Policies," *Journal of Public Policy and Marketing*, 36 (2): 362–78.

Johnson, K. A., R. Memon, A. Alladin, A. B. Cohen, and M. A. Okun (2015), "Who Helps the Samaritan? The Influence of Religious vs. Secular Primes on Spontaneous Helping of Members of Religious Outgroups," *Journal of Cognition and Culture*, 15 (1–2): 217–31.

Johnson, K. A., E. A. Minton, and M. P. McClernon (2021), "Recycling, Relatedness, and Reincarnation: Religious Beliefs about Nature and the Afterlife as Predictors of Sustainability Practices," *Psychology of Religion and Spirituality*. https://doi.org/10.1037/rel0000407.

Johnson, K. A., J. W. Moon, M. A. Okun, M. J. Scott, H. P. O'Rourke, J. N. Hook, and A. B. Cohen (2019), "Science, God, and the Cosmos: Science both Erodes (via Logic) and Promotes (via Awe) Belief in God," *Journal of Experimental Social Psychology*, 84: 103826.

Johnson, K. A., M. A. Okun, and A. B. Cohen (2015), "The Mind of the Lord: Measuring Authoritarian and Benevolent God Representations," *Psychology of Religion and Spirituality*, 7 (3): 227–38.

Johnson, K. A., M. A. Okun, A. B. Cohen, C. A. Sharp, and J. N. Hook (2019), "Development and Validation of the Five-Factor LAMBI Measure of God Representations," *Psychology of Religion and Spirituality*, 11 (4): 339–49.

Johnson, K. A., A. Weinberger, E. Dyke, G. Potter, and A. Green (2022), "Differentiating Personified, Supernatural, and Abstract Views of God across Three Cognitive Domains." Psychology of Religion and Spirituality. http://dx.doi.org/10.1037/rel0000460

Jordan, P. (2003), *Material Culture and Sacred Landscape: The Anthropology of the Siberian Khanty*, Walnut Creek: AltaMira Press.

Jordan, J. J., M. Hoffman, P. Bloom, and D. G. Rand (2016), "Third-Party Punishment as a Costly Signal of Trustworthiness," *Nature*, 530 (7591): 473–6.

Joy, J. (2011), "The Iron Age," in T. Insoll (ed.), *Oxford Handbook of the Archaeology of Ritual and Religion*, 405–21, Oxford: Oxford University Press.

Jung, C. G. (1964), *Man and His Symbols*, New York: Doubleday.

Kahneman, D. (2011), *Thinking, Fast and Slow*, New York: Farrar, Straus and Giroux.

Kalish, C. W. (1996), "Preschoolers' Understanding of Germs as Invisible Mechanisms," *Cognitive Development*, 11 (1): 83–106.

Kaner, S. (2011), "The Archaeology of Religion and Ritual in the Prehistoric Japanese Archipelago," in T. Insoll (ed.), *Oxford Handbook of the Archaeology of Ritual and Religion*, 357–69, Oxford: Oxford University Press.

Kant, I. ([1787] 1929), *Critique of Pure Reason*, N. K. Smith (trans.), New York: St. Martin's Press.

Kapitány, R., N. Nelson, E. R. R. Burdett, and T. R. Goldstein (2020), "The Child's Pantheon: Children's Hierarchical Belief Structure in Real and Non-Real Figures," *PLOS ONE*, 15 (6): e0234142.

Kapitány, R., and M. Nielsen (2015), "Adopting the Ritual Stance: The Role of Opacity and Context in Ritual and Everyday Actions," *Cognition*, 145: 13–29.

Kapogiannis, D., A. K. Barbey, M. Su, G. Zamboni, F. Krueger, and J. Grafman (2009), "Cognitive and Neural Foundations of Religious Belief," *Proceedings of the National Academy of Sciences of the United States of America*, 106 (12): 4876–81.

Karmiloff-Smith, A. (1992), *Beyond Modularity: A Developmental Perspective on Cognitive Science*, Cambridge: MIT Press.

Kay, A. C., D. Gaucher, J. L. Napier, M. J. Callan, and K. Laurin (2008), "God and the Government: Testing a Compensatory Control Mechanism for the Support of External Systems," *Journal of Personality and Social Psychology*, 95 (1): 18–35.

Kay, A. C., D. Gaucher, I. McGregor, and K. Nash (2010), "Religious Belief as Compensatory Control," *Personality and Social Psychology Review*, 14 (1): 37–48.

Kay, A. C., J. A. Whitson, D. Gaucher, and A. D. Galinsky (2009), "Compensatory Control: Achieving Order through the Mind, Our Institutions, and the Heavens," *Current Directions in Psychological Science*, 18 (5): 264–8.

Keesing, R. M. (1984), "Rethinking 'Mana,'" *Journal of Anthropological Research*, 40 (1): 137–56.

Kelemen, D. (1999a), "Beliefs about Purpose: On the Origins of Teleological Thought," in M. C. Corballis and S. E. G. Lea (eds.), *The Descent of Mind: Psychological Perspectives on Hominid Evolution*, 278–94, Oxford: Oxford University Press.

Kelemen, D. (1999b), "The Scope of Teleological Thinking in Preschool Children," *Cognition*, 70 (3): 241–72.

Kelemen, D. (1999c), "Why Are Rocks Pointy? Children's Preference for Teleological Explanations of the Natural World," *Developmental Psychology*, 35 (6): 1440–52.

Kelemen, D. (2004), "Are Children "Intuitive Theists"?," *Psychological Science*, 15: 295–301.

Kelemen, D., and E. Rosset (2009), "The Human Function Compunction: Teleological Explanation in Adults," *Cognition*, 111 (1): 138–43.

Keller, P. S. (2011), "Sleep and Attachment," in M. El-Sheikh (ed.), *Sleep and Development: Familial and Socio-Cultural Considerations*, 49–77, Oxford: Oxford University Press.

Keller, T. (2008), *The Reason for God: Belief in an Age of Skepticism*, London: Penguin Books.

Kent, E. F. (2013), *Sacred Groves and Local Gods: Religion and Environmentalism in South India*, Oxford: Oxford University Press.

Keyes, C. F., and E. V. Daniel, eds. (1983), *Karma: An Anthropological Inquiry*, Berkeley: University of California Press.

Kidwell, C. S., H. Noley, and G. E. Tinker (2020), *A Native American Theology*, Maryknoll: Orbis Books.

Kiessling, F., and J. Perner (2014), "God-Mother-Baby: What Children Think They Know," *Child Development*, 85 (4): 1601–16.

Kim, S., and P. L. Harris (2013), "Belief in Magic Predicts Children's Selective Trust in Informants," *Journal of Cognition and Development*, 15 (2): 181–96.

Kim, S. and P. L. Harris (2014), "Children Prefer to Learn from Mind-Readers," *British Journal of Developmental Psychology*, 32 (4): 375–87.

Kirby, K. R., R. D. Gray, S. J. Greenhill, F. M. Jordan, S. Gomes-Ng, H.-J. Bibiko, D. E. Blasi, C. A. Botero, C. Bowern, and C. R. Ember (2016), "D-PLACE: A Global Database of Cultural, Linguistic and Environmental Diversity," *PLOS ONE*, 11 (7): e0158391.

Kirkpatrick, L. A. (1998), "God as a Substitute Attachment Figure: A Longitudinal Study of Adult Attachment Style and Religious Change in College Students," *Personality and Social Psychology Bulletin*, 24 (9): 961–73.

Kirkpatrick, L. A. (2005), *Attachment, Evolution, and the Psychology of Religion*, New York: Guilford Press.

Kirkpatrick, L. A., and P. R. Shaver (1992), "An Attachment-Theoretical Approach to Romantic Love and Religious Belief," *Personality and Social Psychology Bulletin*, 18 (3): 266–75.

Kitchens, M. B., and R. E. Phillips (2018), "A Curvilinear Relationship between Clear Beliefs about God and Self-Concept Clarity," *Psychology of Religion and Spirituality*, Advance online publication.

Klass, M. (1995), *Ordered Universes: Approaches to the Anthropology of Religion*, Boulder: Westview Press.

Klein, N. (2014), *This Changes Everything: Capitalism vs. the Climate*, Toronto: Alfred A. Knopf.

Knight, N., P. Sousa, J. L. Barrett, and S. Atran (2004), "Children's Attributions of Beliefs to Humans and God: Cross-Cultural Evidence," *Cognitive Science*, 28 (1): 117–26.

Knudson, R. M., A. L. Adame, and G. M. Finocan (2006), "Significant Dreams: Repositioning the Self Narrative," *Dreaming*, 16 (3): 215–22.

Koenig, H. G. (2012), "Religion, Spirituality, and Health: The Research and Clinical Implications," *International Scholarly Research Notices Psychiatry*, 2012, 1–33. https://downloads.hindawi.com/archive/2012/278730.pdf. Accessed August 1, 2022.

Koenig, M. A., and P. L. Harris (2005), "Preschoolers Mistrust Ignorant and Inaccurate Speakers," *Child Development*, 76: 1261–77.

Kokko, H. (2007), *Modelling for Field Biologists and Other Interesting People*, Cambridge: Cambridge University Press.

Koltko-Rivera, M. E. (2004), "The Psychology of Worldviews," *Review of General Psychology*, 8 (1): 3–58.

Kosmin, B. A., A. Keysar, R. Cragun, and J. Navarro-Rivera (2009), *American Nones: The Profile of the No Religion Population: A Report Based on the American Religious Identification Survey 2008*, Hartford: Trinity College.

Kouha, C. (2015), "A Comparison between the God of the Bible and the Tannese Primal Gods: An Apologetic to Educate Tannese Christians," *Melanesian Journal of Theology*, 31 (2): 220–84.

Krause, N. (2015), "Trust in God, Forgiveness by God, and Death Anxiety," *Omega: Journal of Death and Dying*, 72 (1): 20–41.

Krause, N., and G. Ironson (2017), "Forgiveness by God, Religious Commitment, and Waist/Hip Ratios," *Journal of Applied Biobehavioral Research*, 22 (4): 1–12. https://doi.org/10.1111/jabr.12104.

Krejci, M. J. (1998), "Gender Comparison of God Schemas: A Multidimensional Scaling Analysis," *The International Journal for the Psychology of Religion*, 8 (1): 57–66.

Krippner, S., F. Bogzaran, and A. P. De Carvalho (2002), *Extraordinary Dreams and How to Work with Them*, Albany: SUNY Press.

Krupenye, C., and J. Call (2019), "Theory of Mind in Animals: Current and Future Directions," *Wiley Interdisciplinary Reviews: Cognitive Science*, 10 (6): e1503.

Kuiken, D., M.-N. Lee, T. Eng, and T. Singh (2006), "The Influence of Impactful Dreams on Self-Perceptual Depth and Spiritual Transformation," *Dreaming*, 16 (4): 258–79.

Kuiken, D., and S. Sikora (1993), "The Impact of Dreams on Waking Thoughts and Feelings," in A. Moffitt, M. Kramer, and R. Hoffman (eds.), *The Functions of Dreaming*, 419–76, New York: State University of New York Press.

Kuiken, D., and L. Smith (1991), "Impactful Dreams and Metaphor Generation," *Dreaming*, 1 (2): 135–45.

Kunkel, M. A., S. Cook, D. S. Meshel, D. Daughtry, and A. Hauenstein (1999), "God Images: A Concept Map," *Journal for the Scientific Study of Religion*, 38 (2): 193–202.

Kupor, D. M., K. Laurin, and J. Levav (2015), "Anticipating Divine Protection? Reminders of God Can Increase Nonmoral Risk Taking," *Psychological Science*, 26 (4): 374–84.

Kühl, H. S., A. K. Kalan, M. Arandjelovic, F. Aubert, L. D'Auvergne, A. Goedmakers, S. Jones, L. Kehoe, S. Regnaut, A. Tickle, and E. Ton (2016), "Chimpanzee Accumulative Stone Throwing," *Scientific Reports*, 6: 22219.

Kwisthout, J., H. Bekkering, and I. Van Rooij (2017), "To Be Precise, the Details Don''t Matter: On Predictive Processing, Precision, and Level of Detail of Predictions," *Brain & Cognition*, 112: 84–91.

Laato, A., and J. C. de Moor (2003), *Theodicy in the World of the Bible*, Leiden: Brill.

Laine, J. W. (2014), *Meta-Religion: Religion and Power in World History*, Berkeley: University of California Press.

Lambert, N. M., F. D. Fincham, T. F. Stillman, S. M. Graham, and S. R. M. Beach (2010), "Motivating Change in Relationships: Can Prayer Increase Forgiveness?," *Psychological Science*, 21: 126–32.

Lame Deer, J. F., and R. Erdoes (1972), *Lame Deer, Seeker of Visions: The Life of a Sioux Medicine Man*, New York: Touchstone.

Lang, A. (1900), *The Making of Religion*, 2nd ed., London: Longmans, Green, and Co.

Lane, J. D. (2021), "Constructing Ideas of the Supernatural," *Journal of Cognition and Development*, 22 (3): 343–55.

Lane, J. D., P. L. Harris, S. Gelman, and H. M. Wellman (2014), "More than Meets the Eye: Young Children's Trust in Claims that Defy Their Perceptions," *Developmental Psychology*, 50: 865–71.

Lane, J. D., and P. Shafto (2017), "Young Children's Attributions of Causal Power to Novel Invisible Entities," *Journal of Experimental Child Psychology*, 162: 268–81.

Lane, J. D., H. M. Wellman, and E. M. Evans (2010), "Children's Understanding of Ordinary and Extraordinary Minds," *Child Development*, 81: 1475–89.

Lane, J. D., H. M. Wellman, and E. M. Evans (2012), "Socio-Cultural Input Facilitates Children's Developing Understanding of Extraordinary Minds," *Child Development*, 83: 1007–21.

Lane, J. D., H. M. Wellman, and E. M. Evans (2014), "Approaching an Understanding of Omniscience from the Preschool Years to Early Adulthood," *Developmental Psychology*, 50 (10): 2380–92.

Lane, J. E. (2013), "Method, Theory, and Multi-Agent Artificial Intelligence: Creating Computer Models of Complex Social Interaction," *Journal for the Cognitive Science of Religion*, 1 (2): 161–80.

Lane, J. E. (2018), "Strengthening the Supernatural Punishment Hypothesis through Computer Modeling," *Religion, Brain & Behavior*, 8 (3): 290–300.

Lane, J. E. (2015), "Semantic Network Mapping of Religious Material," *Journal for Cognitive Processing*, 16 (4): 333–41.

Lane, J. E. (2017), "Looking Back to Look Forward: From Shannon and Turing to Lawson and McCauley to ...?" in L. H. Martin and D. Wiebe (eds.), *Religion Explained?: The Cognitive Science of Religion after Twenty-Five Years*, 169–80, London: Bloomsbury.

Lane, J. E. (2018), "The Emergence of Social Schemas and Lossy Conceptual Information Networks: How Information Transmission Can Lead to the Apparent "Emergence" of Culture," in S. Mittal, S. Y. Diallo, and A. Tolk (eds.), *Emergent Behavior in Complex Systems Engineering: A Modeling and Simulation Approach*, 329–56, New York: John Wiley.

Lane, J. E. (2019), "Understanding Epistemological Debates in the Humanities and Social Sciences Can Aid in Model Development: Modeling Interpretive and Explanatory Theories," in S. Y. Diallo, W. J. Wildman, F. L. Shults, and A. Tolk (eds.), *Human Simulation: Perspectives, Insights, and Applications*, 67–79, Cham: Springer.

Lane, J. E. (2021), *Understanding Religion through Artificial Intelligence: Bonding and Belief*, London: Bloomsbury.

Lane, J. E., and W. W. McCorkle (2012), "Ancestors in the Simulation Machine: Measuring the Transmission and Oscillation of Religiosity in Computer Modeling," *Religion, Brain & Behavior*, 2 (3): 215–18.

Lang, M., B. G. Purzycki, C. L. Apicella, Q. D. Atkinson, A. Bolyanatz, E. Cohen, C. Handley, E. K. Klocova, C. Lesorogol, S. Mathew, R. A. McNamara, C. Moya, C. D. Placek, M. Soler, T. Vardy, J. L. Weigel, A. K. Willard, D. Xygalatas, A. Norenzayan, and J. Henrich (2019), "Moralizing Gods, Impartiality and Religious Parochialism across 15 Societies," *Proceedings of the Royal Society B: Biological Sciences*, 286 (1898): 20190202.

Lanman, J. A. (2012), "The Importance of Religious Displays for Belief Acquisition and Secularization," *Journal of Contemporary Religion*, 27 (1): 49–65.

Lanman, J. A., and M. D. Buhrmester (2016), "Religious Actions Speak Louder than Words: Exposure to Credibility-Enhancing Displays Predicts Theism," *Religion, Brain & Behavior*, 7 (1): 3–16.

Lansing, J. S. (1987), "Balinese 'Water Temples' and the Management of Irrigation," *American Anthropologist*, 89 (2): 326–41.

Lansing, J. S., and K. M. Fox (2011), "Niche Construction on Bali: The Gods of the Countryside," *Philosophical Transactions of the Royal Society B: Biological Sciences*, 366 (1566): 927–34.

Lansing, J. S., and J. N. Kremer (1993), "Emergent Properties of Balinese Water Temple Networks: Coadaptation on a Rugged Fitness Landscape," *American Anthropologist*, 95 (1): 97–114.

Lansing, J. S., and J. Miller (2005), "Cooperation, Games, and Ecological Feedback: Some Insights from Bali," *Current Anthropology*, 46 (2): 328–34.

Lansing, J. S., S. Thurner, N. N. Chung, A. Coudurier-Curveur, Ç. Karakaş, K. A. Fesenmyer, and L. Y. Chew (2017), "Adaptive Self-Organization of Bali's Ancient Rice Terraces," *Proceedings of the National Academy of Sciences*, 114 (25): 6504–9.

Lantis, M. (1938), "The Alaskan Whale Cult and Its Affinities," *American Anthropologist*, 40 (3): 438–64.

Larrimore, M. (2013), *Job: A Biography*, Princeton: Princeton University Press.

Laughlin, C. D. (2011), "Communing with the Gods: The Dreaming Brain in Cross-Cultural Perspective," *Time and Mind*, 4 (2): 155–88.

Laurence, S., and E. Margolis (2001), "The Poverty of the Stimulus Argument," *British Journal for the Philosophy of Science*, 52 (2): 217–76.

Lawson, E. T. and R. N. McCauley (1990), *Rethinking Religion: Connecting Cognition and Culture*, Cambridge: Cambridge University Press.

le Guen, O., R. Iliev, X. Lois, S. Atran, and D. L. Medin (2013), "A Garden Experiment Revisited: Inter-Generational Change in Environmental Perception and Management of the Maya Lowlands, Guatemala: A Garden Experiment Revisited," *Journal of the Royal Anthropological Institute*, 19 (4): 771–94.

Lebedev, A. V., M. Lövdén, G. Rosenthal, A. Feilding, D. J. Nutt, and R. L. Carhart-Harris (2015), "Finding the Self by Losing the Self: Neural Correlates of Ego-Dissolution under Psilocybin," *Human Brain Mapping*, 36 (8): 3137–53.

Lee, L. (2015), *Recognizing the Non-Religious: Reimagining the Secular*, Oxford: Oxford University Press.

Lee, R. B. (2003), *The Dobe Ju/"Hoansi*, 3rd ed., Belmont: Wadsworth.

Leeson, P. T. (2012), "Ordeals," *The Journal of Law and Economics*, 55 (3): 691–714.

Leeson, P. T. (2017), *WTF?!: An Economic Tour of the Weird*, Stanford: Stanford Economics and Finance.

Leeson, P. T., and C. J. Coyne (2012), "Sassywood," *Journal of Comparative Economics*, 40, 608–20.

Leeson, P. T., and P. A. Suarez (2015), "Superstition and Self-Governance," *New Thinking in Austrian Political Economy*, 19: 47–66.

Legare, C. H., E. M. Evans, K. S. Rosengren, and P. L. Harris (2012), "The Coexistence of Natural and Supernatural Explanations across Cultures and Development," *Child Development*, 83: 779–93.

Legare, C. H., and R. E. Watson-Jones (2015), "The Evolution and Ontogeny of Ritual," in D. M. Buss (ed.), *The Handbook of Evolutionary Psychology*, 829–47, New York: Wiley.

Legare, C. H., and A. L. Souza (2012), "Evaluating Ritual Efficacy: Evidence from the Supernatural," *Cognition*, 124 (1): 1–15.

Legerstee, M. (1991), "The Role of Person and Object in Eliciting Early Imitation," *Journal of Experimental Child Psychology*, 51 (3): 423–33.

Leibniz, G. ([1710] 1986), *Theodicy*, New York: Open Court.

Lerner, M. J., and L. Montada (1998), "An Overview: Advances in Belief in a Just World Theory and Methods," in L. Montada and M.J. Lerner (eds.), *Responses to Victimizations and Belief in a Just World* (Critical Issues in Social Justice), 1–7, New York: Plenum.

Leung, A. K. Y., and D. Cohen (2011), "Within- and Between-Culture Variation: Individual Differences and the Cultural Logics of Honor, Face, and Dignity Cultures," *Journal of Personality and Social Psychology*, 100 (3): 507–26.

Levin, R., and T. A. Nielsen (2009), "Nightmares, Bad Dreams, and Emotion Dysregulation: A Review and New Neurocognitive Model of Dreaming," *Current Directions in Psychological Science*, 18 (2): 84–8.

Levin, R., and T. A. Nielsen (2007), "Disturbed Dreaming, Posttraumatic Stress Disorder, and Affect Distress: A Review and Neurocognitive Model," *Psychological Bulletin*, 133 (3): 482–528.

Levine, M. (2012), "Non-Theistic Conceptions of God," in C. Meister and P. Copan (eds.), *Routledge Companion to Philosophy of Religion*, 272–83, London: Routledge.

Lewis, D. (1969), *Convention: A Philosophical Study*, New York: John Wiley.

Lewis-Williams, D. (2002), *Mind in the Cave: Consciousness and the Origins of Art*, London: Thames & Hudson.

Lewontin, R. C. (1961), "Evolution and the Theory of Games," *Journal of Theoretical Biology*, 1 (3): 382–403.

Lightner, A., T. Bendixen, and B. G. Purzycki (2022), "Cross-Cultural Datasets Systematically Underestimate the Presence of Moralizing Gods in Small-Scale Societies. SocArXiv. https://doi.org/10.31235/osf.io/29at3.

Lillard, A. (1998), "Ethnopsychologies: Cultural Variations in Theories of Mind," *Psychological Bulletin*, 123: 3–32.

Lipton, D. (1999), *Revisions of the Night: Politics and Promises in the Patriarchal Dreams of Genesis*, Sheffield: Sheffield Academic.

Liu, D., H. M. Wellman, T. Tardif, T., and M. A. Sabbagh (2008), "Theory of Mind Development in Chinese Children: A Meta-Analysis of False-Belief Understanding across Cultures and Languages," *Developmental Psychology*, 44 (2): 523–31.

Lohmann, R. I., and S. A. P. Dahl (2013), "Sleep, Dreaming, and the Imagination: Psychosocial Adaptations to an Ever-Changing World," *Reviews in Anthropology*, 42 (2): 56–84.

Lombrozo, T., D. Kelemen, and D. Zaitchik (2007), "Inferring Design: Evidence of a Preference for Teleological Explanations in Patients with Alzheimer's Disease," *Psychological Science*, 18 (11): 999–1006.

Longest, K. C. and C. Smith (2011), "Conflicting or Compatible: Beliefs about Religion and Science among Emerging Adults in the United States," *Sociological Forum*, 26 (4): 846–69.

Loprieno, A. (2003), "Theodicy in Ancient Egyptian Texts," in A. Laato and J. C. de Moor (eds.), *Theodicy in the World of the Bible*, 27–56, Leiden: Brill.

Lovins, C. (2015), "Shangdi Is Watching You: Tasan and Big Moralizing Gods," *Journal of the American Academy of Religion*, 83 (2): 464–89.

Lowe, B. S., S. K. Jacobson, H. Anold, A. S. Mbonde, and K. Lorenzen (2019), "The Neglected Role of Religion in Fisheries Management," *Fish and Fisheries*, 20 (5): 1024–33.

Loy, D. (1982), "Enlightenment in Buddhism and Advaita Vedanta," *International Philosophical Quarterly*, 22 (1): 65–74.

Lucas, A. J., E. R. R. Burdett, V. Burgess, N. McGuigan, L. A. Wood, P. L. Harris, and A. Whiten (2017), "Children's Selective Copying of Their Mother versus an Expert," *Child Development*, 88: 2026–42.

Luckert, K. W. (2013), *Stone Age Religion at Göbekli Tepe: from Hunting to Domestication, Warfare and Civilisation*, Portland: Triplehood.

Lugo, L., A. Cooperman, J. H. Martinez, B. Mohamed, M. Robbins, N. Sahgal, and K. Simmons (2012), "The World's Muslims: Unity and Diversity," *Pew Research Center*, 202, 164. https://www.pewresearch.org/religion/2012/08/09/the-worlds-muslims-unity-and-diversity-executive-summary/.

Luhrmann, T. M. (2011), "Toward an Anthropological Theory of Mind," *Suomen Antropologi: Journal of the Finnish Anthropological Society*, 36 (4): 5–69.

Luhrmann, T. M. (2012), *When God Talks Back: Understanding the American Evangelical Relationship with God*, New York: Knopf.

Luhrmann, T. M. (2020), *How God Becomes Real: Kindling the Presence of Invisible Others*, Princeton: Princeton University Press.

Luhrmann, T. M., K. Weisman, F. Aulino, J. D. Brahinsky, J. C. Dulin, V. A. Dzokoto, C. Legare, M. Lifshitz, E. Ng, N. Ross-Zehnder, and R. E. Smith (2021), "Sensing the Presence of Gods and Spirits across Cultures and Faiths," *Proceedings of the National Academy of Sciences*, 118 (5): e2016649118.

Luna, L. E. (1986), *Vegetalismo: Shamanism among the Mestizo Population of the Peruvian Amazon*, Stockholm: Almqvist & Wiksell International.

Luo, Y., and R. Baillargeon (2010), "Toward a Mentalistic Account of Early Psychological Reasoning," *Current Directions in Psychological Science*, 19 (5): 301–7.

Maarif, S. (2015), "Ammatoan Indigenous Religion and Forest Conservation," *Worldviews*, 19 (2): 144–60.

Macrae, C. N., J. M. Moran, T. F. Heatherton, J. F. Banfield, and W. M. Kelley (2004), "Medial Prefrontal Activity Predicts Memory for Self," *Cerebral Cortex*, 14 (6): 647–54.

Mageo, J., and R. E. Sheriff (2020), *New Directions in the Anthropology of Dreaming*, London: Routledge.

Maij, D. L., and M. van Elk (2019), "Evolved Priors for Agent Detection," *Religion, Brain & Behavior*, 9 (1): 92–4.

Maij, D. L., H. T. van Schie, and M. van Elk (2019), "The Boundary Conditions of the Hypersensitive Agency Detection Device: An Empirical Investigation of Agency Detection in Threatening Situations," *Religion, Brain & Behavior*, 9 (1): 23–51.

Maij, D. L. R., F. van Harreveld, W. Gervais, Y. Schrag, C. Mohr, and M. van Elk (2017), "Mentalizing Skills Do Not Differentiate Believers from Non-Believers But Credibility Enhancing Displays Do," *PLOS ONE*, 12 (8): e0182764.
Mails, T. E. (1979), *Fools Crow*, Lincoln: University of Nebraska Press.
Makris, N., and D. Pnevmatikos (2007), "Children's Understanding of Human and Super-Natural Mind," *Cognitive Development*, 22 (3): 365–75.
Malinowski, B. (1932), *Argonauts of the Western Pacific*, London: George Routledge.
Malinowski, B. (1974), *The Foundations of Faith and Morals: An Anthropological Analysis of Primitive Belief and Conduct with Special Reference to the Fundamental Problems of Religion and Ethics*, Folcroft: Folcroft Library Editions.
Malinowski, B. (1992), *Malinowski and the Work of Myth*, Ivan Strenski (ed.), Princeton: Princeton University Press.
Maquet, P., and G. Franck (1997), "REM Sleep and Amygdala," *Molecular Psychiatry*, 2 (3): 195–6.
Marett. R. R. (1900), "Pre-Animistic Religion," *Folklore* 11 (2): 162–84.
Marett, R. R. (1914), *The Threshold of Religion*, 2nd ed., London: Methuen.
Margolis, E., and S. Laurence (2013), "In Defense of Nativism," *Philosophical Studies*, 165: 693–718.
Markus, H. R., and S. Kitayama (1991), "Culture and the Self: Implications for Cognition, Emotion, and Motivation," *Psychological Review*, 98 (2): 224–53.
Marshall, L. (1962), "!Kung Bushman Religious Beliefs," *Africa*, 32 (3): 221–52.
Martin, L. H. (2014), "Great Expectations for Ara Norenzayan's *Big Gods*," *Religion*, 44 (4): 628–37.
Maryanski, A. (2018), *Émile Durkheim and the Birth of the Gods: Clans, Incest, Totems, Phratries, Hordes, Mana, Taboos, Corroborees, Sodalities, Menstrual Blood, Apes, Churingas, Cairns, and Other Mysterious Things*, London: Routledge.
Masuzawa, T. (2005), *The Invention of World Religions: Or, How European Universalism Was Preserved in the Language of Pluralism*, Chicago: University of Chicago Press.
Mauritsen, A. L., T. Bendixen, and H. R. Christensen (n.d.), Does a Pandemic Increase Religiosity in a Secular Nation? A Longitudinal Examination. https://doi.org/10.31234/osf.io/qsgej.
Mauss, M. (2001), *A General Theory of Magic*, London: Routledge.
May, R., and F. D. Fincham (2018), "Deity Representation: A Prototype Approach," *Archiv Für Religionspsychologie / Archive for the Psychology of Religion*, 40 (2–3): 258–86.
Maynard Smith, J. (1982), *Evolution and the Theory of Games*, Cambridge: Cambridge University Press.
Mayr, E. (2002), *What Evolution Is*, London: Phoenix Press.
mays, b. o., R. Seligman, and D. L. Medin (2020), "Cognition beyond the Human: Cognitive Psychology and the New Animism," *Ethos*, 48 (1): 50–73.
McAuliffe, K., J. J. Jordan, and F. Warneken (2015), "Costly Third-Party Punishment in Young Children," *Cognition*, 134: 1–10.
McCauley, R. N. (2000), "The Naturalness of Religion and the Unnaturalness of Science," in F. Keil and R. A. Wilson (eds.), *Explanation and Cognition*, 61–86, Cambridge: MIT Press.
McCauley, R. N. (2011), *Why Religion Is Natural and Science Is Not*, Oxford: Oxford University Press.
McCauley, R. N., and J. Henrich (2006), "Susceptibility to the Muller-Lyer Illusion, Theory-Neutral Observation, and the Diachronic Penetrability of the Visual Input System," *Philosophical Psychology*, 19 (1): 1–23.

McClenon, J. (2001), *Wondrous Healing: Shamanism, Human Evolution, and Origins of Religion*, DeKalb: Northern Illinois University Press.

McElreath, R., and R. Boyd (2007), *Mathematical Models of Social Evolution: A Guide for the Perplexed*. Chicago: University of Chicago Press.

McKay, R. T., and D. C. Dennett (2009), "The Evolution of Misbelief," *Behavioral and Brain Sciences*, 32 (6): 493–510.

McKay, R., and C. Efferson (2010), "The subtleties of error management," *Evolution and Human Behavior*, 31 (5): 309–19.

McKay, R., and H. Whitehouse (2015), "Religion and Morality," *Psychological Bulletin*, 141 (2): 447–73.

McNamara, J. M., and O. Leimar (2020), *Game Theory in Biology: Concepts and Frontiers*, Oxford: Oxford University Press.

McNamara, P. (2004), *An Evolutionary Psychology of Sleep and Dreams*, Santa Barbara: Praeger.

McNamara, P. (2016), *Dreams and Visions: How Religious Ideas Emerge in Sleep and Dreams*, Santa Barbara: Praeger.

McNamara, P. (2019), *The Neuroscience of Sleep and Dreams*, Cambridge: Cambridge University Press.

McNamara, P., J. Andresen, J. Clark, M. Zborowski, and C. A. Duffy (2001), "Impact of Attachment Styles on Dream Recall and Dream Content: A Test of the Attachment Hypothesis of REM Sleep," *Journal of Sleep Research*, 10 (2): 117–27.

McNamara, P., R. Ayala, and A. Minsky (2014), "REM Sleep, Dreams, and Attachment Themes across a Single Night of Sleep: A Pilot Study," *Dreaming*, 24 (4): 290–308.

McNamara, P., and K. Bulkeley (2015), "Dreams as a Source of Supernatural Agent Concepts," *Frontiers in Psychology*, 6: 1–8.

McNamara, P., P. Johnson, D. McLaren, E. Harris, C. Beauharnais, and S. Auerbach (2010), "REM and NREM Sleep Mentation," *International Review of Neurobiology*, 92 (2010): 69–86.

McNamara, P., B. Teed, V. Pae, A. Sebastian, and C. Chukwumerije (2018), "Supernatural Agent Cognitions in Dreams," *Journal of Cognition and Culture*, 18 (3–4): 428–50.

McNamara, R. A. (2014), *Powers Interview: Sau, Borisi, Mana, Sorcery, Traditional Medicine, Totem Beliefs in Yasawa, Fiji*.

McNamara, R. A., and J. Henrich (2017), "Kin and kinship psychology both influence cooperative coordination in Yasawa, Fiji," *Evolution and Human Behavior*, 38 (2): 197–207.

McNamara, R. A., and J. Henrich (2018), "Jesus vs. the Ancestors: How Specific Religious Beliefs Shape Prosociality on Yasawa Island, Fiji," *Religion, Brain & Behavior*, 8 (2): 185–204.

McNamara, R. A., and B. G. Purzycki (2020), "Minds of Gods and Human Cognitive Constraints: Socio-Ecological Context Shapes Belief," *Religion, Brain & Behavior*, 36 (1): 1–16.

McNamara, R. A., A. Norenzayan, and J. Henrich (2016), "Supernatural Punishment, In-Group Biases, and Material Insecurity: Experiments and Ethnography from Yasawa, Fiji," *Religion, Brain & Behavior*, 6 (1): 34–55.

McNamara, R. A., R. Senanayake, A. K. Willard, and J. Henrich (2021), "God's Mind on Morality," *Evolutionary Human Sciences*, 3 (E6): 1–19.

Medin, D. L., and S. G. García (2017a), "Conceptualizing Agency: Folkpsychological and Folkcommunicative Perspectives on Plants," *Cognition*, 162, 103–23.

Medin, D. L., and S. G. García (2017b), "Grounding Principles for Inferring Agency: Two Cultural Perspectives," *Cognitive Psychology*, 95: 50–78.

Medin, D., S. Waxman, J. Woodring, and K. Washinawatok (2010), "Human-Centeredness Is Not a Universal Feature of Young Children's Reasoning: Culture and Experience Matter When Reasoning about Biological Entities," *Cognitive Development*, 25 (3): 197–207.

Meena, S. L. (2005), "Relationship between State and Dharma in Manusmriti," *Indian Journal of Political Science*, 66 (3): 575–88.

Meyer-Rochow, V. B. (2009), "Food Taboos: Their Origins and Purposes," *Journal of Ethnobiology and Ethnomedicine*, 5 (1): 1–10.

Meylan, N. (2017), *Mana: A History of a Western Category*, Leiden: Brill.

Mikloušić, I., and J. E. Lane (2019), "How the Non-Religious View the Personality of God in Relation to Themselves," *Studia Humana*, 8 (3): 39–57.

Mikulincer, M., P. R. Shaver, and N. Avihou-Kanza (2011), "Individual Differences in Adult Attachment Are Systematically Related to Dream Narratives," *Attachment & Human Development*, 13 (2): 105–23.

Mikulincer, M., P. R. Shaver, Y. Sapir-Lavid, and N. Avihou-Kanza (2009), "What's Inside the Minds of Securely and Insecurely Attached People? The Secure-Base Script and Its Associations with Attachment-Style Dimensions," *Journal of Personality and Social Psychology*, 97 (4): 615–33.

Miller, G. A. (2003), "The Cognitive Revolution: A Historical Perspective," *Trends in Cognitive Sciences*, 7 (3): 141–4.

Miller, J. H., and S. E. Page (2007), *Complex Adaptive Systems: An Introduction to Computational Models of Social Life*, Princeton: Princeton University Press.

Millière, R. (2017), "Looking for the Self: Phenomenology, Neurophysiology and Philosophical Significance of Drug-Induced Ego Dissolution," *Frontiers in Human Neuroscience*, 11, Article 245.

Mir, M. (1991), "Humor in the Qur"an," *Muslim World*, 81 (3–4): 179–93.

Mittermaier, A. (2007), "The Book of Visions: Dreams, Poetry, and Prophecy in Contemporary Egypt," *International Journal of Middle East Studies*, 39 (2): 229–47.

Mittermaier, A. (2010), *Dreams that Matter*, Berkeley: University of California Press.

Mittermaier, A. (2012), "Dreams from Elsewhere: Muslim Subjectivities beyond the Trope of Self-Cultivation," *Journal of the Royal Anthropological Institute*, 18 (2): 247–65.

Moore, J. T., and M. M. Leach (2016), "Dogmatism and Mental Health: A Comparison of the Religious and Secular," *Psychology of Religion and Spirituality*, 8 (1): 54–64.

Morgan, R., R. Fischer, and J. A. Bulbulia (2017), "To Be in Synchrony or Not? A Meta-Analysis of Synchrony's Effects on Behaviour, Perception, Cognition and Affect," *Journal of Experimental Social Psychology*, 72: 13–20.

Morrison, K. M. (2000), "The Cosmos as Intersubjective: Native American Other-than-Human Persons," in G. Harvey (ed.), *Indigenous Religions: A Companion*, 23–36, London: Cassell.

Mu, Y., S. Kitayama, S. Han, and M. J. Gelfand (2015), "How Culture Gets Embrained: Cultural Differences in Event-Related Potentials of Social Norm Violations," *Proceedings of the National Academy of Sciences*, 112 (50): 15348–53.

Murdock, G. P. (1934), *Our Primitive Contemporaries*, Oxford: Macmillan.

Murdock, G. P. (1967), "Ethnographic Atlas: A Summary," *Ethnology*, 6 (2): 109–236.

Murdock, G. P., and D. R. White (1969), "Standard Cross-Cultural Sample," *Ethnology*, 8 (4): 329–69.

Muthukrishna, M., A. V. Bell, J. Henrich, C. M. Curtin, A. Gedranovich, J. McInerney, and B. Thue (2020), "Beyond Western, Educated, Industrial, Rich, and Democratic (WEIRD) Psychology: Measuring and Mapping Scales of Cultural and Psychological Distance," *Psychological Science*, 31 (6): 678–701.

Nash, J. F. (1950), "Equilibrium Points in n-Person Games," *Proceedings of the National Academy of Sciences*, 36 (1): 48–9.

Nettle, D., and W. E. Frankenhuis (2020), "Life-History Theory in Psychology and Evolutionary Biology: One Research Programme or Two?," *Philosophical Transactions of the Royal Society B: Biological Sciences*, 375: 20190490.

Neihardt, J. G. (1984), *The Sixth Grandfather: Black Elk's Teachings Given to John G. Neihardt*, Lincoln: University of Nebraska Press.

Nielbo, K. L., and J. Sørensen (2011), "Spontaneous Processing of Functional and Non-Functional Action Sequences," *Religion, Brain & Behavior*, 1 (1): 18–30.

Nielbo, K. L., D. M. Braxton, and M. A. Upal (2012), "Computing Religion: A New Tool in the Multilevel Analysis of Religion," *Method & Theory in the Study of Religion*, 24 (3): 267–90.

Nielsen, M., and C. Blank (2011), "Imitation in Young Children: When Who Gets Copied Is More Important Than What Gets Copied," *Developmental Psychology*, 47 (4): 1050–3.

Nielsen, T. A., and R. A. Powell (1992), "The Day-Residue and Dream-Lag Effects: A Literature Review and Limited Replication of Two Temporal Effects in Dream Formation. *Dreaming*, 2 (2): 67–77.

Nietzsche, F. (1988), "Jenseits von Gut und Böse," in M. Montanari and G. Colli (eds.), *Kritische Studienausgabe*, vol. 5, 2nd ed., 9–243, Berlin: De Gruyter.

Nietzsche, F. W. (2005), *Thus Spoke Zarathustra: A Book for Everyone and Nobody*, Oxford: Oxford University Press.

Nisbett, R. E., and D. Cohen (1996), *Culture of Honor: The Psychology of Violence in the South*, London: Routledge.

Neiman, S. (2002), *Evil in Modern Thought: An Alternative History of Western Philosophy*, Princeton: Princeton University Press.

Newman, G. E., F. C. Keil, V. A. Kuhlmeier, and K. Wynn (2010), "Early Understandings of the Link between Agents and Order," *Proceedings of the National Academy of Science*, 107: 17140–5.

Nicholson, A. J. (2010), *Unifying Hinduism: Philosophy and Identity in Indian Intellectual History*, New York: Columbia University Press.

Noë, A. (2004), *Action in Perception*, Cambridge: MIT Press.

Noffke, J. L., and S. H. McFadden (2001), "Denominational and Age Comparisons of God Concepts," *Journal for the Scientific Study of Religion*, 40 (4): 747–56.

Norenzayan, A. (2013), *Big Gods: How Religion Transformed Cooperation and Conflict*, Princeton: Princeton University Press.

Norenzayan, A., and W. M. Gervais (2013), "The Origins of Religious Disbelief," *Trends in Cognitive Sciences*, 17 (1): 20–5.

Norenzayan, A., W. M. Gervais, and K. H. Trzesniewski (2012), "Mentalizing Deficits Constrain Belief in a Personal God," *PLOS ONE*, 7 (5), e36880.

Norenzayan, A., and A. F. Shariff (2008), "The Origin and Evolution of Religious Pro-Sociality," *Science*, 322 (5898): 58–62.

Norenzayan, A., A. F. Shariff, A. K. Willard, E. Slingerland, W. M. Gervais, R. A. McNamara, and J. Henrich (2016), "The Cultural Evolution of Prosocial Religions," *Behavioral and Brain Sciences*, 39 (1–65): 331.

Norris, P., and R. Inglehart (2011), *Sacred and Secular: Religion and Politics Worldwide*, Cambridge: Cambridge University Press.

North, D. C. (1990), *Institutions, Institutional Change, and Economic Performance: The Political Economy of Institutions and Decisions*, Cambridge: Cambridge University Press.

Northoff, G., A. Heinzel, M. de Greck, F. Bermpohl, H. Dobrowolny, and J. Panksepp (2006), "Self-Referential Processing in Our Brain: A Meta-Analysis of Imaging Studies on the Self," *NeuroImage*, 31 (1): 440–57.

Nyhof, M. A., and C. Johnson (2017), "Is God Just a Big Person? Children's Conceptions of God across Cultures and Religious Traditions," *British Journal of Developmental Psychology*, 35 (1): 60–75.

O'Flaherty, W. D. (1975), *Hindu Myths: A Sourcebook Translated from the Sanskrit*, London: Penguin Books.

O'Keefe, T. (2010), *Epicureanism*, Berkeley: University of California Press.

Ogata, A., and T. Miyakawa (1998), "Religious Experiences in Epileptic Patients with a Focus on Ictus-Related Episodes," *Psychiatry and Clinical Neurosciences*, 52 (3): 321–5.

Oishi, S., and E. Diener (2014), "Residents of Poor Nations Have a Greater Sense of Meaning in Life Than Residents of Wealthy Nations," *Psychological Science*, 25: 422–30.

Oishi, S., K. O. Seol, M. Koo, and F. F. Miao (2011), "Was He Happy? Cultural Difference in Conceptions of Jesus," *Journal of Research in Personality*, 45 (1): 84–91.

ojalehto, b. l., D. L. Medin, and S. G. García (2017), "Conceptualizing Agency: Folkpsychological and Folkcommunicative Perspectives on Plants," *Cognition*, 162, 103–23.

ojalehto, b. l., D. L. Medin, W. S. Horton, S. G. Garcia, and E. G. Kays (2015), "Seeing Cooperation or Competition: Ecological Interactions in Cultural Perspectives," *Topics in Cognitive Science*, 7 (4): 624–45.

ojalehto mays, b., R. Seligman, and D. L. Medin (2020), "Cognition Beyond the Human: Cognitive Psychology and the New Animism," *Ethos*, 48 (1): 50–73.

Orr, Y., J. S. Lansing, and M. R. Dove (2015), "Environmental Anthropology: Systemic Perspectives," *Annual Review of Anthropology*, 44: 153–68.

Ostrom, E. (1990), *Governing the Commons: The Evolution of Institutions for Collective Action, Political Economy of Institutions and Decisions*, Cambridge: Cambridge University Press.

Overgaard, S. (2006), "The Problem of Other Minds: Wittgenstein's Phenomenological Perspective," *Phenomenology and the Cognitive Sciences*, 5 (1): 53–73.

Paden, W. E. (2017), "Shifting Worldviews: Modeling Sacrality in Naturalistic Perspective," *Religion*, 47 (4): 704–17.

Paden, W. E.(2018), "Behaviors and Environments: Patterns of Religious World Habitation," in A. K. Petersen, G. I. Sælid, L. H. Martin, J. S. Jensen, and J. Sørensen (eds.), *Evolution, Cognition, and the History of Religion: A New Synthesis*, 100–14, Leiden: Brill.

Palagini, L., and N. Rosenlicht (2011), "Sleep, Dreaming, and Mental Health: A Review of Historical and Neurobiological Perspectives," *Sleep Medicine Reviews*, 15 (3): 179–86.

Palmer, M., and V. Finaly (2003), *Faith in Conservation: New Approaches to Religions and the Environment, Directions in Development*, Washington: World Bank.

Pargament, K. I., B. W. Smith, H. G. Koenig, and L. Perez (1998), "Patterns of Positive and Negative Religious Coping with Major Life Stressors," *Journal for the Scientific Study of Religion*, 37 (4): 710–24.

Park, C. L. (2013), "Religion and Meaning," In R. Paloutzian and C. L. Park (eds.), *Handbook of the Psychology of Religion and Spirituality*, 2nd ed., 357–79, New York: Guilford Press.

Park, C. L., and S. Folkman (1997), "Meaning in the Context of Stress and Coping," *Review of General Psychology*, 1 (2): 115–44.

Pazhoohi, F., M. Lang, D. Xygalatas, and K. Grammer (2017), "Religious Veiling as a Mate-Guarding Strategy: Effects of Environmental Pressures on Cultural Practices," *Evolutionary Psychological Science*, 3 (2): 118–24.

Peacock, J. (2008), "Suffering in Mind: The Aetiology of Suffering in Early Buddhism," *Contemporary Buddhism*, 9 (2): 209–26.

Pearl, J., M. Glymour, and N. P. Jewell (2016), *Causal Inference in Statistics: A Primer*, New York: John Wiley.

Peatfeield, A. (1992), "Rural Ritual in Bronze Age Crete: The Peak Sanctuary at Atsipadhes," *Cambridge Archaeological Journal*, 2: 59–87.

Penn, D. C., and D. J. Povinelli (2007), "On the Lack of Evidence that Non-Human Animals Possess Anything Remotely Resembling a 'Theory of Mind'," *Philosophical Transactions of the Royal Society, B*, 362: 731–44.

Peoples, H. C., P. Duda, and F. W. Marlowe (2016), "Hunter-Gatherers and the Origin of Religion," *Human Nature*, 27: 261–82.

Peoples, H. C., and F. W. Marlowe (2012), "Subsistence and the Evolution of Religion," *Human Nature*, 23 (3): 253–69.

Perner, J., T. Ruffman, and S. R. Leekam (1994), "Theory of Mind Is Contagious: You Catch It from Your Sibs," *Child Development*, 65: 1228–38.

Petersen, A. K. (2011), "Rituals of Purification, Rituals of Initiation: Phenomenological, Taxonomical and Culturally Evolutionary Reflections," in D. Hellholm, T. Vegge, Ø. Nordeval, and C. Hellholm (eds.), *Ablution, Initiation, and Baptism. Late Antiquity, Early Judaism, and Early Christianity*, Vol. 1, 3–40, Berlin: De Gruyter.

Petersen, A. K. (2013), "Attaining Divine Perfection through Different Forms of Imitation," *Numen*, 60 (1): 7–38.

Petersen, A. K. (2017), "The Tangled Cultural History of the Axial Age," *Journal of Cognitive Historiography*, 4 (2): 257–72.

Petersen, A. K. (2019a), "Continuity as a Core Concept for a Renewed Scientific Study of Religion," in A. K. Petersen, I. S. Gilhus, L. H. Martin, J. S. Jensen, and J. Sørensen (eds.), *Evolution, Cognitions, and the History of Religion: A New Synthesis. Festschrift in Honour of Armin W. Geertz*, 86–99, Leiden: Brill.

Petersen, A. K. (2019b), "A New Take on Asceticism: Asceticism as Training and Secession Suspended between Individuality and Collectivity," *Numen*, 66 (5–6): 465–98.

Petersen, A. K. (2022a), "Hvad er Religion? - En Samtale med Hans Jørgen Lundager Jensen og en Del Andre," *Religionsvidenskabeligt Tidsskrift* (forthcoming).

Petersen, A. K. (2022b), "From Sacrificed Humans to Self-Sacrificing Humans: A Longue-Durée Bio-Cultural Evolutionary Perspective on Sacrifice," in M. J. Walsh, R. Willerslev, and og S O"Neill (eds.), *The State of Human Sacrifice Research – A Global Perspective from Northern Europe*, London: Routledge.

Petersen, A. K., J. H. Turner, A. W. Geertz, and A. Maryanski (2022), "*Homines Emotionales* and Religion as an Evolutionary Exaptation: A Response to Leonardo Ambasciano," *Journal for Cognitive Historiography*, 6 (1–2): 157–171.

Pettitt, P. B. (2011), "Religion and Ritual in the Lower and Middle Paleolithic," in T. Insoll (ed.), *Oxford Handbook of the Archaeology of Ritual and Religion*, 329–43, Oxford: Oxford University Press.

Pew Research Center (2014), "Religion in America: U.S. Religious Data, Demographics and Statistics," Pew Research Center's Religion and Public Life Project. https://www.pewresearch.org/religion/religious-landscape-study/.

Pew Research Center (2015a), "A Portrait of American Orthodox Jews: A Further Analysis of the 2013 Survey of U.S. Jews." https://www.pewresearch.org/religion/2015/08/26/a-portrait-of-american-orthodox-jews/.

Pew Research Center (2015b), "The Future of World Religions: Population Growth Projects, 2010–2050." https://assets.pewresearch.org/wp-content/uploads/sites/11/2015/03/PF_15.04.02_ProjectionsFullReport.pdf.

Pew Research Center (2021), "In Response to Climate Change, Citizens in Advanced Economies Are Willing to Alter How They Live and Work." https://www.pewresearch.org/global/wp-content/uploads/sites/2/2021/09/PG_2021.09.14_Climate_FINAL.pdf.

Pflueger, L. (2008), "Person Purity and Power in Yogasutra," in K. Jacobsen (ed.), *Theory and Practice of Yoga Essays in Honour of Gerald James Larson*, 29–60, New Delhi: Motilal Banarsidass.

Phillips III, R. E., K. I. Pargament, Q. K. Lynn, and C. D. Crossley (2004), "Self-Directing Religious Coping: A Deistic God, Abandoning God, or No God at All?" *Journal for the Scientific Study of Religion*, 43 (3): 409–18.

Piaget, J. (1929), *The Child's Conception of the World*, London: Harcourt Brace.

Piedmont, R. L., J. E. G. Williams, and J. W. Ciarrochi (1997), "Personality Correlates of One's Image of Jesus: Historiographic Analysis Using the Five-Factor Model of Personality," *Journal of Psychology of Theology*, 25 (3): 364–73.

Pietraszewski, D., and A. E. Wertz (2021), "Why Evolutionary Psychology Should Abandon Modularity," *Perspectives on Psychological Science*, 17 (2): 465–90.

Pinker, S. (2005a), "So How Does the Mind Work?," *Mind & Language*, 20 (1): 1–24.

Pinker, S. (2005b), "A Reply to Jerry Fodor on How the Mind Works," *Mind & Language*, 20 (1): 33–8.

Poirier, S. (2003), "This Is Good Country. We Are Good Dreamers," in R. I. Lohmann (ed.), *Dream Travelers: Sleep Experiences and Culture in the Western Pacific*, 107–26, London: Palgrave Macmillan.

Poling, D. A., and E. M. Evans (2004), "Are Dinosaurs the Rule or the Exception?: Developing Concepts of Death and Extinction," *Cognitive Development*, 19 (3): 363–83.

Power, E. A. (2017), "Discerning Devotion: Testing the Signaling Theory of Religion," *Evolution and Human Behavior*, 38 (1): 82–91.

Powers, W. K. (1975), *Oglala Religion*, Lincoln: University of Nebraska Press.

Prakash, C., K. D. Stephens, D. D. Hoffman, M. Singh, and C. Fields (2021), "Fitness Beats Truth in the Evolution of Perception," *Acta Biotheoretica*, 69 (3): 319–41.

Prasad, H. S. (2000), "Dreamless Sleep and Soul: A Controversy between Vedanta and Buddhism," *Asian Philosophy*, 10 (1): 61–73.

Premack, D. G., and A. Premack (2003), *Original Intelligence: Unlocking the Mystery of Who We Are*, New York: McGraw Hill.

Premack, D. G., and G. Woodruff (1978), "Does the Chimpanzee Have a Theory of Mind?," *Behavioral and Brain Sciences*, 1 (4): 515–26.

Preston, J. L., and A. Baimel (2021), "Towards a Psychology of Religion and the Environment," *Current Opinion in Psychology*, 40: 145–49.

Preston, J., and N. Epley (2009), "Science and God: An Automatic Opposition between Ultimate Explanations," *Journal of Experimental Social Psychology*, 45 (1): 238–41.

Preston, J., R. S. Ritter, and J. Hepler (2013), "Neuroscience and the Soul: Competing Explanations for the Human Experience," *Cognition*, 127 (1): 31–7.

Price, M., and J. Launay (2018), "Increased Wellbeing from Social Interaction in a Secular Congregation," *Secularism and Nonreligion*, 7 (6): 1–9.

Puga-Gonzalez, I., F. L. Shults, W. J. Wildman, and S. Y. Diallo (2018), "InCREDulous Scandinavians: An Agent-Based Model of the Spread of Secularism," *Proceedings of the Winter Simulation Conference*, Piscataway, NJ: Institute for Electrical and Electronics Engineers.

Puga-Gonzalez, I., W. J. Wildman, K. McCaffree, R. T. Cragun, and F. L. Shults (2020), "InCREDulity in Artificial Societies," in P. Ahrweiler (ed.), *Social Simulation, Springer Lecture Notes in Computer Science*, 81–93, Cham: Springer.

Pungetti, G., G. Oviedo, and D. Hooke, eds. (2012), *Sacred Species and Sites*, Cambridge: Cambridge University Press.

Purzycki, B. G. (2011), "Tyvan *Cher Eezi* and the Socioecological Constraints of Supernatural Agents' Minds," *Religion, Brain & Behavior*, 1 (1): 31–45.

Purzycki, B. G. (2013a), "Toward a Cognitive Ecology of Religious Concepts: An Example from the Tyva Republic," *Journal for the Cognitive Science of Religion*, 1 (1): 99–120.

Purzycki, B. G. (2013b), "The Minds of Gods: A Comparative Study of Supernatural Agency," *Cognition*, 129 (1): 163–79.

Purzycki, B. G. (2016), "The Evolution of Gods' Minds in the Tyva Republic," *Current Anthropology*, 57 (S13): S88–S104.

Purzycki, B. G., and T. Arakchaa (2013), "Ritual Behavior and Trust in the Tyva Republic," *Current Anthropology*, 54: 381–8.

Purzycki, B. G., and A. Baimel (2016), "Examining the Minds of Gods," in N. Clemens (ed.), *MacMillan Interdisciplinary Handbooks on Religion: Mental Religion*, 45–60, Farmington Hills: MacMillan.

Purzycki, B. G., and E. C. Holland (2018), "Buddha as a God: An Empirical Assessment," *Method & Theory in the Study of Religion*, 31 (4–5): 1–29.

Purzycki, B. G., and A. Jamieson-Lane (2017), "AnthroTools: An R Package for Cross-Cultural Ethnographic Data Analysis," *Cross-Cultural Research*, 51 (1): 51–74.

Purzycki, B. G., and V. Kulundary (2018), "Buddhism, Identity, and Class: Fairness and Favoritism in the Tyva Republic," *Religion, Brain & Behavior*, 8 (2): 205–26.

Purzycki, B. G., and R. A. McNamara (2016), "An Ecological Theory of Gods' Minds," in Helen de Cruz and Ryan Nichols (eds.), *Advances in Religion, Cognitive Science, and Experimental Philosophy*, 143–67, London: Bloomsbury.

Purzycki, B. G., and R. Sosis (2019), "Resistance, Subversion, and the Absence of Religion in Traditional Societies," in S. Bullivant and M. Ruse (eds.), *The Cambridge Companion to Atheism*, 982–1004, Cambridge: Cambridge University Press.

Purzycki, B. G., and R. Sosis (2022), *Religion Evolving: The Dynamics of Culture, Cognition and Ecology*, Sheffield: Equinox.

Purzycki, B. G., and J. Watts (2018), "Reinvigorating the Comparative, Cooperative Ethnographic Sciences of Religion," *Free Inquiry*, 38 (3): 26–9.

Purzycki, B. G., and A. K. Willard (2016), "MCI Theory: A Critical Discussion," *Religion, Brain & Behavior*, 6 (3): 207–48.

Purzycki, B. G., M. N. Stagnaro, and J. Sasaki (2020), "Breaches of Trust Change the Content and Structure of Religious Appeals," *Journal for the Study of Religion, Nature and Culture*, 14 (1): 71–94.

Purzycki, B. G., C. Apicella, Q. D. Atkinson, E. Cohen, R. A. McNamara, A. K. Willard, D. Xygalatas, A. Norenzayan, and J. Henrich (2016), "Moralistic Gods, Supernatural Punishment and the Expansion of Human Sociality," *Nature*, 530 (7590): 327–30.

Purzycki, B. G., T. Bendixen, A. Lightner, and R. Sosis (n.d.), Gods, Games, and the Socioecological Landscape. https://doi.org/10.31234/osf.io/r9qtm.

Purzycki, B. G., D. Finkel, J. Shaver, N. Wales, A. Cohen, and R. Sosis (2012), "What Does God Know? Supernatural Agents' Access to Socially Strategic and Non-Strategic Information," *Cognitive Science*, 36: 846–69.

Purzycki, B. G., J. Henrich, C. Apicella, Q. D. Atkinson, A. Baimel, E. Cohen, R. A. McNamara, A. K. Willard, D. Xygalatas, and A. Norenzayan (2018), "The Evolution of Religion and Morality: A Synthesis of Ethnographic and Experimental Evidence from Eight Societies," *Religion, Brain & Behavior*, 8 (2): 101–32.

Purzycki, B. G., C. T. Ross, C. Apicella, Q. D. Atkinson, E. Cohen, R. A. McNamara, A. K. Willard, D. Xygalatas, A. Norenzayan, and J. Henrich (2018), "Material Security, Life History, and Moralistic Religions: A Cross-Cultural Examination," *PLOS ONE*, 13 (3): e0193856.

Purzycki, B. G., A. Willard, E. K. Klocová, C. L. Apicella, Q. Atkinson, A. Bolyanatz, E. Cohen, C. Handley, J. Henrich, M. Lang, C. Lesorogol, S. Mathew, R. McNamara, C. Moya, A. Norenzayan, C. Placek, M. Soler, T. Vardy, J. Weigel, D. Xygalatas, and C. T. Ross (2022), "The Moralization Bias of Gods' Minds: A Cross-Cultural Test," *Religion, Brain & Behavior*, 12 (1–2): 38–60.

Purzycki, B. G., T. Bendixen, A. D. Lightner, and R. Sosis (2022), "Gods, Games, and the Socioecological Landscape," *Current Research in Ecological and Social Psychology*, 3: 100057.

Pyysiäinen, I. (2009), *Supernatural Agents: Why We Believe in Souls, Gods, and Buddhas*, Oxford: Oxford University Press.

Radin, P. (1914), "Religion of the North American Indians," *Journal of American Folklore*, 27 (106): 335–73.

Radin, P. (1992), "Monotheism among American Indians," in D. Tedlock and B. Tedlock (eds.), *Teachings from the American Earth: Indian Religion and Philosophy*, 219–47, New York: Liveright.

Raffield, B., N. Price, and M. Collard (2019), "Religious Belief and Cooperation: A View from Viking-Age Scandinavia," *Religion, Brain & Behavior*, 9 (1): 2–22.

Raichle, M. E. (2015), "The Brain's Default Mode Network," *Annual Review of Neuroscience*, 38 (1): 433–47.

Rappaport, R. A. (1968), *Pigs for the Ancestors: Ritual in the Ecology of a New Guinea People*, Long Grove: Waveland Press.

Rappaport, R. A. (1979), *Ecology, Meaning, and Religion*, Richmond: North Atlantic Books.

Rappaport, R. A. (1999), *Ritual and Religion in the Making of Humanity*, Cambridge: Cambridge University Press.

Rath, S., S. Banerjee, and R. John (2020), "Greater Tree Community Structure Complexity in Sacred Forest Compared to Reserve Forest Land Tenure Systems in Eastern India," *Environmental Conservation*, 47 (1): 52–9.

Raymond, H. (2007), "The Ecologically Noble Savage Debate," *Annual Review of Anthropology*, 36 (1): 177–90.

Reddish, P., P. Tok, and R. Kundt (2016), "Religious Cognition and Behaviour in Autism: The Role of Mentalizing," *International Journal for the Psychology of Religion*, 26 (2): 95–112.

Redfield, R. (1952), "The Primitive World View," *Proceedings of the American Philosophical Society*, 96 (1): 30–6.

Regenstein, J. M., M. M. Chaudry, and C. E. Regenstein (2003), "The Kosher and Halal Food Laws," *Comprehensive Reviews in Food Science and Food Safety*, 2 (3): 111–27.

Rescorla, R. A., and A. R. Wagner (1972), "A Theory of Pavlovian Conditioning: Variations in the Effectiveness of Reinforcement and Nonreinforcement," in A. H. Black and W. F. Prokasy (eds.), *Classical Conditioning II: Current Research and Theory*, 64–99, New York: Appleton-Century-Crofts.

Richerson, P., and J. Henrich (2012), "Tribal Social Instincts and the Cultural Evolution of Institutions to Solve Collective Action Problems," *Cliodynamics*, 3: 38–80.

Richert, R. A., and J. L. Barrett (2005), "Do You See What I See? Young Children's Assumptions about God's Perceptual Abilities," *International Journal for the Psychology of Religion*, 15 (4): 283–95.

Richert, R. A., A. R. Saide, K. A. Lesage, and N. Shaman (2017), "The Role of Religious Context in Children's Differentiation between God's Mind and Human Minds," *British Journal of Developmental Psychology*, 35 (1): 37–59.

Richert, R. A., N. J. Shaman, A. R. Saide, and K. A. Lesage (2016), "Folding Your Hands Helps God Hear Hou: Prayer and Anthropomorphism in Parents and Children," *Research in the Social Scientific Study of Religion*, 27: 140–57.

Riel-Salvatore, J. and G. A. Clark (2001), "Grave Markers: Middle and Early Upper Paleolithic Burials and the Use of Chronotopology and in Contemporary Paleolithic Research," *Current Anthropology*, 42: 449–79.

Religion, Brain & Behavior. (2015), *Special Issue on Ara Norenzayan's Big Gods*, 5 (4): 266–342.

Richerson, P. J., and R. Boyd (2005), *Not by Genes Alone: How Culture Transformed Human Evolution*, Chicago: University of Chicago Press.

Rittenhouse, C. D., R. Stickgold, and J. A. Hobson (1994), "Constraint on the Transformation of Characters, Objects, and Settings in Dream Reports," *Consciousness and Cognition*, 3 (1): 100–13.

Rival, L. (2012), "Animism and the Meanings of Life: Reflections from Amazonia," in M. Brightman, V. E. Grotti, and O. Ulturgasheva (eds.), *Animism in Rainforest and Tundra: Personhood, Animals, Plants and Things in Contemporary Amazonia and Siberia*, 69–81, New York: Berghahn Books.

Rivers, W. H. R. (1908), "Totemism in Fiji," *Man*, 8: 133–6.

Rivers, W. H. R. (1909), "Totemism in Polynesia and Melanesia," *Journal of the Royal Anthropological Institute of Great Britain and Ireland*, 39: 156–80.

Rizzuto, A.-M. (1979), *The Birth of the Living God*, Chicago: University of Chicago Press.

Robbins, J. (2008), "On Not Knowing Other Minds: Confession, Intention, and Linguistic Exchange in a Papua New Guinea Community," *Anthropological Quarterly*, 81 (2): 421–9.

Robbins, J., B. B. Schieffelin, and A. Vilaça (2014), "Evangelical Conversion and the Transformation of the Self in Amazonia and Melanesia: Christianity and the Revival of Anthropological Comparison," *Comparative Studies in Society and History*, 56 (3): 559–90.

Roberts, C. W. (1989), "Imagining God: Who Is Created in Whose Image?," *Review of Religious Research*, 30 (4): 375–86.

Roberts, S. O., K. Weisman, J. D. Lane, A. Williams, N. P. Camp, M. Wang, M. Robison, K. Sanchez, and C. Griffiths (2020), "God as a White Man: A Psychological Barrier to Conceptualizing Black People and Women as Leadership Worthy," *Journal of Personality and Social Psychology*, 119 (6): 1290–315.

Rao, R. P., and D. H. Ballard (1999), "Predictive Coding in the Visual Cortex: A Functional Interpretation of Some Extra-Classical Receptive-Field Effects," *Nature Neuroscience*, 2 (1): 79–87.

Roes, F. L. (2009), "Moralizing Gods and the Arms-Race Hypothesis of Human Society Growth," *Open Social Science Journal*, 2 (1): 70–3.

Roes, F. L., and M. Raymond. (2003), "Belief in Moralizing Gods," *Evolution and Human Behavior*, 24 (2): 126–35.

Rogers, A. R. (2020), "Beating Your Neighbor to the Berry Patch," *bioRxiv*. Accessed online: https://www.biorxiv.org/content/10.1101/2020.11.12.380311v8.

Rosmarin, D. H., E. J. Krumrei, and G. Andersson (2009), "Religion as a Predictor of Psychological Distress in Two Religious Communities," *Cognitive Behaviour Therapy*, 38 (1): 54–64.

Rossano, M. J. (2007), "Supernaturalizing Social Life," *Human Nature*, 18 (3): 272–94.

Rossano, M. J. (2012), "The Essential Role of Ritual in the Transmission and Reinforcement of Social Norms," *Psychological Bulletin*, 138 (3): 529–49.

Rossano, M. J. (2019), "How Ritual Made Us Human," in T. Henley, M. J. Rossano, and E. Kardas (eds.), *Handbook of Cognitive Archaeology: Psychology in Pre-History*, 333–53, London: Routledge.

Rossano, M. J. (2020), "Ritual as Resource Management," *Philosophical Transactions of the Royal Society B*, 375: 20190429.

Rossano, M. J. (2021), *Ritual in Human Evolution and Religion*, London: Routledge.

Rossano, M. J., and A. LeBlanc (2017), "Why Add the Supernatural?," *Religion, Brain & Behavior*, 7 (4): 375–7.

Rossano, M. J., and B. Vandewalle (2016), "Belief, Ritual, and the Evolution of Religion," in J. R. Liddle and T. K. Shackelford (eds.), *The Oxford Handbook of Evolutionary Psychology and Religion*, 1–33, Oxford: Oxford University Press.

Rottman, J., L. Zhu, W. Wang, R. Seston Schillaci, K. J. Clark, and D. Kelemen (2017), "Cultural Influences on the Teleological Stance: Evidence from China," *Religion, Brain & Behavior*, 7 (1): 17–26.

Rowatt, W., and L. A. Kirkpatrick (2002), "Two Dimensions of Attachment to God and Their Relation to Affect, Religiosity, and Personality Constructs," *Journal for the Scientific Study of Religion*, 41 (4): 637–51.

Rozin, P., L. Millman, and C. Nemeroff (1986), "Operation of the Laws of Sympathetic Magic in Disgust and Other Domains," *Journal of Personality and Social Psychology*, 50 (4): 703–12.

Ruegg, S. (1976), "On the Supramundane and the Divine in Buddhism," *Tibet Journal*, 1 (3/4): 25–8.

Ruffle, B. J., and R. Sosis (2007), "Does It Pay to Pray? Costly Ritual and Cooperation," *B. E. Journal of Economic Analysis and Policy*, 7 (1), Article 18.

Rüpke, J. (2014), "Is History Important for a Historical Argument in Religious Studies?," *Religion*, 44 (4): 645–8.

Rutjens, B. T., J. van der Pligt, and F. Van Harreveld (2010), "Deus or Darwin: Randomness and Belief in Theories about the Origin of Life," *Journal of Experimental Social Psychology*, 46 (6): 1078–80.

Rutjens, B. T., F. van Harreveld, J. van der Pligt, L. M. Kreemers, and M. K. Noordewier (2013), "Steps, Stages, and Structure: Finding Compensatory Order in Scientific Theories," *Journal of Experimental Psychology: General*, 142 (2): 313–18.

Ryle, J. (2010), *My God, My Land: Interwoven Paths of Christianity and Tradition in Fiji*, London: Routledge.

Saide, A., and R. Richert (2021), "Concepts of God and Germs: Social Mechanisms and Cognitive Heuristics," *Cognitive Science*, 45 (5): e12942.

Saide, A. R., and R. A. Richert (2020), "Socio-Cognitive and Cultural Influences on Children's Concepts of God," *Journal of Cognition and Culture*, 20 (1–2): 22–40.

Saler, B. (1977), "Supernatural as a Western Category," *Ethos*, 5 (1): 31–53.

Samuel, G. (2014), "Between Buddhism and Science, Between Mind and Body," *Religions*, 5 (3): 560–79.

Samuels, R. (2004), "Innateness in Cognitive Science," *Trends in Cognitive Sciences*, 8 (3): 136–41.

Samuels, R., S. Stich, and P. D. Tremoulet (1999), "Rethinking Rationality: From Bleak Implications to Darwinian Modules," in E. LePore and Z.W. Pylyshyn (eds.), *What Is Cognitive Science?*, 74–120, Malden: Wiley-Blackwell.

Sanchez, C., B. Sundermeier, K. Gray, and R. J. Calin-Jageman (2017), "Direct Replication of Gervais and Norenzayan (2012): No Evidence that Analytic Thinking Decreases Religious Belief," *PLOS ONE*, 12 (2): e0172636.

Sanderson, S. K. (2018), *Religious Evolution and the Axial Age: From Shamans to Priests to Prophets*, London: Bloomsbury.

Sándor, P., S. Szakadát, and R. Bódizs (2014), "Ontogeny of Dreaming: A Review of Empirical Studies," *Sleep Medicine Reviews*, 18 (5): 435–49.

Śaṅkarācārya, Ś. (1901), *The Bhagavad-Gita, with the Commentary of Sri Sankaracharya*, trans. A. Mahadevarans, Mysore: G.T.A. Printing Works.

Sarkissian, H., and M. Phelan (2019), "Moral Objectivism and a Punishing God," *Journal of Experimental Social Psychology*, 80: 1–7.

Scarpelli, S., C. Bartolacci, A. D'Atri, M. Gorgoni, and L. De Gennaro (2019), "The Functional Role of Dreaming in Emotional Processes," *Frontiers in Psychology*, 10: 459.

Scarre, C. (2011), "Monumentality," in T. Insoll (ed.), *Oxford Handbook of the Archaeology of Ritual and Religion*, 9–23, Oxford: Oxford University Press.

Schaap-Jonker, H., B. Sizoo, J. Van Schothorst-Van Roekel, and J. Corveleyn (2013), "Autism Spectrum Disorders and the Image of God as a Core Aspect of Religiousness," *International Journal for the Psychology of Religion*, 23 (2): 145–60.

Schaap-Jonker, H., N. van der Velde, E. H. M. Eurelings-Bontekoe, and J. M. T. Corveleyn (2017), "Types of God Representations and Mental Health: A Person-Oriented Approach," *International Journal for the Psychology of Religion*, 27 (4): 199–214.

Schafer, M. H. (2013), "Close Ties, Intercessory Prayer, and Optimism among American Adults: Locating God in the Social Support Network," *Journal for the Scientific Study of Religion*, 52: 35–56.

Schäfer, P. (2017), *Zwei Götter im Himmel: Gottesvorstellungen in der Jüdischen Antike*, München: C. H. Beck Verlag.

Schapera, I. (1930), *The Khoisan Peoples of South Africa: Bushmen and Hottentots*, London: Routledge & Kegan Paul.

Schelling, T. C. (1971), "Dynamic Models of Segregation," *Journal of Mathematical Sociology*, 1 (2): 143–86.

Schieffelin, B. B. (2008), "Speaking Only Your Own Mind: Reflections on Talk, Gossip and Intentionality in Bosavi (PNG)," *Anthropological Quarterly*, 81 (2): 431–41.

Schjødt, U. (2007), "Homeostasis and Religious Behaviour," *Journal of Cognition & Culture*, 7 (3–4): 313–40.

Schjødt, U., and M. Andersen (2017), "How Does Religious Experience Work in Predictive Minds?" *Religion, Brain & Behavior*, 7 (4): 320–3.

Schjoedt, U., H. Stødkilde-Jørgensen, A. W. Geertz, and A. Roepstorff (2009), "Highly Religious Participants Recruit Areas of Social Cognition in Personal Prayer," *Social Cognitive and Affective Neuroscience*, 4 (2): 199-207.

Schjoedt, U., H. Stødkilde-Jørgensen, A. W. Geertz, T. E. Lund, and A. Roepstorff (2011), "The Power of Charisma: Perceived Charisma Inhibits the Frontal Executive Network of Believers in Intercessory Prayer," *Social Cognitive & Affective Neuroscience*, 6 (1): 119-27.

Schjoedt, U., J. Sørensen, K. L. Nielbo, D. Xygalatas, P. Mitkidis, and J. Bulbulia (2013a), "Cognitive Resource Depletion in Religious Interactions," *Religion, Brain & Behavior*, 3 (1): 39-55.

Schjoedt, U., J. Sørensen, K. L. Nielbo, D. Xygalatas, P. Mitkidis, and J. Bulbulia (2013b), "The Resource Model and the Principle of Predictive Coding: A Framework for Analyzing Proximate Effects of Ritual," *Religion, Brain & Behavior*, 3 (1): 79-86.

Schjødt, U. (2018), "Predictive Coding in the Study of Religion: a Believer's Testimony," in A. K. Petersen, G. I. Sælid, L. H. Martin, J. S. Jensen, and J. Sørensen (eds.), *Evolution, Cognition, and the History of Religion: A New Synthesis*, 364-79, Leiden: Brill.

Schloss, J. P., and M. J. Murray (2011), "Evolutionary Accounts of Belief in Supernatural Punishment: A Critical Review," *Religion, Brain & Behavior*, 1 (1): 46-99.

Schmidt, K. (2007), *Sie Bauten die Ersten Tempel: Das Rätselhafte Heiligtum der Steinzeitjäger, die Archäologische Entdeckung am Göbekli Tepe*, München: C. H. Beck Verlag.

Schredl, M. (2017), "Is Dreaming Related to Sleep-Dependent Memory Consolidation?," in *Cognitive Neuroscience of Memory Consolidation*, 173-82, Cham: Springer.

Schultz, W. (1998), "Predictive Reward Signal of Dopamine Neurons," *Journal of Neurophysiology*, 80 (1): 1-27.

Schweickert, R. (2007), "Properties of the Organization of Memory for People: Evidence from Dream Reports," *Psychonomic Bulletin & Review*, 14 (2): 270-76.

Schweickert, R., Z. Xi, C. Viau-Quesnel, and X. Zheng (2020), "Power Law Distribution of Frequencies of Characters in Dreams Explained by Random Walk on Semantic Network," *International Journal of Dream Research*, 192-201.

Schweizer, P. (2019), "Sāṃkhya-Yoga Philosophy and the Mind-Body Problem," *Prabuddha Bharata*, 124 (1): 232-42.

Schweizer, P. (2020), "Advaita and the Philosophy of Consciousness without an Object— CORE Reader," *Prabuddha Bharata*, 125 (1): 156-64.

Segal, G. (1996), "The Modularity of Theory of Mind," in P. Carruthers and P. Smith (eds.), *Theories of Theories of Mind*, 141-57, Cambridge: Cambridge University Press.

Segall, M. H., D. C. Campbell, and M. J. Herskovits (1963), "Cultural Differences in the Perception of Geometric Illusions," *Science*, 39 (3556): 769-71.

Segall, M. H., D. C. Campbell, and M. J. Herskovits (1966), *The Influence of Culture on Visual Perception: An Advanced Study in Psychology and Anthropology*, New York: The Bobbs-Merrill.

Selterman, D., A. I. Apetroaia, S. Riela, and A. Aron (2014), "Dreaming of You: Behavior and Emotion in Dreams of Significant Others Predict Subsequent Relational Behavior," *Social Psychological and Personality Science*, 5 (1): 111-18.

Selterman, D., A. Apetroaia, and E. Waters (2012), "Script-Like Attachment Representations in Dreams Containing Current Romantic Partners," *Attachment & Human Development*, 14 (5): 501-15.

Selterman, D., and S. Drigotas (2009), "Attachment Styles and Emotional Content, Stress, and Conflict in Dreams of Romantic Partners," *Dreaming*, 19 (3): 135-51.

Seltzer, R. M. (1980), *Jewish People, Jewish Thought: The Jewish Experience in History*, Hoboken: Prentice Hall.

Seth, A. K., B. J. Baars, and D. B. Edelman (2005), "Criteria for Consciousness in Humans and other Mammals," *Consciousness and Cognition*, 14 (1): 119–39.

Shahaeian, A., C. C. Peterson, V. Slaughter, and H. M. Wellman (2011), "Culture and the Sequence of Steps in Theory of Mind Development," *Developmental Psychology*, 47 (5): 1239–47.

Shaman, N. J., A. R. Saide, and R. A. Richert (2018), "Dimensional Structure of and Variation in Anthropomorphic Concepts of God," *Frontiers in Psychology*, 9: 1–16.

Shariff, A. F., and A. Norenzayan (2011), "Mean Gods Make Good People: Different Views of God Predict Cheating Behavior," *International Journal for the Psychology of Religion*, 21 (2): 85–96.

Shariff, A. F., A. Norenzayan, and J. Henrich (2010), "The Birth of High Gods: How Cultural Evolution of Supernatural Policing Influenced the Emergence of Complex, Cooperative Human Societies, Paving Way for Civilization," in Mark Schaller, Ara Norenzayan, Steven J. Heine, Toshio Yamagishi, and Tatsuo Kameda (eds.), *Evolution, Culture, and the Human Mind*, 119–36, New York: Taylor and Francis.

Shariff, A. F., and M. Rhemtulla (2012), "Divergent Effects of Beliefs in Heaven and Hell on National Crime Rates," *PLOS ONE*, 7 (6): 1–6.

Sharma, S., H. C. Rikhari, and L. M. S. Palni (1999), "Conservation of Natural Resources through Religion: A Case Study from Central Himalaya," *Society & Natural Resources*, 12 (6): 599–612.

Sharp, C. A., E. B. Davis, K. George, A. D. Cuthbert, B. P. Zahl, D. E. Davis, J. N. Hook, and J. D. Aten (2019), "Measures of God Representations: Theoretical Framework and Critical Review," *Psychology of Religion and Spirituality*, 13 (3): 340–57.

Sharp, C. A., P. J. Rentfrow, and N. J. S. Gibson (2017), "One God but Three Concepts: Complexity in Christians" Representations of God," *Psychology of Religion and Spirituality*, 9 (1): 95–105.

Shaver, J., and J. Bulbulia (2016), "Signaling Theory and Religion," in N. Clements (ed.), *Religion: Mental Religion*, 101–17, Farmington Hills: MacMillian Interdisciplinary Handbooks.

Shaver, J. H., G. Fraser, and J. Bulbulia (2017), "Charismatic Signaling: How Religion Stabilizes Cooperation and Entrenches Inequality," in J. R. Liddle and T. K. Shackelford (eds.), *The Oxford Handbook of Evolutionary Psychology and Religion*, 230–45, Oxford: Oxford University Press.

Shin, F., and J. L. Preston (2019), "Green as the Gospel: The Power of Stewardship Messages to Improve Climate Change Attitudes," *Psychology of Religion and Spirituality*.

Shtulman, A. (2008), "Variation in the Anthropomorphization of Supernatural Beings and Its Implications for Cognitive Theories of Religion," *Journal of Experimental Psychology: Learning, Memory, and Cognition*, 34: 1123–38.

Shtulman, A., R. Foushee, D. Barner, Y. Dunham, and M. Srinivasan (2019), "When Allah meets Ganesha: Developing Supernatural Concepts in a Religiously Diverse Society," *Cognitive Development*, 52: 100806.

Shults, F. L., and W. J. Wildman (2018), "Modeling Çatalhöyük: Simulating Religious Entanglement in a Neolithic Town," in I. Hodder (ed.), *Religion, History and Place in the Origin of Settled Life*, 33–63, Denver: University of Colorado Press.

Shults, F. L., J. E. Lane, and R. N. McCauley (2017), "Bringing Ritual to (Simulated) Minds: A Computational Model of Ritual Competence Theory," *American Academy of Religion*. Accessed online: https://prezi.com/pknor1lp2ji9/erica/?utm_campaign=share&utm_medium=copy.

Shults, F. L., J. E. Lane, W. J. Wildman, S. Diallo, C. J. Lynch, and R. Gore (2018a), "Modeling Terror Management Theory: Computer Simulations of the Impact of Mortality Salience on Religiosity," *Religion, Brain & Behavior*, 8 (1): 77–100.

Shults, F. L., R. Gore, C. Lemos, and W. J. Wildman (2018b), "Why Do the Godless Prosper? Modeling the Cognitive and Coalitional Mechanisms that Promote Atheism," *Psychology of Religion and Spirituality*, 10 (3): 218–28.

Shults, F. L., R. Gore, W. J. Wildman, C. J. Lynch, J. E. Lane, and M. D. Toft (2018c), "A Generative Model of the Mutual Escalation of Anxiety between Religious Groups," *Journal of Artificial Societies and Social Simulation*, 21 (4): 1–24.

Shults, F. L., W. J. Wildman, J. E. Lane, C. Lynch, and S. Y. Diallo (2018e), "Multiple Axialities: A Computational Model of the Axial Age," *Journal of Cognition and Culture*, 18: 537–64.

Shweder, R. A., N. C. Much, M. Mahapatra, and L. Park (1997), "The 'Big Three' of Morality (Autonomy, Community, Divinity) and the 'Big Three' Explanations of Suffering," in A. M. Brandt and P. Rozin (eds.), *Morality and Health*, 119–69, London: Routledge.

Sibley, C. G., and J. Bulbulia (2012), "Faith after an Earthquake: A Longitudinal Study of Religion and Perceived Health before and after the 2011 Christchurch New Zealand Earthquake," *PloS One*, 7 (12): e49648.

Silberbauer, G. B. (1972) "The G/Wi Bushmen," in *Hunters and Gatherers Today*, 271–326. Prospect Heights: Waveland Press.

Silver, M. (1995), *Economic Structures of Antiquity*, London: Greenwood Press.

Silverman, G. S., K. A. Johnson, and A. B. Cohen (2016), To believe or not to believe, that is not the question: The complexity of Jewish beliefs about God, *Psychology of Religion and Spirituality*, 8 (2): 119–30.

Sims, A. (2017), "The Problems with Prediction—The Dark Room Problem and the Scope Dispute," in T. Metzinger and W. Wiese (eds.), *Philosophy and Predictive Processing*: 23. Frankfurt am Main: MIND Group. doi: 10.15502/9783958573246. https://openscience.ub.uni-mainz.de/bitstream/20.500.12030/648/1/56665.pdf. Accessed August 1, 2022.

Sinding Bentzen, J. (2019), "Acts of God? Religiosity and Natural Disasters Across Subnational World Districts," *Economic Journal*, 129: 2295–321.

Singer, T. (2006), "The Neuronal Basis for Empathy and Fairness," *Empathy and Fairness: Novartis Symposium*, 278: 20–30.

Singer, T., B. Seymour, J. P. O"Doherty, K. E. Stephan, R. J. Dolan, and C. C. Frith. (2006), "Empathic Neural Responses are Modulated by the Perceived Fairness of Others," *Nature*, 439 (26): 466–9.

Singh, M., and Z. H. Garfield (n.d.), "Evidence for Third-Party Mediation but not Punishment in Mentawai Justice," https://psyarxiv.com/bjaxd/.

Singh, M., T. J. Kaptchuk, and J. Henrich (2021), "Small Gods, Rituals, and Cooperation: The Mentawai Water Spirit Sikameinan," *Evolution and Human Behavior*, 42 (1): 61–72.

Sinha, D. (2002), "Culture and Psychology: Perspective of Cross-Cultural Psychology," *Psychology and Developing Societies*, 14 (1): 11–25.

Skali, A. (2017), "Moralizing Gods and Armed Conflict," *Journal of Economic Psychology*, 63: 184–98.

Skipper, A., T. J. Moore, and M. Loren (2018), 'The Prayers of Others Helped': Intercessory Prayer as a Source of Coping and Resilience in Christian African

American Families," *Journal of Religion & Spirituality in Social Work: Social Thought*, 37: 373–94.
Skoggard, I., C. R. Ember, E. Pitek, J. C., and C. Carolus (2020), "Resource Stress Predicts Changes in Religious Belief and Increases in Sharing Behavior," *Human Nature*, 31 (3): 249–71.
Skórka, P., M. Żmihorski, E. Grzędzicka, R. Martyka and W. J. Sutherland (2018), "The Role of Churches in Maintaining Bird Diversity: A Case Study from Southern Poland," *Biological Conservation*, 226: 280–7.
Škrabáková, L. (2014), "Amerindian Perspectivism and the Life of Plants in Amazonia," in K. Pauknerová, M. Stella, and P. Gibas (eds.), *Non-Humans in Social Science: Ontologies, Theories and Case Studies*, 165–86, Červený Kostelec: Pavel Mervart.
Skyrms, B. (2003), *The Stag Hunt and the Evolution of Social Structure*, Cambridge: Cambridge University Press.
Slingerland, E., and B. Sullivan (2017), "Durkheim with Data: The Database of Religious History," *Journal of the American Academy of Religion*, 85 (2): 312–47.
Sloterdijk, P. (2009), *Du mußt dein Leben ändern. Über Anthropotechnik*. Frankfurt am Main: Suhrkamp.
Smith, A. E., and R. G. Veldman (2020), "Evangelical Environmentalists? Evidence from Brazil," *Journal for the Scientific Study of Religion*, 59 (2): 341–59.
Smith, D. M. (1998), "An Athapaskan Way of Knowing: Chipewyan Ontology," *American Ethnologist*, 25 (3): 412–32.
Smith, E. A., and M. Wishnie (2000), "Conservation and Subsistence in Small-Scale Societies," *Annual Review of Anthropology*, 29 (1): 493–524.
Smith, J. Z. (1978), *Map Is not Territory: Studies in the History of Religions*, Leiden: Brill.
Smith, J. Z. (1990), *Drudgery Divine: On the Comparison of Early Christianities and the Religions of Late Antiquity* (Jordan Lectures in Comparative Religion 14, 1988), Chicago: University of Chicago Press.
Smith, M. L. (2019), *Cities: The First 6,000 Years*, New York: Viking.
Smith, J. M., and R. T. Cragun (2019), "Mapping Religion's Other: A Review of the Study of Nonreligion and Secularity," *Journal for the Scientific Study of Religion*, 58 (2): 319–35.
Smither, J. W., and A. G. Walker (2015), "The Relationship between Core Self-Evaluations, Views of God, and Intrinsic/Extrinsic Religious Motivation," *Psychological Reports: Sociocultural Issues in Psychology*, 116 (2): 647–62.
Smuts, B. B., and J. M. Watanabe (1990), "Social Relationships and Ritualized Greetings in Adult Male Baboons (*Papio cynocephalus anubis*)," *International Journal of Primatology*, 11: 147–72.
Snarey, J. (1996), "The Natural Environment's Impact upon Religious Ethics: A Cross-Cultural Study," *Journal for the Scientific Study of Religion*, 35 (2): 85–96.
Snow, C. P. (2012), *The Two Cultures*, Cambridge: Cambridge University Press.
Sørensen, J. (2007a), *A Cognitive Theory of Magic*, Lanham: AltaMira Press.
Sørensen, J. (2007b), "Acts that Work: A Cognitive Approach to Ritual Agency," *Method & Theory in the Study of Religion*, 19 (3–4): 281–300.
Sørensen, J. (2020), "Må Kraften Være med Dig [May the Force Be with You]," *Religion: Tidsskrift for Religionslærerforeningen for Gymnasiet og HF*, 1: 46–55.
Sørensen, J. (2021), "Force and Categorization: Reflections on Marcel Mauss and Henri Hubert's *Esquisse d'une Théorie Générale de La Magie*," in J. F. Sørensen and A. K.

Petersen (eds.), *Theoretical and Empirical Investigations of Divination and Magic*, 246–73, Leiden: Brill.

Soler, M. (2012), "Costly Signaling, Ritual and Cooperation: Evidence from Candomblé, an Afro-Brazilian Religion," *Evolution and Human Behaviour*, 33: 346–56.

Solomon, S., J. Greenberg, and T. Pyszczynski (2015), *The Worm at the Core: On the Role of Death in Life*, New York: Random House.

Sosis, R. (2003), "Why Aren"t We All Hutterites?" *Human Nature*, 14 (2): 91–127.

Sosis, R. (2009), "The Adaptationist-Byproduct Debate on the Evolution of Religion: Five Misunderstandings of the Adaptationist Program," *Journal of Cognition and Culture*, 9 (3–4): 315–32.

Sosis, R. (2019), "Why Cultural Evolutionary Models Need a Systemic Approach," in A. K. Petersen, I. S. Gilhus, L. H. Martin, J. S. Jensen, and J. Sørensen (eds.), *Evolution, Cognition, and the History of Religion: A New Synthesis. Festschrift in Honour of Armin W. Geertz*, 45–61, Leiden: Brill.

Sosis, R., and C. Alcorta (2003), "Signaling, Solidarity and the Sacred," *Evolutionary Anthropology*, 12 (6): 264–74.

Speed, D., T. J. I. Coleman, and J. Langston (2018), "What Do You Mean, 'What Does It All Mean?' Atheism, Nonreligion, and Life Meaning," *Sage Open*, 8 (1): 2158244017754238.

Sperber, D. (1996), *Explaining Culture: A Naturalistic Approach*, Malden: Blackwell.

Sperber, D. (2002), "In Defense of Massive Modularity," in E. Dupous (ed.), *Language, Brain and Cognitive Development: Essays in Honor of Jacques Mehler*, 47–57, Cambridge: MIT Press.

Spilka, B., P. Armatas, and J. Nussbaum (1964), "The Concept of God: A Factor-Analytic Approach," *Review of Religious Research*, 6 (1): 28–36.

Sponsel, L. (2012), *Spiritual Ecology: A Quiet Revolution*, Santa Barbara: Praeger.

Spunt, R. P., and R. Adolphs (2015), "Folk Explanations of Behavior: A Specialized Use of a Domain-General Mechanism," *Psychological Science*, 26 (6): 724–36.

Sriraman, B., and W. Benesch (2005), "Consciousness and Science: An Advaita-Vedantic Perspective on the Theology—Science Dialogue," *Theology and Science*, 3 (1): 39–54.

Staal, F. (1979), "The Meaninglessness of Ritual," *Numen: International Review for the History of Religions*, 26 (1): 2–22.

Standing Bear, L. ([1928] 1975), *My People the Sioux*, Lincoln: University of Nebraska Press.

Stark, R. (2009), *Discovering God: The Origins of the Great Religions and the Evolution of Belief*, New York: HarperCollins.

Stark, R., and W. S. Bainbridge (1985), *The Future of Religion*, Berkeley: University of California Press.

Stark, R., and W. S. Bainbridge (1987), *A Theory of Religion*, New Brunswick: Rutgers University Press.

Stark, R., and W. S. Bainbridge (1996), *Religion, Deviance and Social Control*, London: Routledge.

Starmans, C., and P. Bloom (2012), "Windows to the Soul: Children and Adults See the Eyes as the Location of the Self," *Cognition*, 123 (2): 313–18.

Stausberg, M. (2014), "*Big Gods* in Review: Introducing Ara Norenzayan and His Critics," *Religion*, 44 (4): 592–608.

Stefanakis, H. (1995), "Speaking of Dreams: A Social Constructionist Account of Dream Sharing," *Dreaming*, 5 (2): 95–104.

Stepansky, R., B. Holzinger, A. Schmeiser-Rieder, B. Saletu, M. Kunze, and J. Zeitlhofer (1998), "Austrian Dream Behavior: Results of a Representative Population Survey," *Dreaming*, 8 (1): 23–30.

Steward, J. H. (1972), *Theory of Culture Change: The Methodology of Multilinear Evolution*, Chicago: University of Illinois Press.

Stewart, V. M. (1974), "A Cross-Cultural Test of the 'Carpentered World' Hypothesis using the Ames Distorted Room Illusion," *International Journal of Psychology*, 9 (2): 79–89.

Stolle, D. (2001), "Clubs and Congregations: The Benefits of Joining an Association," in K. S. Cook (ed.), *Trust in Society*, 202–44, New York: Russell Sage Foundation.

Strassmann, B. I. (1992), "The Function of Menstrual Taboos among the Dogon," *Human Nature*, 3: 89–131.

Strauch, I., and B. Meier (1996), *In Search of Dreams: Results of Experimental Dream Research*, Albany: SUNY Press.

Strauss, C., and N. Quinn (1997), *A Cognitive Theory of Cultural Meaning*, Cambridge: Cambridge University Press.

Strawn, B. D., and M. Alexander (2008), "Correlation of Self-Perception and Image of Christ Using the Five-Factor Model of Personality," *Pastoral Psychology*, 56 (3): 341–53.

Stites, R. (1988), *Revolutionary Dreams: Utopian Vision and Experimental Life in the Russian Revolution*, Oxford: Oxford University Press.

Stoll, M. (2015), *Inherit the Holy Mountain: Religion and the Rise of American Environmentalism*, illustrated ed., Oxford: Oxford University Press.

Stulp, H. P., J. Koelen, A. Schep-Akkerman, G. G. Glas, and L. Eurelings-Bontekoe (2019), "God Representations and Aspects of Psychological Functioning: A Meta-Analysis," *Cogent Psychology*, 6 (1): 1–50.

Swanson, G. E. (1960), *The Birth of the Gods: The Origin of Primitive Beliefs*, Ann Arbor: University of Michigan Press.

Swanson, L. R. (2016), "The Predictive Processing Paradigm Has Roots in Kant," *Frontiers in Systems Neuroscience*, 10: 79.

Sword, G., and J. R. Walker (1992), "Oglala Metaphysics," in *Teachings from the American Earth: Indian Religion and Philosophy*, 205–8, New York: Liveright.

Talmy, L. (2000), *Towards a Cognitive Semantics*, Cambridge: MIT Press.

Tam, K.-P., and H.-W. Chan (2017), "Environmental Concern Has a Weaker Association with Pro-Environmental Behavior in Some Societies than Others: A Cross-Cultural Psychology Perspective," *Journal of Environmental Psychology*, 53: 213–23.

Taves, A. (2016), *Revelatory Events: Three Case Studies of the Emergence of New Spiritual Paths*, Princeton: Princeton University Press.

Taves, A. (2020), "Mystical and Other Alterations in Sense of Self: An Expanded Framework for Studying Nonordinary Experiences," *Perspectives on Psychological Science*, 15 (3): 669–90.

Taves, A., and E. Asprem (2018), "Scientific Worldview Studies: A Programmatic Proposal," in A. K. Petersen, I. S. Gilhus, L. H. Martin, J. S. Jensen, and J. Sørensen (eds.), *Evolution, Cognition, and the History of Religion: A New Synthesis*, 297–308, Leiden: Brill.

Taves, A., E. Asprem, and E. Ihm (2018), "Psychology, Meaning Making, and the Study of Worldviews: Beyond Religion and Non-Religion," *Psychology of Religion and Spirituality*, 10 (3): 207–17.

Taylor, B. (2016), "The Greening of Religion Hypothesis (Part One): From Lynn White, Jr and Claims That Religions Can Promote Environmentally Destructive Attitudes and

Behaviors to Assertions They Are Becoming Environmentally Friendly," *Journal for the Study of Religion, Nature and Culture*, 10 (3): 268–305.

Taylor, B., G. Van Wieren, and B. Zaleha (2016), "The Greening of Religion Hypothesis (Part Two): Assessing the Data from Lynn White, Jr, to Pope Francis," *Journal for the Study of Religion, Nature and Culture*, 10 (3): 306–78.

Taylor, C. (2007), *A Secular Age*, Cambridge: Belknap Press of Harvard University Press.

Taylor, J. B. (2006), *My Stroke of Insight: A Brain Scientist's Personal Journey*, London: Viking Penguin.

Teehan, J. (2013), "The Cognitive Bases of the Problem of Evil," *The Monist*, 96 (3): 325–48.

Teehan, J. (2014), "Cognitive Science and the Limits of Theology," in J. L. Barrett and R. Trigg (eds.), *The Roots of Religion: Exploring the Cognitive Science of Religion*, 167–87. Farnham: Ashgate.

Teehan, J. (2016), "Religion and Morality: Evolution of the Cognitive Nexus," in J. Liddle and T. Shackelford (eds.), *Oxford Handbook of the Evolutionary Psychology of Religion*, 117–34, Oxford: Oxford University Press.

Teehan, J. (2021), "Hypocrites and the Pure in Heart: Religion as an Evolved Strategy for In-Group Formation," in R. Roitto, C. Shantz, and L. Luomanen, *Social and Cognitive Perspectives on the Sermon on the Mount*, 239–63, Sheffield: Equinox.

Teehan, J., and F. L. Shults (2019), "Religion, Empathy, and Cooperation: A Coase Study in the Promises and Challenges of Modeling and Simulation," in S. Y. Diallo, W. J. Wildman, F. L. Shults, and A. Tolk (eds.), *Human Simulation: Perspectives, Insights, and Applications*, New Approaches to the Scientific Study of Religion series, 157–78, Cham: Springer.

Tempesta, D., V. Socci, L. De Gennaro, and M. Ferrara (2018), "Sleep and Emotional Processing," *Sleep Medicine Reviews*, 40: 183–95.

Templeton, J. M. (1981), *The Humble Approach: Scientists Discover God*, London: Templeton Foundation Press.

Thomas, K. ([1971] 1991), *Religion and the Decline in Magic*, London: Penguin Books.

Thomassen, E. (2014), "Are Gods Really Moral Monitors? Some Comments on Ara Norenzayan's *Big Gods* from a Historian of Religion," *Religion*, 44 (4): 667–73.

Thomson, B. (1895), "The Kalou-Vu (Ancestor-Gods) of the Fijians," *Journal of the Anthropological Institute of Great Britain and Ireland*, 24: 340–59.

Thomson, R. A., and P. Froese (2018), "God, Party, and the Poor: How Politics and Religion Interact to Affect Economic Justice Attitudes," *Sociological Forum*, 33 (2): 334–53.

Thornton, C. (2017), "Predictive Processing Simplified: The Infotropic Machine," *Brain & Cognition*, 112: 13–24.

Throop, C. J. (2012), "On the Varieties of Empathic Experience: Tactility, Mental Opacity, and Pain in Yap," *Medical Anthropology Quarterly*, 26 (3): 408–30.

Tibenderana, P. K. (1980), "Supernatural Sanctions and Peace-Keeping among the Bakiga of Western Uganda during the Nineteenth Century," *Journal of African Studies*, 7 (3): 144–51.

Tillich, P. (1955), *The Shaking of the Foundations*, New York: Charles Scribner and Sons.

Tomasello, M. (2019), *Becoming Human: A Theory of Ontogeny*, Cambridge: Bellknap Press of Harvard University Press.

Tomlinson, M. (2007), "Mana in Christian Fiji: The Interconversion of Intelligibility and Palpability," *Journal of the American Academy of Religion*, 75 (3): 524–53.

Tomlinson, M., and T. P. Kāwika Tengan (2016), *New Mana: Transformations of a Classic Concept in Pacific Languages and Cultures*, Acton ACT, Australia: Australian National University Press.

Tomasello, M., A. P. Melis, C. Tennie, E. Wyman, and E. Herrmann (2012), "Two Key Steps in the Evolution of Human Cooperation: The Interdependence Hypothesis," *Current Anthropology*, 53: 673–92.

Toren, C. (2004), "Becoming a Christian in Fiji: An Ethnographic Study of Ontogeny," *Journal of the Royal Anthropological Institute*, 10 (3): 221–40.

Toren, C. (2009), "Intersubjectivity as Epistemology," *Social Analysis*, 53 (2): 130–46.

Townsend, C., A. Aktipis, D. Balliet, and L. Cronk, (2020), "Generosity among the Ik of Uganda," *Evolutionary Human Sciences*, 2: E23.

Toyoda, Y. (1998), "To Which Bird Do You Belong?: Totemic Belief among the Mari, Papua New Guinea," *Senri Ethnological Studies*, 47: 61–77.

Tremlin, T. (2016), *Minds and Gods: The Cognitive Foundations of Religion*, Oxford: Oxford University Press.

Triandis, H. C. (1995), *Individualism and Collectivism*, Boulder: Westview Press.

Trimèche, S., G. Vinsonneau, and E. Mullet (2006), "Individual Differences in the Theological Concept of God," *International Journal for the Psychology of Religion*, 16 (2): 83–100.

Trimmer, P. C., A. I. Houston, J. A. R. Marshall, M. T. Mendl, E. S. Paul, and J. M. McNamara (2011), "Decision-Making under Uncertainty: Biases and Bayesians," *Animal Cognition*, 14 (4): 465–76.

Trivers, R. (1971), "The Evolution of Reciprocal Altruism," *Quarterly Review of Biology*, 46: 35–57.

Trueblood, E. (1964), *The Humor of Christ*, New York: Harper & Row.

Tuominen, J., T. Stenberg, A. Revonsuo, and K. Valli (2019), "Social Contents in Dreams: An Empirical Test of the Social Simulation Theory," *Consciousness and Cognition*, 69: 133–45.

Tuominen, J., H. Olkoniemi, A. Revonsuo, and K. Valli (2022), "'No Man is an Island': Effects of Social Seclusion on Social Dream Content and REM Sleep," *British Journal of Psychology*, 113 (1): 84–104.

Turin, M. (1999), "The Chenchu of the Indian Dekkan," in R. B. Lee and R. Daly (eds.), *The Cambridge Encyclopedia of Hunters and Gatherers*, 252–6, Cambridge: Cambridge University Press.

Turner, J. H., A. Maryanski, A. K. Petersen, and A. W. Geertz (2018), *The Emergence and Evolution of Religion: By Means of Natural Selection*, London: Routledge.

Turner, L. M. (1894), *Ethnology Ungava District*, Washington, DC: Smithsonian Institution.

Tuzin, D. F. (2001), *Social Complexity in the Making: A Case Study among the Arapesh of New Guinea*, London: Routledge.

Tybjerg, T. (2018), "Marett og Mana," *Religionsvidenskabeligt Tidsskrift* (67): 67–76.

Tylor, E. B. ([1871] 2016a), *Primitive Culture: Researches into the Development of Mythology, Philosophy, Religion, Art, and Custom: Volume I*, London: John Murray.

Tylor, E. B. ([1871] 2016b), *Primitive Culture: Researches into the Development of Mythology, Philosophy, Religion, Art, and Custom: Volume II*, London: John Murray.

Unnever, J. D., F. T. Cullen, and J. P. Bartkowski (2006), "Images of God and Public Support for Capital Punishment: Does a Close Relationship with a Loving God Matter?," *Criminology*, 44 (662): 835–66.

Unsworth, S. J., W. Levin, M. Bang, K. Washinawatok, S. R. Waxman, and D. L. Medin (2012), "Cultural Differences in Children's Ecological Reasoning and Psychological Closeness to Nature: Evidence from Menominee and European American Children," *Journal of Cognition and Culture*, 12 (1–2): 17–29.

Upal, M. A. (2005), "Simulating the Emergence of New Religious Movements," *Journal of Artificial Societies and Social Simulation*, 8 (1). https://www.jasss.org/8/1/6.html.

Upal, M. A. (2010), "An Alternative Account of the Minimal Counterintuitiveness Effect," *Cognitive Systems Research*, 11 (2): 194–203.

Valéry, P. (1978), *Variété I et II*, Paris: Gallimard.

Valli, K., A. Revonsuo, O. Pälkäs, K. H. Ismail, K. J. Ali, and R.-L. Punamäki (2005), "The Threat Simulation Theory of the Evolutionary Function of Dreaming: Evidence from Dreams of Traumatized Children," *Consciousness and Cognition*, 14 (1): 188–218.

Van Elk, M., and A. Aleman (2017), "Brain Mechanisms in Religion and Spirituality: An Integrative Predictive Processing Framework," *Neuroscience & Biobehavioral Reviews*, 73: 359–78.

Van Elk, M., B. T. Rutjens, J. van der Pligt, and F. Van Harreveld (2016), "Priming of Supernatural Agent Concepts and Agency Detection," *Religion, Brain & Behavior*, 6 (1): 4–33.

Van der Helm, E. and M. P. Walker (2011), "Sleep and Emotional Memory Processing," *Sleep Medicine Clinics*, 6 (1): 31–43.

Van der Sluys, C. (1999), "The Jahai of Northern Peninsular Malaysia," in R. B. Lee and R. Daly (eds.), *The Cambridge Encyclopedia of Hunters and Gatherers*, 307–11, Cambridge: Cambridge University Press.

Van Leeuwen, N., and M. Van Elk (2019), "Seeking the Supernatural: The Interactive Religious Experience Model," *Religion, Brain & Behavior*, 9 (3): 221–51.

Van Mulukom, V., and M. Lang (2021), "Religious Experiences Are Interpreted through Priors from Cultural Frameworks Supported by Imaginative Capacity Rather Than Special Cognition," *Journal for the Cognitive Science of Religion*, 7 (1): 39–53.

Van Mulukom, V., H. Turpin, R. Haimila, B. G. Purzycki, T. Bendixen, E. Kundtová Klocová, D. Řezníček, T. J. Coleman III, K. Sevinç, E. O. Maraldi, U. Schjoedt, B. Rutjens, and M. Farias (2021), "What Do Non-Religious Non-Believers Believe in? Secular Worldviews around the World," *Psychology of Religion and Spirituality*. Accessed online: https://doi.org/10.1037/rel0000480.

Vann, B., and N. Alperstein (2000), "Dream Sharing as Social Interaction," *Dreaming*, 10 (2): 111–19.

Veissière, S. P. L., A. Constant, M. J. D. Ramstead, K. J. Friston, and L. J. Kirmayer (2020), "Thinking through Other Minds: A Variational Approach to Cognition and Culture," *Behavioral and Brain Sciences*, 43 (e90): 1–75.

Vidal, C. (2008), "Wat Is een Wereldbeeld? (What is a worldview?)," in H. v. d. Van Belle and J. Veken (eds.), *Nieuwheid Denken: De Wetenschappen en Het Creatieve Aspect van de Werkelijkheid*, 71–86, Leuven: Acco.

Virupakshananda, S. (2015), *Sāṃkhya kārikā of Īśvara Kṛṣṇa with the Tattva-Kaumudī of Sri Vācaspati Miśra*, Morrisville: Lulu Press.

Visuri, I. (2012), "Could Everyone Talk to God? A Case Study on Asperger's Syndrome, Religion, and Spirituality," *Journal of Religion, Disability & Health*, 16 (4): 352–78.

Visuri, I. (2018), "Rethinking Autism, Theism and Atheism: Bodiless Agents and Imaginary Realities," *Archive for the Psychology of Religion*, 1: 1–31.

Visuri, I. (2020), "Sensory Supernatural Experiences in Autism," *Religion, Brain & Behavior*, 10 (2): 151–65.

Von Neumann, J., and O. Morgenstern (1953), *Theory of Games and Economic Behavior*, Princeton: Princeton University Press.
Vosniadou, S. (2002), "On the Nature of Naïve Physics," in M. Limón and L. Mason (eds.), *Reconsidering Conceptual Change: Issues in Theory and Practice*, 61–76, New York: Kluwer Academic.
Wacholtz, A. B., and K. I. Pargament (2005), "Is Spirituality a Critical Ingredient of Meditation? Comparing the Effects of Spiritual Meditation, Secular Meditation, and Relaxation on Spiritual, Psychological, Cardiac, and Pain Outcomes," *Journal of Behavioral Medicine*, 28: 369–84.
Waghorne, J. P., and N. Cutler with V. Narayanan, eds. (1985), *Gods of Flesh/Gods of Stone: The Embodiment of Divinity in India*, New York: Columbia University Press.
Wagner, R. (2018), "Totemism," in H. Callan (ed.), *The International Encyclopedia of Anthropology*, 1–3, New York: John Wiley.
Wagner, U., S. Gais, and J. Born (2001), "Emotional Memory Formation Is Enhanced across Sleep Intervals with High Amounts of Rapid Eye Movement Sleep," *Learning & Memory*, 8 (2): 112–19.
Walker, J. R. (1991), *Lakota Belief and Ritual*, Lincoln: University of Nebraska Press.
Walker, M. P., and R. Stickgold (2006), "Sleep, Memory, and Plasticity," *Annual Review of Psychology*, 57 (1): 139–66.
Walker, M. P., and E. van der Helm (2009), "Overnight Therapy? The Role of Sleep in Emotional Brain Processing," *Psychological Bulletin*, 135 (5): 731–48.
Wamsley, E. J., and R. Stickgold (2010), "Dreaming and Offline Memory Processing," *Current Biology*, 20 (23): R1010–R1013.
Wamsley, E. J., and R. Stickgold (2011), "Memory, Sleep, and Dreaming: Experiencing Consolidation," *Sleep Medicine Clinics*, 6 (1): 97–108.
Ward, K. (1998), *Concepts of God: Images of the Divine in Five Religious Traditions*, London: Oneworld.
Watanabe, J. M. (1990), "From Saints to Shibboleths: Image, Structure, and Identity in Maya Religious Syncretism," *American Ethnologist*, 17 (1): 131–50.
Watson-Jones, R. E., and C. H. Legare (2016), "The Social Functions of Group Rituals," *Current Directions in Psychological Science*, 25 (1): 42–6.
Watts, J., S. J. Greenhill, Q. D. Atkinson, T. E. Currie, J. Bulbulia, and R. D. Gray (2015), "Broad Supernatural Punishment but Not Moralizing High Gods Precede the Evolution of Political Complexity in Austronesia," *Proceedings of the Royal Society B: Biological Sciences*, 282 (1804): 20142556.
Watts, J., J. C. Jackson, C. Arnison, E. M. Hamerslag, J. H. Shaver, and B. G. Purzycki (2022), "Building Quantitative Cross-Cultural Databases From Ethnographic Records: Promise, Problems and Principles," *Cross-Cultural Research*, 56 (1): 62–94.
Watts, J., O. Sheehan, S. J. Greenhill, S. Gomes-Ng, Q. D. Atkinson, J. Bulbulia, and R. D. Gray (2015), "Pulotu: Database of Austronesian Supernatural Beliefs and Practices," *PLOS ONE*, 10 (9): e0136783.
Watts, J., O. Sheehan, J. Bulbulia, R. D. Gray, and Q. D. Atkinson. (2018), "Christianity Spread Faster in Small, Politically Structured Societies," *Nature Human Behaviour*, 2 (8): 559–64.
Waytz, A., K. Gray, N. Epley, and D. M. Wegner (2010), "Causes and Consequences of Mind Perception," *Trends in Cognitive Sciences*, 14 (8): 383–8.
Weber, M. (1920), 'Zwischenbetrachtung: Theorie der Stufen und Richtungen Religiöser Weltablehnung," *Gesammelte Aufsätze zur Religionssoziologie, Vol. 1*, 546–54. Tübingen: Mohr-Siebeck.

Weber, M. (1993), *The Sociology of Religion*, Boston: Beacon Press.
Wegner, D. M., and K. Gray (2017), *The Mind Club: Who Thinks, What Feels, and Why It Matters*, London: Penguin.
Weiskopf, D. A. (2020), "Representing and Coordinating Ethnobiological Knowledge," *Studies in History and Philosophy of Science Part C: Studies in History and Philosophy of Biological and Biomedical Sciences*, 84: 101328.
Wellman, H. M., D. Cross, and J. Watson (2001), "Meta-Analysis of Theory of Mind Development: The Truth about False Belief," *Child Development*, 72 (3): 655–84.
Wen, N. J., A. K. Willard, M. Caughy, and C. H. Legare (2020), "Watch Me, Watch You: Ritual Participation Increases In-Group Displays and Out-Group Monitoring in Children," *Philosophical Transactions of the Royal Society B: Biological Sciences*, 375 (1805): 20190437.
Wendt, A. (1999), "Afterword: Tatauing the Post-Colonial Body," in V. Hereniko and R. Wilson (eds.), *Inside Out: Literature, Cultural Politics, and Identity in the New Pacific*, 399–412, Lanham: Rowman & Littlefield.
Westheimer, G. (2008), "Was Helmholtz a Bayesian?," *Perception*, 37 (5): 642–50.
Whicher, I. (1998), "The Mind (Citta): Its Nature, Structure and Functioning in Classical Yoga (2)," *Nagoya Studies in Indian Culture and Buddhism*, 19: 23–82.
White, C. J. M., and A. Norenzayan (2019), "Belief in Karma: How Cultural Evolution, Cognition, and Motivations Shape Belief in Supernatural Justice," *Advances in Experimental Social Psychology*, 60: 1–63.
White, C. J. M., and A. Norenzayan (2022), "Karma and God: Convergent and Divergent Mental Representations of Supernatural Norm Enforcement," *Psychology of Religion and Spirituality*, 14 (1): 70–85.
White, C. J. M., A. Norenzayan, and M. Schaller (2019), "The Content and Correlates of Belief in Karma across Cultures," *Personality and Social Psychology Bulletin*, 45 (8): 1184–201.
White, C. J. M., J. M. Kelley, A. F. Shariff, and A. Norenzayan (2019), "Supernatural Norm Enforcement: Thinking about Karma and God Reduces Selfishness among Believers," *Journal of Experimental Social Psychology*, 84: 103787.
White, C. J. M., A. K. Willard, A. Baimel, and A. Norenzayan (2021), "Cognitive Pathways to Belief in Karma and Belief in God," *Cognitive Science*, 45 (1): e12935.
White, C. J., M. Muthukrishna, and A. Norenzayan (2021), "Cultural Similarity among Coreligionists within and between Countries," *Proceedings of the National Academy of Sciences*, 118 (37): e2109650118.
White, C. (2021), *An Introduction to the Cognitive Science of Religion: Connecting Evolution, Brain, Cognition, and Culture*. London: Routledge.
White, L. (1967), "The Historical Roots of Our Ecologic Crisis," *Science*, 155 (3767): 1203–7.
White, P. A. (2006), "The Role of Activity in Visual Impressions of Causality," *Acta Psychologica*, 123: 166–85.
White, R. (2003), *Prehistoric Art: The Symbolic Journey of Humankind*, New York: Henry H. Abrams.
Whitehouse, H. (2004), *Modes of Religiosity: A Cognitive Theory of Religious Transmission*, Lanham: Rowman Altamira.
Whitehouse, H. (2011), "The Coexistence Problem in Psychology, Anthropology, and Evolutionary Theory," *Human Development*, 54 (3): 191–99.
Whitehouse, H., and J. A. Lanman (2014), "The Ties That Bind Us: Ritual, Fusion, and Identification," *Current Anthropology*, 55: 674–95.

Whitehouse, H., K. Kahn, M. E. Hochberg, and J. J. Bryson (2012), "The Role for Simulations in Theory Construction for the Social Sciences: Case Studies Concerning Divergent Modes of Religiosity," *Religion, Brain & Behavior*, 2 (3): 182–224.

Wiebe, D. (2014), "Milestone or Millstone: Does Norenzayan's Book Live Up to the Hype?," *Religion*, 44 (4): 674–83.

Wierzbicka, A. (2006), "On Folk Conceptions of Mind, Agency and Morality," *Journal of Cognition and Culture*, 6 (1–2): 165–79.

Wiese, W. and T. Metzinger (2017), "Vanilla PP for Philosophers: A Primer on Predictive Processing," in T. Metzinger and W. Wiese (eds.), *Philosophy and Predictive Processing*, 1–18, Frankfurt am Main: MIND Group.

Wigger, J. B., K. Paxson, and L. Ryan (2013), "What Do Invisible Friends Know? Imaginary Companions, God, and Theory of Mind," *International Journal for the Psychology of Religion*, 23: 2–14.

Wildman, W. J., and R. Sosis (2011), "Stability of Groups with Costly Beliefs and Practices," *Journal of Artificial Societies and Social Simulation*, 14 (3). https://www.jasss.org/14/3/6.html.

Wildman, W. J., F. L. Shults, S. Y. Diallo, R. Gore, and J. E. Lane (2020), "Post-Supernatural Cultures: There and Back Again," *Secularism and Nonreligion*, 9 (6): 1–15.

Willard, A. K., and R. A. McNamara (2019), "The Minds of God(s) and Humans: Differences in Mind Perception in Fiji and North America," *Cognitive Science*, 43 (1): e12703.

Willard, A. K., and A. Norenzayan (2017), ""Spiritual But Not Religious": Cognition, Schizotypy, and Conversion in Alternative Beliefs," *Cognition*, 165: 137–46.

Wilt, J. A., J. J. Exline, J. B. Grubbs, C. L. Park, and K. I. Pargament (2016), "God's Role in Suffering: Theodicies, Divine Struggle, and Mental Health," *Psychology of Religion and Spirituality*, 8 (4): 352–62.

Wimmer, H., and J. Perner (1983), "Beliefs about Beliefs: Representation and Constraining Function of Wrong Beliefs in Young Children's Understanding of Deception," *Cognition*, 13 (1): 103–28.

Windt, J. M. (2010), "The Immersive Spatiotemporal Hallucination Model of Dreaming," *Phenomenology and the Cognitive Sciences*, 9 (2): 295–316.

Windt, J. M. (2015), *Dreaming: A Conceptual Framework for Philosophy of Mind and Empirical Research*, Cambridge: MIT Press.

Windt, J. M., and V. Noreika (2011), "How to Integrate Dreaming into a General Theory of Consciousness: A Critical Review of Existing Positions and Suggestions for Future Research," *Consciousness and Cognition*, 20 (4): 1091–107.

Wittgenstein, L. (1997), *Lectures and Conversations on Aesthetics, Psychology and Religious Belief*, Cyril Barrett (ed.), Berkeley: University of California Press.

Wolle, R. G., A. McLaughlin, and L. Heiphetz (2021), "The Role of Theory of Mind and Wishful Thinking in Children's Moralizing Concepts of the Abrahamic God," *Journal of Cognition and Development*, 22 (3): 398–417.

Wood, C., and R. Sosis (2019), "Simulating Religions as Adaptive Systems," in S. Y. Diallo, W. J. Wildman, F. L. Shults, and A. Tolk (eds.), *Human Simulation: Perspectives, Insights, and Applications*, 209–32, Cham: Springer.

Woolley, J. D., and V. Cox (2007), "Development of Beliefs about Storybook Reality," *Developmental Science*, 10 (5): 681–93.

Woolley, J. D., and M. E. Ghossainy (2013), "Revisiting the Fantasy-Reality Distinction: Children as Naïve Skeptics," *Child Development*, 84 (5): 1496–510.

Woolley, J. D., and K. E. Phelps (2001), "The Development of Children's Beliefs about Prayer," *Journal of Cognition and Culture*, 1: 51-79.

Wright, R. M. (2018), "The Kuwai Religions of Northern Arawak Speaking Peoples: Initiation, Shamanism, and Nature Religions of the Amazon and Orinoco," *Boletín de Antropología*, 33 (55): 123-50.

Xygalatas, D., S. Kotherová, P. Maňo, R. Kundt, J. Cigán, E. K. Klocová, and M. Lang (2018), "Big Gods in Small Places: The Random Allocation Game in Mauritius," *Religion, Brain & Behavior*, 8 (2): 243-61.

Yaden, D. B., J. Haidt, R. W. Hood, D. R. Vago, and A. B. Newberg (2017), "The Varieties of Self-Transcendent Experience," *Review of General Psychology*, 21 (2): 143-60.

Yamagishi, T., and N. Suzuki. (2009), "An Institutional Approach to Culture," in M. Schaller, A. Norenzayan, S. J. Heine, T. Yamagishi, and T. Hameda (eds.), *Evolution, Culture and the Human Mind*, 185-203, London: Psychology Press.

Young, M. J., M. W. Morris, J. Burrus, L. Krishnan, and M. P. Regmi (2011), "Deity and Destiny: Patterns of Fatalistic Thinking in Christian and Hindu Cultures," *Journal of Cross-Cultural Psychology*, 42 (6): 1030-53.

Zhang, D., Q. Li, H. Shen, H. Song, K. Xu, F. Liu, J. Wang, and D. Liu (2018), "The Dreams of Monks: Studies on Chinese Buddhists' Dream Content," *Dreaming*, 28 (3): 235-44.

Zuckerman, P. (2008), *Society without God*, New York: New York University Press.

Zuckerman, M., C. Li, and E. Diener (2018), "Religion as an Exchange System: The Interchangeability of God and Government in a Provider Role," *Personality and Social Psychology Bulletin*, 44 (8): 1201-13.

Index

Abrahamic traditions 33, 38, 39, 58, 90, 97, 113, 115, 123, 130
   Christianity 13, 22–6, 28, 30, 32, 34–5, 37, 38, 41–8, 59, 65, 74, 89–90, 92, 99, 101, 108–10, 118–19, 121, 130–1, 151, 159–62, 167, 179, 181, 190, 196 nn.1, 4, 198 n.5, 199 n.10
   Judaism 26, 32, 41–2, 45, 87, 92, 108–9, 161, 177
   Islam 22, 24, 26, 32, 41, 42, 44–7, 59, 92, 109, 142, 162, 166
Abrahamsen, Adele 8
adaptationist approach 31, 124, 166, 173, 185–6
adaptation, religion as, *see* adaptationist approach
adjudication 155–6
Advaita Vedanta 111, 113–17
Aengus (Celtic deity) 29
Aesop 104
Afghanistan 106
Africa, archaeology of 81–2
African peoples
   Bakiga (Uganda) 29
   Canary Islanders 121
   Dogon (Mali) 129
   Egyptians
      Ancient 50, 84, 91, 106–7
      contemporary 59
   general 6, 34, 154
   Hadza 132
   Ik 155
   Liberians 155
   Mauritius 132
   Nuer 129
   San (!Kung) 129, 156, 201 n.3
   G/wi 129
agency 3, 12, 16, 18–21, 56–9, 63–7, 70–4, 93, 97, 113, 185, 189, 196–7 n.5

agency detection 2, 12–14, 16, 18–19, 32, 65, 80, 93–4, 113, 137, 185
Agent Zero 177
Aghababaei, Naser 190
agnosticism, *see* unbelief
agricultural revolution 169, 198 n.7
agricultural transition, *see* agricultural revolution
ALAN Analytics 179
Alexander the Great 106
Allah, *see* Abrahamic traditions, Islam
Allport, Floyd 29
Alzheimer's disease 19, 190
Amazon, *see* Native South Americans
American samples 161–2, 168, 187, 190
Amerindian Perspectivism 116–19
anattā 115
ancestral 32, 84, 118, 124, 132, 137
Andersen, Marc 13
angel 26, 41, 49, 58, 171
animatism 63–5, 69–70, 73
animism 64–5, 80, 116–19, 122, 185
anicca 115
anthropocentric hypothesis 20, 161
anthropomorphism 2, 12, 18, 20–6, 33–5, 38, 65, 68, 70, 113, 117, 137
antisocial 130, 165
apatheism 186–7, 192
Archbishop of Canterbury 159
Arctic, *see* Native North Americans
Aristotle 103
Arjuna 116
artificial intelligence 2, 4, 170, 172, 176
asceticism 108–10, 113
Asian peoples
   Ammatoans 156
   Bactrian 107
   Balinesians 3, 142–3, 154, 165
   Batak 153, 156, 201 n.3
   Batek 154
   Birhor 154

Chenchu 156
India 3, 23, 46, 48, 111, 113–15, 119, 154, 156, 164
Indonesians 22, 26 (*see also* Ammatoans, Mentawai)
Jahai 155
Mentawai 155
Mro 164
Paliyans 129
Russians 86
Semang 156
Tyvans 24, 36, 132, 145, 165
atheism, *see* unbelief
Ātman, the 114
Atran, Scott 94, 153, 171
Australia, *see* Oceanic peoples
autism spectrum disorder 15, 186
autoregressive integrated moving average models 39
Axelrod, Robert 171
Axial Age 102, 170, 198 nn.2, 5–6, 199 n.10
axiology 190–1
Aztec temples, archaeology of 84

Bactrian, *see* Asian peoples
Badi Shitala Mata (Hindu deity) 29, 43
Bainbridge, William S. 172–3, 175
Bardi, *see* Australian peoples
Baron-Cohen, Simon 13–15
Barrett, Justin 13, 21–2, 26, 50, 111
Barsalou, Lawrence W. 8
Bayes, Thomas 9
Bayes' theorem 9–11, 13
Bechtel, William 8
Begouen, Count Henri 82
Belfast 173
beings
  general 19, 25, 44, 59–60, 66–7, 70, 91, 95, 98, 111–12, 115–19, 171–4, 177–8, 180–1
  supernatural 12, 15, 58–60, 66, 94, 98, 111, 169–70, 176, 181, 197 n.9
belief, *see also* unbelief
  religious 31, 32–3, 39, 119, 137, 172, 177, 184, 189–90, 192
    function of 190
  supernatural 31, 80, 93, 117, 158, 169–70, 177–8, 184

Bhagavad Gita 115–16
bhakti 116
bias 20, 25, 30, 33–5, 39, 55, 95, 122, 129
  cognitive 12–13, 17–19, 24–5, 30, 33, 138
  content 25, 158
  context (*see* bias, cultural learning)
  cultural learning 25, 27, 158
  payoff 158
Bina48 robot 178
bodhisattvas 115
Boehm, Christopher 130
bonobos 104
Boyer, Pascal 97, 149, 171, 198 n.6
Brahman (Hindu deity), Brahminical 42, 114–16
Braxton, Donald 174
Brazil 162, 188
Bryson, Joana 174
Buddhism 111, 113, 115–17, 161–2, 179, 196 n.1
Bunyoro (Ugandan deity) 29
Burdett, Emily 2, 26
by-product hypothesis 54, 185–7

cairns, ritual 165
Caluori, Nava 187
Canada 46, 188
Carney, James 174
Çatal Höyük 102
causal 3, 51, 70–2, 74, 102, 106, 110, 113, 125–6, 170, 191, 196 n.1
  inference 170, 175
  model 125
Cassian, John 110
Chaos (Greco-Roman deity) 29
Charles, Sarah J. 188
chi (Chinese spiritual force) 196 n.1
chimpanzees 32, 79–80, *see also* bonobos
China 19, 27, 59, 104
Chinese, *see* Asian peoples
Christianity, *see* Abrahamic traditions
climate
  activists 162
  change 2, 4, 159–62, 166
  crisis 159–63, 166–8
  scientists 162, 166
Codrington, Robert Henry 66

cognitive architecture 5
  modules 7–9, 15
  schemas 16, 53–5, 195 n.1
Colace, Claudio 61
collaboration 179, 187, 189
colonization 118–19
Columbus, Christopher 121
commitment 27, 50, 56, 63, 78, 85, 87, 131–2, 142, 151, 155, 158, 160–3, 165, 168, 180, 186–7
commons problems, *see* tragedy of the commons
complexity 31, 38, 127, 130, 153, 170–1, 175, 177
  social 124–5, 127–9, 131, 200 n.7
computational modeling 173
computational models, *see* computational modeling
Conan Doyle, Sir Arthur 134
connectionism 8, 16, 195 n.1
constructivism 21–3
control 11, 30, 37. 59, 64, 85, 109, 125–6, 141, 175, 186, 190–1
continuity theory of dreaming 53
conventions 134–5, 138, 143, 155
cooperation 2–3, 30, 43, 78, 85–8, 95–6, 124, 138–42, 145, 150, 152–3, 160, 163, 165, 166, 168–9, 172, 177, 188, 199 n.11
  defection 32, 96, 139–42, 145, 150, 152–3, 157–8
  fairness 95–8, 104
  game theory, evolutionary 133–46
  large-scale 36, 102, 169
  mechanization of 87
  professionalization of 88
  reciprocity 95–8, 153–4, 156, 201 n.2
  scientific study of 169
cooperator, *see* cooperation
coordination 3, 134–5, 141–4, 146, 152, 167
correlational 15, 174, 189
cosmology 190
cost 36, 95–6, 137, 140, 144, 155, 159, 176
counterfactuals 56, 173
counterintuitive 33, 55, 111
Coyote (trickster) 45
credibility-enhancing displays (CREDs) 27, 186, 192
Crete, archaeology of 83

critical thinking 189
Croatia, archaeology of 81
cross-cultural 1–3, 14–15, 34–5, 59, 65, 67, 69, 122–3, 125–6, 129, 131, 149–52, 154, 157, 162–3, 187, 189, 192, 196 n.1
cultural cybernetics 176
cultural evolution 31–3, 36, 39, 64, 151–2, 157–8
cultural-group selection 158
cultural schemas 16, 195 n.1
cultures of honor 151
curvilinear 189
Cyburg 172
Czech Republic 188

D-PLACE database 39, 126–7, 200 nn.4–5
Dahl, Shayne A. P. 57
Dalai Lama 115, 179
Damasio, Antonio 9
Darwin, Charles 31–2, 38, 190
Darwinian, *see* Darwin, Charles
Database of Religious History (DRH) 39, 178, 200 n.6
Dávid-Barrett, Tamás 174
Death Tape 181
defect, *see* defection
defection, *see* cooperation
deity 41–6, 48–50, 65, 92, 107, 109, 115, 121, 123, 130, 149, 156–7, 179–80, 201 n.3
Deloria Jr., Vine 65, 70, 73
DeMallie, Raymond J. 68, 196 n.4
demons 41, 60, 94, 105, 118, 121, 171
Denmark, *see* European peoples
Descartes, René 14, 31, 112
Descartes' problem, *see* Descartes, René
Devoted Actor Theory 177
dharma 46, 114
discernment folk theory of dreams 58
djinns 171
Dogrib, *see* Native North Americans
domain specificity 5, 7–8, 71
Domhoff, G. William 53–5
Dreaming, the (Aboriginal Australian concept) 164
dreams 2–3, 45, 51–61, 115
Driving Game 134, 138, 141
dual inheritance theory 187

dualism, mind/body 112, 114
dukkha 115
Durkheim, Émile 38, 64–5, 69–70, 103, 105, 171, 199 nn.8, 13
Durkheimian, *see* Durkheim, Émile

Ecumenical Patriarch Bartholomew 159
education 19, 72, 178
effectance 34
egocentrism 2, 30, 34, 96
Egypt, archaeology 84, *see also* African peoples
Egyptian, *see* African peoples
elicited agent knowledge 34
Emmons, Robert A. 44
emotions 7, 9, 19, 48, 52–6, 64, 73, 77–8, 85, 88, 96, 100, 103–5, 171, 177, 199 nn.8–12
emotional memory 55
England, *see* European peoples
England, archaeology of 84
environment 4, 6–7, 9, 11–14, 16, 18, 32–4, 48, 60, 63–4, 71–3, 93–4, 106, 112, 136, 153, 156, 160, 162, 166, 168, 172, 175–6, 197 n.9
environmental influence 7, 32, 38, 103, 106, 125, 146, 150, 153, 159, 161–4, 166–8
environmentalism 159–68
Epicurus 89–91, 97 n.5
Epstein, Joshua 170–1, 174, 177
equality 189
equilibria 134
equilibrium 135, 176
    Nash 133, 138
error management theory 137
Estsanadehi (Diné deity) 29
ethnocentrism 130–1
Ethnographic Atlas 125–6, 131, 200 nn.2, 5–6
Europe, *see* European peoples
European Enlightenment 171
European peoples
    Austrians 22
    British 104
        Medieval 163
    Danes 104, 188
    Finns 19, 188
    Greek 105, 108, 111
    Minoans 83
    Polish 164
Evangelicals 59, 161–2
Evans-Pritchard, Edward Evan 102, 124, 130
evil, *see* Problem of Evil
evolutionary game theory, *see* cooperation
evolutionary stable strategy 138
Eysenck, Michael W. 7

fairness, *see* cooperation
fitness
    biological 136–45
    cultural 106
    physical 50
Fodor, Jerry 5–7, 11
Foucault, Paul-Michel 109–10
France, archaeology of 81–2
Frazer, James G. 103
free-list method 152, 154, 156, 167
Freud, Sigmund 17–18, 20, 37, 171
Freudian theory, *see* Freud, Sigmund
Friston, Karl J. 53
Frith, Uta 15

//*gangwasi* (San ancestor spirits) 129
Galton's problem 125
game theory, *see* cooperation
Ganesha 24, 43
generative folk theory of dreams 58
Genesis 43, 58, 106
Germany, archaeology of 84
Gervais, Will 186–7
ghosts 18, 26, 94, 115, 118, 171, 195 n.3
Gilgamesh 29, 105
Glaskin, Katie 58
god-problems 149, 152–3, 155–8, 201 n.2
gods
    big 32, 101–3, 198 nn.6, 7, 199 n.11
    high 34, 36, 41–3, 50, 123–31, 200 nn.2–5, 7, 201 n.1
    moralistic/moralizing 3, 32, 36–7, 43, 121–32, 140, 142, 146, 149–51, 200 n.7
Goodall, Jane 32
Göbekli Tepe 77–8, 80, 198 n.7
Granqvist, Pehr 56
Great Britain, *see* European peoples

Great Mystery, Great Spirit, see
    wakan tanka
Grim, John A. 196 n.3
Groark, Kevin P. 58
guru 170, 179–81
Guthrie, Stewart 12–13, 93, 137–8
G/wi, *see* African peoples

Hadot, Pierre 108–9
Hadza, *see* African peoples
Hawk-Dove Game 144–6
Heider, Fritz 12
Heiphetz, Larissa 24, 27
Henrich, Joseph 57, 150, 176, 201 n.2
Heschel, Abraham 45
Hewitt, John Napoleon Brinton 196 n.2
Hindus, Hinduism 23–4, 29, 41–3, 46–8,
    50, 113, 195 n.1, 196 n.1
Hobson, J. Allan 53
Hobson, Nicholas M. 78
Hochberg, Michael 174
Hoder (Norse deity) 29
Hohwy, Jakob 11
Homo heidelbergensis 81
Homo neanderthalensis 81
Horton, Robin 60
Hubert, Henri 65, 76, 69–71, 74
Human Relations Area Files (HRAF)
    database 200 n.3
Hume, David 171
hyperactive agency detection, *see* agency
    detection

Icarus 105
Ignerssuak (Inuit deity) 29
India, *see* Asian peoples
Indonesians, *see* Asian peoples
Industrial Revolution, the 163
Inglehart, Ronald 186
innateness 5–7, 11, 16, 70, 96
insecurity, *see* security
institutions 64, 106, 138, 142, 146, 151, 153,
    156, 161, 163, 187, 192
    secular 152, 157, 164, 187
integration problem 169
intuitions 31, 72, 92, 98, 152
    evolved 136
Inuit, *see* Native North Americans
Iraq, archaeology of 81

irreligion, *see* unbelief
Isaac (biblical) 58, 106
Islam, *see* Abrahamic traditions
Īśvara 116

Jacob (biblical) 58–9
James, William 38, 171
Japan, *see* Asian peoples
Japan, archaeology of 84
Jerusalem 173
Jesus 24, 42–4, 48–9, 74, 119, 181
Jews, Jewish, *see* Abrahamic traditions
Jnana 116
Job (biblical) 29, 89–91, 98–9, 197 n.3
Johnson, Carl 26
Johnson, Dominic D. D. P. 198 n.6
Johnson, Kathryn 2, 47
Jones, Jim 179–81
Judaism, *see* Abrahamic traditions
Jukurrpa (Aboriginal Australian concept)
    144
Jung, Carl 171

Kaaba 74
Kahn, Ken 174
kaivalya 115
kalapas 115
Kalou-vu (ancestor spirit) 118
karma, karmic 113–16, 195 n.1, 196 n.1,
    196–7 n.5
Keane, Mark 7
Keesing, Roger M. 67
Kelemen, Deborah 94
Keller, Timothy 42
kinship 112, 118
Kirkpatrick, Lee 56
Koresh, David 180
kosmos religion 103, 106–10, 198 n.6,
    199 n.10
Krishna (Hindu deity) 24, 46, 49, 116
Kṛṣṇa, *see* Krishna

Lactantius 89
Lake Tanganyika 164
LAMBI measure of god representations 46
Lane, Jonathan D. 25
Lane, Justin 4
Lang, Andrew 123
Lawson, Thomas 171, 174

Lee, Lois 184–5, 202 n.3
Leslie, Alan M. 15
Leibniz, Gottfried 90
Liberia, *see* African peoples
life-history theory 150
Lillard, Angeline 14
liminality 80–1
Lohmann, Roger Ivar 57
Luhrmann, Tanya 15, 59
Luther, Martin 35

Macedonia 106–7
machine learning 170
Malinowski, Bronislaw 102, 124
mana (Polynesian spiritual force) 3, 63, 66–7, 70, 72–4
manitou (Ojibwe spiritual force) 65, 196 nn.3, 4
Maori, *see* Oceanic peoples
Marett, Robert R. 63–5, 71
marginal likelihood 10–11
Martu, *see* Australian peoples
materialism 102, 112, 115
materialist, *see* materialism
Matsigenka, *see* Native South Americans
Mauritius, *see* African peoples
Mauss, Marcel 65, 67, 69–71, 74
maya 114
Maya 58, 117
   Itza (*see* Native South Americans)
   Lowlands of Guatemala 153, 164
Mayan temples, archaeology of 84
McCauley, Robert 171, 174
McNamara, Patrick 2
McNamara, Rita Anne 3, 151
meaning 79, 94, 102, 183, 186, 190–1
   existential 190
meaning-making 188
meditation 85, 87, 113–14
Medea (biblical) 108
mentalizing 12, 14–16, 66, 112–13, 186
message folk theory of dreams 58
meta-data 131
Mexico 165
Mickey Mouse 111
mind of god 17, 92, 96–7, 112, 167, 178
mind-control 109
mind perception, *see* agency detection

minimal counterintuitiveness theory 33, 55, 11
Minoans, *see* European peoples
missionaries 102, 112, 118–19, 121, 125, 130
Mittermaier, Amira 59
model of mind 3, 113
   cultural 119
   folk 111
   informal 111–12, 116, 118
   local 119
   opacity 118–19
   Western 112
modularity of mind 5–9, 12–16
mokṣa 114
morality 3, 41, 102–5, 123, 126, 132, 150, 198 n.6, 201 n.1
   evolved 96
motivations 2, 30, 35, 39, 100, 163
   maintenance cognitive control 30, 37
   maintenance of psychological safety 30, 38
   prosocial (*see* prosociality)
   punishment of norm violations 36
Mro, *see* Asian peoples
Müller-Lyer illusion 6, 11, 14
Muslim, *see* Abrahamic traditions
mysticism 177

Najle, Maxine B. 187
nāma-rūpa 115
Native North Americans
   Arctic (general) 117
   Dogrib 130
   Inuit 29, 130
   Lakota (*see* Sioux)
   Navajo (Diné) 29
   Plains peoples (general) 58, 64, 154
   Sioux 65, 67–8, 130, 196 n.4
Native South Americans
   Abipón Indians 121, 200 n.2
   Amazonians 3, 112, 116–18
   Aztec, ancient 84
   Caribbeans 122
   Itza (Maya) 153–4, 164
   Matsigenka 130
   Mayans (*see also* Itza, Tzotzil)
      ancient 84
      general 117

Tzotzil (Maya) 58
natural selection 93, 104, 106, 136–8
naturalism 1–2, 116, 118
Near-Oriental religions 105
Netherlands, the 188
Nielbo, Kristoffer 174
Nietzche, Friedrich 37
nirvana 115
nonreligion, *see* unbelief
nonsense folk theory of dreams 58
Norenzayan, Ara 101–2, 186–7, 198 n.7
Norris, Pippa 186
norm 1, 27, 33, 36–7, 45, 85, 97, 102–3, 105, 117–18, 129, 134–5, 151, 154–6, 163, 174, 185–6, 199 n.8, 201 n.2
  adherence 165
  moral 150
  opacity 117–19
  violation 150, 152, 165
Nuer, *see* African peoples
Nyhof, Melanie 22, 26

Oceania, *see* Oceanic peoples
Oceanic peoples
  Australian peoples
    Aboriginal Australians (general) 123
    Australians 188
    Bardi 58
    Martu 3, 143–4, 154, 163–4
  Fijians 118–19, 132, 151, 155
  general 29, 112, 116, 118–19
  Maori 84
  Melanesians 66–7
  Samoans 157
  Tannese (Vanuatu) 132, 154
Odysseus 105
Oishi, Shigehiro 27
omnibenevolence 90
omnipresence 44, 68, 101
omniscience 3, 18, 20, 22–3, 26, 44, 68, 90, 97, 140, 151, 182
ontology 57, 190
orenda (Iroquois spiritual force) 65, 69, 73, 196 n.2
Ovid 29

Pacific, the, *see* Oceanic peoples
Paden, William 60

Pakistan, history of 106
Paleolithic 18, 82
Pāli Abhidhamma 115
Paliyan, *see* Asian peoples
paracosms 59
Pascal, Blaise, *see* Pascal's Wager
Pascal's Wager 135–6
Patañjali 115
paternity certainty 155–6
Paul (biblical) 42, 108
People's Temple, the 179–81
Perner, Josef 14
perspectivism 112, *see also* Amerindian Perspectivism
Piaget, Jean 17–18, 20–1
Piagetian theory, *see* Piaget, Jean
Plato 108
pneuma (Christian spiritual force) 196 n.1
Poirier, Sylvie 58
Poland, *see* European peoples
Pope Francis 159
prakṛti 115–16
praxeology 190
predictive coding, *see* predictive processing
predictive processing
  hyperpriors 11, 16, 71
  posteriors 9–11
  priors 9–14, 200 n.7
preparedness hypothesis 20–5
Preston, Jesse 168, 191
Prisoner's Dilemma 139–41, 145
Problem of Evil 3, 89–92, 98–100
projection, psychological 30–40
Prometheus 105
prosociality 49–50, 78, 85–6, 95–6, 102, 124, *see also* cooperation
Protestant 26, 119
Pulotu database 38, 130, 200 n.6
puruṣa 115–16
Purzycki, Benjamin Grant 2–3, 6, 36, 107, 151, 167

Ram Dass 179
Ramanuja 42
rapid eye movement (REM) 52–3, 55–7, 60
Rappaport, Roy 79, 124, 172, 199 n.8
rational actor theory 95, 169
reciprocity, *see* cooperation

religiosity 14, 27, 63, 162, 176, 187, *see also* unbelief
religiously unaffiliated, *see* unbelief
resource management 85, 151, 154, 160, 164–5, 201 n.3
Richert, Rebekah 22, 26
Rizzuto, Ana-Marie 47
Roman antiquity 29, 50, 105
Rossano, Matt J. 3
Ruamoko (Polynesian deity) 29
Russians, *see* Asian peoples
Rutjens, Bastiaan T. 190

sacrifice 31, 44, 64, 66, 85, 105, 107–10
Sāmkhya 111, 113, 115–16
saṃsāra 114–15
samyoga 115
San, *see* African peoples
Sanderson, Stephen K. 106
Sándor, Piroska 61
Śaṅkarācārya, Sri 114, 116
sankaras 115
Santa Claus 111
Sasaki, Joni 167
Satan 90, 99
Schelling segregation model 172
Schjoedt, Uffe 2, 13
Schweickert, Richard 55
secularism, *see* unbelief
secularization theory 187
security
  existential 178, 186
  material 150–1, 202 n.8
segregation 172–3
Selterman, Dylan F. 56
sensory deprivation 13
Serbia, archaeology of 84
SESHAT 178
shaman(s) 70, 74, 78, 80, 82–4, 117, 196 n.2
Shitala Mata (Hindu deity) 43
Shiva (Hindu deity) 42
Shtulman, Andrew 26
signaling 27, 60, 105, 111, 141–3, 146, 151, 155, 158, 165, 200 n.14
Simmel, Marianne 12
simulation, computational 169–82
simulation theory, *see* Social Simulation Theory
Sioux, *see* Native North Americans

social bonding 188, 192, *see also* cooperation
social ecology 16, 30, 36, 149, 151, 157, 160, 162–3, 166–8
Social Simulation Theory 54, 59
sociocultural hypothesis 21, 24–5
Sosis, Richard 174–5
soul travel theory of dreams 58
source credibility 13
Sørensen, Jesper 3, 74
Spain, archaeology of 81, 83
Sperber, Dan 7, 171
spirit-masters 145–6
spirits 1, 3, 12, 14–16, 31–2, 36, 58, 60, 63–9, 71–3, 90, 94, 97, 117, 123, 126, 129, 131–2, 138, 146, 149, 151–7, 164, 171, 195 n.3, 200 n.4
Stag Hunt 141–2, 144
Stagnaro, M. Nicholas 167
Standard Cross-Cultural Sample (SCCS) 125–7, 131, 200 nn.2, 6
Stark, Rodney 172–3
subak 142–3
subjective well-being, *see* well-being
Sunday Assembly 185, 188
supernatural punishment 124, 129, 139–42, 146, 150, 152, 154, 156, 158, 201 n.5
superstition 136–7, 201 n.4
sustainability, *see* environmentalism

taboos
  animal 156
  bathing 32
  food 154–5
  general 85, 129, 154
  menstrual 155
  resource use 153–4, 157, 164
  sexual 45, 154–5
Taku Skan Skan (Siouan deity) 68
Tate (Siouan deity) 68
Taves, Ann 60, 189
teleological 18–19, 138, 158, 190
teleology 94, 190
temple 48, 84, 105, 107, 142–3, 154, 165, 179–80
Templeton, Sir John 44
tevoro 118
theodicy, *see* Problem of Evil
theological (in)correctness 34, 41, 45

theory of mind 2, 12, 14–15, 18, 23, 61, 94, 186
Theory of Ritual Competence 175
Theravāda 115
therianthropy 82, 92
Thich Nhat Hahn 179
Tillich, Paul 99
totemism 29, 118
tragedy of the commons 139–40, 163
Trickster 41, 45–7, 118
truth 42, 102–3, 110, 114–15, 137, 189
Tuominen, Jarno 54
Turing Test 178, 181
Turkey 77, 188
Tylor, Edward B. 38, 64, 103, 122–3
Tyvans, *see* Asian peoples

unbelief 183–7, 191–2
  inCREDulous atheism 186–7, 192
  secularism 2, 113, 184, 187–8, 192, 199–200 n.13, *see also* secularization theory
  skepticism 176
  unaffiliated, religiously 183
United Kingdom, *see* UK
United Kingdom 27, 167, 188
United States of America 22, 24, 26, 35, 37, 46, 104, 161–2, 188
Upal, M. Afzal 173–4

van Elk, Michiel 13
Van Leeuwen, Neil 13
van Mulukom, Valerie 4
Vanuatu 131, 154
Vedas 114
Veresaev, Vikenty 86
Vergil 104
Vishnu (Hindu deity) 42

visitation folk theory of dreams 59–9
Visuri, Ingela 15

wakan (Siouan spiritual force) 3, 64–5, 67–70, 73
wakan tanka (Siouan spiritual entities) 45, 66–70, 72–3, 196 n.4
Wakinyan (Siouan deities) 69
Ward, Keith 45
water temples 142–3, 154, 165. *see also subak*
Watts, Alan 179
Watts, Joseph 130
Weber, Max 38, 171, 200 n.13
well-being
  personal 150
  psychological 189
  subjective 48
Whitehouse, Harvey 102, 174–5
White, Cindel 197 n.5
White, Lynn 161
Wildman, Wesley 4, 174
Windt, Jennifer 54
Wittgenstein, Ludwig 103
Wohpe (Siouan deity) 69
Wood, Connor 175
worldview approach 183, 189–92

Xenophanes 33

Yahweh, *see* Abrahamic traditions, Judaism
yoga 115–16, 188
Yoga Sutras 113, 115–16

Zeus 111
Zhang Fei (Chinese deity) 29
Zuckerman, Phil 186

www.ingramcontent.com/pod-product-compliance
Lightning Source LLC
Chambersburg PA
CBHW052218300426
44115CB00011B/1741